ERIC J. HANSON'S FINANCIAL HISTORY OF ALBERTA | 1905–1950

ERIC J. HANSON'S FINANCIAL HISTORY OF ALBERTA | 1905–1950

edited by

Paul Boothe and Heather Edwards

Institute for Public Economics
University of Alberta

UNIVERSITY OF
CALGARY
PRESS

Published by the University of Calgary Press
2500 University Drive NW, Calgary, Alberta, Canada T2N 1N4
www.uofcpress.com

National Library of Canada Cataloguing in Publication Data

Hanson, Eric J., 1912–
  Eric J. Hanson's financial history of Alberta, 1905–1950 / Eric J.
Hanson ; Paul Boothe, Heather Edwards, editors.

Includes bibliographical references and index.
ISBN 1-55238-090-4

  1. Finance, Public—Alberta—History—20th century. 2.
Alberta—Economic conditions—1905-1945.* 3. Alberta—Economic
conditions—1945-1991.* 4. Fiscal policy—Alberta—History—20th
century. I. Boothe, Paul Michael, 1954- II. Edwards, Heather, 1976-
III. Title. IV. Title: Financial history of Alberta, 1905-1950.
HJ795.A6H36 2003   336.7123'09'041   C2003-910982-8

The editors gratefully acknowledge the financial support of the Alberta Treasury. The University of Calgary Press acknowledges the financial support of the Government of Canada through the Book Publishing Industry Development Program (BPIDP) for our publishing activities.

Printed and bound in Canada by Transcontinental Printing
∞This book is printed on acid-free Eco Book, 100% post-consumer fibre

Cover and page design by Mieka West; typesetting by Liz Gusnoski.

CONTENTS

LIST OF FIGURES

LIST OF TABLES

LIST OF ABBREVIATIONS, SYMBOLS, AND TERMS

ABBREVIATIONS

C.A.R.	Canadian Annual Review
Conference	Dominion-Provincial Conference on Reconstruction
C.J.E.P.S.	Canadian Journal of Economics and Political Science
C.Y.B.	Canada Year Book
D.B.S.	Dominion Bureau of Statistics
P.A.	[Government of Alberta] Public Accounts
Sirois Report	Report of the Royal Commission on Dominion-Provincial Relations

SYMBOLS

n.a.	figures not available
0 or 0.0	nil or zero
—	amount too small to be expressed or "trace"

TERMS

provincial income	national income produced in Alberta, 1906–21 and personal income of residents for 1922–50 (see Appendix A)
revenue	includes capital and ordinary revenues wherever used unless qualified
expenditure	includes capital and ordinary expenditures wherever used unless qualified
surplus or deficit	refer to differences between revenue and expenditure in the overall sense above unless qualified

See the appendices for further explanations of terms and source materials.

INTRODUCTION

Eric Hanson said it best: this "… is a story of ups and downs, of feast and famine, of Cadillacs and Bennett buggies." This is the story of Alberta from its creation in 1905 to prosperity in 1950. In this book, Hanson gives readers a first-hand account of some of the momentous events that shaped the province of Alberta. He chronicles the birth of the province, and the railway loans that would cripple the province in later years. He details the misery of the Great Depression and one of the great political experiments of this century – the rise of Social Credit. Hanson gives us an hour-by-hour account of Alberta's failed negotiations with the federal government and the province's debt default, followed by its near miraculous financial recovery over the next decade. Finally, he sets the stage for modern Alberta, describing the heady days surrounding the oil strike at Leduc #1 in 1949.

In addition to weaving this fascinating story, Hanson gives scholars his meticulous documentation of the activities of the provincial economy and government, providing a level of detail and scope unavailable from any other account, or indeed for any other province. We believe that Hanson's work ranks among the very best economic histories ever produced in Canada, and yet it sat, virtually forgotten, in the provincial archives for more than forty years.

Our goal in publishing this edited edition of Hanson's doctoral thesis is to preserve the fine work set out in its pages and make it accessible both to scholars and to anyone interested in the economic and political history of Alberta. As it becomes known, we believe that Hanson's efforts will provide the foundation for much future research and will thus help expand our understanding of the history of Western Canada and how that history affects the world we live in today. It will also stand as a fitting tribute to Alberta's greatest economist of the century.

FINDING THE MANUSCRIPT

In 1990, Paul Boothe began to work on a study of Alberta government spending. Supported by the Canadian Tax Foundation, a key component of the study was a set of time-consistent data for spending and revenue that spanned the period from 1905 to 1991. After several years of searching for key missing statistics, Boothe came across a copy of Eric Hanson's thesis in the University of Alberta library in 1994. Unfortunately, the thesis was printed on microcards that could no longer be read. A librarian suggested that the provincial archives might have a readable copy, and so Boothe was put in contact with Mr. David Leonard, an historian who was at that time serving as Provincial Archivist. Mr. Leonard not only knew of the only copy of the Hanson manuscript in the province, but also allowed Boothe to make a second copy for research purposes.

After reading the manuscript, Boothe quickly became aware of the enormous value of Hanson's work as a source of data and as a chronicle of Alberta's history. Hanson had an enormous contribution to make to the understanding of Alberta's economic and fiscal history, yet it was virtually unknown among students of the subject. Boothe sought and was granted permission by Clark University's Economics Department and Mrs. Hanson to publish an edited version of the study, and the Provincial Treasurer, the Honourable Jim Dinning, agreed to fund the publication of the book as a celebration of Alberta Treasury's 90th anniversary. It would now be possible for Boothe to achieve his aims of preserving and circulating this important text.

ERIC HANSON – ALBERTA'S GREATEST ECONOMIST

Eric Hanson was born in Alfta, Sweden, in 1912. When he was 13 years old, he immigrated with his family to a farm in Alberta. Eric studied to be a school teacher, graduating from Camrose Normal School in 1931. He taught in various schools in rural Alberta before earning his Bachelor of Arts degree from Queen's University in 1942. Thereafter, he served as a principal in rural Alberta for two years before moving to Edmonton to teach and begin work on a Master of Arts degree in Political Economy, which was granted by the University of Alberta in 1946.

That same year he began to work as a sessional lecturer in the Department of Political Economy where he taught returning servicemen. Hanson was quickly promoted to Lecturer in 1947 and began work on his Ph.D. at Clark University in Worchester, Massachusetts, under Professor James Maxwell. He took a leave from the University of Alberta in 1949–50 to spend the year at Clark University and completed his degree in 1952 with a doctoral thesis entitled "A Financial History of Alberta, 1905–1950." Meanwhile, Hanson continued to advance steadily in the department of Political Economy at the University of Alberta, gaining promotion to Assistant Professor in 1950, Associate Professor in 1953, and acting as the department's Administrative Officer between 1952 and 1957. He served as Professor and Head from 1957 to 1964, overseeing its transformation into the departments of Economics and Political Science. He stepped down as Head to become Associate Dean of Graduate Studies from 1964 to 1967, and then served on the Board of Governors from 1968 to 1971. In 1974 he retired, and was appointed Professor Emeritus.

In these positions, Hanson had a formative hand on the direction that economics developed in the province of Alberta. Apart from being in a position to guide ideas and methods, he taught individuals who would have an impact themselves, such as A.D. O'Brien, retired Deputy Provincial Treasurer of Alberta. The influence Hanson could have is perhaps better reflected in his own interest in the policy implications that economics could have, as demonstrated by the subjects he covered in his publications.

Hanson was a prolific writer and an insightful analyst throughout his professional career, and his work spanned all aspects of the discipline of public finance. Alberta's first, and arguably greatest economist, he wrote a number of influential books on federal-provincial relations, education finance, health care finance (for the Hall Royal Commission), and energy economics. Hanson's early experience as a teacher may explain the avid interest in education finance, and his continued association with the Alberta Teacher's Association. Other areas that Hanson wrote papers or books on include local government, the oil industry (wherein he revised the skeptical opinion he voiced in his doctoral thesis), the Carter Report, the beginnings of Syncrude, unification of the Edmonton Metropolitan area, tax reform and the history of the University of Alberta's Department of Economics. Recognition for his work earned Hanson fellowships in the Royal Society of Canada and the Royal Society of Health.

Eric Hanson passed away in 1985. To commemorate his contribution to his profession and the University, each year the Department of Economics sponsors the Eric J. Hanson Memorial Lecture featuring a distinguished Canadian addressing an important public policy question.

HOW WE EDITED THE MANUSCRIPT

The challenge we faced as editors was to transform a doctoral thesis of more than 800 pages into a book for contemporary readers. To prepare the book for publication, we began by retyping the entire manuscript. Following this, all tables and figures were recreated in electronic form. The next challenge was to reduce the size of the manuscript while maintaining the substance of Hanson's work. In the end we reduced the size by about a third, in large part by eliminating the repetition of ideas and figures. We also condensed the sizeable section

Hanson had included on the location and geography of Alberta, believing that this information was more fully available elsewhere, as well as being least central to his thesis.

We have tried to maintain Hanson's style throughout the book. While his diction and phrasing may be unfamiliar to some readers (he refers to the federal government as the Dominion government, for example), we believe that these are nonetheless important to giving readers the benefit of Hanson's firsthand experience with many of the events he describes. This account of Alberta's financial history is not just the result of careful study, it is also the result of having lived through the times in question; in this text, "the present" is 1950, and the words are from the pen of one who was there. Finally, it is important to realize that any book in the area of social science is a product of its time. Some of Hanson's views and conjectures reflect the economic conditions and predominant thinking of the era in which this study was written – the early 1950s. As editors, we have tried to preserve Hanson's attitudes as much as possible, while at the same time adding editorial footnotes when knowledge of subsequent events is useful.

STRUCTURE OF THE BOOK

The book is organized into nine chapters. The first sets out the historical, geographical, political and structural background of the province; the next six are dedicated to the five temporal sections into which Hanson divides Alberta's development; the eighth chapter summarizes and synthesizes the important aspects previously discussed; and in the last chapter Hanson presents his key findings. A variety of calculations and details on Hanson's methodology can be found in the appendices.

Chapter 1 provides Alberta's setting and background in terms of geography, history, structure and politics. This helps to conceptualize Alberta in relation to the rest of Canada and to introduce the agricultural and migration issues that were to have a significant effect on the province's development. Reaching back into the period when Alberta was an undistinguished section of Canada's territories, Hanson identifies key factors that influenced the province's being established as it was. The new provincial government's attempts to fulfill its functions are sketched, and the economic background within which these efforts occurred is clearly illustrated. This chapter also discusses the provincial government's evolution with regards to division of labour, revenue sources and expenditures. The relationship between the different levels of government (federal, provincial and municipal) is explained, and the place of schools within this is given special attention, no doubt due to Hanson's personal interest in education. A brief word about the different provincial administrations is also included, thus rounding out Hanson's explanation of the political forces at play in Alberta.

Each of the chapters dedicated to a slice of Alberta's history follows the same organization. The chapters begin with a comment on the general state of economic development, and highlight any noteworthy events during the time period. They then proceed to examine the government's general policies, and to give a detailed account of the Alberta's expenditures and sources of revenue. These chapters also consider the province's general assets and liabilities and are particularly interested in the impact the government had on the economy. A glance at the table of contents will reveal the same methodological progression through expenditures and resources for each time period. The only exception is the period of 1936 to 1951, where analysis is spread over two chapters to accommodate a discussion of Alberta's debt default in 1936, for intertwined in this methodological approach are the unique developments that distinguish one period from another. This method of analysis is sometimes prone to repetition (the worst instances of which have been eliminated), but nonetheless results in a very comprehensive history of Alberta.

Chapter 3 chronicles the investment boom between 1906 and 1913, a period characterized by great optimism and unprecedented growth. Yet this period also contains the story of the Great Waterways Railway, which remains couched in scandal. Hanson tells this tale from the early pressures that induced government involvement through to its procession through the court system. Hanson also tackles the less than clear system of bookkeeping used during this time, providing a much more cohesive account of the province's fiscal activities than is elsewhere available, and revealing the disparity between spending and revenue that would later lead to financial difficulties.

The boom broke in 1913, and in his fourth chapter Hanson examines the consequences of this and the First World War. During this period Alberta was stricken with drought and labour unrest, as well as general unease due to the war. Yet the war also created a demand for many of Alberta's resources, and Hanson examines the interaction of these two forces. The building of infrastructure (health system, telephone lines, roads) continued to be important, and despite developing new taxation schemes, the provincial government laid the seeds of its soon-to-be overwhelming debt burden during this period. Hanson precisely describes the forces, ideologies and personalities that led to this situation as he uses these historical circumstances to advance his theories on the impact of debt and default.

The fifth chapter describes Alberta through the post-war depression, when it lost most of the remnants of its initial optimism. The final chapter in the ongoing saga of the railways is told, as is the province's acquisition of public domain lands from the federal government, a development which Hanson recognized as important with the benefit of seeing Alberta's oil discoveries. He also shows how the Liberal government tried to respond to drastic drops in livestock and grain prices concurrently with increasing demands from its population, but finally lost to the United Farmers of Alberta, which began cutting back and seeking new sources of revenue. The province weathered this period without undue injury, but the government's policies have been subject to substantial criticism. Hanson's analysis shows that even if the critics' advice had been followed, very little more of Alberta's growing debt could have been retired. Recovery started in the later twenties, and it was beyond the government's ability to hasten the process.

Unfortunately, recovery was short-lived, for the Great Depression began in the 1930s. Chapter 6 covers the period from 1930 to 1935 wherein the Depression hit Alberta particularly hard because of the debts incurred by both the government and by private citizens in the twenties. Hanson explains the combination of forces that placed many Albertans in particularly dire financial straits, leading the government to provide relief it could scare afford, and enact legislation to protect citizens from losing their farms. The difficulties surrounding the irrigation and telephone systems are examined, and the government's increasingly desperate attempts to secure funds and reduce debt are related. Special attention is given to the political and economic forces that created and compounded Alberta's debt situation, leading up to default in 1936.

Chapter 7 tells more fully how the default came about as it considers the years 1936 to 1950, and examines the consequences that it engendered. Hanson provides a detailed and engaging account of the personalities, the negotiations, and the passing telegraphs that led immediately to the default. Further, he grounds this story within a wider view of the social, political and economic forces that the players were immersed in. The chapter also comments on the lackluster agricultural and economic situation before the Second World War, on the dynamic between the federal government's pricing policies and the dramatic increase in agriculture prices during the war, on Social Credit initiatives the government attempted in the early part of this period, and on the provincial budgets that Alberta enacted following its default.

Analysis of the years 1936 to 1951 is continued in Chapter 8, focusing on the specific fiscal developments rather than on the general conditions discussed in the previous chapter, and with an emphasis on the 1940s. Hanson provides an analysis of the general trends in expenditure and revenue, discussing, among other things, new funding arrangements for education and hospitals, various agreements between the provincial and federal governments, and the rise of public domain revenues with the advent of large oil and gas discoveries. Of interest to contemporary readers is Hanson's constant skepticism over the likelihood of continuing energy resource revenues in Alberta; he flatly disbelieved that Alberta was to become a province whose economy was influenced more by the energy industry than by agriculture. In subsequent writings, he revised his opinion somewhat in light of the evidence. (See, for example, *Dynamic Decade: the evolution and effects of oil industry in Alberta* [McClelland and Stewart, 1958], and *Regional Employment and Income Effects of the Petroleum Industry in Alberta* [1966].) Hanson also discusses the various certificates that the government issued, relations between the province and its municipalities, and the changing composition of Alberta's assets and liabilities.

Chapter nine is a review of the previous six chapters, pulling out the larger trends. Hanson follows the same format that he used for analyzing each of the individual sections, going through the various government expenditures, revenues, and debt loads, but applies it to the entire period, 1905 to 1950. He also considers the influence of the inequity and instability of income distribution, the shift in expenditures between municipalities and the province, the changing importance and size of government, the relationship between expenditure and income, and compares Alberta with the other provinces on all these counts. This chapter is especially rich in tables and figures, used to give visual representation of the trends Hanson seeks to highlight.

Having reviewed the forty-five-year span, Hanson uses Chapter 10 to present the elements that were most important to making Alberta and its economy follow the course that they did. These include a variety of physical factors such as Alberta's location and population density; historical happenings including the rate and time of Alberta's development; political decisions regarding the size of the Western province, and provision of relief and services; and economic policies, especially guarantees. Hanson concludes the chapter with an interesting analysis of Alberta's most controversial fiscal event, the debt default. In it, he suggests that contrary to some of the opinions prevailing at his time, defaulting on its debt in 1936 did Alberta little benefit in terms of making it a prosperous, and often envied, province in the confederation.

ACKNOWLEDGEMENTS

A number of people and organizations contributed to make this project possible. Special thanks goes out to the Honourable Jim Dinning, who agreed to support production of this book as part of Alberta Treasury's 90th anniversary celebrations. The Deputy Provincial Treasurer, A. D. O'Brien provided support and encouragement throughout the project.

David Leonard gave us initial access to the manuscript. Charlene Hill painstakingly retyped it, and Grant Hilsenteger recreated every chart and table. Finally the Economics Department of Clark University and Mrs. Hanson gave us permission to publish this version of Hanson's work almost half a century after it was undertaken. On behalf of all those interested in the history of our province, we offer our sincere thanks.

Paul Boothe
Heather Edwards
Edmonton, November 2002

AUTHOR'S PREFACE

This study of the government finances of the Canadian province of Alberta implicitly examines the level of government intermediate between the federal and local governments in Canada and the United States.

In the explicit sense, however, it is more than that. It is the story of a province affected by geographic and economic factors shared only with the other two prairie provinces and some western American states. For example, transportation costs bulk large in Alberta because of sheer geography, a condition which aggravates the cyclical and structural economic changes that have affected the province from time to time. The province was settled and developed rapidly in response to changes in demand and cost factors which made wheat growing both feasible and profitable on the prairies. Cyclical and structural changes in the demand for wheat and other agricultural products in the world's export markets during the 1920s and 1930s called for readjustments that created serious private and public financial problems. The increase in the demand for agricultural products during World War II led to rapid recovery from the Depression of the 1930s. Post-war developments in the petroleum industry have generated a high level of investment activity and provided the provincial government with greatly increased revenues. It is a story of ups and downs, of "feast" and "famine," of Cadillacs and "Bennett buggies."

Two events are of special importance. One is the provincial public debt default and partial interest repudiation of 1936–46. The other is the emergence of Alberta as one of the "haves" of the ten provinces in the sphere of public finance. A discussion of the factors underlying these events, as well as of the events themselves, forms a considerable portion of this treatise. To deal adequately with these two developments as well as to examine the financial problems of the province as the intermediate unit of government in the Canadian federation, such factors as the geography of Alberta, the economic development of the province, its governmental structure and political development, expenditure and revenue policies, and local public finance are discussed at some length.

Aside from the interpretation of data and the actual writing of the treatise, the main tasks which faced the writer were the selection of facts to be presented, the organization of the material selected, and the construction of statistical series with intertemporal consistency. With respect to the first, the sins of commission are perhaps greater than those of omission. As to the second, the chronological method adopted facilitated progress in collecting and selecting data covering such a long period as 1905–50. The third consumed the major portion of the writer's time; classificatory decisions were not always easy to make without deliberation, existing data had to be obtained from many sources, and they had to be adjusted to fit the classifications made. Various estimates were also necessary. The appendices set out the sources and processes utilized to secure the statistical series.

The writer is greatly indebted to Professor James A. Maxwell of Clark University, who gave most patient, encouraging, and valuable guidance over a period of almost two years. He is indebted to the members of the staff of the Legislative Library of the Government of Alberta who assisted him in obtaining access to provincial government documents and newspaper files. Staff members of various provincial and city government departments answered queries and supplied documents; this is herewith gratefully acknowledged. Dr. H.B. Mayo, Professor of Political Science, University of Alberta, read parts of the manuscript at various points and made welcome suggestions. The writer is also grateful to members of the staff of the Rutherford Library, University of Alberta, who permitted him to take out reference works for long periods of time. Last, but not least, is the debt he owes his wife, who sacrificed much time and effort in assisting him in typing and revising the manuscript and who constantly encouraged him to complete this dissertation.

GEOGRAPHIC, HISTORICAL, AND STRUCTURAL
BACKGROUND

1

The physical environment conditions the policies of governments. While these factors cannot supply a complete explanation of what governments have done, they cannot be ignored, for often they supply useful first approximations and working hypotheses. Also important for government policies are the parameters imposed by their structure and responsibilities. Therefore, some attention to these aspects is justified in a work on public finance.

THE GEOGRAPHY OF ALBERTA

Alberta has abundant and varied physical resources, but Alberta's location with reference to world markets and the rather scattered nature of its resources combine to produce a relatively high level of transportation costs. This limits resource utilization and makes for high overhead costs; indeed, during the downswings of gross income, overhead is precariously high in relation.[1] Hence, fluctuations in net income can be extremely wide in amplitude.

These fluctuations are the result of both internal and external factors. The variable weather from year to year is an especially important internal cause because of the dominant position of agriculture in the economy of the province. Scanty, unreliable rainfall, especially in the southeast, and frosts in the north and west, make for variability from year to year in the yield of grain crops. Hot and dry summer winds and hailstorms make for even greater unpredictability.[2] While diversification of agricultural production can ameliorate this condition somewhat, it is not very feasible in the brown and dark brown soil zones (see Figure 1.1).[3] Also, only a limited portion of the land can be successfully cultivated (see Figure 1.2). The most important external factor is the dependence of the province upon outside markets for most of its agricultural products, markets in which wide price fluctuations have been very characteristic in the past. These fluctuations have been mitigated to some extent by federal government marketing policies in recent years, but the future success of such policies

Figure 1.1 Soil Zones in Alberta, adapted from Alberta Soil Surveys

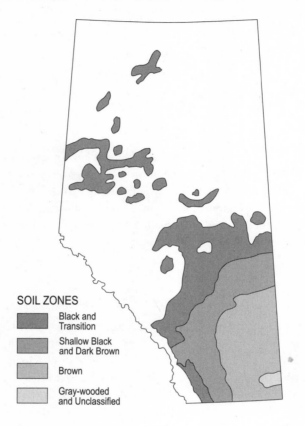

SOIL ZONES

- Black and Transition
- Shallow Black and Dark Brown
- Brown
- Gray-wooded and Unclassified

is difficult to predict. Public finance policies must accordingly be studied and interpreted in the light of these basic conditions.

The recent discovery of petroleum on a large scale, along with the growth of manufacturing during the last decade promise to reduce income variability somewhat. Yet, considerable income fluctuations will continue to occur because agriculture still promises to outweigh all other industries in value of production for some time to come.[4] Further, petroleum is a raw material subject to price and output uncertainties. The extension of pipelines to reach eastern markets will tend to reduce prices received by petroleum producers since Alberta oil will then be in competition with other sources of oil.[5] The discovery of oil has, however, provided large windfall revenues in the form of purchase prices of leases for the provincial government during recent years; the public domain has come

Figure 1.2 Wheat Zones in Alberta from A. Stewart, Crop Insurance in Alberta

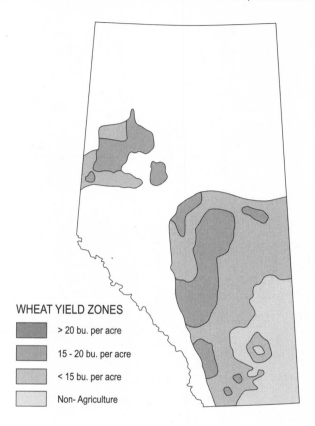

WHEAT YIELD ZONES

> 20 bu. per acre

15 - 20 bu. per acre

< 15 bu. per acre

Non- Agriculture

into its own with a vengeance (see Table 1.1). Royalties on production will provide considerable revenue of a recurring nature.

The rapid population growth and economic development during the early decades of the province's history created a pressing demand for capital, which was met by much borrowing, both public and private. Consequently, with a tapering off in population growth and with depression in the 1930s, the debt problem was a matter of paramount concern.[6] The distribution and sparse nature of population have tended to make for relatively high costs of government services (see Figure 1.3).

Rapid urbanization in recent years is leading to increasing debts among urban municipalities. In the past, welfare costs in the form of old age pensions and unemployment relief have not been as great relatively as in the older regions with more old people and greater urban populations. In the future these promise

Table 1.1 Revenue of the Government of Alberta from Petroleum and Natural Gas, 1945–1951 (millions of dollars).

Fiscal year	Royalties	Fees and rentals	Leases	Other	Total	Total as per cent of revenue
1945–46	0.6	0.4	0.0	0.0	0.9	1.5
1946–47	0.5	0.3	0.0	0.0	0.8	1.6
1947–48	0.8	0.7	0.0	0.0	1.5	2.4
1948–49	1.6	2.2	8.7	0.0	12.5	15.6
1949–50	3.4	5.7	23.2	0.1	32.4	29.2
1950–51	4.8	9.0	28.0	0.1	41.9	31.2

Source: Government of Alberta, *Public Accounts* (henceforth P.A.), 1945–51.

to be considerably greater in Alberta, the one secularly as the proportion of old people increases (see Table 1.2), and the other cyclically as a larger proportion of the population moves to the cities and becomes engaged in occupations subject to greater employment fluctuations than agriculture.

Agriculture has provided a subsistence living for most of its practitioners in the past during periods of unemployment in other industries. But the highly specialized nature of agriculture in some areas of the province necessitated government relief payments on a large scale during the prolonged depression of the 1930s. At the same time there was considerable under employment and excess capacity in the agricultural industry of the whole province. The agrarian discontent generated by these conditions is basic in any attempt to explain the experiments with new political parties, both in 1921 and 1935, and the adoption of unconventional financial policies.[7]

THE TERRITORIAL PERIOD
ECONOMIC DEVELOPMENT

Fur traders penetrated to Alberta in the latter half of the eighteenth century. The Hudson's Bay Company and the Northwest Company ruled the Northwest Territories and Rupert's Land until 1867 when the Dominion government purchased Rupert's Land from the company. In the interim before the 1874 arrival of the Northwest Mounted Police, whiskey traders from Montana established themselves in southern Alberta. After 1874 they were forced to confine themselves

Figure 1.3 Distribution of Population, Alberta, 1946, Census Divisions and Regions

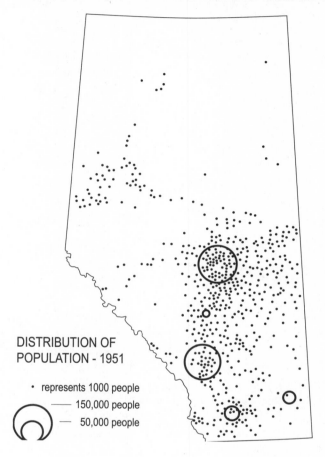

DISTRIBUTION OF
POPULATION - 1951

• represents 1000 people
—— 150,000 people
—— 50,000 people

to the legal export of buffalo hides. In the 1870s, cattle ranching began to develop in southern Alberta, but the industry's development was hampered by poor stock and a lack of market outlets. New regulations, improved enforcement and the development of railways allowed cattle ranching to prosper in the 1880s, but the industry was still far from stable. There was also some horse ranching, but sheep grazing was discouraged in response to demands from the cattlemen. There was very little agriculture before 1895.

A number of settlements were in existence in northern Alberta as early as 1871.[8] The completion of the Canadian Pacific Railway in 1885 offset the advantage of the northern water routes over the southern and the population of the newly accessible south began to overtake that of the north. Still, the rate

Table 1.2 Population of Alberta by Age Groups for Census Years 1901–1946

Year	Percentage of Population of Alberta				
	0 to 4	5 to 14	16 to 64	65 and over	Age not stated
1901	14.9	24.1	58.3	1.8	0.9
1906	13.3	21.5	62.7	1.8	0.7
1911	12.9	19.2	64.9	1.6	1.4
1916	14.2	21.0	62.0	1.9	0.9
1921	13.3	23.0	61.2	2.4	0.1
1926	11.7	23.9	61.4	3.0	–
1931	10.7	22.0	63.8	3.5	–
1936	9.8	20.8	65.2	4.2	–
1941	9.4	19.3	66.1	5.2	0.0
1946	10.6	18.1	65.0	6.3	0.0

Sources: *Dominion Census*, 1901, 1911, 1921, 1931, and 1941;
Census of the Prairie Provinces, 1906, 1916, 1926, 1936, and 1946.

of settlement in both Alberta and Saskatchewan remained slow due to fears of Indian rebellions,[9] the lack of transportation routes, the belief that all of southern Alberta was an arid waste, and the short frost-free period.[10] It was the rapid rise in wheat prices during the late 1890s, coupled with no increase in transportation costs, which gave a great stimulus to settlement.[11]

After 1897 the favourable price and transportation cost conditions, the disappearance of the frontier in the United States, and a vigorous immigration policy of the Dominion government[12] were major factors which led to rapid settlement in the Canadian West.[13] The Canadian investment boom before 1913 has been so adequately analysed elsewhere that it need not be treated further here.[14] It is sufficient to note that between 1900 and 1905, construction activity of all kinds generated incomes which formed a large percentage of the total income of the prairie economy. Agricultural income was low, especially in Alberta where the field crop average was less than 30 acres per farm before 1906.[15] The remuneration from construction work was a welcome supplement to many struggling settlers, and provided others with sufficient capital to start life on a farm.

Despite this boom period, Alberta lagged behind Manitoba and Saskatchewan in the 1890s. In 1891 Alberta had only 8 per cent of the prairie's farms, and only 7 per cent of the total expansion in field crop acreage.[16] In

Alberta, there were greater obstacles to land clearance, markets for farm products were less accessible, and the frost-free period was shorter than in the other two prairie provinces. Wheat crops were not feasible until after 1900,[17] so lower priced oats and barley were sown, and livestock played a larger role than elsewhere, even though livestock prices fluctuated greatly.

Alberta was very much the junior of the three prairie provinces in 1906. It had only 23 per cent of the total population of the three provinces, and not much over 10 per cent of the gross agricultural income. Consequently, its provincial government did not have a wide revenue base when it began operations. Perhaps the granting of provincial status in 1905 was somewhat premature.

TERRITORIAL GOVERNMENT

In June, 1870, The Hudson's Bay Company surrendered its charter and Rupert's Land to the British Crown, and the Crown transferred Rupert's Land and the Northwest Territory beyond it to the Dominion of Canada.[18] Thus the Dominion found itself in possession of Crown lands in the prairies, whereas in the rest of Canada the provincial governments held the title to the Crown lands. When the province of Manitoba was carved out of the new territory in 1870, the Dominion retained title to the Crown lands in that province because it wanted to use them to build a Pacific railway, and because it wanted to adopt a homestead policy. Similarly, it retained title to them when Alberta and Saskatchewan became provinces in 1905 because it wanted to continue the latter policy. Thus the basis for the natural resources controversy between the Dominion government and the three prairie provinces was laid. Several writers have told that story.[19]

The Manitoba Act of 1870 provided that the lieutenant-governor of the new province was to act as lieutenant-governor of the Northwest Territories as well. A Northwest council, chiefly residents of Manitoba, was appointed by the Dominion to advise the lieutenant-governor in administering the territories. Until 1873, the Dominion Secretary of State for the provinces dictated much of the policy to the lieutenant-governor and his council. Between 1873 and 1876 the Minister of the Interior assumed this function. It was an unsatisfactory arrangement for the nominated council knew little about the territories, and its ability to act was hampered by delays in approval of legislation by the Dominion government.

In 1875 the Dominion parliament passed the Northwest Territories Act (38 Vic. Cap. 49). It provided for a lieutenant-governor and a council which was to be nominative until the settlement of the territories would warrant some elective members.[20] It was, in effect, a crown colony form of government. The Dominion government still provided for its approval or disallowance of territorial legislation and this often led to much delay and to the ensuing dissatisfaction of council members.

The council possessed both legislative and administrative powers. It could legislate on territorial administrative offices, civil justice, education, municipal government, local public works, property and civil rights in the territories, and on all matters of a purely local or private nature. But it could not borrow money on the credit of the territories, charter railways, provide hospitals and asylums, or administer criminal justice. These limitations continued to be effective until provincial status was granted in 1905.

The chief source of revenue consisted of grants made by the Dominion government to be spent for purposes specified by that government subject to recommendations made by the council. The council was permitted to issue various licenses and to impose fines in enforcing territorial ordinances. It had no power to impose direct taxation except in electoral districts.

The early territorial government, then, was subject to much direction from Ottawa. There was little effective reaction against this condition of affairs before 1885, but demands for self-government and a legislative assembly began to be made as the number of elected members on the council increased.[21] The half-breed rebellion of 1885 lent strength to these requests since it was felt that the Dominion government, through ignorance of local conditions and even neglect, had failed to take steps to prevent the 1885 uprising despite repeated warnings of the council.

Several years passed before the Dominion government yielded to these demands. In 1886 the Northwest Territories were given representation in the Dominion parliament, a measure which relieved the council of much work in the preparation of memorials to the Dominion government with respect to adjustments in land laws and other statutes administered by the Dominion in the territories. In 1887 the Dominion government expressed its willingness to consider changes in the constitution of the territorial government and requested the council to propose "some inexpensive form of government that would give the people greater control over the management of their affairs."[22] The council proposed a wholly elected assembly presided over by a speaker and a responsible executive council to be chosen by the assembly. The Dominion government met these proposals in part in 1888 and in that year the first legislative elective assembly met.[23]

Under the new dispensation, a speaker chosen by the assembly replaced the lieutenant-governor in presiding over the deliberations of the assembly. The lieutenant-governor chose four members of the assembly to form an advisory council on finance. The assembly and the lieutenant-governor were soon at odds over the status of the advisory council of finance and on the manner of proposing revenue and expenditure measures. By 1891 the assembly had its way with regard to control over the purse.[24] In that year the Dominion government amended the Northwest Territories Act by giving the assembly power to make ordinances with respect to the expenditure of territorial funds and those portions of the Dominion appropriations to the territories which the lieutenant-governor had been authorized to spend in concurrence with the assembly. In 1892 the Dominion parliament adopted the suggestion of F.W.G. Haultain, a member of the executive committee who had gone to Ottawa to make various representations of voting a lump sum for the expenses of government in the territories instead of itemized votes.[25]

In 1897 a further step toward responsible government was taken. The executive committee appointed by the assembly was replaced by an executive council chosen by the lieutenant-governor with the support of the majority of the assembly. This event coincided with the beginning of the remarkable population growth and economic development which characterized the area until World War I. Yet the territorial government continued to lack a number of provincial rights. It could not borrow money on its own credit, charter railways, or administer criminal justice. The lack of these rights, the lack of formulae for determining the yearly Dominion grant, and the insistent demand for public services in keeping with the rapid growth of the population after 1897, do much to explain the drive for provincial status which culminated in 1905 with the formation of the two new provinces of Alberta and Saskatchewan.

This is not the place, however, to analyse all the forces that permeated Dominion-territorial relationships and the movement that ultimately succeeded in procuring provincial autonomy. The story has been told elsewhere.[26]

THE BEGINNINGS OF LOCAL GOVERNMENT

Despite the existence of various legislations providing for municipal incorporation since the 1875 Northwest Territories Act, there were no incorporated municipalities in Alberta until Calgary became a town in 1884. Edmonton was incorporated next, in 1891, and only after that did municipal institutions grow in number.[27]

To a large extent the early territorial legislatures left the creation of urban municipal units to local initiatives. Some degree of coercion was used to secure some form of local government for very small places, and special legislation dealing with unincorporated towns and hamlets was put on the statute books in the 1890s. Special statutes in response to local requests incorporated the first cities and towns. The revised municipal ordinance of 1897 left cities free to draw up their own charters. Thus a legacy of separate city charters was left the new provinces in 1905.[28]

Rural local government proceeded very slowly because settlers were so pre-occupied with searching and consolidating their new homes and holdings that little energy and few resources were left for devotion to organized public services. Under these conditions only the most rudimentary scheme of local government proved practicable,[29] and even this had to be prodded by the senior government. These organizations eventually became known as local improvement districts; they comprised from three to six townships, had an elected council, collected taxes, and were responsible for the non-educational public services.

The School Ordinance was passed in 1884, providing for the erection of both Protestant and Catholic schools. The school board of the district could levy taxes on real property. The Dominion government was requested to provide for a school grant in its appropriations to the territories, and this was done in 1885. The organization of schools proceeded rapidly, and in 1885 there were fifty-nine public schools in operation throughout the territory.[30]

The number of schools in operation increased from 76 in 1886 to 917 in 1904 for all the territories. The number of pupils enrolled increased from 2,553 to 41,033 in the same period. Grants paid to schools rose from $9,000 to $239,000.[31] School districts were quite separate from and independent of other local government units. For example, each town and village school district embraced much rural territory around the town or village. Rural school districts often included parts of two or more local improvement districts. The school districts often levied their own taxes and controlled expenditures on education. Some districts, however, arranged to have their taxes collected by the municipalities concerned. Dominion and territorial grants for education were paid directly to the treasurers of the districts or to teachers as part salary. By 1905, the separation of school and municipal units had become firmly established and has remained a traditional principle until the present.[32]

GOVERNMENTAL FUNCTIONS AND EXPENDITURES

The Dominion government performed a large part of the function of the administration of justice in the territories. It provided a police force on which it spent larger sums annually than it granted to the territorial government (see Table 1.3). This force not only administered and enforced criminal justice,

Table 1.3 Dominion Government Expenditure on Territorial Government and Upon Some Items Closely Related to the North-West Territories, 1886–1905 (in thousands of dollars)

Year	Territorial Government Mounted Police	North-West Mounted Police	Dominion Lands	Immigration	Yukon Territory	Total
1886	3,235	1,029	195	257	0	4,716
1887	110	782	196	341	0	1,429
1888	105	863	185	245	0	1,398
1889	177	830	189	202	0	1,398
1890	181	753	174	110	0	1,218
1891	249	741	158	181	0	1,329
1892	245	702	133	178	0	1,258
1893	276	615	136	181	0	1,208
1894	277	611	133	202	0	1,223
1895	304	646	130	196	0	1,276
1896	331	533	120	120	0	1,124
1897	321	526	111	127	0	1,085
1898	348	865	91	261	47	1,612
1899	357	403	93	256	1,098	2,207
1900	354	844	105	435	332	2,070
1901	504	912	133	445	275	2,269
1902	492	948	159	495	267	2,361
1903	802	990	186	643	808	3,429
1904	894	950	247	745	638	3,474
1905	1,259	1,013	277	972	476	3,997

Source: C.Y.B., 1906. The amounts spent on territorial government from 1893 to 1905 inclusive do not equal the amounts set out in the public accounts of the territorial government because a part of the Dominion government appropriation was spent on territories and functions outside the jurisdiction of the territorial government and because of differences in the fiscal years of the territorial and the Dominion governments.

but also assisted settlers in many other respects.[33] In addition, the Dominion government administered the land laws.[34] The territorial government administered civil justice and provided for the administration of laws generally. By and large, however, it may be said that the Dominion government assumed responsibility for Adam Smith's two basic functions of government.[35]

With respect to Smith's third function, that of "erecting and maintaining those public institutions and those public works, which though they are in the highest degree advantageous to a great society, are, however, of such a nature, that the profit could never repay the expense to any individual...,"[36] the territorial and municipal governments played a major role, although the Dominion government provided much of the revenue for it. Outlays on education, roads, bridges, and ferries were the most prominent items among these expenditures "for economic and social ends" to use the modern phrase adopted by Mrs. Hicks.[37] Aid to agricultural societies, inspection of coal mines and steam boilers, hail insurance, destruction of noxious weeds, hospital grants-in-aid, and indigent relief were among the items of a much smaller order of magnitude (see Table 1.4). The Dominion government provided most of the funds, and indeed before 1893 it specified how expenditures were to be made. In addition, municipal governments spent increasing amounts on education and public works.[38]

Table 1.5 indicates the growth of population (and the subsequent need for public works), and the rapid rise in the number of school children, which help explain the upward trend in territorial government expenditures during the two decades before 1905. Table 1.6 sets out the trends in the relative importance of each major type of expenditure.

An examination of this table reveals a decline in the percentage of total expenditure devoted to schools from 1892, as the territorial government shifted more of the burden of education expenditures upon the localities as direct taxation of property was developed by them. An increasing proportion of expenditures was assigned to public works until it was more than one-half in 1904. Hail insurance indemnities constituted an uncontrollable item which could have disrupted the territorial budget seriously. But since the government did not enter the hail insurance business until 1903, it escaped the difficulties the provincial governments encountered in this field in later years.

THE DOMINION GOVERNMENT APPROPRIATION

The Dominion government appropriation provided most of the revenue for the territorial government until 1905. Before 1892, it was split into a number of different itemized votes and was spent for purposes specified by

Table 1.4 Revenues and Expenditures of the North-West Territories, 1904 and Jan. 1 to Aug. 31, 1905 (in thousands of dollars)

Revenue	1904	1905
1. Dominion of Canada	641	786
2. Taxes	0	–
3. Licences, permits, and fees	46	46
4. Liquor control	64	73
5. Fines and penalties	6	6
6. Public domain[a]	43	62
7. Sale of commodities	6	4
8. Hail insurance	23	38
9. Refunds of expenditure	3	2
10. Interest on bank deposits	8	8
Total revenue	842	1,026

Expenditure	1904	1905
1. Legislation	29	7
2. General government	105	78
3. Administration of justice	6	7
4. Education	300	188
5. Roads, bridges, and ferries	566	247
6. Agriculture	29	30
7. Public welfare	37	38
8. Public domain[b]	10	2
9. Hail insurance[c]	12	1
10. Other (chiefly government printer)	27	57
Total expenditure	1,121	655

Source: Government of the North-West Territories, Public Accounts, 1904 and 1905.
(a) Chiefly from school lands fund held in trust by the Dominion government.
(b) Coal mine inspection and game law enforcement.
(c) The territorial liquidator paid out over $72,000 in hail indemnities during the fall of 1905.

Table 1.5 Population and the Number of School Children in the North-West Territories, 1886–1905 (in thousands)

Year	Population[a]	School Children[b]
1886	78	3
1887	82	3
1888	86	3
1889	91	5
1890	95	5
1891	99	6
1892	110	6
1893	121	8
1894	132	11
1895	143	12
1896	154	13
1897	163	15
1898	173	17
1899	183	19
1900	193	20
1901	164	24
1902	221	27
1903	278	33
1904	336	41
1905	402	50

Sources:
(a) From *C.Y.B.*, 1936, 141. The figures include Yukon and the present North-West Territories up to and including the year 1900. For 1901 to 1905 inclusive, the figures include only the area comprised by the provinces of Alberta and Saskatchewan. In 1901 the population of all the territories was 211,000.
(b) From Shortt and Doughty, *Prairie Provinces*, 155. The figure for 1905 is estimated.

the Dominion government, acting if it wished, upon the advice of the territorial council. The latter body communicated with the Dominion government repeatedly on this method of appropriation. The question of subsidies comparable to those paid to provinces was mooted and so was the question of public lands. In 1892 the senior government yielded to the extent of voting a lump sum actually to the territorial government, to be spent on different items determined by the territorial assembly.

Nevertheless, the appropriation continued to be a focus of controversy until 1905. Its level continued to be determined to a large extent with reference to the overall budgetary position of the Dominion government, certainly sound

Table 1.6   Expenditures on Major Functions of the North-West Territories Government Expressed as Percentages of Total Expenditure

Function	Percentage of total expenditure		
	1892–93	1901	1904
Grants to schools	43	30	24
Public works	35	43	55
Other	22	27	21

Source: Government of the North-West Territories, *Public Accounts, 1892–93, 1901,* and *1904.*

financial procedure. The territorial government made estimates of its requirements which were forwarded annually to the Dominion government. It stressed the principle of fiscal need and pointed to the continuous growth of population and the accompanying need for schools and public works. At the same time, the demand for a subsidy fixed according to an agreed formula grew. This demand became part and parcel of the autonomy movement of the early 1900s.[39] Many reviews of this controversy tend to make the senior government a villain and territorial premier F.W.G. Haultain as a knight in shinning armour, but there seems to be no real need to view the situation in this light. Assessed in terms of the Dominion–provincial financial arrangements of the era, the Dominion government's policy with respect to territorial appropriations can hardly be called "penurious."

In terms of the need for roads, bridges, public buildings, and public services engendered by the rapid growth of population after 1897, the annual appropriations were small. They were sufficient to alleviate somewhat the lack of public works and services in a region which had to build up these from almost nothing. There was never enough to meet many urgent demands for expenditure, but no government anywhere can satisfy all demands made upon it, and few can meet fully even urgent demands.

LOCAL REVENUES

The small magnitude of the local receipts of the territorial government during the early years is indicated in Table 1.7. The local receipts came chiefly from liquor permits, billiard licences, and fines. Smaller amounts were derived from auctioneers' licences, marriage licences, ferry licences, legal fees, and the sale of stray horses. The receipts from liquor permits and licenses provided more than 80 per cent of total local receipts until 1900.

Table 1.7 Receipts of the North-West Territorial Government and Dominion
Government Appropriations to the Territorial Government, 1874–87
(in thousands of dollars)

Year	Local	Dominion
1874	0	13
1875	0	32
1876	0	4
1877	0	18
1878	0	18
1879	–	11
1880	–	10
1881	–	18
1882	–	19
1883	4	29
1884	7	35
1885	8	49
1886	7	3,235
1887	11	110

Sources: Local receipts data are derived from the Government of the North-West Territories, *Public Accounts, 1885–87*. The Dominion Government appropriations are figures obtained from *C.Y.B.*, 1906, 356.

Local revenues of the territorial government remained small throughout the entire territorial period. In most years from 1893 to 1905 they provided from 10 per cent to 15 per cent of the total revenue (see Table 1.8). Although the territorial council was given the power to levy direct taxes for territorial purposes in 1886, it was reluctant to levy direct taxes upon the general public, and this became characteristic of subsequent provincial administrations. The levying of such taxes on any significant scale was delegated to local governments. An ordinance in 1903 provided for the imposition of succession duties, but collections were negligible for the country was new.

Municipal governments levied direct taxes on property and income. At first, the level of taxation was low by any standards, but by 1903 it rose substantially – almost to the level of the territorial revenue, including the Dominion appropriation. The figures for the city of Edmonton in Table 1.8 are indicative of the trend of urban taxation; from 1900 to 1905, the tax levy quadrupled in that city. Before 1897 there was little rural taxation, except for school purposes, but with

Table 1.8   Revenues of the Government of the North-West Territories, 1886–1905, and Tax Levies of the City of Edmonton, 1892–1905 (in thousands of dollars)

Year	Revenue of the Territorial Government			Edmonton		
	Dominion Government	Local Sources	Total	Property Assessment	Tax Levy	Mill Rate
1886	0	6	6			
1887	0	11	11			
1888	0	17	17			
1889	0	16	16			
1890	0	20	20			
1891	0	19	19			
1892	60	46	106	674	6	8.0
1893	220	31	251	964	14	11.3
1894	234	34	268	989	19	16.1
1895	228	30	258	1,132	18	12.9
1896	213	30	242	915	15	14.3
1897	384	28	412	769	16	15.9
1898	284	196	480	1,031	21	17.0
1899	303	42	345	1,188	22	15.5
1900	420	47	467	1,245	28	19.5
1901	472	73	545	1,396	33	21.5
1902	549	101	650	1,724	37	19.5
1903	988	120	1,108	3,208	55	16.5
1904	683	159	842	3,960	76	17.0
1905	848	178	1,026	6,621	116	16.0

Sources: The data on revenues of the territorial government were obtained from the Government of the North-West Territories, *Public Accounts, 1886–1905*. The figures under "Dominion government" include payments to the territorial government on account of the school lands. The 1905 figures are eight-month totals. The liquidator received some additional revenues between September 1 and November 24, 1905, which are not included here.

The Edmonton data were obtained from the City of Edmonton, *Financial and Departmental Report*, 1912, 250. School tax levies are included for all years except 1892. The mill rate is obtained by adding the mill rates for municipal, debenture, and Protestant school purposes. The Catholic school rates were higher than the Protestant school rates. Edmonton was incorporated as a town in 1892 and as a city in 1904.

the increasing settlement of the territories and the establishment of improvement districts, levies rose significantly.

Urban municipalities and school districts, in contrast to the territorial government which at the most could overdraw its accounts with the banks in anticipation of receipt of the Dominion grant, could float debentures. By the end of 1905 Edmonton had a debenture debt exceeding $400,000, or close to $40 per capita. At the end of the same year town and village school districts in Alberta had debenture liabilities of $397,000, while those of the rural districts amounted to $227,000.[40] These were modest beginnings in the accumulation of public debt. But the floodgates opened after 1905, and the above figures look paltry beside the ones of 1913, the last year of the Canadian investment and settlement boom before World War I.

GOVERNMENT AND THE ECONOMY

The impact of the government upon the economy was more significant in less direct ways than by outright expenditures. Here the Dominion government was very influential. It spent large sums upon immigration and upon the transcontinental railways. In addition, its railway land policy and its railway construction guarantees provided much stimulus to private investment and economic activity in the territories. These policies were, of course, undertaken deliberately to stimulate development of the Canadian Northwest.

The consensus of students of Dominion-territorial relationships before 1905 seems to be that the financial embarrassment of the territorial government was a very important factor leading to pressure for increased grants and constant negotiations after 1900 on the question of autonomy. In his budget speech of 1901, the territorial treasurer, Arthur Sifton, complained that "we are not getting and cannot get under present conditions the amount of money proper to carry on the affairs of the country."[41] The opposition leader, R.B. Bennett, after taking Sifton to task for claiming a budget surplus (a Siftonian habit perpetuated for many years in Alberta), wound up his speech by saying that the Dominion government should pay the territories an annuity of one million dollars. In his budget speech of 1902, Sifton called the Dominion grant "totally inadequate."[42] Haultain called it a "starvation allowance."[43] Territorial members of parliament expressed similar sentiments. By 1903 most of these opinions and sentiments had become sufficiently focused as a demand for provincial autonomy to lead the Dominion government to take action.

Early in 1905 Sir Wilfrid Laurier brought down the autonomy bills for debate in the Canadian parliament. These were passed after various amendments, chiefly with respect to the education clauses and the public lands subsidy, and the government of the Northwest Territories ceased to exercise jurisdiction after August 31. A liquidator was appointed to collect accrued revenues, to make deferred and previously authorized expenditures, and to divide the assets of the old government between those of the two new provinces.

GOVERNMENT STRUCTURE OF ALBERTA

The geographical and historical background has been sketched in the previous sections. It remains to examine briefly the governmental structure and procedure of the province.

GENERAL FRAMEWORK

The constitution of Alberta is the Alberta Act passed by the Canadian parliament in 1905. This federal statute made Alberta a province subject to the clauses of the British North America Act of 1867, and also provided for special clauses pertaining to Alberta with respect to education, public lands, and Dominion government subsidies.[44] Thus the new province was given the powers and functions of other provinces of Canada except as modified by special clauses in the Alberta Act. These special clauses provided for the establishment of separate public schools where a religious group so desired, for federal administration and ownership of the unalienated lands, and for special subsidies based upon the principle of compensation for the lack of public domain revenues, the need for public buildings, and a fictitious debt allowance.[45] In 1930, after a long period of controversy and negotiation, the Dominion government transferred the control and ownership of the public lands to the province. The subsidy clauses were changed in 1907 by an amendment of the British North America Act which revised provincial subsidies upward. There were also modifications which did not involve constitutional amendments. For example, special provisions were made with respect to unemployment and agricultural relief in the 1930s, tax fields in 1941 and 1947, and debt adjustment in 1945.

The province has had a single-chambered legislature from the beginning which has been changed in size from time to time by provincial legislation.[46] The first premier served as provincial treasurer and minister of education. Succeeding premiers have tended to assume only one of these two portfolios or none at all.[47]

PROVINCIAL GOVERNMENT FUNCTIONS

The chief function of a province is to serve as an agency of self-government on all matters which are not of direct Dominion importance. It differs from the small local governments in size, in the possession of parliamentary institutions, and in its status as a constitutionally autonomous community.[48] The functions and powers of all provinces are enumerated in Section 92 of the British North America Act of 1867 and its amendments. Alberta became subject to the provisions of this act by the Alberta Act of 1905, and consequently its functions as a province are those listed in Section 92 of the 1867 Act. It has not always been easy to distinguish between Dominion and provincial jurisdictions with respect to various matters mentioned in the section, and there have been many disputes. Therefore, it is more useful in terms of subsequent discussions of provincial finance to present a short sketch of the activities of government departments, rather than to repeat the phraseology of Section 92.

Originally, there were six departments:

The department of the attorney-general is responsible for discharging "the second duty of the sovereign," the administration of justice. It administers and enforces all Dominion laws in the province, as well as the provincial laws; it supervises the work of the courts and it collects a variety of fees, licences, fines and penalties. During the first two decades, the department licensed the liquor trade, but in the 1920s, this function was transferred to a newly constituted liquor control board under the jurisdiction of the treasury department.

The agriculture department has concerned itself from the first with the encouragement and development of agriculture. It has also supervised provincial creameries, and has established agricultural schools and experimental farms. Very early on, it was also responsible for public health.

The education department has concerned itself mainly with the supervision of teaching and of schools. It also disburses the provincial grants to schools and determines the scheme of allocation of these grants among the various districts.

The public works department is concerned with the construction and maintenance of highways, bridges, and public buildings of all departments. It licences trucks and buses, it administers highway traffic regulations, and was responsible for the telephone system in the first few years. It also provides for the inspection of steam boilers, elevators, and a number of similar matters.[49]

The department of the provincial secretary is responsible for all communications between the province and the other governments. It has also administered the provincial corporation acts, collected corporation and railway taxes, issued marriage licences, licensed automobiles and theatres, and administered various matters pertaining to jails and to hospitals for the insane, but some of these functions have since been transferred to other departments.

The treasury department completes the list of the first departments formed. It is responsible for the financial administration of the province. The work of the department is dealt with at a later point in connection with the budgetary procedure.

As established functions expanded in scope and as new ones were undertaken, additional departments were organized. Thus the department of railways and telephones was organized out of the public works department in 1912. The department of municipal affairs is an outgrowth of the local improvement branch of the department of public works. This department advises and supervises the local governments of the province. It also collects most of the property taxes of the provincial government when such taxes exist. The department of industries and labour was organized in the 1930s to regulate such matters as collective bargaining, union organization, labour practices, industrial standards, hours of labour, minimum wages, workmen's compensation, and many other related matters. A department of economic affairs was organized in the 1940s to promote development of immigration and cultural activities, to develop tourist and travel facilities, and to publicize the province generally.

The department of public health and welfare was established in 1918 to deal with various functions previously performed by the department of agriculture and provincial secretary. More lately, it has been split to form the departments of public health and of public welfare. The public health department has a wide variety of duties: the operation of provincial hospitals, asylums, and sanatoriums; the supervision and enforcement of public health regulations; the issue of marriage licences; the collection of vital statistics; the registration of nurses, the allocation and distribution of grants to hospitals. The public welfare department supervises various social services such as old age and blind pensions, mothers' allowances, unemployment relief, child welfare, and homes for the aged and indigent relief. The expenditures of both these departments have increased steadily as more services have been provided and higher minimum standards have been set.

The department of lands and mines was established after 1930 when the province obtained title to the public lands. Recently it has been split to form the department of mines and minerals and of lands and forests. The former administers the provincial laws with respect to coal mining and petroleum and natural gas production. The department of lands and forests regulates the fishing, trapping, hunting, grazing, homesteading, and the cutting of timber, as well as a number of minor related matters.

In terms of expenditures, the departments of public works, education, health, and public welfare bulk the largest at the present time.[50] During the early years the departments of the attorney-general and agriculture absorbed much larger proportions of expenditure than now. An analysis of expenditures on a functional basis must, of course, cut across departmental lines. This is done in subsequent chapters.

REVENUE STRUCTURE

The most striking external characteristic of the provincial revenue system has been, and still is, the great number and variety of sources of revenue.[51] The province relied heavily upon Dominion subsidies and the school lands fund during the early years, and only slightly upon taxation, this power having been delegated to the municipalities.

In the World War I period, however, a number of new taxes were imposed and the rates of old ones were raised. Thus revenue from taxes rose to considerable prominence during the period between the two world wars, especially since further taxes (e.g. income tax) were imposed during the 1930s. Recent Dominion-provincial agreements and the buoyancy of other provincial revenues have made direct provincial taxes less important. The gasoline tax is now the chief source of tax revenue. Revenue from public domain has come to form the largest item in the provincial total in recent years due to petroleum discoveries. Liquor profits are also a significant item. In addition, the province receives large amounts from the Dominion government in lieu of taxes, and grants-in-aid for a number of social services. The province also collects smaller but nonetheless substantial sums through licences, fees and fines on an ever widening array of services.[52] The sales of commodities and resources has also brought in revenues.

A word about Dominion subsidies and the School lands fund will help explain the revenues derived from these two sources:

Dominion Subsidies: The financial terms of the autonomy measures of 1905 were substantially the same for both Alberta and Saskatchewan. For several years to come, the subsidy comprised the major source of provincial revenue, but rapid development and growth necessitated the tapping of other sources of revenue. The subsidies became less and less significant as a proportion of total revenues although they continued to be a bone of contention between the Dominion government and the province. The provinces have persistently outdone Oliver Twist in asking for more and the Dominion government has been reluctant to provide second helpings.[53]

The original subsidy terms for Alberta were as follows:[54]

(1) A per capita subsidy of 80 cents based on an estimated population of 250,000 in 1905, and to be revised every 2.5 years until the population reached 800,000;
(2) $50,000 for the support of the government;
(3) A debt allowance of $405,375 being the equivalent of interest at 5% on an assumed debt of $8,107,500;
(4) $375,000 in lieu of revenue from public lands retained by the Dominion government, to be increased to $562,500 when the population exceeded 400,000, to $750,000 when the population exceeded 800,000, and to $1,125,000 when the population exceeded 1,200,000;
(5) $93,750 per annum for five years only, as an additional allowance in lieu of public lands, and to provide for the construction of necessary public buildings.

The initial subsidy to the province amounted to $1,124,125 according to the above stipulations. The 1907 revision of all Dominion subsidies led to an increase of $130,000 per annum for government, bringing this subsidy up to $180,000. But the increased subsidies utterly failed to meet the much greater increase in provincial expenditures. This failure is the origin of the provincial request for control of public domain lands. The first Alberta government resolution containing such a request was in 1910, but not until 1930 would the Dominion government transfer title of public lands to the province.

The School Lands Fund: By the Dominion Lands Act of 1872 (35 Vict., c. 23, s. 22), Sections 11 and 29 in every surveyed township throughout the extent of Dominion lands were set apart as an endowment for education. The school lands were administered by the Minister of the Interior of the Dominion government, who arranged for the sale of such lands. The proceeds were to be invested in Dominion securities, and the interest thereon, after deducting the cost of management, was to be paid annually to the government of the province or territory in which the lands sold were situated. Sales were made by public auctions. By and large, the system and timing of sales were successful and there seems to be no major criticism of the Dominion land policy with respect to the school lands administration.[55]

The provincial government receipts from this source increased rapidly. During the early years the fund provided for a substantial portion of the grants to schools, sometimes more than half the grants. The fund helped to ease the financial burden of education during the early years when it was not always easy to collect school taxes in cash from struggling settlers, and when the provincial government itself had not developed a local revenue system yielding substantial and adequate sums.

BUDGETARY PROCEDURE

One of the first statutes to be passed by the first Alberta legislature dealt with the duties and powers of the treasury department and with the auditing of public accounts.[56] The fiscal structure erected by the first act has not been altered substantially although some changes have been made. It bears mentioning that the fiscal year was changed in 1927 to run from April 1 to March 31, and that accounting procedures have undergone change by refinement in techniques.

The Treasury Department was set up to manage and control the revenue and expenditure of the province. At present, the Treasury Board exercises much the same kinds of power as the treasury board of the Dominion government. It reviews the estimates, allocates appropriations during the fiscal year wherever allocation is called for, approves accounting methods and procedures in the treasury and operating departments, and generally serves as the arbiter and investigator when accounts or expenditures are questioned. The treasury department receives the provincial revenues collected by various departments; it also collects revenue directly. Thus it receives the Dominion subsidy, and the Dominion government tax subsidy; it collects interest on provincial investments and bank balances. It collects a number of refunds, public utility commission fees, and proceeds from the sale of gazettes and statutes, and it receives payments of various kinds of advances. Until the phenomenal rise of public domain, the department was the major collector of revenue. The department is also custodian of provincial funds and disburses provincial moneys. Finally, it assembles and tabulates the budget estimates for the provincial treasurer.

The early public accounts are haphazard and contain large miscellaneous categories in which one finds immersed such substantial items as bank loans and interest on such loans.[57] Following the reorganization of accounting techniques and procedures in 1924, the Alberta public accounts have been models for other public accounts. The chief criticism of them attests to the high standard of work of present-day provincial accountants: that the accounting techniques and classifications used have been refined so much that the layman or the average legislator is just as confused as he would be with the early accounts. It may be asking a great deal, of course, to request a simple annual statement of provincial revenues and expenditures, lumping together items now classified as income and capital items, which would be intelligible to the average layman who has enough initiative to devote some time to the study of the financial position of his province.[58] Nevertheless, democracy cannot progress unless there is a growth in the number of participating and informed citizens.

The provincial treasurer delivers the budget speech usually in February or March, but many speeches have been delivered in other months. The treasurer usually outlines the general economic conditions which obtained during the previous year, reviews of the financial operation of the government during that year, and presents the revenue and expenditure estimates for the coming year. Once passed and after the lieutenant-governor signs it, the budget becomes law.

The executive council has the power to issue special warrants to provide for unforeseen expenditures which arise when the legislature is not in session. Such warrants have also been used to augment appropriations which run out earlier in the fiscal year. The provincial auditor must include in the public accounts all special warrants issued during the fiscal year, stating both amounts and purposes. Weather conditions, sudden economic changes which often have arisen from weather factors, and changes in government are major factors which have given rise to the use of warrants on a considerable scale.

LOCAL GOVERNMENT

Rural Local Government: The territorial ordinance of 1903 with respect to local improvement districts continued in force until 1912. In 1905 the local improvement districts were put under the jurisdiction of the local improvement branch of the provincial department of public works, and the clerk in charge of this branch became known as the tax commissioner. The organization of small districts proceeded rapidly. So many requests for organization in new areas were made that the provincial government considered that the time was ripe for the creation of full-fledged municipalities. Accordingly, a Rural Municipality Act was passed in 1912, providing for the establishment of rural municipal corporations and for a provincial department of municipal affairs.[59]

The large local improvement districts were dissolved. The province was divided into nine-township squares beginning at the south eastern corner of the province.[60] Residents of such units could request incorporation of the unit as a rural municipality if it had a density of at least one person per square mile. They also had the option of applying for the setting up of the unit as an organized local improvement district to be operated in accordance with the regulations of the Local Improvement Act of 1907.[61] The administration unit for unorganized territory administered by the department of municipal affairs become the nine-township square.[62]

The organized local improvement district was more popular than the rural municipality. In 1912, 90 units became local improvement districts. Most of these districts were located in the areas which had been settled longest and which had been in organized areas before. Rural municipalities numbered 55; most of these were set up in newly settled areas, which had previously been unorganized. There was considerable opposition, especially in the older areas, to the organization of rural municipalities. This opposition rose from the fear of increased taxation, the fear of going into debt, and the dislike of electing councillors at large rather than by wards.[63] When various changes in regulations failed to encourage the formation of municipalities, the provincial government passed legislation, which compelled all existing organized local improvement districts to organize as municipalities in 1918. This step doubled the number of municipal districts in the province.[64]

The municipal districts met with varying fortunes in the years that followed.[65] Many drought-stricken districts became unable to operate without substantial external assistance,[66] and most of these were disorganized and amalgamated as Special Areas, administered by the provincial government. The remainder became improvement districts. A few municipal districts along the western fringe of settlement also reverted to the improvement form of organization whereby they became administered by the provincial government.

The next step of reorganization came in 1942 when the provincial government dissolved most municipal districts and organized new, larger units.[67] Finally, in 1950, the provincial legislature passed a measure that provided for the organization of counties with omnibus authority over all kinds of local governments within a given area. Organization of such counties is optional. The first one of these counties was set up on January 1, 1951.

A brief summary of present organization is in order. Rural areas are divided into municipal districts and improvement districts. The functions of these districts are to provide for public works, local public welfare, protection of persons and property, sanitation and health. The districts levy taxes not only for their own functions, but also for school and hospital purposes. Towns and villages inside the boundaries of the districts are not under the jurisdiction of the districts; they are separate incorporated municipalities. Elected councils govern the municipal districts and secretary-treasurers and their staffs carry on the day-to-day administration. Thus responsibility for local government functions, policies, and the collection of all local taxes is vested in local residents. The improvement districts are merely administrative areas in which the provincial government through the Department of Municipal Affairs levies taxes for the provision of local services, the level of expenditure and levies being decided by the provincial government. In these areas, then, the senior government is responsible for local government functions and tax collections.

Urban Local Government: Urban municipal organization proceeded with far less prodding and supervision by the provincial government than rural organization. If anything, the provincial government had to exercise restraint to prevent small centres from acquiring too elaborate a government structure. Nevertheless, centres with only 2,000 people secured city charters.

There have been no major changes in urban municipal organization since 1905, except to provide for uniform city charters in 1951. The functions and organization of urban centres are similar to those elsewhere in North America. Consequently, there is little need here for an elaboration of the structure of urban municipalities. There are three kinds of urban units: cities, towns, and villages. From the beginning, the basis for differentiation has been population within a defined area. The required population has been revised upward from time to time for the three kinds of units.

Special charters granted by the provincial government govern Cities. Towns and villages are subject to the stipulations of one act, *The Town and Village Act*. Towns have a more elaborate governmental structure than villages. For example, a town has five councillors and a mayor, while a village has three councillors, one of whom is known as the reeve. There are at present about 500 hamlets in the province. These are under the jurisdiction of municipal or improvement districts. Table 1.9 shows the graph of urban incorporations for census years since 1891.

The chief revenue sources of urban centres are the property tax and the business tax. Licences provide a minor part of total revenues. Municipally owned public utilities provide substantial revenues in some centres. During the early 1900s the urban centres tried the experiment of assessing land only, leaving all other property tax-free. Fiscal need and the collapse of urban land values reversed this trend. Since World War I there has been an increasing tendency to assess and tax buildings and improvements, at least on a partial basis.[68]

School Districts: The scheme of organization for school districts inherited from the territorial regime was continued without much modification until 1936. Since then there have been various reorganizations, and districts have become larger, but fewer in number.

Both urban and rural school districts have obtained most of their revenues from taxation of local property and from provincial government grants. Until quite recently there was little uniformity in tax collection procedure. Many

Table 1.9   Number of Incorporated Urban Municipalities in Alberta
for Census Years Since 1891

Year	Cities	Towns	Villages	Total
1891	0	2	0	2
1901	1	7	20	28
1906	5	23	36	64
1911	6	44	65	115
1916	6	49	105	160
1921	6	54	119	179
1926	6	54	125	185
1931	7	54	145	206
1936	7	52	146	205
1941	7	53	145	205
1946	7	54	134	195

Sources: *North-West Gazette, Alberta Gazettes*, and the Department of Municipal Affairs,
Annual Reports.

school districts collected their own taxes, while others made arrangements
for municipalities, urban or rural, to collect their taxes for them. In 1945, it
became compulsory for all school districts to send requisitions of its local revenue requirements to the various municipal governments within its area. These
municipal governments, rural and urban, strike school mill rates on assessed
property accordingly and collect the school taxes.[69] They pay the requisitions of
the school districts, however, on the basis of what the latter request, and not on
the basis of tax collections for a given period.[70]

Hospital Districts: These are analogous to the school districts. They
comprise integral areas that are often under the jurisdiction of several municipalities. Hospitals are built to provide hospital and medical facilities for
residents. These districts obtain their revenues from requisitions on municipalities, which levy a hospital tax on property, and from provincial grants.

PROVINCIAL ADMINISTRATION

The province has had three administrations since 1906, Liberal, United Farmers
of Alberta, and Social Credit. In 1905, only the two traditional Canadian parties, Liberal and Conservative, were active in the provincial political arena. The
Liberals won overwhelmingly in the election of the fall of 1905, obtaining 23
seats out of 25. They were re-elected, though with somewhat smaller majori-
ties, in the elections of 1909, 1913, and 1917. They went down to defeat in the

election of 1921 when the United Farmers of Alberta entered politics and won easily. Neither the Liberals nor the Conservatives have made much headway in the political field since that date. The Liberal party built up the framework of the administrative machinery of the province and during the first five years pursued rather conservative policies. In 1910, the party split into two factions in connection with the Alberta and Great Waterways Railway case. In any event, the administration tended more and more to take its cue from the more radical and extravagant spirits within the party and from the United Farmers of Alberta, a rapidly growing organization which made continuous demands upon the government for a variety of rural expenditures and policies.[71] A.L. Sifton, the chief justice of Alberta, became premier in 1910, and he was able to reconcile the various conflicting elements, which threatened to lead to the disintegration of the Liberal party and administration. He left in 1917 to join the Union government formed at Ottawa, and the long-threatened break-up of the Liberal party became complete in 1921.

The Liberal administration obtained a reputation for extravagance, reckless incurrence of debt, and corruption. A statement in the report of the Bank of Canada on provincial finance in Alberta published in 1937 is as follows: "After making full allowance for the rapid economic development of the province, and the legitimate cost of facilities provided by the government to aid and stimulate this development, it remains the case – in our opinion – that the 1905–22 period was characterised by waste, loose administration, and incurrence of debt to an extent which could not be justified even when allowance is made for the optimistic spirit of the times."[72] The language used by the contemporary daily papers and the man on the street was much stronger. The Liberals have been unable to live down the reputation of their early administration almost until this day. Yet the judgement is too harsh. If the Liberal administration had pursued a more conservative policy, it would have been replaced by another administration that would have done much the same things as those that were done. The platforms of both parties contained proposals for government ownership and operation of several kinds of enterprises such as railways, grain elevators, packing plants, creameries, hail insurance, and farm credit institutions. If anything, the Conservative opposition was more vociferous about government ownership than the Liberal administration which felt the burden of office. Outside the two parties stood the strong organization of the United Farmers of Alberta (U.F.A.), which could deal a moral blow whenever it so desired. Until the end of World War I this organization supported the Liberals. But when the Liberals failed to usher in an "agricultural utopia" and the severe depression of 1921 struck the province, the U.F.A. entered policies and formed an administration.[73]

The U.F.A. remained in power for fourteen years. It was sustained by the electorate in 1926 and 1930, but was swept out of power by the newly formed Social Credit party in 1935. The U.F.A. administration pursued surprisingly conservative policies during its term of office. It found it just as difficult as the previous administration to solve the economic problems which beset farmers, and acquired a reputation for good administration along conventional lines. The severe depression of the early 1930s coupled with the personal scandals, real and alleged, involving cabinet ministers (including the premier), ensured their defeat when the Social Credit party was organized and entered provincial politics. The Liberals had high hopes of forming another administration in 1935, but the sudden decision of the Social Credit organization to enter the contest blasted their hopes.

The Social Credit party captured 56 seats out of 63 in the 1935 election. The chief opposition, as usual in the Alberta legislature, consisted of members elected by the two largest cities. But the Social Credit party did obtain more urban support than either of the other two previous administrations. The U.F.A. failed to elect a single member even in the rural constituencies. Social Credit, incidentally, received somewhat more than half of the popular vote, a rather high proportion in a four-party contest. The new administration attempted unsuccessfully to implement Social Credit proposals. One of its most well-known acts was the repudiation of part of the interest on Alberta government bonds and the default of such bonds. It won the election of 1940 by a rather narrow margin as Liberals, Conservatives, and many U.F.A. members combined to contest the election as the Independent party. More radical U.F.A. members supported the third entry in the contest, the Cooperative Commonwealth Federation, commonly known as the C.C.F. and regarded as the socialist party of Canada. The Independent party elected a substantial number of members and formed a strong opposition in the legislature along with the single C.C.F. member. The Independent party fell apart, however, and although the C.C.F. appeared to be a potential threat in the election of 1944, the Social Credit administration won a landslide victory in which almost all opposition was obliterated.

The present administration has gained a reputation among both rural and urban voters for honest and efficient government. In addition, the purely Social Credit appeal is still relatively strong in the rural constituencies. The opposition has been fragmentary and there has been no economic recession since the 1930s. The present premier is generally regarded as a man of integrity and sincerity, both because of his fundamentalist religious beliefs and Sunday radio broadcasts, and because he has proved to be an able administrator. The administration won an easy victory in the election of 1948. There are few indications that it would not win handily again if an election were held now.[74] A severe depression, especially if it were coupled with any substantial evidence at all of mismanagement or corruption, could lead to the defeat of the present party. Armament programs militate against the occurrence of large-scale depression; charges of corruption lack any substantiation in fact. One hears in all walks of life in the province that Alberta has "good honest government." Albertans would be sadly disillusioned if evidence should be found to the contrary.[75]

This is not the place to provide any detailed explanation of the political philosophy of Albertans. But the Alberta electorate, especially the rural part, has never subscribed wholeheartedly to a *laissez-faire* philosophy of government.[76] Agitation for government intervention and for expenditures on economic and social development was no weaker before and during World War I than in subsequent years. There has been little doubt among Albertans that governments play an influential part in the functioning of the economy. They have also subscribed to ideas which have fallen on barren ground elsewhere. The single tax movement was strong before World War I, and many municipalities had a whirl at the single tax on land, while the provincial government levied a tax on increases in land values or "unearned increments." The U.F.A. ideas of "co-operation instead of competition" and "production for use instead of profit" found uncritical acceptance. Social Credit theories provided new faith in economic salvation where the old slogans failed, and they were novel enough to make them distinguishable from previous slogans and theories. Finally, the political ideas of referendum and recall have found a place in all party platforms, including the Conservative.

The explanation of these manifestations is a very complex task, and one can only hazard the mention of a few prominent factors. One should not forget the shortage of capital in a new region, the hardships of pioneers who often fought a futile fight against the elements and declining agricultural prices, the resentment against middlemen in the distributive industries, the isolation and harshness of life on many western farms which favoured introspection concerning the economic systems which did not seem to offer any guarantees of security to farmers and which seemed to dash their hopes to the ground when the elements did not, the comparative lack of alternative economic opportunities within the region, and the high degree in which transportation costs and protective tariffs accentuated fluctuations in agricultural net income. Farmers in Manitoba and Saskatchewan were affected by the same factors but in lesser degree. Further, many of them had enjoyed more sustained prosperity at a higher level than Alberta farmers before 1930, a large number of whom were still pioneers at that date. Perhaps, too, as Professor Innes suggests, the Liberal government at Ottawa did more to "sweeten" the eastern Prairie Provinces when Alberta turned "sour." [77]

THE INVESTMENT BOOM, 1906–13

2

ECONOMIC DEVELOPMENT

Economic growth in terms of capital formation and productive capacity continued at a rapid pace after Alberta became a province. Thousands of new farms
were established; urban centres grew in number and in size; railways, roads,
bridges, public buildings, schools, hospitals, factories, warehouses, retail estab-
lishments, and office buildings were constructed at an accelerated rate until
1913. Investment was slowed up in 1908 by the financial crisis in the United
States and the poor crop in Alberta in 1907, but the setback was temporary for
investment recovered by 1909 and gained momentum until 1912. In that year,
immigration and railway mileage added reached peaks which have never been
exceeded,[1] while the value of building permits taken out in Alberta cities was
not exceeded until 1948. Table 2.1 reveals the growth of investment activity
between 1906 and 1912.

A high proportion of provincial income was generated by investment
expenditures. On the other hand, the income produced by agriculture was
relatively low compared to subsequent periods. This is indicated by the figures in Table 2.2.

The agricultural potential, of course, was being built up during the investment and settlement boom. The number of farms doubled between 1906 and
1911, and the field crop acreage more than tripled. The value of the wheat crop
in 1913 was seven times that of 1906.[2] The rapid expansion in wheat production was largely attributable to the opening up of the southeast for settlement.
Dairying and swine production made steady progress. Although the settlement
of the south and southeast made heavy inroads into the ranching industry, the
number of cattle in the province decreased until 1911. After that date the cattle
population began to rise again with the establishment of many new farms in the
central and northern parts of the province.

Table 2.1   Selected Indicators of Investment Activity in Alberta, 1906–1913

Year	Immigration (thousands)	Building Permits Edmonton & Calgary (millions)	Railway Mileage Added	Annual Population Increase
1906	23	$3.0	179	19
1907	31	4.4	87	51
1908	28	3.6	40	30
1909	43	4.5	149	35
1910	45	7.8	275	35
1911	46	16.7	318	38
1912	48	34.8	955	26
1913	44	17.9	592	29

Sources: The immigration figures are based on records at Canadian ports of entry and were taken from *Facts and Figures*, 51–52. Immigrants have been, and still are, required to state the province of intended destination. It does not necessarily follow that this is the province of eventual residence. The building permits data were obtained from the records of the two cities. Railway mileage added was obtained from *Facts and Figures*, 309. The figures on annual population increases were obtained from C.Y.B., 1946, 127.

Some other industries also grew to significance, manufacturing and coal mining being the most notable. The growth of manufacturing was partly dependent upon the increasing quantity and variety of agricultural products and partly upon the rise of urban markets for so-called "local" products such as bread, dairy products, and meats. The number of employees in manufacturing rose from less than 2,000 in 1905 to about 7,000 in 1910, and the gross value of manufactured products increased from $5 million to $19 million.[3]

A number of tertiary activities developed to distribute goods and provide services. Probably one-third of the working force was engaged in trade, transportation, communication, finance, services, and professions. The urban population growth of 138 per cent between 1906 and 1911 is indicative of the great expansion of such activities.

The economic development of the province was highly dependent upon capital drawn from outside the province. The commercial banks tapped the idle funds of their branches elsewhere in Canada and provided short-term funds for business concerns and governments on the prairies. Corporation securities and government bonds and debentures were sold in England, United States, and Eastern Canada, the English market absorbing the major share of such issues. Loan, trust, and insurance companies lent large sums on mortgages, chiefly to farmers.[4] Finally, many immigrants, particularly Americans, brought substantial

Table 2.2   Provincial Income and Net Value of Agricultural Production in Alberta, 1906–1913 (in millions of dollars)

Year	Provincial Income	Net Value of Agriculture
1906	41	13
1907	53	14
1908	60	19
1909	73	23
1910	88	25
1911	130	55
1912	168	52
1913	165	58

Sources: The provincial income figures are based upon estimates made by the writer (see Appendix A), and they are to be regarded as indications of the trends in economic activity. The net values of agricultural production are also estimates and are components of the provincial income estimates (see Appendix A, Table A3).

amounts of capital with them. The "marginal efficiency of capital"[5] was high, and rising interest rates throughout 1912 and 1913 failed to deter investors from borrowing. English lenders were not too selective in their extension of funds to Canadian borrowers. In the urban centres, real estate speculation became rife by 1911, "a natural product of exotic progress, an outgrowth of Western enthusiasm."[6] The break in investment activity and urban real estate booms seemed far off in 1912, but interest rates were turning upward by the end of the year. In 1913 the long investment boom tapered off, and it sputtered to a stop by 1914.

FISCAL POLICIES OF THE PROVINCIAL GOVERNMENT

INITIAL POLICIES AND COMMITMENTS

The first budget for the province was presented to the legislature on May 7, 1906, by Premier A.C. Rutherford who also served as provincial treasurer. By present-day standards it was small indeed, but by territorial standards it seemed large.[7] Rutherford outlined the terms of the Dominion subsidy agreement and expressed great satisfaction with them. Other revenues were to be obtained from railway taxation, land registration fees, corporation taxes and educational tax on lands outside school districts. About half the estimated expenditures were appropriated to public works.

The next three budgets followed much the same pattern. There were references to the general economic situation in each year. The Dominion subsidy amendments of 1907 found favour with the premier, while the 1905 terms were referred to as being only "fairly good" in the budget speech of 1908. Continued reference was made to the need for increased population. Estimated surpluses were announced in each year. Such surpluses were arrived at in two ways. First, total appropriations were not spent in 1906, and the province ended the year with over $500,000 in its treasury. By including this amount in 1907 revenue estimates, Rutherford was able to predict a surplus for the year. Secondly, in 1909 a capital account was set up, a device which was, no doubt, forced upon the premier by the government supporters who felt that the provincial government was proceeding altogether too stodgily. In any event, Rutherford defended borrowing and the setting up of a capital account by quoting the provincial treasurer of Manitoba at some length on these matters, and by stressing the need for further public works and buildings.

Thus the Rutherford administration, after a cautious start, soon found the pressure for a more rapid rate of construction of highways, telephones, and public buildings to be irresistible. In 1907 it found itself manoeuvred into adopting a policy of government ownership of telephones. At that time the Bell Telephone Company served urban centres but refused to make substantial rural expansions despite continuous pressure for rural telephone service. Mr. Cushing, the Minister of Public Works, reflected rural opinion in a statement in the legislature in 1907:

> The Alberta government believes that if it has any function at all it
> is to protect the people from such monopolies (The Bell Telephone
> Company). The opinion of the government is that the only way to
> regulate such a monopoly is to enter into competition and ensure low
> rates and proper service. It desires to create the means by which the
> farmers will secure the business advantages that will result from a
> system of municipal telephones throughout the province of Alberta.
> Last session's legislation made it possible for people to operate their
> own system and for the province to supply the trunk lines.[8]

In 1908 the provincial government bought out the Bell Telephone Company and floated a bond issue of $2 million in London to finance this transaction and to provide funds for expansion. The telephone venture was to prove an expensive one in which expenditures were often tempered by political expediency.

But it was the railway question that was the paramount issue. When the province was formed there were no railroads north or west of Edmonton; the city lacked connections to the east; and the whole central eastern part of the province lacked railroad services. The south was served well enough by the main line of the Canadian Pacific Railway and there was a trunk line running from Macleod in the south to Calgary and Edmonton. It was felt that the Canadian Pacific, the Canadian Northern, and other companies chartered and aided by the Dominion government were proceeding too slowly. The provincial Conservatives and a number of Liberals on the government side suggested provincial government construction, ownership and operation. A veritable railway "fever" gripped the legislature in 1909, an election year, and the government finally brought down the long-awaited railway legislation.

Thus after a careful start by Premier Rutherford, who tried to hold down borrowing, the electorate in a raw and expanding economy was not to be denied. It wanted government assistance to provide facilities for exploiting the resources of the region: highways, railways, telephones, and agricultural marketing agencies. As a consequence, the provincial government was highly committed in the telephone business and railway construction as early as 1909. In addition, it had inherited the hail insurance scheme initiated by the territorial government and the creameries of the Dominion government. The former was showing signs of snowballing into heavy expenditures in 1909 and the latter did not improve the condition of the provincial treasury in any way. The seeds of future fiscal difficulties of Alberta governments had been sown.

THE ALBERTA AND GREAT WATERWAYS RAILWAY

By the legislation of 1909 the government guaranteed the bonds of three companies in three separate bills. The Canadian Northern and the Grand Trunk Pacific were given guarantees totalling over $17 million to build railways in the central and northern part of the province. The Alberta and Great Waterways Railway Company headed by W.R. Clarke, a Kansas city banker and railway man, was given a guarantee of $20,000 per mile and $400,000 for terminals at Edmonton, the total guarantee running up to $7,400,000. This railway was to be built to Fort McMurray in the northeast where water transportation to the Mackenzie River was available and where extensive tar sand discoveries had been made. At the same time it was to open up agricultural territories in the north for settlement.

The two Canadian companies proceeded with the construction of the railways projected for them, although at a slower rate than the general public expected and desired. But these companies were also engaged in the construction of transcontinental lines guaranteed by the federal government. Consequently, it took time to get the provincially guaranteed branch lines started and completed.

Late in 1909 the London branch of J.P. Morgan and Company floated $7,400,000 of Alberta and Great Waterways first mortgage bonds in London. They were to carry interest at 5%, to mature in 50 years, and sold at a price of 110.[9] Mr. Clark organized the Canada West Construction Company under Dominion charter, arranged with his company, the Alberta and Great Waterways Railway Company to construct the railway and to receive $7,400,000 for such construction. The proceeds of the sale of bonds, amounting to $7,400,000, were deposited in chartered banks in Edmonton.[10] Mr. Clarke then assigned to the construction company any rights he and the original company held, and also assigned the net proceeds of the bond issue to the construction company. The latter in turn assigned its rights to the Royal Bank of Canada, which held $6 million of the proceeds, as collateral security for the advances made or to be made.[11]

It was an ill-starred venture. Some members of the legislature from Southern Alberta had opposed it from the start. Other members began to have doubts about the integrity of the promoters. There were many allegations with respect to the Morgan transaction, and it was charged that the government had not safeguarded the province sufficiently in getting construction of the railway started and completed. The Rutherford administration, which had been re-elected by a large majority at the polls in 1909, split wide open over the issue as Mr. Cushing, the public works minister, resigned. The reasons for this split are clouded in obscurity. There were other members in the Liberal party in Alberta, too, who felt that the premier was going much too slowly and was merely giving Alberta a prosaic, routine sort of government. It may be said this faction considered the railway issue a convenient one on which to break with Rutherford and to discredit him among the electors, because the public was thoroughly aroused, not only by the delay in building a northern railway, but by the Morgan transaction.

The reorganized Rutherford cabinet barely escaped defeat in the legislature on several occasions by insurgent Liberals and the Conservatives, who now joined forces. The cabinet ministers, uncertain of their tenure with every vote taken, finally drew up a resolution appointing a royal commission "for the purpose of ascertaining whether any and if any, which officer, or officers of the Government, or member, or members, of the Legislature of the Province, were or are interested, directly or indirectly, by themselves, or through others in the erection, incorporation or organization of the Alberta and Great Waterways Railway Company, or in the making of, or entering into, or carrying out a certain contract between the Government and the Province and the Alberta and Great Waterways Railway Company, or the guaranteeing by the province of the securities of the said company or the sale thereof or in the proceeds of, or the amount realized from, the disposition or sale of the said securities or otherwise, howsoever, in connection with the said Company." The resolution was passed unanimously, the legislature adjourned, and a commission was appointed.

The commission began its hearings late in March 1910. It gathered volumes of testimony and evidence. Members of the government and of the provincial legislature gave evidence, and so did E.A. James, general manager of Clark's railway company. Clarke himself refused to give evidence, a fact which Albertans regarded as a direct affront to their province and which made distrust of financial promoters even more deeply ingrained than before. A letter was received from the Morgan's in London stating that no rake-off had been paid to any one and that the sale of bonds had been a straight transaction.[12] In November the commission submitted its report to the legislature. The majority report, signed by Chief Justice Harvey and Justice Scott, stated that the government had not taken all the precautions it could have done in its dealings with Clarke and associates, accepted the denial of Premier Rutherford and Attorney General Cross that they had no personal interest in the enterprise and concluded that there was no evidence that they had any such interest. Justice Beck, who made a minority report, exonerated the Rutherford government. The general consensus of the press and the public was that the commission had failed to clear the government of stigma in the affair.

Whether Rutherford or any members of his party had any personal interest in the whole transaction has never been shown. It seems inconceivable that the premier had any such interest. The record of his public life indicates that he was a methodical, sincere, and well-meaning man who did not know everything that his henchmen were doing. He and his cabinet resigned in May 1910, before the commission completed its hearings, and the lieutenant governor called upon Chief Justice Sifton to form a new Liberal administration.

Premier Arthur Sifton was a forceful leader with a strong and somewhat arrogant personality. He had to perform both as a tightrope walker and a strong man to maintain a Liberal administration. He performed adroitly and forcefully until he left Alberta in 1917 to become a member of the federal cabinet. He found himself in a difficult position when he took office. There was a clamour for a railway for the North Country; there was continuous pressure for increased expenditures on telephones and highways; and there was the problem of who should pay the interest on Alberta and Great Waterways bonds.

On July 11, 1910, the Sifton administration paid the half-yearly interest on the railway bonds, giving as its reason for so doing that the railway company had defaulted. The $7,400,000 was still in the hands of the banks and was drawing interest at 3.5%, but the provincial government was unable to obtain either the principal or bank interest. In November 1910, Premier Sifton introduced a bill in the legislature in which he proposed to lay claim to the proceeds of the bond issue in order to provide revenues for general expenditure of the province. He pointed out that the railway company had failed to proceed with construction and that it had defaulted on the payment of interest. The province, by taking over the proceeds, would incur a direct liability, and the railway company would be freed of any claims under the bond issue. A number of Liberals opposed the measure, and R.B. Bennett, the Conservative leader who subsequently became prime minister of the federal government, said that the measure meant confiscation, repudiation of a contract (for the first time) by a British legislature and that it would lead to much litigation.[13] But the measure passed after much debate. Clarke immediately protested and made appeals to Ottawa to prevent the province from taking over the bond issue proceeds. The province, however, failed to collect anyway because the banks refused to pay the money deposited with them to the government on the grounds that they had no right, under the circumstances, to pay it to anyone. Consequently, the case went to the courts.

The government now found its position financially precarious and legally embarrassing. It made the semi-annual interest payments on the bonds in question by resorting to borrowing from the banks. It entered suit against the Royal Bank of Canada to collect money, both principal and accrued interest, belonging to Alberta and Great Waterways. In addition, the government was itself sued by the Royal Bank of Canada for reimbursement of $398,000 paid out by the bank in connection with railway construction. A number of other parties, chiefly railway suppliers and engineering firms, also entered suit against the provincial government for reimbursement for materials and services supplied the railway company and for damages because of the failure to fulfil contracts.

The Chief Justice of Alberta, C.A. Stuart, dealt with the suit filed by the government in October 1911, by a decision of November 6. He said that he had done so hurriedly on the presumption that the case would go to a higher court and to the Privy Council.[14] He declared the provincial legislation to be effective: the province had the power to collect the money involved. The banks still refused to pay. An unsuccessful appeal was made to the federal government to disallow the provincial legislation, and the case went to the Supreme Court of Alberta *en banc*. This body dismissed the appeal. The arguments of both sides were most complex, and the case itself had become so seriocomic that it would have made excellent material for a Gilbert and Sullivan opera.[15]

The case went to the Privy Council late in 1912. On December 12 of that year the Lord Chancellor stated, "The question was so difficult, and involved such grave constitutional issues, that the Judicial Committee must take time to consider it."[16] There the matter rested until 1913 when the final settlement was made.

The Judicial Committee of the Privy Council delivered its decision on January 31, 1913. It upheld the appellants on the ground that the statute of 1910 would have precluded the bank from fulfilling its legal obligations to return the money to the bondholders whose right to this return was a civil right arising and enforceable outside the province.[17] Thus the statute was beyond the powers of the Alberta legislature. The provincial government found its position very embarrassing as a result of the decision. It had a large temporary indebtedness at the time; the payment of interest on bonds still had to be made; an election was in the offing; Edmonton and the north were still clamouring for a northern railway. The *Edmonton Bulletin* declared, "The decision, on the reasons which are given for it, is a particularly flagrant case of protection of private or corporate interest against public right. The province is being ground between the upper and nether millstone of the Imperial Privy Council and the Royal Bank."[18] No doubt this reflected the reaction of a large part of the public, for financial institutions and distant judicial bodies have never been especially beloved in the Canadian West.

Premier Sifton left no stone unturned to find a solution to the government's problem and he found one by late summer. After negotiations with J.D. McArthur who was building the Edmonton, Dunvegan, and British Columbia Railway to the Peace River and the Hudson's Bay Railway for the Dominion government, the government reached an agreement with this railway contractor. McArthur agreed to build the railway under the original guarantees with respect to the date limits of construction and branch lines. The bondholders and the institutions concerned were satisfied with the arrangement. Construction and operation of the railway was to be undertaken in the name of the original company, the Alberta and Great Waterways. The legislature passed a bill accordingly on October 18. The banks then turned over the bond proceeds of $7,400,000 to McArthur, and reimbursed the government $950,000 for interest earned on the bonds since 1910.

The solution relieved the government of further interest payments, at least for the time being, and released the funds held by the banks for use during a period when construction activity generally was falling off. But it still committed the province to a railway venture of dubious long-run values, and left the provincial government liable for operation deficits of the railway. It was unfortunate that Sifton's original solution could not have been adopted. Expenditures on highways, schools, and telephones in settled territory certainly would have provided higher economic and social benefits than a railway through muskegs and rocks to a mirage called the "great northland." They would have assisted materially to increase productivity and well-being in those parts of Alberta where the marginal productivity was much higher than in the north. The construction of the railway did little for many years in increasing the total value product of the Alberta economy. And in the period following World War I the railway became a serious source of embarrassment to the provincial treasury.

THE BUDGETS OF PREMIER SIFTON

Premier Sifton's budgets were brief and yet verbose, for the premier was given to using long, complex sentences. Sifton made no spectacular announcements on policy, but contented himself with outlining estimated expenditures and revenues in summary fashion, and predicting surpluses by dubious accounting measures. He presented budgets in 1910, 1912, and 1913.[19] Throughout, Sifton justified continued borrowing, tried to make costly ventures appear to be paying their way, and appealed to popular opinions (such as public optimism or the general distrust of chartered banks). He also, in 1912 and 1913, called for the Dominion to transfer natural resources to the province to provide it with an "elastic revenue." The premier was subject to justified opposition criticism for lack of public accounts for 1911, and for the misleading statement that there was a surplus. There had been large deficits on an overall basis in every year after 1906 despite the insistence of both Rutherford and Sifton that there were surpluses. There was little wrong with this state of affairs in view of the urgency of expenditures from which economic and social benefits would be derived. But one finds it more difficult to excuse the administration for its failure to design a revenue structure appropriate to rising expenditure and its downright jiggling of accounts to obscure to the electorate the financial position of the province. Neither course is justifiable in a democracy.

Rutherford believed that the Dominion subsidy would suffice and attempted to cut the provincial cloth accordingly. But he fell almost unwittingly into the capital account pitfall and yielded to the great pressure for a northern railway. Sifton, on the other hand, saw clearly that the Dominion subsidy was much too small in relation to the level of expenditures demanded. He had to cope with financial, legal, and political problems posed by the Alberta and Great Waterways affair. But he relied upon agitation for the transfer of the public domain and upon an easy money market instead of devising a revenue structure that might approach adequacy.

An event of interest was the first meeting of the Committee on Public Accounts in the history of the province. The *Edmonton Journal* commented, "One way to reveal the mystery of the financial affairs in Alberta is to investigate public accounts." [20] The committee found that the province had borrowed in excess of legislative authority in 1912, and provided some clearer statements on public debt than those current in the legislature at the time. Domination of the committee by the government members prevented "too much" probing by the opposition members. Further, the latter proved relatively ineffective in their questions which were designed to cast aspersions on persons rather than to clarify broad financial issues.

THE GROWTH OF THE PROVINCIAL DEBT

It is time to assess quantitatively the growth of the provincial debt. Table 2.3 shows actual surpluses and deficits for 1906 to 1913 on an overall basis. The size of the deficit of 1910 in relation to revenue is particularly striking. It was a consequence of the Alberta and Great Waterways affair. Rutherford brought down only temporary estimates before he resigned, and Sifton carried on during the remainder of the year by use of warrants financed largely by bank loans. The ease with which such loans were obtained at first undoubtedly tempted the government to give in to the pressure for spending and reduced government resistance to delegations of various groups in subsequent years. The Alberta and Great Waterways issue hung like a black cloud over the administration after 1910. It created uncertainty as to future railway policy; it embarrassed the government financially because of the default of the railway company of interest payments. It is little wonder that the government drifted into debt on a large scale in 1910 and in subsequent years.

Some direct debt had been incurred before 1910 (see Table 2.4). Temporary loans amounting to over $1,200,000 were obtained to finance the telephone expenditures and these loans were paid out of a debenture issue of $2 million sold in London at 4 per cent. Temporary loans for capital expenditure for general purposes were obtained in 1909. During 1910 such loans increased to almost $3.5 million.

Table 2.3 Revenue and Expenditure of the Government of Alberta, 1905–1913 (in millions of dollars)

Fiscal Year	Overall basis[a]			Overall basis[b]			Income account[c]		
	R	E	S or D(−)	R	E	S or D(−)	R	E	S or D(−)
1905	0.7	0.2	0.5	0.7	0.2	0.5	0.6	0.2	0.5
1906	1.5	1.5	−	1.5	1.5	0.1	1.4	1.3	0.1
1907	1.9	2.5	−0.5	1.9	2.2	−0.3	1.8	1.8	−
1908	2.6	3.9	−1.4	2.4	2.8	−0.4	2.8	2.1	0.7
1909	2.8	4.3	−1.5	2.5	3.5	−1.0	2.5	2.6	−0.1
1910	2.5	5.8	−3.3	2.1	4.6	−2.5	2.1	3.7	−1.6
1911	3.3	6.2	−2.9	2.8	4.7	−1.9	2.8	3.0	−0.2
1912	4.1	8.4	−4.3	3.4	5.7	−2.3	3.4	3.4	0.1
1913	5.6	9.5	−3.9	4.5	6.6	−2.1	4.5	4.4	0.1

Abbrev.: R is revenue; E is expenditure; S is surplus; D is deficit.

(a) This includes the telephone system. Data were obtained from an analysis of Government of Alberta, *P.A., 1905–13*. Revenues include those receipts which improved the condition of the treasury without increasing liabilities; expenditures include cost outlays, that is, payments which worsened the condition of the treasury without reducing liabilities. See Appendix B for details of procedures used to analyze the public accounts.

(b) This excludes the telephone system. The data were derived in the same way as in (a).

(c) Obtained directly from Government of Alberta, *P.A., 1950–51*, Statement No. 18. Capital revenues and expenditures are excluded.

In 1911 the government borrowed over $9 million on a temporary basis. These loans were renewed from time to time, and not until the end of 1912 did the government decide to float debentures, chiefly for telephone expenditures, to make the debt more permanent. Accordingly, a bond issue of $4,867,000 at 4 per cent was easily sold in London late in 1912 through Lloyd's Bank. The government realized about $12.5 million from the sale of debentures totalling over $13 million in par value in 1913. This total was comprised of several issues. A temporary debenture issue of $4,804,000 was sold through Lloyd's Bank late in 1912 at 97, the debenture carrying a rate of 4 per cent. A thirty-year issue of $4,867,000 at 4.5 per cent was sold through the same channels late in 1913. Finally, a ten-year issue of $3,600,000 at 4.5 per cent was sold through Spencer, Trask, and Company, New York, late in the year. Most of the proceeds were used to retire the temporary indebtedness of the province, almost $11 million. This included the retirement of treasury bills amounting to £1,500,000 carrying a rate of 5.75 per cent, which had been issued in anticipation of receiving the proceeds from Alberta and Great Waterways bonds that had been renewed periodically. Finally, over $3.5 million was obtained through temporary loans.

Table 2.4   Public Debt of the Government of Alberta, 1906–1913
(in millions of dollars)

As at Dec. 31	1906	1907	1908	1909	1910	1911	1912	1913
Direct debt:								
Net funded debt	0.0	0.0	0.0	2.0	2.0	2.0	6.9	15.3
Unfunded debt	0.0	0.0	1.2	1.0	3.4	7.3	10.7	3.7
Total	0.0	0.0	1.2	3.0	5.4	9.3	17.6	19.0
Indirect debt:	0.0	0.0	0.0	19.6	19.6	19.6	34.1	37.2
Total debt	0.0	0.0	1.2	22.6	25.0	28.9	51.7	56.2

Source: Government of Alberta, *Public Accounts*. Indirect debt consists of railway bonds guaranteed
by the provincial government.

Thus borrowed funds in 1913 totalled $16 million, revenue amounted to $5.5 million, repayment of loans came to nearly $11 million, and expenditures reached about $9.5 million (see Table 2.5 for a summary of sources and uses of funds for 1913 and previous years). The province paid for its accommodation in the form of discount and expenses of over $1 million on the debenture issues. Interest rates, too, had risen by 1913; thus a bond rate of 4.5 per cent had to be set on the last two issues of the year instead of the 4 per cent set on the previous issues.

Why was the policy of borrowing on a temporary basis pursued for years? The answer is found in the conditions surrounding the Alberta and Great Waterways case. After Sifton assumed office in 1910, he secured the passage of legislation which would appropriate the proceeds of the bond issue by Alberta and Great Waterways Company for general revenue purposes and, of course, have the province assume the debt of the defaulting railway company. But it took the courts three years to decide on the validity of the 1910 statute, and the decision was unfavourable. The province paid dearly. The interest on the defaulted bonds had to be met. Temporary loans piled up to meet growing expenditure and in anticipation of funding the debt through the railway bond proceeds.[21] When the province failed to obtain these proceeds for general purposes it had to go to the capital market at a time when interest rates had risen, investors had become more selective than before, and the credit standing of the province had deteriorated.

The indirect or guaranteed debt was also increased in 1912 and 1913. Table 2.6 indicates the growth of such debt. The pressure for the construction of railway did not abate after 1910. The public awaited the construction of branch lines and northern railways impatiently, and expected the provincial

Table 2.5 Sources and Uses of Funds of the Government of Alberta, 1905–1913 (in millions of dollars)

	1905	1906	1907	1908	1909	1910	1911	1912	1913
SOURCES									
Revenue	0.7	1.5	1.9	2.6	2.8	2.5	3.3	4.1	5.6
Temporary loans	0.0	0.0	0.0	1.2	1.0	3.4	12.7	11.2	3.7
Debentures	0.0	0.0	0.0	0.0	1.9	0.0	0.0	0.0	12.4
Total	0.7	1.5	1.9	3.8	5.8	5.9	16.0	15.3	21.7
USES									
Expenditures	0.2	1.5	2.4	3.9	4.3	5.8	6.2	8.4	9.5
Temporary loans	0.0	0.0	0.0	0.0	1.2	1.0	8.8	7.8	10.7
Total	0.2	1.5	2.4	3.9	5.5	6.8	15.0	16.2	20.2
NET PROCEEDS									
Revenue	0.5	–	–0.5	–1.3	–1.5	–3.3	–2.9	–4.3	–3.9
Temporary loans	0.0	0.0	0.0	1.2	–0.2	2.4	3.9	3.4	–7.0
Debentures	0.0	0.0	0.0	0.0	1.9	0.0	0.0	0.0	12.4
Total	0.5	–	–0.5	–0.1	0.3	–0.9	1.0	–0.9	1.5
Cash balance, year end	0.5	0.5	–	–0.1	0.2	–0.7	0.3	–0.6	0.9
Cash balance, General Revenue Fund, year end	0.5	0.6	–	–	–	0.7	2.0	–1.6	0.5

Sources: Government of Alberta, *Public Accounts, 1905–1913.* The data from this source were classified and arranged in accordance with the categories above. Thus the classifications are not those of the accounts for the period, which showed temporary loans and debenture proceeds under revenue and repayments under expenditure. The last item, Cash Balance, General Revenue Fund, is derived directly from the public accounts.

government to take action soon to secure such railways. On February 6, 1912, Sifton announced his railway policy, asserting that it was the duty of the provincial government to provide railways, telephones, and roads.

The people who came to Alberta, he said, in characteristic style, were not prepared to wait like the pioneers of Quebec, the Maritimes, and the western plains of the United States; they were entitled to "all the accessories of civilization they had in the countries they came from." [22] Consequently, the province stood ready to guarantee bonds to finance the construction of 1,813 miles of railroad at a rate from $13,000 to $20,000 per mile for a 350-mile railway to the Peace River country, the government to hold the

Table 2.6   Contingent Liabilities of the Government of Alberta, 1905–1913
(in millions of dollars)

As at Dec. 31	1905	1908	1909	1910	1911	1912	1913
Railway bonds:							
A.&G.W.	0.0	0.0	7.4	7.4	7.4	7.4	7.4
C.N.R.	0.0	0.0	9.7	9.7	9.7	9.7	9.7
G.T.P.	0.0	0.0	2.4	2.4	2.4	3.6	3.6
E.D. & B.C.	0.0	0.0	0.0	0.0	0.0	7.0	7.0
C.N.W.	0.0	0.0	0.0	0.0	0.0	6.4	9.2
L. & N.W.	0.0	0.0	0.0	0.0	0.0	0.0	0.3
Total	0.0	0.0	19.6	19.6	19.6	34.1	37.2
Other:	none						

Source: *P.A., 1925,* 103.
Abbrev.: A. & G.W. is the Alberta and Great Waterways Railway; C.N.R. is the Canadian Northern
Railway; G.T.P. is the Grand Trunk Pacific Railway; E.D. & B.C. is the Edmonton, Dunvegan,
and British Columbia Railway; C.N.W. is the Canadian Northern Western Railway; L. & N.W.
is the Lacombe and North Western Railway.

first mortgage on the railway and its equipment, fifty miles to be constructed before the money was advanced, a hundred miles to be completed
by the end of 1912, and the whole line to be completed by the end of 1914.
These provisos were designed to prevent the occurrence of a facsimile of
the Alberta and Great Waterways case. Similar guarantees and provisos applied to other railway companies. The Canadian Northern was to build
from Saskatoon to Calgary, the government guaranteeing the section of this
line within Alberta. The Grand Trunk Pacific was to build a railway to the
coalmines at Coal Branch almost 200 miles west of Edmonton. Finally, the
Canadian Northern-Western was to construct ten different lines throughout the province, including the north. The total amount involved in these
guarantees was almost $26 million.

Almost one thousand miles of railways were built in the province during 1912, an all-time high for any year in its history. The federal government
guaranteed part of the mileage, but the province guaranteed the major portion. The construction of the Alberta and Great Waterways Railway hung
in abeyance pending the decision of the Privy Council and the securing of a
suitable construction company. Ironically enough, the province was already
implementing the guarantee of a railway that was not under construction.

Table 2.7 Expenditures of the Government of Alberta, 1905–1913
(in millions of dollars)

Fiscal Year	General Government				Social Expenditure				Economic Expenditure					Debt Int.	Other	Total
	Leg.	Adm.	Just.	Total	Educ.	P.H.	P.Wel	Total	Ag.	P.D.	Hwys	Tel.	Total			
1905	–	–	–	0.1	–	–	–	–	–	–	0.1	0.0	0.1	0.0	–	0.2
1906	0.1	0.2	0.1	0.3	0.2	0.1	–	0.3	0.3	–	0.5	–	0.8	0.0	–	1.5
1907	0.1	0.4	0.1	0.6	0.4	0.1	–	0.5	0.3	–	0.7	0.3	1.3	0.0	0.1	2.4
1908	0.1	0.6	0.3	1.0	0.4	0.1	–	0.6	0.5	–	0.7	1.1	2.3	–	–	3.9
1909	0.1	0.9	0.4	1.4	0.4	0.2	–	0.7	0.6	–	0.6	0.7	1.9	0.2	0.1	4.3
1910	0.2	0.7	0.8	1.7	0.7	0.4	–	1.1	0.8	0.1	0.7	1.0	2.6	0.2	0.3	5.8
1911	0.1	1.1	0.6	1.8	0.5	0.4	–	1.0	0.6	0.1	0.5	1.4	2.6	0.4	0.4	6.2
1912	0.2	1.1	0.6	1.9	0.7	0.3	0.1	1.1	0.4	0.1	1.5	2.5	4.4	0.5	0.5	8.4
1913	0.5	1.2	0.7	2.4	0.9	0.2	0.1	1.2	0.7	0.1	1.2	2.6	4.6	0.9	0.4	9.5

Source: *P.A., 1905–13.* For methods of classification used to reclassify the data in the public accounts, see Appendix B. Capital expenditures are included, so no distinction is being made here between expenditures on income and capital account. The classifications in the early public accounts were made along departmental lines with a large miscellaneous category; consequently they were of little use for a functional analysis of expenditure.
Abbreviations: Leg. is legislation; Adm. is administration; Just. is justice; Educ. is education; P.H. is public health; P.Wel is public welfare; Ag. is agriculture; P.D. is public domain; Hwys is highways; Tel. is telephones.

THE LEVEL OF PROVINCIAL GOVERNMENT SERVICES

The railway question overshadowed other aspects of government policy. But these aspects were far from neglected, for the Rutherford government set up the administrative machinery of the province and began the construction of many buildings. The Sifton administration followed up with a vigorous telephone policy and the completion of the public buildings; it did its best to "expand in all directions." Table 2.7 shows the various expenditures.

GENERAL GOVERNMENT

Expenditure on general government was relatively high during the 1906–13 period. Large capital expenditures were required to provide the physical facilities for the government, and low population density made for a high per capita cost. The substantial increase after 1907 is attributable to several factors that took some time to become operative: the land titles office, the law courts, payments to the Royal Northwest Mounted Police, and the public buildings construction program.

Construction expenditures absorbed between 40 and 50 per cent of the outlays on general government after 1908. Rural residents were critical of the expenditures on public buildings; they felt that there were better uses for the money spent on structures that they considered too elaborate. The province paid, or rather incurred debts, for the cause of provincial status. Simpler structures would have served just as well as the more elaborate ones built, even though they would have been less aesthetic and ostentatious. In terms of increasing the productivity of the economy, a more rapid rate of construction of market roads for farming areas could have been a more economical policy. On the other hand, such roads tend to disintegrate if they are not properly maintained. The tendency of government legislators and administrators at all levels of government to build for "all time" and for display led to priority being given to the construction of buildings containing large quantities and varieties of imported stones and materials.[23]

SOCIAL EXPENDITURE

Education accounted for most of the social expenditure during the 1906–13 period. The provincial department of education drew up school curricula, provided a school inspection staff, and made grants to schools according to statutory stipulations and ministerial direction. In 1908 a provincial university was set up as a separate entity that derived its revenue from student fees and provincial government appropriations voted annually. Agricultural schools began to be established in 1912 and more than half of the federal agricultural assistance grants which began to be received in that year was devoted to expenditure on such schools.

The provincial government concerned itself with providing acceptable educational services to its citizens from the beginning. Its grants-in-aid system encouraged the hiring of teachers with good qualifications and the operation of schools for a maximum number of days. Although the provincial grants diminished relatively to school district revenues between 1906 and 1913, the grant per pupil increased somewhat (see Table 2.8). Teacher training facilities were provided in 1907, and a provincial university was provided in the following year. Special efforts were made to cope with the problem of education among the foreign-born by appointing supervisors to deal exclusively with education in so-called "foreign" districts.

In the fields of public health and welfare government action was less vigorous, but an attempt was made to provide a tolerable minimum of services. One pressing problem was the provision of facilities for mental patients, who

50

Table 2.8   Provincial Government Grants to Schools, 1906 and 1913

	1906	1913
Per pupil	$4.93	$5.76
As % of total revenue of:		
(a) Urban school districts	14.4	9.0
(b) Rural school districts	26.3	19.0
(c) All school districts	20.4	12.8

Source: Government of Alberta, Department of Education, Annual Reports, 1906 and 1913.

had to be sent to Manitoba institutions for several years after 1905. By 1913 the government had succeeded in constructing enough hospital space, and Alberta patients were no longer sent to Manitoba. The provincial government operated mental hospitals and spent considerable money on buildings after 1908. General hospitals were operated by local governments, by religious orders, or by private individuals, and the provincial government provided steadily increasing grants-in-aid. Provision was made for child welfare services in 1910. But the total effort in the field of social expenditure was not spectacular. Social expenditure rose rapidly enough until 1910, and then levelled off at a figure somewhat over one million dollars annually. In 1913 it took about 12 per cent of total expenditure. Albertans cannot be accused of building up a "welfare state" during this period. Instead they were acutely concerned with economic expenditures, notably provision of transportation and communication facilities, which might enable individuals to increase their incomes.

ECONOMIC EXPENDITURE

This category, which might well be called developmental expenditure, includes outlays on bridges, roads, railways, agricultural assistance and promotion, aid to industries, public domain, and trading services.

The need for roads and bridges has always been acute in Alberta and no government can long neglect to meet it. In 1906 there were few roads in Alberta worthy of the name, and bridges were scarce. Many ferries had to be provided at river crossings pending bridge construction or where traffic density did not justify a bridge. All roads built by the provincial as well as local governments during this period were graded dirt highways. There were never enough of them and they became seas of mud during rains. The number of automobiles was not yet sufficient to justify the construction of gravelled or paved highways. Despite relatively large expenditures on highways, the standard of service provided was low. Distances were too great and expenditures were therefore spread thinly.

The assistance and promotion of agriculture assumed many forms. Provincial government expenditures were made upon grants to agricultural societies and exhibition associations, exhibition judges, the destruction of noxious weeds and wolves, stock inspection, brand registration, dairy promotion, demonstration farms and fairs, stock shows, seed grain advances, bounties to the sugar beet industry, and many other items. Such expenditures were justified in a province in which agriculture was the main industry, but there were questionable appropriations. Probably the grants to agricultural societies were in this category, and perhaps the expenditure on demonstration farms.

Expenditures on public domain include outlays on fire protection, the inspection of coal mines, immigration and colonization publicity, and the enforcement of the game laws. The order of magnitude of these expenditures was small before 1913.

Economic expenditures absorbed about one-half of provincial government expenditures throughout the period. Telephone expenditures accounted for the largest share, especially after 1910 when capital expenditure on rural extensions was accelerated. The discontinuance of hail insurance in 1911 and the declining advances to the government creameries led to a decrease in agricultural expenditure after 1910. The level of highway expenditure remained almost constant until 1912 when an ambitious trunk highway program was launched. The constancy of highway expenditure in money terms is interesting in view of the insistent demands for roads and priority given highway expenditures by the territorial government. Provincial status certainly did not solve the internal transportation problem. Furthermore, with its power to incur debt, a power denied the territorial government; the provincial government was able to spend increasing amounts on telephone extensions while highways were relatively neglected until 1912.

OTHER EXPENDITURES

Interest charges of the provincial government were non-existent until 1908. They grew rapidly after that date as temporary loans and debentures increased, and in 1913 they almost equalled the expenditure on education. They were becoming a burden of great consequence.

Refunds, remissions, rebates, advances to the government printer, and grants to various clubs and organizations accounted for a miscellaneous group of expenditures. In addition, the bond interest paid on the Alberta and Great Waterways bonds constituted a major expenditure item between 1910 and 1913.

THE DEVELOPMENT OF GOVERNMENT REVENUES

The total revenue of the provincial government, including the gross earnings of the telephone system, rose from about $1.5 million in 1906 to $5.6 million in 1913 (see Table 2.9). This increase is not impressive in the light of the rapid population and income increases during the period. Provincial government revenue constituted a declining percentage of the provincial income after attaining a peak of 4.3 per cent in 1908 (see Table 2.10).

The early hopes that the Dominion subsidy would cover a substantial part of the expenditures of the provincial government were not realized. As it formed an increasingly smaller portion of total revenue, the demand for provincial control of the public lands grew accordingly, although the provincial government did not become vociferous about this matter until after 1911 when a Conservative government came into power at Ottawa.

There was a general failure to develop a revenue structure in keeping with the growth of expenditures, population, and provincial income. It was hoped, Micawber-like, that with the increase in population something would turn up to provide more revenue. There were no attempts to impose taxation on a widespread basis; such taxation, on the other hand, was imposed by the municipalities in the form of property taxes. The provincial government attempted to levy a heavy tax on railroads, ran into constitutional difficulties, and finally had to settle for reduced amounts fixed by negotiations with the railways. It set up the beginnings of an elaborate corporate tax structure, which discriminated against financial, transportation, and communication companies. The level of rates, however, was low before 1913 so that the provincial corporation taxes cannot have deterred corporate investment significantly in the province. Furthermore, in the end the tax would tend to be shifted to the general public in view of the rising demand for goods and services. The education tax failed to produce substantial amounts of revenue due to a restricted tax base, while succession duties could not be expected to produce significant revenue in a new country.

An unearned interest tax on land was imposed in 1913. It provided that there should be payable upon registration of land transfers a tax of 5 per cent on the increased value of uncultivated land, based upon an original value of $25 per acre for land outside any incorporated centre and upon the last assessed value within incorporated centres. The value of the improvements made on the property was exempt, and agricultural land valued at $50 and less per acre was exempt if 10 per cent of the land was under cultivation twelve months before the sale. This tax solved no revenue problem because it was imposed just at the time when urban land values were beginning to collapse and because it practically exempted all agricultural land.

Table 2.9 Revenues of the Government of Alberta, 1905–13
(in thousands of dollars)

	1905	1906	1907	1908	1909	1910	1911	1912	1913
Dom. of Canada	562	1124	1148	1444	1273	1024	1217	1260	1285
Taxes	1	1	152	211	211	194	164	467	324
Lic. and fees	5	48	225	316	407	357	742	967	1246
Public domain	0	0	4	2	4	6	14	19	25
School lands	0	3	60	51	67	99	166	236	224
Liquor control	2	58	71	70	77	85	93	108	128
Fines	3	12	22	22	29	33	49	90	69
Sales	–	251	202	270	356	290	271	167	223
Refunds	103	1	20	19	4	4	10	9	975
Interest	4	27	29	32	128	85	196	219	319
Repayments	0	0	0	21	52	21	7	67	11
Miscellaneous	1	–	–	–	2	–	1	9	15
Telephones	0	0	4	106	179	290	376	483	737
Total revenue	683	1525	1935	2565	2792	2489	3309	4100	5580

Source: See Appendix B.

Table 2.10 Revenue of the Government of Alberta as a Percentage of Provincial
Personal Income and of its Own Total Expenditures, 1906–13

Year	Percentage of provincial income	Percentage of expenditure
1906	3.7	103
1907	3.7	79
1908	4.3	66
1909	3.8	65
1910	2.8	43
1911	2.5	53
1912	2.4	49
1913	3.4	59

Sources: See Appendices A and B.

Attempts were made to earmark revenues from corporation and educational taxes for education expenditures. Some grants to school districts and to the provincial university were made on this basis, but they were paid rather sporadically. The government found itself too hard-pressed for cash to indulge in the luxury of earmarked funds on any consistent basis.

The government also failed to charge adequate rates for telephone services and hail insurance. This failure stemmed from the reluctance to impose any provincial government financial burdens directly on agriculture. The telephone rate policy was to charge much higher rates in the urban centres than in the rural areas to recoup losses in the latter to as great a degree as possible. Hail insurance premiums, though raised in 1908, failed to meet indemnities paid out in most years. On the other hand, provincial creameries did not commit the province financially to any significant extent.

Although revenue from licences and fees grew rapidly until 1913, expenditures on services rendered and on collections were large. Court and legal fees fell far short of meeting the costs of administration of justice.[24] Liquor licence fees approximately paid for liquor control. The cost of land titles transfer and registration office formed from 20 to 30 per cent of the land titles fees collected, exclusive of capital expenditure on buildings. Cost of inspection services absorbed the major share of the fees collected in connection with the inspection of steam boilers and coal mines, and with the regulation of such activities as the recording of brands for ranchers and the survey of town sites. In short, increasing revenue from fees did little to alleviate the pressure on the provincial budgets.

GOVERNMENT AND THE ECONOMY

The rising expenditures of all governments contributed to economic progress by providing collective facilities and services of various kinds, which tend to make the economy more productive. The provision of railways, roads, bridges, and telephones meant more rapid and efficient facilitation of exchange processes among producers and consumers. Some telephone extensions were of dubious value from the economic point of view, for by providing such services in sparsely settled areas when they might have been provided in somewhat more densely settled areas marginal value products were not equated, and hence total "provincial" product was not maximized. Such a criticism can be levelled at railway policies as well. For example, the area northeast of Edmonton along both sides of the North Saskatchewan was a fertile farming district heavily populated by settlers from Central Europe. Yet legislators insisted on toying with railway construction in the less fertile and less-known north while this eastern area lacked railway facilities. Some of the debt incurred for railways and telephones, too, was to prove detrimental to economic progress in later years because of high debt charges and additional investments induced by the desire to salvage previous investments and by pressure exerted by inhabitants of settlements established by virtue of such investments. Generally speaking, future benefits were given too high an estimate and were not discounted at a significantly high rate, while future costs were underestimated or ignored or discounted to a high degree with the reckless optimism of the day. Finally, urban centres easily exceeded the provincial government in optimism and ill-advised expenditures.

Social expenditures, such as those on education, contributed toward increased activity in subsequent years by reducing illiteracy and increasing skills and enlightenment. It is difficult to see any unjustified expenditure in this sphere.

Some expenditures represented interference with the private economy and may have acted as a deterrent to private investment. The telephone system is an outstanding example. But the government provided a service to many areas that would otherwise have gone without for many more years. An appraisal of this policy involves a weighing of social benefits against social costs, rather than of relative demand and supply prices. Many urban trading services were municipally owned. These excluded private enterprise in these spheres, but they also avoided problems of public utility regulation, a type of regulation undeveloped before 1915. The operation of government creameries may have impinged upon investments in the dairy industry. The railway policies, however, stimulated private investment. Administration and economic expenditure, aside from the trading services, facilitated transportation and provided for law enforcement in the private sector. In addition, capital expenditures stimulated investment in the construction industry and industries providing construction materials. In short, government expenditures, despite the bias for government ownership and operation of a variety of enterprises, probably on balance stimulated rather than hindered private investment.

The level of taxation was not yet burdensome. The property taxes of local governments, though considerable, were still relatively low. Provincial taxes were not high enough to deter investment. Not even the corporation taxes and fees were significant enough to discourage the incorporation of companies, and the entrance into the province of "foreign" companies.

It remains to examine some cyclical aspects and to gauge quantitatively the impact of government revenues and expenditures upon the provincial economy. The annual increase in debenture debt and the magnitudes of deficits

Table 2.11 Gross Debt, Overall Deficits, and Interest Charges of All Governments in Alberta, 1906–13 (in millions of dollars)

	1906	1907	1908	1909	1910	1911	1912	1913
Gross debenture debt	2.0	5.5	7.9	13.0	17.5	22.2	36.4	69.3
Overall deficit	0.8	4.1	3.7	4.4	7.9	7.7	13.5	25.8
Interest charges	0.1	0.1	0.2	0.4	0.6	0.8	1.0	1.6

Sources: Appendices B and C. Gross debenture debt does not include guaranteed ones (e.g. railway bonds). Interest charges are computed on the basis of 4.5 per cent of the gross debt outstanding of all governments at the end of the previous year. Direct interest data for all governments are not available.

are rough measures of annual capital expenditures. Measured in these terms, the capital expenditures of local governments were much greater than those of the provincial government. The combined impact of both levels of government can be gauged from Table 2.11. For example, the overall deficit of all governments was nearly $26 million in 1913, or about one-sixth of the provincial income in that year. Whatever else may be said about ill-advised projects undertaken by urban local governments in 1913, they cushioned the urban depression, which began in that year, considerably. In the same year all expenditures of both levels of government equalled about 28 per cent of the provincial income, a peak percentage that was not attained again until the 1930s. Governments, in other words, were still pulling the stops out while private business had begun to push them in.

Revenue collections within the economy reduce the cash balances of individuals in contrast to expenditures, which augment them. Governments have, in the past, tended to attempt to increase collections when economic recessions have set in. Alberta governments were no exception at this time. The provincial government increased tax and fee rates in 1913; the local governments raised property tax rates in the same year. This augmented yields already increased from expanding revenue bases. Thus tax revenue absorbed more than 6 per cent of provincial income in 1913 as against less than 4 per cent in 1912 (see Table 2.12). Again the local governments accounted for the bulk of the collections. The latter were much more important generally than the provincial government as is indicated by Table 2.13.

A measure of fiscal impact, which combines revenues and expenditures, is that of "net income-increasing expenditure." [25] In the first instance it enables one to judge if fiscal impact is positive or negative – that is, whether fiscal

Table 2.12 Total Taxation of Alberta Governments, 1906–13
(in millions of dollars)

	1906	1907	1908	1909	1910	1911	1912	1913
Provincial	–	0.2	0.2	0.2	0.2	0.2	0.5	0.3
Urban locals	0.6	0.7	1.2	1.4	1.7	2.1	3.6	8.1
Rural locals	0.6	0.7	0.9	1.1	1.3	1.5	1.8	2.3
Total taxes	1.2	1.6	2.3	2.7	3.2	3.9	5.9	10.6
Total as a per cent of Provincial income	3.0	3.0	3.9	3.7	3.6	3.0	3.5	6.4

Sources: Appendices B and C.

Table 2.13 Comparisons of the Provincial and Local Governments in Alberta, 1913
(as percentage of total)

	Provincial	Local	Total
Revenue	35	65	100
Expenditure	20	80	100
Debenture debt excluding guarantees	22	78	100
Debenture debt including guarantees	49	51	100

Sources: Appendices A and B.

policy added to the income of the economy or diminished it. In the second instance, the trend of the impact and the relative magnitude of it with respect to income may be detected. Table 2.14 sets out the results of calculations and estimates made for the 1906–13 period. The positive nature of the governmental contribution to the income stream of the economy and the extraordinarily high level of it in 1913 are evident. In addition, the provincial government exerted an indirect positive influence upon the size of the provincial income stream by its railway guarantee policy. Similar guarantees by the Dominion government had the same effect.

Table 2.14 Net Income-Producing Expenditures of the Provincial and Local
Governments in Alberta, 1906–13 (in millions of dollars)

Year	Dominion Subsidy	School Lands Fund	Overall Deficit less Interest Payments	Total	Total as Per Cent of Prov. Income
1906	1.1	–	0.7	1.8	4
1907	1.1	0.1	4.0	5.2	10
1908	1.4	0.1	3.5	5.0	8
1909	1.3	0.1	4.0	5.4	8
1910	1.0	0.1	7.3	8.4	10
1911	1.2	0.2	6.9	8.3	7
1912	1.3	0.2	12.5	14.0	8
1913	1.3	0.2	24.2	25.7	16

Sources: Appendices A and B.

THE WORLD WAR I PERIOD, 1914–20

3

ECONOMIC DEVELOPMENT

Investment and speculative activities fell off rapidly in Alberta in 1913 and the two following years in keeping with the general Canadian decline. Immigration became merely a trickle by 1915. Urban building activity fell off to almost nothing in the same year. Railway construction, however, remained at a substantial level even in 1915, partly because of government guarantees and partly because projects already begun had to be finished to meet stipulations in construction contracts. But it dropped rapidly after 1915 and came to a virtual standstill in 1917, although some additional mileage was added in 1919 and 1920. Investment activity generally remained at low levels throughout the war period because of the difficulty of borrowing funds from external sources, and because of the shortage of materials and labour. In 1919 and 1920, however, such activity increased substantially with the removal of these restrictions and in response to increasing prices. Table 3.1 shows the trends for the whole period.

The decline in investment activity just before and during the war brought little, if any decline in provincial income. There were business failures and unemployment in the urban centres, and there was a serious drought in the southeast in 1914, which led the Dominion and provincial governments to provide emergency relief. Despite these setbacks, the value of agricultural production and income for the whole province was maintained because agricultural prices rose substantially. In following years, agriculture came to the fore almost dramatically, and its increasing contributions to the provincial income stream more than compensated the loss of investment income in previous years. In 1915, agriculture enjoyed a banner year with crop yields that have never been exceeded in the history of the province.[1] The war period was marked by the expansion of agricultural production and rising agricultural prices. The annual value of agricultural production and field crop acreage doubled between 1915 and 1920. Particularly great stimulus was given to wheat production, which became the leading branch of the agricultural industry.

Table 3.1 Selected Indicators of Investment Activity in Alberta, 1913–1920

Year	Immigration (thousands)	Building Permits, Edmonton & Calgary (millions)	Railway Mileage Added	Annual Population Increase (thousands)
1913	44	$17.9	592	29
1914	18	8.3	450	30
1915	7	0.5	326	31
1916	12	0.9	134	16
1917	17	0.9	−52	12
1918	12	1.5	14	14
1919	20	3.1	131	19
920	18	6.1	46	24

Sources: Immigration figures were taken from *Facts and Figures*, 51–52; building permits from ibid., 274; railway mileage data from ibid., 309; and annual population increase from *C.Y.B.*

Table 3.2 Provincial Income and Net Value of Agricultural Production in Alberta, 1913–1920 (in millions of dollars)

Year	Provincial Income	Net Value of Agriculture	Agriculture as % Share of Provincial Income
1913	165	58	35
1914	164	75	46
1915	183	109	60
1916	259	168	64
1917	308	197	64
1918	253	127	50
1919	325	164	50
1920	365	198	54

Source: Appendix A.

Table 3.3 Wheat Yields, Wheat Prices, Field Crop Acreage, and Value of Field Crops in Alberta, 1913–1920

Year	Wheat Yield (bu. per acre)	Wheat Price (cents per bu.)	Field Price Average Crop (millions)	Value of Field Crops (millions)
1913	22.7	61	3.7	$47
1914	21.1	91	3.4	60
1915	32.8	79	4.0	93
1916	25.0	133	5.4	149
1917	18.3	174	6.7	177
1918	6.0	192	7.7	113
1919	8.0	231	8.2	149
1920	20.5	152	8.4	204

Source: All data were obtained from *C.Y.B.*

The rapid rise of agriculture to a position of dominance in the provincial economy may be seen by examining Table 3.2.

But the upward trend in agricultural production was far from smooth as can be surmised from Table 3.2. In 1918 and 1919 the southern part of the province was drought-ridden, and other parts of the province were also affected by the lack of precipitation. In addition, frosts made heavy inroads in northern districts. The wheat crop fell from 53 million bushels in 1917 to 24 million bushels in 1918, but price increases cushioned the fall in value. After the two bad crop years of 1918 and 1919 a record crop was harvested in 1920, but the break in agricultural prices in that year diminished the total value of the crop. Table 3.3 indicates the violent yield fluctuations, the rapid rise in wheat prices until 1919, the great increase in field crop acreage, and the high levels attained by field crop values during this period.

Production was also uneven though upward in other spheres of production. Coal production declined from 4.3 million tons in 1913 to 3.4 million tons in 1915 as demand decreased. Unemployment appeared accordingly in mining towns. The war period brought recovery, and coal production rose steadily to over 6 million tons in 1918. Strikes, market uncertainties, and transportation difficulties led to reduced production in 1919, but in 1920 production rose to almost 7 million tons as strike settlements were made and coal prices became firm. The production of natural gas declined in 1915, rose until 1919, and then fell off in 1920 with the decline in reserves. Some petroleum discoveries were made near Calgary in 1913 and there was a little bubble of speculation in oil stocks during the next two years. This bubble burst in 1915 when the wells drilled failed to become substantial producers. The total annual value of mineral production fell from $15 million in 1913 to $10 million in 1915.[2] It rose, however, every succeeding year, except 1919, to a high of almost $34 million in 1920. Coal accounted for between 80 per cent and 90 per cent of annual mineral values. The annual value of manufacturing declined in 1914 and 1915, but rose rapidly throughout the war years in response to increasing demands for flour, meat, and dairy products. The gross value of manufactured products rose from $29 million in 1915 to a high of $89 million in 1920.[3] The latter figure was not exceeded until 1929, and again until 1940. A major share of the rise in the value of production was attributable to price increases from year to year.

In general, prices advanced throughout the whole period. There were some slight declines in 1913, but with the war in 1914 an immediate upward pressure developed (see Table 3.4). It should be noted that when prices were at their peak before the declines of May 1920, they were considerably higher than the averages shown in Table 3.4 for 1920. The decline in agricultural prices after 1917 should also be noted. While wheat prices continued to climb until nearly 1920, the price of oats and other grain fell in late 1918, and the prices of livestock, particularly cattle, fell in the same year and continued to do so until 1922. At the same time the cost of agricultural purchases and interest rates rose to very high peaks in 1920. The good crop of 1920 kept farmers solvent, but when the drought of 1921 struck the province, farmers generally were in serious difficulties.

Although the decline in investment activity was not reflected in a serious decline in provincial income, the slowing flow of funds into Alberta in 1913 had other ramifications. Urban municipalities and the provincial government experienced greater difficulties in floating debentures, and private borrowers found it increasingly difficult to get loans. English lenders became more selective than before in their overseas investments. In spite of this, Alberta cities, especially Edmonton, managed to sell large debenture issues in 1913, but at the cost of discounts and higher interest rates. In April 1913, Edmonton sold debentures aggregating over $11 million at 95 net, while the provincial government sold a bond issue of $5 million in London at 97. The servicing of such debts, both public and private, soon became a burden of consequence. During the war years the provincial government managed to raise substantial amounts in the United States before that country became fully engaged in the war. The two post-war years, however, brought renewed borrowings as funds became available from the outside again. Farmers borrowed heavily at high interest rates to expand field acreage, to purchase more land at inflated prices, and to obtain field equipment. They paid heavily and dearly after 1920. Governments, especially the Province of Alberta, also became heavily committed

Table 3.4   Selected Price Indicators, Canada and Alberta, 1913–1920

Year	Wholesale 1926=100 Canada	Agricultural Products, Alberta 1926=100	Cost of Living Canada 1935–39=100	Cost of Farm Purchaes, W. Canada 1935–39=100	Intereest Rates, Canada 1935–39=100
1913	64	81	79	n.a.	125
1914	65	125	80	84	121
1915	70	108	81	88	149
1916	84	161	87	97	139
1917	114	216	102	125	171
1918	127	174	116	147	171
1919	134	186	127	158	163
1920	156	125	145	179	183

Sources: All series except interest rates and part of the farm purchase index are annual averages. The wholesale price index is for Canada, and the data were obtained from the D.B.S., *Prices and Price Indexes, 1944–1947*, 8. The index of prices of agricultural products is a measure of farm prices actually received by farmers in Alberta; the data come from D.B.S., *Quarterly Bulletin of Agricultural Statistics*, Jan. 1937, 29. The cost-of-living index is the Canadian urban one; data are taken from the *Department of Labour Gazette*, Ottawa, June 1950, 967. The price index of commodities and services purchased by farmers pertain to Western Canada, and the data are derived from D.B.S., *Prices and Price Indexes, 1944–1947*, 51. The index of interest rates is calculated from yields of Ontario provincial bonds; the indexes given above are for December of each given year; the data come from ibid., 95.

FISCAL DEVELOPMENT

PROVINCIAL BUDGETS

A new treasurer, C.R. Mitchell, delivered the budget speech of 1914. He emphasized the need for going to money markets despite unfavourable conditions in them. At the same time he indicated that the government was not yet inclined to raise its tax levies. An estimated surplus was declared by including loans among revenues. The following year a deficit was reluctantly predicted, and once the breach had been made, deficits were admitted thereafter. Still, as long as funds could be obtained externally, the provincial government was going to take the easy way out and hope that some day the full bloom of economic development would somehow provide more revenue without unpleasant political ramifications. It had not yet adopted the habit of older governments of raising rates and imposing new taxes during recessions to attempt to balance budgets.[4]

Yet, in face of successive deficits, Mr. Mitchell began to place increasing emphasis upon the need for increased taxation as the years went by. In 1916 and 1917 he contented himself with stressing the necessity of collecting a larger proportion of the levies imposed under existing tax laws. In 1917 an amusement tax was imposed; in 1918 came a general tax on land (the supplementary revenue tax) and a tax on coal production. In the 1918 budget speech the treasurer said that the government had hesitated to impose new taxation while "men's minds were more or less upset and there were uncertainties about business conditions in the future." But in his 1919 budget speech he told the legislature bluntly that the people of Alberta must face direct taxation whether they liked it or not because "we have a very considerable number of very active organizations in this country that are continually pressing upon this government for social legislation." Finally, in the 1920 budget speech he remarked:

> I think one of the chief assets of this province is the character of the
> people, the character of the administration, and last but not least,
> our ability to impose a tax which will, in the long run, be sufficient
> to meet maturing obligations from year to year. The real security
> which stands behind our financial program as well as the security of
> our bonds is our annual revenue and our power to increase taxation
> to the limit of requirements to which we might properly go without
> imposing an undue hardship upon the people.[5]

But the demands upon the public purse were too great to permit balanced over-all budgets, and there were sizeable deficits in every year from 1914 to 1920. Agricultural relief strained the treasury during and after the drought years of 1918 and 1919; the government was too deeply committed in its telephone and railway ventures; the Dominion government withdrew the Northwest Mounted Police from non-military duties, a step which led to heavy expenditures on a provincial police force; the rapid growth in the number of automobiles called for better roads; the pressure for social legislation became too insistent to be resisted after the war. The provincial government, saddled with economic expenditures of dubious value, added to its social and highway expenditure reluctantly and almost wearily by 1920. In that year it outdid itself with an overall deficit of over $8 million while the election year 1921 saw a deficit of $16 million. The administration was pressed too hard to be able to retrench expenditures, and having gone so far it was but a short step to go much farther.[6]

Table 3.5 indicates the revenue and expenditure record of the government from 1914 to 1920 inclusive. Including the telephones, there was an overall

Table 3.5 Revenue and Expenditure of the Government of Alberta, 1914–1920 (in millions of dollars)

Fiscal Year	Overall Basis[a]			Overall Basis[b]			Income Account[c]		
	R	E	S or D(–)	R	E	S or D(–)	R	E	S or D(–)
1914	5.3	8.0	–2.7	4.4	6.3	–1.9	4.4	4.4	–0.1
1915	5.2	9.4	–4.1	4.2	8.0	–3.8	4.1	4.7	–0.6
1916	5.4	7.3	–1.9	4.4	6.1	–1.8	4.2	5.0	–0.8
1917	6.4	8.4	–2.0	5.2	7.2	–2.0	5.1	5.7	–0.6
1918	7.8	9.7	–1.9	6.6	8.1	–1.5	6.3	7.1	–0.8
1919	9.8	13.2	–3.4	8.1	9.9	–1.8	8.0	7.9	0.1
1920	13.0	21.3	–8.3	11.1	15.0	–4.0	9.0	8.5	0.5

(a) Includes telephones. Derived by methods outlined in Appendix B.
(b) Excludes telephones. Derived by methods outlined in Appendix B.
(c) From *P.A., 1950–51*, Statement No. 18.

deficit in every year, a peak of more than $8 million being reached in 1920. Excluding the telephones, there was also an overall deficit in every year. Finally, there were deficits on income account from 1914 to 1918 inclusive.

CONTINUED GROWTH OF THE PUBLIC DEBT

The war years restrained provincial borrowing because of the closing of the English capital market during the early war years, the growing difficulty of obtaining American funds, and the priority of Canadian federal government issues in all markets open to Canadian securities. The latter irked provincial governments in Canada generally, and Alberta was no exception. There seemed to be a lack of realization that there was a limit to the factors of production that could be devoted to internal resource development while the country fought a war, a limitation that could not have been remedied by making funds easily available to provincial governments unless the resources devoted to war were at the same time diminished.

Despite the limitations upon borrowing, the Alberta government succeeded in making substantial additions to its debt (see Table 3.6). Early in 1914 a $7.4 million bond issue at 4.5 per cent, due in 1924, was sold through Spencer, Trask, and Company in Great Britain and about $7.1 million was realized. Treasury bills sold in 1913 totalling $3.5 million were repaid in November 1914. The province began 1915 with practically no unfunded debt; its cash position was relatively strong; its credit standing was good. By 1915 it was becoming

Table 3.6 Public Debt of the Province of Alberta, 1914–1920 (in millions of dollars)

As at Dec. 31	Direct Debt			Indirect Debt			Total
	Net Funded	Unfunded	Total	Class I	Class II	Total	
1914	22.7	0.0	22.7	41.6	0.0	41.6	64.4
1915	26.7	0.0	26.7	41.6	0.0	41.6	68.4
1916	28.6	0.0	28.6	41.6	0.0	41.6	70.3
1917	30.0	0.8	30.8	22.7	19.0	41.6	72.4
1918	30.7	2.3	33.1	22.8	19.0	41.7	74.8
1919	33.7	2.0	35.6	20.9	22.5	43.4	79.1
1920	40.8	3.8	44.5	25.2	22.5	47.8	92.3

Source: *P.A., 1914–1920* and *1950–1951*, Statements No. 19 and 20. Class II indirect debt consists of railway debentures originally guaranteed by the province but later assumed by the Canadian National and Canadian Pacific Railways. The province still remained liable in the event of the financial failure of the railways.

quite difficult to obtain funds overseas, but the province succeeded in selling a $4 million bond issue maturing in 1925. It realized less than $3.5 million and had to set a bond rate of 5 per cent so it was a costly achievement. Further debenture issues of smaller magnitude were sold in 1916 and 1917.

In 1917 the government found itself unable to sell debentures on the scale it desired and resorted to temporary loans from the banks. It also began to issue demand certificates of various denominations bearing interest at 5 per cent compounded annually. This measure was adopted to raise money at a lower interest rate than that charged by the eastern money markets and the banks. Stress was also put upon the desirability of reducing the government's dependence upon outside markets. The certificates constituted a potential threat to the cash position of the province as the years went by and as the amounts issued grew to exceed provincial cash balances many times over.

In 1919 and 1920, the government once again began to rely heavily upon the sale of debentures (see Table 3.7). The bond rate on the 1919 issues was 5.5 per cent; in 1920 it rose to 6 per cent as the province marketed heavy offerings. Except for a small amount purchased on the market in 1920, no debentures were redeemed since no issue was due before 1922.

A sinking fund on a partial basis for debt repayment was set up in 1915. It was decided to set aside 0.5 per cent of the outstanding debt in each year. Larger amounts were to be set aside in the future with the expected rise in population and revenue. It was argued by the treasurer that full provision for

Table 3.7 Sources and Uses of Funds of the Government of Alberta, 1914–1920 (in millions of dollars)

	1914	1915	1916	1917	1918	1919	1920
SOURCES							
Revenue	5.3	5.2	5.4	6.4	7.8	9.8	13.0
Temporary loans	0.0	0.0	0.0	0.8	1.3	2.0	2.5
Debentures	7.1	3.3	2.0	1.5	0.9	3.0	7.3
Savings certificates	0.0	0.0	0.0	0.4	1.2	2.0	2.8
Total	12.4	8.5	7.4	9.1	11.2	16.8	25.6
USES							
Expenditure	8.0	9.4	7.3	8.4	9.7	13.2	21.3
Temporary loans	3.6	0.0	0.0	0.4	0.4	2.9	1.8
Debentures	0.1	–	–	0.0	0.0	0.0	0.2
Sinking fund	0.1	0.1	0.1	0.1	0.2	0.2	0.2
Savings certificates	0.0	0.0	0.0	–	0.5	1.4	1.7
Total	11.8	9.5	7.4	8.9	10.8	17.7	25.2
NET PROCEEDS							
Revenue	−2.7	−4.1	−1.9	−2.0	−1.9	−3.4	−8.3
Temporary loans	−3.6	0.0	0.0	0.4	0.9	−0.9	0.7
Debentures	7.0	3.3	2.0	1.5	0.9	3.0	7.1
Sinking fund	−0.1	−0.1	−0.1	−0.1	−0.2	−0.2	−0.2
Savings certificates	0.0	0.0	0.0	0.4	0.7	0.6	1.1
Total	0.7	−0.9	0.1	0.1	0.4	−1.0	0.4
Cash balance, year end	1.6	0.7	0.8	0.9	1.3	0.3	0.7

Source: *P.A., 1914–1920.*

debt repayment should not be made in the immediate present since money could be used to greater advantage for current expenditures. If this was so, why set aside anything at all? And since the government was increasing its debt annually there seems to be little justification for a sinking fund contribution which in effect led to increased pressure to obtain funds by borrowing.

MITCHELL JUSTIFIES THE GROWTH OF PUBLIC DEBT

The government did not incur increased debt without some qualms. The treasurer, Mr. Mitchell, did his best to set up a rationale of borrowing and to defend the expenditures made out of borrowed funds. Essentially his argument was that the developmental expenditures by the government would not only provide amenities for settlers but would also increase the productivity and resource utilization of the economy to such an extent that a solid revenue base would be evolved. His "progress with economy" passage in the 1917 budget speech is a lucid and consistent argument for the incurring of public debts by young regions:

> A young province with great resources is naturally progressive. It must either develop its latent wealth or let it lie dormant. Development requires capital. New settlers require transportation facilities in order to reach the markets with their produce. Prudence is a good thing, but too much prudence means stagnation, and it should be the policy of any progressive government to so use its capital that good returns would be manifest from the beginning. This is the meaning of progress, and there should be no hesitation, once the necessity is shown, in putting a just proportion of our assets against initial development. When capital is withheld development must wait, and it is clear that a slightly larger investment at the beginning for such work, in advance of population, is far better than doling out aid in the wake of pioneers who have to suffer until roads and railways reach them. We point to these things as justification of our action in borrowing, from time to time, considerable sums of money in the financial markets of the world. We feel that in borrowing this money we have carried out our bounden duty to the people of a young and progressive province. Up to the present time at least, nothing has occurred to make us regret any expenditure undertaken. So far as initial outlay is concerned, we should hesitate to incur whatever expenditure is necessary to care for the pioneering projects of this country. In a

young country, temporizing with such matters means loss, for returns from investments will quickly follow.[7]

Mitchell expressed the sentiments of the Alberta electorate. Government was expected to provide transportation and communication facilities as rapidly as possible so that individuals could utilize and develop resources. The argument presented above is sound if it is modified by the principle of selectivity of projects and if a reasonable degree of economic stability can be expected.[8] But it was too facilely assumed that almost any capital investment made within the region would pay dividends in the near future. Thus railway and telephone extensions into new territory were approved without considering too carefully what an equal increment of investment might produce in areas already settled. Again, Alberta's economy is fundamentally unstable. It is highly dependent upon the sale of exportable surpluses in unreliable world markets; it suffers from both external and internal transportation handicaps which the provincial government attempted to overcome; it is subject to fluctuations from unpredictable weather vicissitudes and from a marginal climate generally. Under such conditions there are years during which it can be very difficult to meet the high fixed interest charges arising out of a rapidly growing debt.

It was not wrong to incur debt; it was the uses to which borrowed funds were put which were wrong in terms of economic return. The danger of default is ultimately a danger to an economy and its government only insofar as loanable funds cannot be obtained in the future should such funds be desired for further development. How real this danger is has not been demonstrated conclusively by historical experience: some defaulting governments have made successful re-entries into the capital markets of the world while others have had more difficulty in doing so. Probably if the political conditions are basically stable, governments can stage comebacks in the capital markets. If this is so, default is not such a serious matter for a government on the North American continent. Defaults, in other words, are more or less temporary.[9] Finally, there is the question of stigma attached to default. Perhaps this is the ultimate limitation, which checks government borrowing. It was a strong enough consideration in Mitchell's time, but in his Alberta optimism was too great to entertain the thought of default since the province had "limitless resources."

THE LEVEL OF GOVERNMENT SERVICES

GENERAL GOVERNMENT

Total expenditure on general government declined somewhat after 1913, and was stabilized at a level of about $2 million until 1919. The decline and subsequent stabilization was largely attributable to the decrease in the construction of administration buildings.

Various factors led to substantial increases in total expenditure on general government after 1917 (see Table 3.8). Social services were expanded, entailing an increase in administrative staff. Bonuses were paid to civil servants to compensate them for rising living costs. The Dominion government withdrew the Northwest Mounted Police from non-military duties during the war, and the provincial government then organized its own police force. Further, the enforcement of prohibition called for a larger police force than before. Thus in 1916, the government paid only $75,000 for a police force, the agreed payment to the Dominion government for the services of the Northwest Police; in 1920 it paid $493,000 to maintain its own police force.

SOCIAL EXPENDITURE

Social expenditure rose from $1.2 million in 1913 to $1.5 million in 1914 when there were substantial increases in expenditures on agricultural schools and mental hospitals. During the next three years social expenditure stabilized, but there was a sharp increase in the post-war period for which there are several reasons.

First, in the sphere of education, grants to schools were stepped up to improve the new school system. The university appropriation rose, and the school inspection staff were strengthened. A policy of making advances to financially embarrassed school districts was begun in the drought years of 1918 and 1919; these advances were made to enable the districts to meet their debenture obligations and teachers' salaries. In addition, loans were made to normal school students to stimulate the recruitment of teachers since there were many schools closed in the province because of the lack of teachers. Finally, substantial capital expenditures were made in 1919 and 1920 with the construction of the Institute of Technology at Calgary and of additional agricultural schools.

Second, health expenditures rose. A department of public health was organized in 1918, with duties as outlined in Chapter 2; previously public health had been a branch of the municipal affairs department. The influenza epidemic of 1918 made the department a very strategic one from the beginning.

Table 3.8 Expenditures of the Government of Alberta, 1914–1921, According to Functions (in millions of dollars)

Fiscal year	General Government				Social Expenditure				Agr.	P.D.	Economic Expenditure				Debt int.	Other	Total
	Leg.	Adm.	Just.	Total	Educ.	P.H.	P.Wel	Total			Hwys	Tel.	Rwys	Total			
1914	0.1	1.0	0.8	2.0	1.1	0.4	0.1	1.5	0.7	0.1	1.0	1.3	0.0	3.1	1.0	0.3	8.0
1915	0.3	1.0	0.7	2.0	1.1	0.4	0.1	1.7	0.7	0.1	1.0	1.0	1.9	4.6	1.1	–	9.4
1916	0.2	1.0	0.6	1.8	1.2	0.5	0.1	1.7	0.7	0.1	0.9	0.7	0.0	2.4	1.3	0.1	7.3
1917	0.3	1.0	0.7	2.1	1.3	0.3	0.1	1.7	0.9	0.1	1.2	0.8	0.1	3.1	1.3	0.1	8.4
1918	0.2	1.1	0.9	2.1	1.3	0.6	0.1	2.0	1.1	0.1	0.9	1.1	–	3.2	1.5	0.9	9.7
1919	0.2	1.3	1.0	2.5	1.9	1.0	0.2	3.1	1.2	0.1	1.1	2.8	0.4	5.6	1.8	0.2	13.2
1920	0.2	1.4	1.2	2.8	2.4	1.0	0.5	3.8	3.3	0.2	1.6	5.7	1.3	12.0	2.5	0.2	21.3
1921	0.5	1.7	1.2	3.4	3.4	1.0	0.6	5.1	4.3	0.2	2.3	5.4	4.4	16.5	3.8	0.2	29.0

Source: See Appendix B.
Abbrev.: Leg. is legislation; Adm. is administration; Just. is justice; Educ. is education; P.H. is public health; P.Wel is public welfare; Agr. is agriculture; P.D. is public domain; Hwys is highways and bridges; Tel. is telephones; Rwys is railways; Debt int. is debt interest and exchange.

Expenditures grew during the war, and after the expansion of mental hospital facilities and the construction of hospitals for returned soldiers added to the public health costs. An inter-provincial agreement in 1916 secured some economies with respect to the care of the handicapped and feeble-minded children. Manitoba was to look after the deaf and dumb children of the four western provinces; Saskatchewan, the blind; Alberta the feeble-minded; and British Columbia, the incurably insane.

Third, public welfare expenditures rose rapidly in 1919 and 1920. A mothers' allowance act was passed in 1919 under which allowances were to be paid out by the provincial government to widows or mothers in custody of children under 15 years of age if they were boys and under 16 years of age if they were girls. The municipalities were required to pay 50 per cent of the cost. Employment offices were established in 1919 under the Dominion government program, which the province was required to help operate. The organization of a veterans' welfare advisory commission absorbed over $75,000 in 1920. Most of this was spent in the form of grants to the Great War Veterans' Association, to the next-of-kin home, and to the Boy Scouts' Association. Loans were also made to returned soldiers who became regular school students.

Social expenditure, despite an increase in dollar amounts, did not absorb an increasing percentage of total expenditure. In 1920 it accounted for 18 per cent of the total, the same as in 1913. These expenditures can hardly be called extravagant or ambitious; they were necessary if not overdue. Insofar as economic expenditures opened up remote territory for settlement, additional school grants were required, not to mention hospitalization and relief outlays. By and large, the social expenditures provided a very bare minimum of services. The economic expenditures, as suggested previously, might have increased the productive capacity of the provincial economy if they had been confined to proven, well-settled areas. Greater social services in these areas too, would have been conducive not only to greater well-being, but also to greater productivity in settled areas that were often raw and crude. Instead public funds were frittered away on sparsely settled areas in the south and on fringe areas. Perhaps the Dominion government, itself a villain in the piece, should have drawn the northern boundary of Alberta at the 55th or 56th parallel instead of the 60th parallel.

ECONOMIC EXPENDITURE

Despite large advances made to railways in 1915 that led to an increase equal to the 1913 level, there was a considerable reduction in economic expenditure during the rest of the war years, chiefly because of the monetary stringency and the difficulty of obtaining men and materials for railway and telephone construction. Once debentures could be floated in volume again, economic expenditures rose (see Table 3.8). Advances to the Alberta Farmers' Cooperative Elevator Company and to the government creameries accounted for increased expenditures during the early war years, then the drought of 1918 and 1919 came, which hit the southeast particularly hard. Agriculture relief became necessary, and both the Dominion and provincial government spent large sums and guaranteed loans to farmers.[10]

By 1919 both governments combined their forces to provide feed and seed for farm operation in the drought areas, and to provide food and coal for drought-ridden farmers. In municipal districts, the councils were required to supervize and distribute relief, with the money borrowed guaranteed by the province. The Department of Public Works was to do the same job in the improvement districts. The whole system of granting relief was based upon guarantees of loans from the banks by governmental agencies that re-loaned to individuals. It involved the province in relatively small immediate expenditures but laid the basis for substantial ones in the future. The main direct expenditures were made in order to distribute and sell hay and feed throughout the province during the exceptionally long and cold winter of 1919–20, over $2 million being spent altogether of which about $1.2 million was recouped.

There were continual pressures to induce the government to enter the field of agricultural credit. There was much dissatisfaction with the tightening of credit by the banks during the pre-war depression. Premier Sifton voiced the sentiments of farmers on January 25, 1916, in speaking to the Canadian Club at Calgary:

> The time was ripe for amendments to the existing legislation governing these institutions (the commercial banks) by which some more definite control, in the disposal of their deposits should be secured for the people.[11]

The U.F.A. (United Farmers of Alberta)[12] convention which met in Calgary in January, 1916, passed a resolution urging provincial legislation setting up co-operative farm mortgage associations to provide long-term loans, co-operative credit associations to provide short-term loans, and an agricultural bank to provide farmers with loans at lower interest rates than those charged by the chartered banks.

The government took action in 1917 and passed the Livestock Encouragement Act. Under this act, the so-called "cow bill," the government guaranteed the loans of farmers at 6 per cent interest for the purchase of livestock. Over $0.5 million was advanced in this way in 1917, and greater amounts in subsequent years. Legislation providing for long-term and short-term agricultural loans was not put into effect because the provincial government was unable to obtain funds at rates much below 8 per cent.

The hail insurance problem plagued the government from year to year. Provision had been made for municipal hail insurance districts in 1912. A hail insurance tax was imposed upon all assessable land in such districts. The districts were supervised by a Hail Insurance Board of three members, two of which were elected by the municipalities and one of which was to be appointed by the provincial government. Heavy losses were incurred in 1916. Tax rates were raised and indemnities were reduced accordingly in subsequent years. The provincial government managed to avoid expenditures in this sphere despite pressures of the U.F.A.

In 1920 irrigation legislation was passed to provide for irrigation districts. Such districts were to be governed by elected boards under the supervision of a provincial irrigation council. They were empowered to issue debentures subject to a 30-year term and sinking fund provisions. Another act dealt with the Lethbridge Northern Irrigation District, which had been previously formed by private promoters. The Dominion government had made irrigation surveys in the Lethbridge area, but the people of the area looked to the provincial government for direct aid. About $5 million was required for an initial program and about $15 million for the ultimate scheme. The Dominion government was ready to provide the immediate funds if the provincial government guaranteed the bonds. The provincial government refused to do this despite pressure exerted by the Lethbridge residents, the promoters, and the Western Canada Irrigation Association. The provincial government argued that if anyone was to guarantee the bonds, it should be the Dominion government because of its control over water rights, its authority over the irrigation laws, and its retention of natural resources.[13] The act passed by the provincial government provided for a guarantee of two years' interest on bonds issued by the district. Such interest was to be paid only if the debentures of the district became overdue and unpaid; the government did not commit itself to pay any of the principal in such a case. This legislation far from satisfied all the parties immediately concerned with the project because they were unable to obtain sufficient funds to begin operations. The administration, however, was obviously afraid of further guarantees since a number of previous ones had come home to roost.

There was little expenditure on highways during the war, although towards its conclusion, the increasing number of automobiles called for a system of trunk roads, both paved and unpaved. Legislation was passed in 1918 that classified provincial highways as main, district, and local. The province was to meet 75 per cent of the cost of construction of main highways and 25 per cent of that of district highways. The cost of local highways was to be borne by the local authorities. The construction of main and district highways stepped up somewhat in 1919 and 1920 as construction materials and steel for bridges became available in quantity once again. But the price increases absorbed a large part of increased appropriations so that there was relatively little improvement of highway conditions.

Maintenance and operation expenditures on the telephone system increased steadily although construction expenditure dropped. After the war the deterioration of the system called for replacements while political pressures dictated a policy of new extensions. When materials and borrowed money became available again, an ambitious extension program was begun and construction expenditure especially increased.

Railway construction tapered off during the war. On March 9, 1916, according to a statement of Mr. Mitchell, 2,535 miles of railroad had been executed out of a total of 3,510. Grand Prairie in the Peace River country had been reached, and the Alberta and Great Waterways Railway was almost complete. Some direct advances had to be made by the government in 1915 to the Central Canada Railway Company for the purpose of connecting the Edmonton, Dunvegan, and British Columbia Railway with the town of Peace River Crossing. The government's railway policy was under continual fire from the opposition. Criticisms consisted of charges that railways were not built rapidly enough and that they cost too much to build. This criticism stemmed largely from disappointment in the end results as railways were completed; utopias failed to materialize as the "miraculous" North Country with its "fabulous" riches failed to deliver the goods. Nevertheless, the administration passed legislation in 1917 providing for a number of railway extensions to be guaranteed by the province, including one that was to run almost 300 miles northward from Peace River. The difficulty of obtaining men, materials, and money fortunately saved the province from its own folly in this case for the railway could not be built at the time. After the war the northern railways were mostly in financial difficulties, and this precluded consideration of further construction.

By 1920 the Alberta and Great Waterways Railway was in serious financial straits. The section beyond Lac La Biche went through practically uninhabited territory; the section from Edmonton to Lac La Biche also ran through considerable tracts of waste land. In short, it was very poor territory, and direct operation and maintenance costs could not be covered by revenues. The tar sands at the end of the line were undeveloped; nobody had yet discovered a technique, let alone an economic one, for exploiting them. The provincial government stepped in and paid the interest on bonds and also gave an outright subsidy of $400,000 to the railway. Then, after sporadic attempts by the railway company to maintain service, the government took possession and control of this controversial and ill-fated railway on July 28, 1920. The Edmonton, Dunvegan, and British Columbia Railway to the Peace River region was also having difficulty. The railway line was in such poor condition that regular operation schedules were disrupted. The company defaulted on its bond and interest payments in late 1919. The provincial government took no action immediately to meet these obligations because it was negotiating with the Dominion government to have the railway made part of the Canadian National Railway system. Legislation was passed in April 1920, to provide for financial assistance in the event that the Dominion government refused to take over the Peace River railroads. The provincial cabinet stressed the obligation of the province with respect to the guaranteed bonds and the predicament in which settlers would find themselves if railway services were discontinued.

The negotiations with the Dominion government fell through. The provincial government accordingly paid $122,000 in interest on bonds and advanced $750,000 to the railway to enable it to repair its roadbed and to maintain operational schedules. Finally, negotiations were begun with the Canadian Pacific Railway Company, which agreed to manage and control the line beginning in July 1920.

Other railways also received assistance. The Lacombe and Blindman River Electric Railway was paid considerable amounts for construction beginning in 1917, the total for 1917 to 1920 being almost $400,000. Interest was paid on defaulted bonds on branch lines of the Grand Trunk Pacific by the provincial government in 1919 and 1920. But the Dominion government reimbursed the Alberta government on this account.

DEBT CHARGES

Interest payments and other expenses connected with the public debt rose from $1.0 million in 1914 to $2.5 million in 1920.[14] Interest defaults of the railways and higher interest rates on new loans than previously accounted for the sharp rise in these expenditures in 1920. Thus in fifteen years the provincial government had increased obligations that carried an annual charge greater than twice the Dominion statutory subsidies.

Table 3.9   Revenue of the Government of Alberta as a Percentage of the Provincial Income and of its Own Expenditure, 1914–1920

Year	Percentage of Provincial Income	Percentage of Expenditure
1914	3.2	67
1915	2.9	56
1916	2.1	74
1917	2.1	66
1918	3.1	80
1919	3.0	74
1920	3.6	61

Sources: See Appendices A and B.

OTHER EXPENDITURES

Miscellaneous expenditures varied considerably from year to year. The most notable expenditure in this category in 1914 was for the purchase of oats and other grain to be donated to Great Britain and Belgium. The total involved was $286,000. Gifts of this proportion were not made after the first flush of excitement and patriotism, and after the government realized that it was not going to be called upon to contribute to the "last man and the last dollar" as Premier Sifton had suggested in a 1914 speech. Contemporary accounts seem to indicate that both the general public and the provincial government expected the war effort to be more "total" in nature and more disruptive of everyday life than became the case. However, in 1918, the provincial government contributed $800,000 to the "patriotic fund" and in 1919 and 1920 smaller amounts were paid to assist in the rehabilitation of veterans.

THE DEVELOPMENT OF REVENUE

Despite the imposition of new taxes and fees in 1913 and 1914 the revenue of the provincial government declined in 1914, and despite some subsequent increases the totals were inadequate in every year to meet the rising tide of expenditure. Only in 1918 did the government collect as revenue an amount equal to 80 per cent of its expenditure (see Table 3.9).

Despite the imposition of new taxes, then, the provincial government absorbed much the same proportions of provincial income as in the pre-war

Table 3.10 Revenues of the Government of Alberta, 1914–1920
(in millions of dollars)

	1914	1915	1916	1917	1918	1919	1920
Dom. of Canada	1.7	1.6	1.7	1.7	1.6	1.7	1.8
Taxes	0.4	0.6	0.9	1.3	1.9	2.5	3.5
Lic. and fees	1.2	0.8	0.8	1.0	1.3	1.6	1.7
Public domain	0.1	0.1	–	–	0.2	0.2	0.3
School lands	0.2	0.3	0.2	0.3	0.5	0.6	0.7
Liquor control	0.2	0.2	–	–	–	0.3	0.5
Fines	0.1	0.1	0.1	0.1	0.1	0.1	0.2
Sales	0.3	0.4	0.4	0.5	0.6	0.8	1.9
Refunds	–	–	–	–	–	–	0.1
Interest	0.5	0.5	0.6	0.6	0.6	0.6	0.9
Repayments	0.1	–	0.1	–	–	0.1	0.1
Telephones	0.5	0.6	0.7	0.8	1.0	1.2	1.4
Total revenue	5.3	5.2	0.4	6.4	7.8	9.8	13.0

Source: See Appendix B.

period. The revenue structure was too closely geared to urban economic activity in 1913 and consequently total revenue fell in 1914. It failed to tap the rising income from agriculture until several years later when a general provincial land tax was imposed.[15] Even then tax levies could have been higher if the level of provincial income is a reliable criterion of the ability to pay. The aggregates, of course, do not tell the whole story for there is tax delinquency in Alberta in any year because of drought, frost, and hail which strike various parts of the province; there is never a year when crop conditions are even close to uniform throughout the province. Under these circumstances there was hesitancy in imposing large provincial taxes and a considerable degree of leniency developed through the years in dealing with delinquency.

Table 3.10 sets out the provincial government's sources of revenue.

The Dominion subsidy was increased by 25 per cent in 1914 when the provincial population exceeded the 400,000 mark. The total subsidy shrank relatively, however, from one-third of total revenue in 1914 to about 14 per cent in 1920. In 1914 it equalled 21 per cent of total expenditure; in 1920 it was less than 8 per cent. Truly, it was ceasing to perform its original function of providing a large core of stable revenue.

Several conditional grants-in-aid began to be received from the Dominion government during this period. These included small amounts for seed fairs, an agricultural assistance grant,[16] small amounts to induce the province to co-operate in the "greater production" war program of the Dominion government, a grant for the organization of employment offices, and grants for technical education and for venereal disease control. The aggregate grants-in-aid received by the province rose from $60,000 in 1913 to $133,000 in 1920. None of the grants eased the financial strain on the provincial treasury in any way; on the contrary, most of them induced the province to provide additional services, which entailed the use of some provincial as well as federal funds.

In 1914 the government imposed a tax on "wild lands" at the rate of 6.25 cents per acre ($10 per quarter section). Wild lands were defined as unused and uncultivated lands held by their owners for mere speculative purposes. Land held by the Canadian Pacific Railway Company was exempt. Actual collections amounted about one-tenth of the expected total. There were difficulties in obtaining the names and locations of owners, as many of were scattered throughout the world. Many assessment notices came back to the Department of Municipal Affairs as the post office was unable to find the addresses of such notices. In fact, these difficulties had plagued the department for years in collection of local improvement district and educational taxes.

The Educational Tax Act was amended in 1915 to provide for the taxation of lands held under grazing leases from the Dominion government, whether within or without the boundaries of school districts. Despite this and other amendments, the educational tax was not a prolific producer of revenue, nor was it very responsive to changes in economic conditions.

In 1918 a general tax on all alienated land, with certain exemptions, was levied by the province. It was called the supplementary revenue tax and represented an attempt to get "taxation that is equitable and widely distributed in proportion to the ability of people to pay."[17] This tax became a major revenue producer, and in 1920 almost $1.5 million was collected or more than 40 per cent of all tax revenue. Originally it was designed to provide revenue for the "patriotic fund" of the province. The war ended in 1918 after the tax had been levied for one year. The provincial government, however, retained the tax in view of the pressure upon expenditure. It represented too, the first attempt by the province to levy a tax on a broad base.

The tax on railways rose from $74,000 in 1915 to a new level of $111,000 in 1916 as more railway lines became subject to tax. Revenue from this source remained at the same level during subsequent years. The corporation tax was extended in 1916 to apply to all companies operating in the province and including those under Dominion charter, the Farmers' Cooperative Elevator Company being the only exemption. The *Financial Times* of Montreal described the amendment as "most extreme and burdensome" and as "drawn up in a spirit of gross and deliberate hostility."[18] It also questioned the constitutionality of the act since it affected extra-provincial companies. There was no question, however, as to the latter for it was a tax of general application. An amendment of 1918 provided for increased rates on banks and privately-owned gas and power companies. The yield of the corporation tax rose from $130,000 in 1914 to $308,000 in 1920; this was the result of higher rates and the growth of the number of companies induced by increasing prosperity. A tax on theatre and moving picture admissions was imposed beginning in 1916 at the rate of from one cent to twenty-five cents per admission. Its yield increased rapidly in every year, and $170,000 was collected in 1920. Collections from succession duties fluctuated from year to year; here was an unpredictable revenue generator that yielded over $200,000 in the occasional year. Exemptions were lowered and rates increased in 1918; this, however, had little visible effect upon yields during the next few years. Finally, the unearned increment tax contributed little revenue before 1918 when over $100,000 was collected in any one year for the first time. Collections reached a peak of $153,000 in 1920 in response to increased real estate turnover.

Public domain began to produce significant revenue after 1918 when a tax was imposed on sales of coal by coal mine operators.[19] This levy was most ill timed for it imposed an additional burden upon the coal industry which was hard-hit by rising transportation costs and strikes during the post-war years. In any event, public domain revenue increased substantially and reached $319,000 in 1920.

The natural resources controversy was revived at the end of the war. The most notable development was the statement submitted by the Alberta cabinet to the federal government in December, 1920, to the effect that Alberta would be willing to have the public lands subsidy cancelled and to pay back the Dominion government all that it had received in the way of public land subsidies if the senior government would give an accounting for and payment of all it had taken from provincial lands from the beginning of its control. This proposition was not inherently unreasonable, but the question of "accounting" was fraught with endless controversy. It took another ten years to settle the controversy in part.

The revenue from school lands rose rapidly after 1916 in response to increased land sales and higher interest rates. The annual total rose from $220,000 in 1914 to $692,000 in 1920. Mr. Mitchell attacked the Dominion government management of the fund in the 1917 budget speech. The fund had been drawing 3 per cent until 1917 in the form of bank deposits. The Alberta treasurer felt that the money should be invested in Dominion government bonds, which were currently paying 5 per cent. The Dominion government did transfer the funds, an action hastened by the need for money to finance the war. Mr. Mitchell, however, went further for he suggested that the Dominion Act should be amended to permit investment in provincial and municipal bonds and in rural credit bonds to provide "cheap money" (5 per cent) for farmers. Such a policy would have meant the diversion of productive agents from direct war production but Mr. Mitchell failed to point out this aspect of the question.

The revenue from liquor control shrank to almost nothing by 1916 as prohibition was approved by the electorate by a plebiscite in 1915. But in 1919, in response to the influenza epidemic, the sales of the government stores increased greatly as doctors made wholesale prescriptions. The liquor question was very controversial, and enforcement was a major issue. The costs of enforcement were high, and much of the time and energy of the Alberta Provincial Police were devoted to liquor law enforcement. If a system of government sales without prohibition had been adopted in 1915, government deficits would have been reduced by at least one million dollars annually. But the temperance movement was strong and Alberta tried the prohibition experiment for eight years.

Revenue from sales of goods and services increased at much the same rate as provincial revenue until 1920 when the sale of hay to farmers in conjunction with the Dominion-provincial agricultural relief program brought the total to $1.9 million. Advances continued to be made to the government creameries without interest, the repayments constituting the chief item in the category of sales goods and services in ordinary years.

The revenue from the telephone system increased from $0.9 million in 1914, including interest paid on debt, to over $1.9 million in 1920. Without allowing for depreciation the system showed a surplus in every year. But even conservative depreciation estimates would have converted these surpluses into substantial deficits. A telephone expert from Chicago, J.G. Wray, was called upon late in 1918 to review the provincial telephone situation. He reported to the legislature on March 25, 1920, and recommended that toll rates be increased by 25 per cent, exchange rate by 20 per cent and rural rates by 100 per cent. As an alternative to the increase in rural rates he proposed a tax of $8.00 per annum on each quarter-section of land within 300 feet of rural telephone lines. But on May 27, 1920, Premier Stewart stated to the legislature that there would be no increase in rates; he felt that the farmers could not afford to pay. At the same time a large program of extension was approved and begun. The pressure of farm groups, especially the U.F.A., was too strong to be resisted.

Revenue from interest, exclusive of the telephone interest, fluctuated between $100,000 and $200,000 between 1914 and 1919. In 1920 a reimbursement of $225,000 made by the Dominion government on account of interest paid by the province on defaulted Grand Trunk Pacific bonds brought the total up to $352,000. Bank deposits and investments of the government were small and the interest earned on these did not exceed $50,000 annually until 1920. In 1919 the Central Canada Railway discontinued its interest payments due to the province on advances made. The Lacombe and Blindman Valley Electric Railway failed to meet its obligations to the government in 1920. Very small amounts were received as interest from farmers, on account of seed grain and relief advances, or from school districts, which had been given loans. It was a difficult task to make collections in these instances. On the other hand, the United Grain Growers, who had taken over the Alberta elevators, and which had also been given advances in 1915, continued to meet both interest payments on funds advanced by the government.

Some repayments were made throughout the period on seed grain, school district advances, normal school student loans, and drought relief advances. The elevators met their obligations faithfully. Refunds of expenditure increased somewhat in 1920 when the municipal share of mothers' allowances rose to $53,000 and the administrative cost charged to the improvement districts was increased from $10,000 to $25,000. Other refunds and miscellaneous revenue items were not very significant.

GOVERNMENT AND THE ECONOMY

The provincial government continued to emphasize aid to agriculture and settlement in this period. The spectacular rise of agriculture in filling the income gap left by the collapse of the investment boom justified such a policy. But one can question specific projects. The demonstration farms were not absolutely essential, and probably gave rise to more resentment than education. Some interest might have been charged on creamery advances, which in effect, constituted a revolving fund. The advance in 1915 to the Central Canada Railway was questionable as were the northern railway projects generally. Aside from the advance to the Central Canada, the province did not make direct expenditures for railways, but its guarantee policy was not cautious. However, in view of its inability to scotch the Waterways railway project, the poorest investment in the lot, it could hardly turn down guarantees for Peace River railways which had much more to commend them from an economic standpoint than the Waterways railway. The Peace River railways laid the basis for the Peace River settlement boom of the 1920s. Unfortunately, World War I and its economic consequences delayed this development.

The provincial government also fostered agriculture by its reluctance to levy widespread taxes on farmers. The level of rural taxation was low even if one includes the levies of the local governments. Rural governments levied only about one-third of the property taxes in the province throughout the period even though the rural population constituted over 60 per cent of the total population. The provincial government confined its rural property taxation to lands owned largely by speculators and absentee owners. This taxation policy was conducive to agricultural development, but it did not solve the problem of rising debt engendered by expenditures that were too high from year to year in relation to revenues.

Urban municipalities overreached themselves in the years before 1914 in terms of subsequent economic development. Edmonton was the most conspicuous example, for it paved streets, laid out street railway tracks, installed sewers, and many other improvements in outlying sections of the city, in anticipation of a population growth that did not materialize for many years. Indeed, many of the facilities provided were not fully utilized until the 1940s. As a consequence, the city was saddled with high debt and tax burdens, and urban economic development tended to be retarded accordingly.

The war years slowed up both government and private investment in Alberta. After the war, government investments grew rapidly, but at the same time large sums had to be spent to provide agricultural relief and to assist railways. The failure of various railways, both provincial and Dominion government sponsored, dampened the enthusiasm of private promoters and Alberta did not experience a post-war investment boom. Higher taxes, both provincial and municipal, as well as a continued rise in public debt may have acted as a deterrent to investment.

Government shrank in relative importance during this period. Total expenditure of both the provincial and local governments equalled 28 per cent of provincial income in 1913; in 1914 expenditures fell to 24 per cent of income. By 1915 the urban units, the main actors on the public finance stage were "played out," and in that year total government expenditures equalled only 14 per cent of provincial income. From 1916 to 1919 the expenditures varied between 8 per cent and 11 per cent of income. Heavy provincial expenditures in 1920 raised the percentage to 14 in that year.

Tax collections, however, absorbed a somewhat greater proportion of provincial income during the 1914–20 period than previously, somewhere between 4 per cent and 7 per cent annually. Net income-producing expenditures became negligible after 1914. Retrenchment by the municipalities and heavy interest payments arising out of debts contracted in the pre-war period accounted for this failure of government to make a positive contribution to income. Finally, construction expenditures were pinched off because of urban collapse and then by war conditions. However, in 1919 and 1920 the provincial government spent large amounts on public works.

DEPRESSION, STAGNATION, AND RECOVERY, 1921–29

4

ECONOMIC DEVELOPMENT

In Alberta, the 1920s were marked by a sharp and short downturn in prices, income and employment in 1921; by several years of depressed economic activity until 1925, broken by one good crop in 1923; and by intermittent and unspectacular recovery until 1929. After the setback of 1921, Alberta largely marked time until the middle of the decade, and prosperity was not sustained when it did come. It was a decade, too, in which Albertans lost much of their optimism, and many of them left the province, especially between 1921 and 1923.

The most significant fact about the post-war depression was the unprecedented fall in prices. These are set out in Table 4.1. Farm costs and prices were seriously dislocated and agricultural net income shrank materially. In addition, many farmers had previously purchased land at high prices with low cash payments. The payments on farm mortgages accordingly became very heavy in real terms.[1] The long winter of 1919–20 had left many a livestock raiser with a legacy of debt incurred for feed. The cattle industry was very hard hit by the United States Emergency tariff of 1921 and the Fordney-McCumber tariff of 1922.[2] The yearly average price of steers in Edmonton dropped by 43 per cent between 1920 and 1921; for the 1920–23 period the decline was 51 per cent.[3] In the long run, of course, the whole cattle industry suffered a decline. Thus between 1921 and 1929 the number of cattle in Alberta declined from 1,383,000 to 1,010,000, or by 27 per cent.[4] Both the cattle and dairy industries declined absolutely and relatively throughout the decade. Hog and sheep production, however, rose somewhat.

Throughout the first half of the twenties, agriculture was inhibited by either low yields (1924), low prices (1923), or both (1921 and 1922), as is shown in Table 4.2. Price and cost relationships became more favourable towards 1925 (see Table 4.1), and this helped induce a resumption in agricultural expansion. 1927 stands out from the other years, for in that year the value of field crops reached a high that was not exceeded until 1946. It seemed that there would be a recovery, but poor yields returned in 1928, accompanied by poor prices in 1929.

Table 4.1   Selected Price Indicators, Canada and Alberta, 1920–1929

Year	Wholesale Canada 1926=100[a]	Agricultural Products Alberta 1926=100[b]	Cost-of Living Canada 1935–39=100[c]	Cost of Farm Purchases Western Canada 1935–39=100[d]	Interest Rates Canada 1935–39=100[e]
1920	156	125	145	179	183
1921	110	72	130	152	163
1922	97	81	120	134	154
1923	98	55	121	131	146
1924	99	107	119	131	135
1925	103	103	120	130	136
1926	100	100	122	128	135
1927	98	98	120	127	124
1928	96	81	121	126	131
1929	96	106	122	124	139

(a)   From D.B.S., *Prices and Price Indexes, 1944–1947*, 8.
(b)   From D.B.S., *Quarterly Bulletin of Agricultural Statistics*, Jan. 1937, 29. The prices used in computing these indexes are, as closely as can be determined, the prices which were actually received by farmers.
(c)   From Government of Canada, Department of Labour, *Labour Gazette*, June 1950, 967.
(d)   From D.B.S., *Prices and Price Indexes, 1944–47*, 51. This includes farm wage rates, tax and interest rates, and equipment and materials.
(e)   From ibid., 95. This index is calculated from yields of Ontario provincial government bonds. The indexes in the series above are as of December of each given year.

Agriculture attained an economic importance in the 1920s that has not been attained since. Between 1923 and 1928, the net value of agricultural production exceeded 70 per cent of total net value of production annually. Since 1929 it has fluctuated between 50 per cent and 60 per cent in most years, and has never exceeded 65 per cent.[5] A notable fact, too, was the great expansion in the wheat acreage, which rose from 4.1 million acres in 1920 to 7.6 million acres in 1929. The oats acreage, on the other hand, fell from 3.1 million acres to 1.9 million acres respectively. New varieties of wheat, which ripened in a shorter time than previous ones, and field crop acreage expansion, generally accounted for the greatly increased importance of wheat.

Investment activity followed a similar trend. As shown in Table 4.3, the first half of the 1920s saw very little activity. Things improved slightly around 1926 and 1927, and provincial income reached a high for the decade in 1927.[6] But Alberta enjoyed only a brief spell of prosperity in the 1920s; its economy

Table 4.2 Wheat Yields, Wheat Prices, Field Crop Acreages, and Value of Field Crops in Alberta, 1920–1929

Year	Wheat Yield (bu per acre)	Wheat Price (cents per bu.) (cents)	Field Crop Average (millions)	Value of Field Crops (millions)
1920	20.5	152	8.4	$204
1921	10.4	77	9.4	83
1922	11.2	77	10.0	95
1923	28.0	65	10.5	151
1924	11.0	120	11.0	160
1925	18.3	119	8.5	157
1926	18.5	105	10.7	202
1927	27.4	98	11.0	273
1928	23.2	175	11.7	221
1929	12.3	102	12.4	157

Source: *C.Y.B.*, 1922–1931.

was too dependent upon the fortunes of agriculture to participate in the urban prosperity generated in many parts of North America.

Oil wells at the Turner Valley field became producers in this time period, but in general the 1920s saw little expansion in the value of mineral production. After a fall in the net value in the first four years of the twenties, it was a struggle just to regain the 1920 levels by 1929. Construction, custom and repair, forestry, electric power and manufacturing all also had a large dip in the first few years, but recovered slightly better and surpassed the 1920 levels by 1929.

The decade of the 1920s was marked by the depopulation of some areas of the province and the settlement of others. These changes are set out in Table 4.4. Urban growth accounted for the largest part of the population increases between 1926 and 1931 in the southwest and in the centre.

FISCAL DEVELOPMENT AND PROBLEMS

THE RECORD DEFICIT OF 1921

The year 1921 was keynoted by depression with falling agricultural prices, rising urban unemployment, and drastically reduced grain yields brought on by drought. At the same time, the provincial government was subjected to a variety

Table 4.3   Selected Indicators of Investment Activity in Alberta, 1920–1929

Year	Immigration (thousands)	Building Permits Edmonton & Calgary (millions)	Cnstruction Contracts (millions)	Railway Mileage Added	Annual Population Increases (thousands)
1920	18	$6.1	n.a.	46	24
1921	12	3.9	n.a.	93	23
1922	9	5.4	n.a.	−11	4
1923	10	2.3	n.a.	0	1
1924	11	3.3	7	44	4
1925	13	2.7	4	182	5
1926	16	3.9	10	57	6
1927	15	4.9	8	125	25
1928	16	9.7	18	156	25
1929	15	17.1	29	226	26

Sources: Immigration figures were taken from *Facts and Figures*, 51–52; building permits data from ibid., 274; construction contracts awarded in Alberta from ibid., 270; railway mileage added from ibid., 309; and annual population increase from *C.Y.B.*, 1946, 127.

Table 4.4   Population in Alberta Regions, 1921–31 (in thousands)

Region	1921	1926	1931
Southeast (A)	79	62	71
Southwest (B)	183	193	226
Centre (C)	235	252	284
Northeast (D)	42	46	64
Peace River (E)	12	11	27
North and west (F)	42	42	59
Total, Alberta	586	608	732

Sources: From *Dominion Census*, 1921 and 1931, and *Census of the Prairie Provinces*, 1926. For location of the regions, see Fig. 1.3.

of pressures to spend, especially from the farming community, spearheaded by the U.F.A. They pressed for more spending on telephones, highways, rural credit facilities, schools and irrigation. Other communities wanted money for northern railways, assistance with defaulted municipal bonds, and urban unemployment relief. The provincial administration was desperate because it was losing hold of the electorate and an election was not far in the offing. In the minds of a large part of the electorate it was judged that the government had failed to bring prosperity and economic development up to anticipated levels. Albertans expected their provincial government to perform functions far beyond the traditional, constitutional, and financial powers of Canadian provinces.[7] The Alberta government accordingly passed a mass of legislation in the 1921 session and appropriated record sums of expenditures.

In his budget speech of 1921, Mr Mitchell introduced the idea of taxes, but did not actually add to the tax burden. He expected to balance the budget, with an additional two million dollars expected to come from increases in liquor sales, school lands fund receipts, telephone revenue, land titles fees, and the Dominion subsidy. Expenditure estimates exceeded those of 1920 by two million dollars. The treasurer emphasized that every effort had been made to keep the appropriations within the bounds of the expected revenue, and that "all the demands for new services or extensions of services were by no means granted." Yet there were numerous increases in expenditures. No direct mention was made in the speech of the many millions of dollars to be spent on capital account and to be financed by borrowing; the amounts involved were shown in the capital account estimates, which were tabled separately.

The revenue collected on income account in 1921 fell short of the estimates by $1.7 million, while actual expenditures on income account exceeded the estimates by almost $0.4 million. But the deficit on income account was trivial compared to the overall deficit, which amounted to nearly $17 million (see Table 4.5). There was an unprecedented amount of spending on telephone extensions, highway construction, railway assistance, and agricultural relief. It was an election year and the government was prepared to spend as long as it was able to obtain funds from the money markets. Most of the deficit was financed by floating debentures totalling more than $17.5 million in terms of both par value and proceeds at a bond rate of 6 per cent. Funds were also obtained through bank loans and savings certificates. The interest on these loans was to add almost one million dollars annually to future expenditures. It was an amazing performance but one which failed to prevent the election of a new administration. Most of the electorate felt that the government was not doing enough while only a part realized at all, and then only in part, that

Table 4.5 Revenue and Expenditure of the Government of Alberta, 1921–1929 (in millions of dollars)

Fiscal Year	Overall Basis[a] R	E	S or D (–)	Overall Basis[b] R	E	S or D (–)	Overal Basis[c] R	E	S or D (–)
1921	12.1	29.0	–16.9	9.6	22.7	–13.1	8.5	10.6	–2.1
1922	13.3	23.2	–9.9	10.6	19.1	–8.5	9.3	11.2	–1.9
1923	14.4	17.6	–3.2	11.9	14.8	–2.9	10.4	11.0	–0.6
1924	14.7	20.9	–6.2	12.2	18.0	–5.9	10.5	11.1	–0.6
1925	15.4	21.3	–5.9	12.8	18.2	–5.4	11.5	11.3	0.2
1926	16.5	22.1	–5.6	13.6	19.0	–5.4	11.9	11.9	–
1927–28	22.9	26.1	–3.2	18.7	22.1	–3.4	16.1	15.9	0.3
1928–29	22.8	24.9	–2.1	19.1	21.4	–2.2	15.3	13.7	1.6
1929–30	27.6	26.6	1.0	23.7	22.2	1.5	15.8	15.4	0.4

(a) Including telephones. See Appendix B for sources.
(b) Excluding telephones. See Appendix B for sources.
(c) *P.A., 1950–51*, Statement No. 18.
(d) The 1927–28 fiscal year covers the fifteen months from January 1, 1927 to March 31, 1928. Subsequent fiscal years cover the period from April 1 to March 31 annually.

the government was adding very rapidly to its debt. In the 1921 provincial elections, the Liberals lost to the U.F.A.

THE U.F.A. RETRENCHES

The U.F.A. administration reaped the whirlwind, which ironically enough, had in large measure been generated by the U.F.A. as a non-partisan pressure group in previous years. Faced with interest payments on the debt exceeding $4.5 million, insolvent northern railways, drought relief problems, an overextended telephone system, substantial debt repayments, and a stationary revenue, the new administration emphasized economy. The rapid increase in debt charges brought a realization that the growth of debt had to be checked. Premier Greenfield struck the keynote of "economy" in his budget speech of 1922:

Alberta now enters upon a new phase of its history in that it may be said that we have reached the stage where we must mark time in the trend of over-expansion that has overtaken by a considerable margin the extreme limit of our sources of revenue.

The time has arrived when we cannot view with complacency a growing debt while our population and the resultant limitations of our taxing ability remains more or less stationary.[8]

But it was not easy to retrench on any great scale for there were too many "uncontrollable" expenditures to use the term of the provincial treasurer. Interest on the debt, advances to railways for the purpose of maintaining service, the implementation of seed grain guarantees, and the completion of public works projects begun in previous years absorbed about $8 million, or almost two-thirds of provincial revenue. Expenditures on general government, highways and telephones were all reduced but social expenditures rose. For 1922 the overall deficit was almost $10 million (see Table 4.5). This was financed by the cash surplus of over one million dollars which the treasury possessed at the beginning of the year, by an addition of more than six million dollars to the debenture debt, by proceeds from savings certificates, by temporary loans, and by a bank overdraft. Taxes on gasoline and on grain elevators were imposed for the first time, while the rates of many old taxes were increased. Nevertheless, these changes did little to ease the financial situation in 1922 when the deficit on income account was almost as great as that of 1921 (see Table 4.5).

The government began to use the axe with a vengeance in 1923. Further cuts were made in almost every area, but on the other hand, interest on the public debt rose to more than $5 million or more than one-third of the total revenue. Total expenditure was reduced to $17.6 million in 1923 from $23.2 million in 1922 and $29.0 million in 1921.

A number of new revenue measures were introduced. New taxes were imposed on mineral rights, slot machines and soft drinks. Succession duties were increased, and the coal tax was amended so as to make the gross revenue of coal companies the tax base. The total revenue collected increased, but this was attributable just as much to the record crop of 1923, which made revenue collections easier, as to the increase in tax rates and the tapping of new revenue sources. And there was still a deficit.

Attempts to reduce expenditures and to increase revenue continued in 1924 despite growing opposition. Opposition members took the government to task for increasing tax rates. The supplementary revenue tax was attacked in particular. The new treasurer, Mr. R.G. Reid, took critics to task in his budget speech in 1924. He said:

> It should be apparent to the most casual financier that any proposal that would reduce taxation, when the province, with the most rigid economies, cannot balance the budget, must be the result of the natural antipathy of all men to taxation, and cannot be the fruit of mature consideration.[9]

There was indeed much "natural antipathy" to taxes in Alberta as elsewhere. Much of it stemmed from the failure to see the government services provided because they were too thinly spread in a sparsely settled region as to be barely visible to any but the most discerning observer. Complicating the problem was the lack of uniformity of crop conditions in any given year, the unreliability of precipitation conditions from year to year, and price fluctuations. All of these combined to make it difficult to set up a provincial revenue structure that could be depended upon to produce stable revenue.

The outlook was gloomy in 1924. The provincial economy was not prospering and population growth was at a standstill. Albertans, including their government, had lost their early optimistic enthusiasm. Many individuals, mostly farmers, were still heavily in debt, and only the efforts of a provincial debt adjustment board had prevented large-scale court proceedings by securing negotiated agreements between creditors and debtors. The provincial government, despite earnest endeavour to reduce expenditures and to increase revenues, had added $20 million to its debt in the three years of 1922, 1923, and 1924 (see Table 4.6). It kept hoping for another period of economic expansion, for a series of good crop years, and for greater stability in agricultural prices so that revenues would increase enough to cope with the ever-growing debt. Remarkably enough, the capital market continued to be receptive to Alberta bonds despite the widening disparity between debt charges and provincial revenues.

THE REDUCTION OF DEFICITS, 1925–29

The administration continued to reduce expenditures on income account wherever feasible after 1924. But it increased the expenditures on capital account, and this more than offset income account reductions. Revenues rose from year to year in response to improved economic conditions. Consequently, surpluses on income account began to appear and the overall deficits diminished steadily. In 1929–30 there was an overall surplus for the first time since 1906 (see Table 4.5). It arose, however, not from drastic reductions in capital expenditures, but from the sale of the provincial railways in that year.

SOURCES AND USES OF FUNDS

The government continued to be hard-pressed for cash during the 1920s and its cash balances seldom exceeded one million dollars (see Table 4.7). After 1924, the government set up a special investment fund for the purchase of its own

Table 4.6 Public Debt of the Government of Alberta, 1921–1930
(in millions of dollars)

As at end of fiscal year	1921	1922	1923	1924	1925	1926	1928	1929	1930
DIRECT DEBT									
Net funded	57.5	65.7	71.8	76.9	79.5	84.5	87.7	92.8	102.4
Unfunded	5.7	7.3	5.0	6.3	9.2	10.3	13.8	13.1	11.8
Total direct	63.2	72.9	76.8	83.2	88.6	94.8	101.5	105.9	114.2
INDIRECT DEBT									
Class I	30.4	30.7	31.6	28.0	25.6	25.3	26.3	25.8	9.5
Class II (a)	22.5	22.5	22.5	22.5	22.5	22.5	22.5	22.8	32.2
Total indirect	52.9	53.3	54.1	50.5	48.2	47.8	48.8	48.6	41.7
Total debt	116.1	126.2	130.9	133.7	136.8	142.7	150.3	154.6	155.9

Source: *P.A., 1921–30.*

(a) Railway debentures assumed by the two national railway systems.

securities on the market and those of the Dominion government, other provinces, and Alberta municipalities. Attempts were made yearly to increase such investments, and from 1924 to 1930 there were net increases in total holdings (see Table 4.7).

There was considerable borrowing on a temporary basis. The sale of savings certificates exceeded withdrawals in every year except fiscal 1928–29 (see Table 4.7). The sale of debentures continued to provide the main source of cash except for revenue, and there were substantial net increases in debenture debt in every year except 1924.

THE PUBLIC DOMAIN SETTLEMENT

The controversy with the Dominion government in regard to the ownership of public domain was finally settled at the end of this period, after many years of protracted negotiations. An agreement transferring the natural resources from the Dominion government to the Alberta government was signed on December 14, 1929, the same day as the agreement with Manitoba was signed. The Saskatchewan transfer was not made until March 20, 1930. The history of the natural resources question has been told so adequately elsewhere that only a short summary is presented here.[10]

Table 4.7 Sources and Uses of Funds of the Government of Alberta, 1921–1930 (in millions of dollars)

Fiscal year end[a]	1921	1922	1923	1924	1925	1926	1928	1929	1930
SOURCES									
Revenue	12.1	13.3	14.4	14.7	15.4	16.5	22.9	22.8	27.6
Temporary loans	2.0	2.9	1.4	2.8	2.5	2.2	5.0	3.4	8.0
Savings certificates	4.4	3.7	2.6	6.3	6.1	10.5	10.1	7.8	9.5
Debenture proceeds	17.6	9.7	15.8	6.9	6.7	9.2	7.9	8.2	3.9
Sinking fund	0.0	0.3	0.6	0.5	0.2	0.2	0.2	0.2	0.2
Spec. invest. fund	0.0	0.0	0.0	0.4	0.2	2.5	6.6	1.6	5.1
Total sources	36.1	30.0	34.8	31.6	31.1	41.2	52.7	44.0	54.3
USES									
Expenditure	29.0	23.2	17.6	20.9	21.3	22.1	26.1	24.9	26.6
Temporary loans	1.0	2.0	3.9	2.4	1.8	3.5	3.3	3.9	9.5
Savings certificates	3.5	3.0	2.3	5.4	4.0	8.0	8.5	7.9	9.3
Debentures	0.8	3.6	5.2	7.0	4.0	4.6	4.0	3.1	2.0
Sinking fund	0.1	0.2	0.2	0.3	0.3	0.4	0.5	0.5	0.6
Spec. invest. fund	0.3	0.0	0.0	0.1	0.8	4.4	8.8	3.3	6.9
Total uses	34.7	32.1	29.2	36.2	32.2	43.2	51.3	43.7	55.0
NET PROCEEDS									
Revenue	−16.9	−9.9	−3.2	−6.2	−5.9	−5.6	−3.2	−2.1	1.0
Temporary loans	1.0	0.9	−2.5	0.4	0.7	−1.3	1.7	−0.5	−1.5
Savings certificates	0.9	0.7	0.3	0.9	2.1	2.5	1.6	−0.1	0.2
Debentures	16.8	6.1	10.6	−0.1	2.7	4.6	3.9	5.1	1.9
Sinking fund	−0.1	0.1	0.4	0.2	−0.1	−0.2	−0.3	−0.3	−0.4
Spec. invest. fund	−0.3	0.0	0.0	0.3	−0.6	−1.9	−2.2	−1.7	−1.8
Other[b]	−1.2	1.6	−0.3	0.4	0.8	0.2	−0.2	−0.2	−0.1
Cash surplus or deficit(−)	0.2	−0.5	5.3	−4.1	−0.3	−1.7	1.3	0.2	−0.7
Cash balance, year end[c]	0.7	0.2	5.6	1.5	1.2	−0.5	0.9	1.1	1.3

Source: *P.A., 1921–30*. Telephone revenue and expenditure are included.
(a) December 31 for 1921 to 1926 and March 31 for subsequent years.
(b) Trust fund transactions, superannuation receipts and payments, and miscellaneous items.
(c) General revenue fund balance as per statements in the public accounts.

The Alberta government took no measures designed to lead to natural re-sources transfer negotiations while Sir Wilfrid Laurier and his party headed the Dominion government.[11] The sole exception was a resolution of the legislature, passed in 1910, which requested transfer of the resources in Northern Alberta and those of "purely local concern."[12] In 1913, Premier Arthur Sifton is credited with taking the lead in persuading the other two prairie province premiers, Scott and Roblin, to make a joint request for not only the transfer of the natural resources but also for a continuation of the public lands subsidy. They knew this would not be acceptable to Prime Minister Robert Borden, but as far as Premier Sifton was concerned, the fact that he had pressed for a settlement of the natural resource question satisfied the Alberta electorate for the time being.

In 1920, Arthur Meighen, then prime minister of Canada, initiated the ques-tion of resource transfer, but as Manitoba would not consider the discontinuance of the public lands subsidy, the matter was dropped until a new Dominion cabinet assumed power in 1921.[13]

The Alberta government began separate negotiations with the new Dominion government. In 1926, an agreement was reached whereby Alberta was to receive its inalienable domain and a continuance of the land subsidy for a period of three years. Unfortunately some Quebec members in the House of Commons chose to inject the question of educational rights for the Catholic minority in Alberta, during the debate on the agreement. The Dominion and Alberta governments did not wish to stir up sectarian controversies in connec-tion with the natural resources, and after attempting to make amendments that failed to overcome the objections of the Quebec members, dropped the matter. The premier made it clear that the Alberta government was satisfied with the terms agreed on for the transfer of the resources, and that the school question was the only difficulty. On the latter point he expressed a desire to let well enough alone, "we are living in peace here and wish to continue to live at peace."[14]

As matters turned out, Alberta was to receive more than the 1926 agreement provided for. The Dominion government found itself less able to take a strong line on the natural resources question after the report on the Maritimes by the Duncan Commission and after the provincial conference of 1927.[15] The government ap-pointed the Turgeon commission in 1928 to investigate the case of Manitoba. This commission recommended that the inalienable public lands in Manitoba be trans-ferred to the provincial government, that a lump sum of $4,584,000 representing arrears of land subsidy computed on a very questionable basis be paid to Manitoba, and that the public lands subsidy continue to be paid.[16] After the Manitoba pre-mier, Mr. Bracken, and the Dominion Prime Minister, Mr. King, had reached an agreement in June 1, 1929, on the basis of the findings of the commission; Mr. King announced that his government was prepared to give similar treatment to Alberta and Saskatchewan.

In December, 1929, the Dominion government and the Alberta government reached agreement on the following points: (1) inalienable resources in Alberta were to be turned over to the Alberta government; (2) the public lands subsidy was to be continued; and (3) a royal commission was to be set up to enquire whether or not any further compensation should be given. Saskatchewan also came to an agreement on a similar basis in 1930. The resources were accordingly transferred to the two provinces in 1930 after the agreements had been debated and passed by the Dominion Parliament and the provincial legislatures.

The question of what additional compensation should be awarded to the provinces, if any, remained. Two royal commissions, one for each province, were set up to enquire into the matter. After exhaustive testimony presented at hearings and after making elaborate calculations to justify their end results, both commissions awarded a lump sum of $5 million to each province.[17] One of the Saskatchewan commissioners, Mr. H.V. Bigelow, dissented, and on the basis of very dubious assumptions arrived at a figure of $58,242,700 as proper recompense for Saskatchewan. This minority recommendation contributed to make the Saskatchewan government refuse the offer of $5,000,000 made by the Dominion government. Alberta, which had been prepared to accept $5,000,000, also refused the offer of this sum in the final settlement, because she was naturally not going to jeopardize her chances of getting more in the event that Saskatchewan did.

The terms secured were certainly favourable to the provinces. The Dominion government had not received much net revenue from its western lands in view of its homestead policy. The provinces would not likely have done any better for they would have been torn between the desire for more revenue by means of the sale of land and the desire for rapid economic development, which a homestead policy made possible. The latter desire would no doubt have outweighed the former.

In the case of Alberta there was a presumption that the public domain could have become a prolific revenue producer before 1930.[18] This proposition needs to be examined. First, it should be noted that the province levied a tax on coal from 1918 to 1927 when it was declared to be unconstitutional. This tax yields between $131,000 to $283,000 annually until 1927. The annual yields obtained after 1930 by the imposition of royalties, fees, and rentals, fluctuated between $250,000 to $310,000 during the 1930s. Thus the transfer of the public domain did little more in this sphere than to make it constitutional for the government to obtain a revenue of the same order of magnitude as that obtained before 1927. During the intervening period, 1927–30, the Alberta government was, of course, not receiving the coal tax revenue.

Secondly, the volume of petroleum and natural gas produced in the province before 1930 was small. Thus in 1921 the combined produced value of these two products was only $1.5 million; a royalty of one-eighth on this would have yielded revenue of less than $200,000. The annual value of petroleum production rose to more than one million dollars for the first time in 1927. In 1928 the combined value of the two products exceeded $5 million for the first time. Royalties and fees on such a low level of production would not have eased the financial problem of the government significantly. Not until the latter part of the 1930s did petroleum production raise to such a level that rentals and royalties on such production came to form a fairly important source of government revenue. During the late 1940s, of course, revenue from petroleum production and leases reached levels that had not been anticipated. The fact remains that, before 1930, revenue arising from mineral rights held by the province would have been small both in relative and absolute terms. Indeed, the officials who set up the lands and mines department of Alberta in 1930 had serious doubts about whether their department would be self-sufficient or not.

Thirdly, there were considerable expenditures attached to the ownership of the public domain. The net gain to the provincial treasury did not exceed $200,000 annually during the first five years of the 1930s. If account could be taken of increases in general administration expenditures induced by the public domain transfer, the amount is still smaller. If the provincial government had obtained the resources before 1930 and had devised a more productive public domain revenue structure in terms of rates charged, it is very doubtful if annual net revenue could have reached half a million dollars annually during the latter 1920s.

EXPENDITURE POLICIES

GENERAL GOVERNMENT

Expenditure on general government reached a high of $3.4 million in 1921 (see Table 4.8) and formed about 12 per cent of total expenditure. The U.F.A. administration "wrung the fat" out of administrative appropriations and the total spent fell to a low of $2.5 million in 1925. Increases during the following years were relatively small and largely attributable to the construction of administration buildings. The proportion of expenditure absorbed by general government remained almost constant throughout the 1920s for in 1929–30 it was still 12 per cent of the total.

Table 4.8   Expenditures of the Government of Alberta, 1921–1930, According to Functions (in millions of dollars)

Fiscal Year	General Government				Social Expenditure				Economic Expenditure						Debt Int.	Other	Total
	Leg.	Adm.	Just.	Total	Educ.	P.H.	P.Wel	Total	Ag.	P.D.	Hwys	Tel.	Rwys	Total			
1921	0.5	1.7	1.2	3.4	3.4	1.0	0.6	5.1	4.3	0.2	2.3	5.4	4.4	16.5	3.8	0.2	29.0
1922	0.3	1.4	1.2	2.9	3.6	1.6	0.7	5.9	3.8	0.3	1.4	2.9	1.2	9.6	4.7	0.2	23.2
1923	0.4	1.3	1.1	2.9	2.7	1.4	0.5	4.6	1.2	0.2	0.9	1.6	0.5	4.4	5.1	0.7	17.6
1924	0.2	1.2	1.1	2.5	4.8	1.1	0.5	6.4	0.9	0.3	2.1	1.6	0.6	5.5	5.7	0.7	20.9
1925	0.2	1.2	1.1	2.5	3.7	1.2	0.6	5.5	1.3	0.7	2.7	1.9	0.5	7.0	5.5	0.7	21.3
1926	0.4	1.2	1.1	2.6	2.7	1.3	0.6	4.5	0.5	1.0	3.1	1.8	2.2	8.6	5.7	0.7	22.1
1927–28	0.4	1.6	1.3	3.3	3.8	1.8	0.8	6.4	0.6	0.9	2.8	2.4	1.3	8.0	7.3	1.0	26.1
1928–29	0.2	1.3	1.1	2.7	3.5	1.8	0.7	6.0	1.1	0.7	3.4	2.4	1.8	9.4	6.1	0.8	24.9
1929–30	0.2	1.6	1.2	3.0	3.8	2.7	1.2	7.7	0.5	0.9	4.1	3.1	–	8.6	6.2	1.1	26.6

Source: Appendix B
(a)   January 1 — December 31 for 1921–26 inclusive; January 1, 1927 to March 31, 1928 for 1927–28; April 1 to March 31 for 1928–29 and 1929–30.

SOCIAL EXPENDITURE

Social expenditure, despite attempts at retrenchment, increased by about 50 per cent between 1921 and 1930. It formed 17 per cent of total expenditure in 1921; in 1929–30 it absorbed 28 per cent of the total.

Education: The post-war years saw much attention being given to education by the government. Grants to schools rose to assist school districts in obtaining teachers due to a teacher shortage. Special additional grants were made to financially weak rural districts. Finally, special grants were given to districts providing high school instruction. Nevertheless, the provincial grant still provided only 14 per cent of total revenue of all school districts. The university appropriation grew as a result of increasing enrolment after the war. The operational expenditure on agricultural schools increased in 1921, and a technical school was opened in 1920 in response to the Dominion grant for the promotion of industrial, technical, and commercial education; the Dominion government paid 50 per cent of certain expenditures for this purpose. The school inspection staff was increased gradually until 1922. Expenditure on the construction of education buildings such as agricultural and technical schools rose. In 1923, however, there were reductions in most of these education appropriations, some of which were severe.

Expenditure remained at the reduced level of 1923 until 1927 except for the extraordinary outlays involved in assisting the university in 1924 and 1925. Debentures issued in 1914 became due in 1924, and the University was not able to meet payments because World War I and the depression had restricted the number of people available and able to pay tuition. The provincial government had to step in and implement its guarantee on these debentures. After 1927 there was a marked increase arising chiefly from higher school grants and the resumption of the construction of buildings. The government not only reversed its decisions of 1923 and reopened the normal school at Edmonton as well as agricultural schools, but also embarked on the construction of a new large normal school in Edmonton and new agricultural school buildings. Local pressures and desire to have a teacher training institution near the provincial university were the chief factors motivating this building program of the late 1920s.

Public Health: Expenditure on public health rose to a peak of $1.6 million in 1922 chiefly because of heavy construction expenditures on mental hospitals and a sanatorium for tuberculosis patients. Construction expenditures were cut back thereafter, and only a minimum of work was undertaken. The pressure upon existing facilities led to heavy capital expenditure again by 1928, and in 1929–30 almost $1.0 million was spent to expand mental institutions and sanatorium facilities. Annually increasing amounts were also spent on the operation and maintenance of mental institutions, but even then there were constant complaints with respect to the inadequacy of the accommodation available. Only in the sphere of general health services was the government able to reduce expenditures, but even the cuts made here were questionable. In 1923 the number of health nurses stationed in outlying areas to render medical services was reduced from twenty-six to eleven, a very questionable step in sparsely settled regions where doctors were few and far between.

Public Welfare: Unemployment relief payments in 1921 and the operation of veterans' welfare advisory committee from 1920 to 1922 created a temporary bulge in public welfare expenditure. In 1923 unemployment relief payments were eliminated; the veterans' welfare committee became defunct; mothers' allowances and child welfare payments were reduced. The result was a fall in expenditure to less than $500,000. Annual expenditure rose somewhat after 1923 as the number of mothers receiving allowances increased. Increases in numbers of recipients led to higher payments in subsequent years. Two items added almost half a million dollars to the total public welfare expenditure in 1929–30: old age pensions and unemployment relief payments. Both items were destined to swell to major proportions in the 1930s.

ECONOMIC EXPENDITURE

Economic expenditure continued to be the most important expenditure category throughout the 1920s, although it shrank absolutely and relatively. It equalled about 57 per cent of total expenditure in 1921. With the curtailment of telephone, highway, and railway expenditure there was shrinkage to about 42 per cent of total expenditures. Drastic reductions in 1923 cut economic expenditure even further, but irrigation ventures, railways and highways came to absorb increasing amounts in succeeding years and 1929–30 economic expenditure was about one-third of total provincial expenditure. It was a field in which it was not easy for the government to undertake a systematic program of economy; questions of implementation of guarantees and of subsidization cropped up constantly and unexpectedly.

Agriculture: Expenditure on agriculture attained a peak of $4.3 million in 1921 because of heavy outlays for seed grain guarantees and agricultural relief, and declined thereafter because of the discontinuation of the previous seed grain and relief policy. There was still some expenditure on relief through the Livestock Encouragement Act.[19]

There were various other policy changes with respect to expenditure on agriculture. The demonstration farms were sold in 1923 and agricultural agents were hired instead. Grants to agricultural societies were continually reduced after 1923. The government creameries were gradually eliminated after 1922 and working advances made to them ceased after 1924. On the other hand, large amounts were spent during the early years of the 1920s on grasshopper destruction. Measured in terms of expenditure, agricultural functions performed diminished in importance during the latter half of the 1920s.

Public Domain: Expenditure on public domain rose to prominence during the decade chiefly because of ventures in irrigation. The story of how the government saddled itself with another unprofitable venture in resource utilization goes back to 1920 when it was approached by promoters and Lethbridge area residents to guarantee the bonds of the Lethbridge Northern Irrigation District. The government had its misgivings for the guarantee was refused for the time being. But the pressure on government was relentless and the promoters were unable to market the debentures of the district.

In April, 1921, the Liberal administration, which was on its last legs, relented and passed a bill guaranteeing the principal up to $5,400,000 and interest of the bonds of the district. The legislature supported the bill almost unanimously. The district sold 30-year 6 per cent debentures during the summer of 1921 and proceeded with the construction of dams and ditches. The government, however, was bombarded with requests to guarantee the bonds of almost a dozen other irrigation districts that were hastily organized. The new administration inherited these requests. It sparred for a time by doing a sensible thing: it set up an investigative body, the Southern Alberta Survey Board, to report on the possibilities of irrigation in southern Alberta.

The board made an elaborate report, indicated the irrigable acreage, and estimated the cost of the development of the irrigable area to be at least $70 million. In general, it cautioned the government to proceed slowly and to do so on the basis of the progress made in the Lethbridge Northern Irrigation District. The government did commit itself to the extent of guaranteeing bonds of other districts to the extent of $800,000. In addition, it guaranteed the bonds of drainage districts to the amount of $600,000.

The government, of course, was already heavily committed in the Lethbridge Northern venture, which soon showed symptoms of becoming expensive. It was difficult to attract suitable settlers because immigration was low during this period, and relatively few plains farmers had any experience with irrigation. It was questionable, too, whether the traditional crops of wheat and oats would yield the economic returns required to pay the costs of construction, interest on the investment, water rates, and other annual expenses. By 1925 there were only 300 farmers established in the district. The government was obliged to pay defaulted interest on the irrigation district bonds by 1923. Little was collected from the farmers in the district. In 1925 the government waived water rights charges in an effort to induce more settlers to come. It made advances to the district annually to enable it to meet operating and maintenance expenses for the five-year period 1925–29; these advances exceeded $2.5 million.

Other irrigation districts and drainage obtained advances totalling almost $0.8 million during the same period. In addition, the government paid the interest on bonds that had been issued by these districts.

Highways: The roads of Alberta were hopelessly inadequate at the beginning of the 1920s. Few main highways were even gravelled and hard-surfaced roads were non-existent. A motor trip between Edmonton and Calgary was an arduous affair and was regarded as a feat of no small magnitude. The two hundred mile journey would take at least a day under favourable conditions; it would take two or more if it rained. Other highways were no better and often worse than the main highway between the two cities.

The government had begun an ambitious program of road improvement in 1919 and expenditures reached a peak of $2.3 million in 1921. The U.F.A. administration retrenched greatly in this sphere, but it could not resist the pressure exerted by the automobile associations and members of the legislative assembly. To a large extent, Alberta constituents gauge a government by the state of the roads.[20] The government, too, could no longer resist taking advantage of federal grants for highways.

In 1924 the Alberta government came to an agreement with the Dominion government with respect to routes and type of construction. It also set up a Good Roads Board, which was to plan a highway system and to make recommendations on yearly extensions, grading, and surfacing of roads. The provincial auditors set up a special Highway Account and bonds were sold for the express purpose of constructing the highways. This segregation served the purpose of indicating to the legislature and the public, the portion of increasing debt that went to pay for the ever-popular expenditure of outlays for highways.

Telephones: The post-war program of making telephone extensions was continued throughout 1921 and into 1922 despite the fact that the existing system was far from self-liquidating. It was a very suitable field for political patronage and for a government that was going to the electorate: it was easy, though unfortunately wasteful, to give small contracts to farmers to cut and deliver poles. Urban residents were very critical of the extensions being made. There were many charges of corruption and graft, none of which was proved but which have survived in numerous anecdotes of people living in Alberta at the time. Probably the best that can be said about the heavy expenditures of 1920–22 is that they provided cash income to many a farmer hard-hit by the depression of 1921; they were, in other words, counter-cyclical. But the cost of materials was still high during this period. Not until after the government put an end to its construction program in 1922 were costs falling substantially.

Railways: The railway issue was one of the most pressing during the decade and it kept the government financially embarrassed until the railways were sold in 1929. The northern railways and the Grand Trunk Pacific branch lines had defaulted in their interest payments on provincially guaranteed bonds beginning during World War I. By 1920 all of them were in bad straits. The Dominion government reimbursed the province with respect to the interest payments on the bonds of the Grand Trunk Pacific branch lines and took over these lines. But it resisted the requests of the provincial government to have it take over the northern provincial railways.

The provincial government spent $4.4 million in 1921 on the northern railways (including the Lacombe and Northwestern) to complete construction of lines and to bring them into condition to perform regular and reliable service. In addition to this it paid the interest on the bonds of the railways from 1921 to 1925. There were also additional advances each year. Further construction projects were undertaken in the 1926–28 period in response to the Peace River settlement boom. Expenditures on construction and operation fell off abruptly in 1929 with the sale of the railways to the Canadian Pacific and the Canadian National, but a substantial amount of bond interest continued to be the responsibility of the province. At the end of the fiscal year 1929–30, the government had made advances exceeding $16 million to the railways over the ten-year period beginning in 1920. In addition, it had paid over $6 million in interest on guaranteed railway bonds during the same period. The sale of the railways was a happy stroke of business for the provincial government and it was miraculously timed. Yet the negotiations of the sale were lengthy and protracted, for both parties believed during the 1926–29 era that the railways might become profitable ventures.

The Canadian Pacific Railway operating lease of the two Peace River railways, the E.D. & B.C. and the Central Canada Railway, expired in July 1925. The Alberta government was anxious to have the lease renewed. The British Columbia government was, at the same time, trying to secure funds to extend the Pacific Great Eastern Railway into the Peace River country; and it was making representations to the Dominion government and the Canadian Pacific Railway to provide such funds. The situation was complicated further by a claim by the Royal Bank of Canada for $3,000,000 with respect to its owner-ship of the common stock of the E.D. & B.C. Railway. The bank had come into possession of this stock through its purchase of the Union Bank of Canada, which had made advances to the original promoters of the railway. The Royal Bank of Canada forthwith offered to sell its claim to the Alberta government for $1,700,000 in provincial bonds at 3 per cent. Pending acceptance of this of-fer the bank signified that it would not consent to the new lease.[21]

The Alberta government found itself in an uncomfortable position. It was financially responsible in the case of the Peace River Railways already constructed. By continuing under the old lease it was still responsible for main-taining the railways in good condition and for interest on the railway bonds. A new lease under which the Canadian Pacific or the Canadian National would assume greater financial responsibility than under the old Canadian Pacific lease could only be obtained by much cajolery and bargaining and the terms were subject to assent by the Royal Bank. This assent involved the addition of $1,700,000 to the provincial debt in order to establish full ownership of a rail-way which was not paying its way and which to all intents and purposes was already a provincial responsibility. The fact that the recipient of the proposed land issue was a bank would not endear the government to the electorate and an election was looming on the horizon. Finally, if the British Columbia govern-ment and the residents of the Peace River area succeeded in persuading either the Dominion government or the Canadian Pacific Railway or both to connect the Peace River area with Vancouver, the Alberta railways would become more unprofitable than ever and the city of Edmonton, the distribution centre for the north, would suffer.

There were conferences in Ottawa in January and April 1925, attended by the premiers of the two western provinces and by representatives of the Dominion government, the Canadian National, and the Canadian Pacific Railway. The Dominion government and the two railways were reluctant to un-dertake to construct a Pacific outlet from the Peace River. Five engineers were appointed to study the whole Peace River railway situation. In the meantime the Canadian Pacific continued to operate the Peace River railways in Alberta under the old lease. The Alberta Legislature was called together for a special session on August 4, 1925, to consider the terms of new leases that had been offered by the Canadian Pacific and the Canadian National railways. Nothing was decided by the legislature, for the Royal Bank issue stood in the way. Thus the railway continued to be operated under the old lease.[22]

In April 1926, the new premier, J.E. Brownlee, announced that the gov-ernment had come to terms with the Royal Bank, which had scaled down its claim to $1,275,000. He said that the government had tried to interest the Dominion government and the Canadian Pacific in buying the Alberta railways. Nothing came of this, however.

In the meantime the five engineers appointed by the Canadian Pacific and the Canadian National railways to study the Peace River railway question made their report in June 1926. They pointed out that the ultimate cost of an outlet to the Pacific coast would be more than $80 million, that the traffic would have to be many times greater than the existing traffic to pay even the operating expenses, that higher rates would not make such a railway self-supporting, and that it would be more economical to continue to handle the Peace River traffic on existing lines.[23] Thus the idea of a Pacific outlet was spiked and all parties concerned, except the government of British Columbia and the residents of the Peace River area, were prepared to let the matter drop. The British Columbia government continued to press for an extension to the Peace River in the hope that it might solve the financial problems of its own railway, the Pacific Great Eastern, and to colonize the Peace River Block which was located in British Columbia.

The Alberta government reached a cash settlement with the Royal Bank of Canada and paid $1,275,000 on July 31, 1926, and therefore came into full possession of the E.D. & B.C. and Central Canada railways. The lease of the Canadian Pacific railway was cancelled on November 11, 1926, and it was decided to operate the lines through the Department of Railways, which had been in charge of the Alberta and Great Waterways Railway and the Lacombe and Northwestern railway since 1920.[24] A traffic interchange agreement with the Canadian National Railways was also made in order to transfer freight from the north at Edmonton.

The Alberta government, as well as the British Columbia government, continued to strive to relieve themselves of the heavy financial burdens imposed by the ownership and operation of its railways. The Alberta government continued to negotiate with the Canadian Pacific Railway with respect to an acceptable lease. An offer was made to the Dominion government to sell the E.D. & B.C. Railway to the Canadian National Railways. As an alternative the province proposed that the Canadian National Railway undertake to operate the Alberta railways as colonization lines. The Dominion government rejected both alternatives, but made counter offers separately and jointly with the Canadian Pacific Railway.

The Canadian National and the Canadian Pacific made a joint offer early in 1928 to purchase the E.D. & B.C. Railway and Central Canada Railway.[25] The Canadian National Railway made a separate offer for the Alberta and Great Waterways Railway at the same time.[26] The Canadian Pacific Railway offered to buy the Lacombe and North-Western Railway. The railway company was to pay the government $1,500,000 and to assume from the date of the transfer of the capital stock the payment of bonds amounting to $273,000. Further it was to complete the railway to Telfordville, west of Leduc, during 1929. [27]

Premier Brownlee and his government on February 15, 1928, rejected the first two offers. The third offer was accepted and the Lacombe and Northwestern railway was sold accordingly to the Canadian Pacific Railway. In dealing with the first two offers, Premier Brownlee objected chiefly to the interest payments for which the province would continue to be responsible for the next decade. He pointed out that during the previous fiscal year the northern railways had shown an operating surplus of $270,000, a sum which represented a substantial contribution to interest payments. He argued that surpluses in the future might grow so as to exceed the savings in interest to the province that would accrue if the offer were accepted.

The three northern railways showed an operating surplus of $894,000 in 1928, but this represented net earnings of 3.0 per cent on the capital investment before making any allowance for capital recovery. Table 4.9 is indicative of the unprofitable nature of the Alberta government railways. It is clear that the main Peace River railway, the Edmonton, Dunvegan, and British Columbia, was the only one that could be said to be close to being self-liquidating in 1928. The low gross earnings of the Alberta and Great Waterways in each of the years 1921, 1925, and in 1928 in relation to the capital investment are very striking. There can be no question but that the Alberta government stood to gain by almost any sale of the railways that reduced its future railway bond interest payments, and operating deficits. It was the stipulation as to the continuation of interest payments on most of the bonded debt, which chiefly led to the government's rejection of the offers made. It also felt it could do better in view of the increasing prosperity of the period.

The railway question was finally settled in 1929 on terms that were more favourable to the province than the previous offers. The Canadian Pacific Company made an offer on September 17, 1928, on the following basis:

(1) The purchase price was to be $25,000,000. This was to be paid (a) by the first mortgage bonds of the Edmonton, Dunvegan, and British Columbia Railway to the extent of $9,420,000 and, (b) by payment of a sum of $15,580,000 in three instalments, $5,000,000 to be paid on June 1, 1929, and $5,000,000 to be paid on June 1, 1933, and $5,580,000

to be paid on June 1, 1939 with interest at 4 per cent.

(2) The purchaser was to assume all payments made and com-
mitments entertained in the extensions being made to the
Peace River railways. These extensions involved about
$1,000,000. The purchaser also agreed to complete another
sixty miles of extensions within five years. No commitment
was made with respect to the Pacific coast outlet from the
Peace River country.[28]

This offer still left the Alberta government with the liability of the old
Alberta and Great Waterways bond issue of $7,400,000 and responsibility
for further interest payments thereon. It was, nevertheless, a very good offer, and the Alberta cabinet expressed acceptance of it almost immediately
on condition that the Canadian National Railways were to be given an opportunity, exercisable up to December 31, 1928, to participate on a share
and share basis. It was felt that the Dominion government, which owned
the Canadian National Railways, should have a "stake" in the north country, and that the Canadian Pacific railway should not be given sole control
of the northern railways. Somehow, many residents of Edmonton, which
served as a distributing centre for the north, and residents of the north felt
that railway extensions would be made and service would be maintained
if the Dominion government were involved directly in the affair. A mass
meeting in Edmonton on November 21, 1928, passed an almost unanimous
resolution requesting the Dominion government to take action.[29] The senior government yielded and on November 26, 1928 Ottawa announced that
the Canadian National Railways had decided to assume a half interest in
the purchase, subject to ratification by the Dominion parliament.

Both the Alberta legislature and the Dominion parliament ratified the
agreement in February 1929. The Northern Alberta Railway Company was
incorporated to take over all the Northern Alberta railways. It was to be jointly
owned and managed by the two great transcontinental railway companies.

The Alberta government had finally divested itself of ventures that had
proved to be a great strain on its treasury. It wrote off a loss of $11.4 mil-
lion on the basis of the agreement made. In view of the difficulties looming
up during the 1930s, however, it was a very fortunate stroke of business for
the government. Even in 1929, all members of the legislature voted for the
agreement; they realized that a good bargain had been made.

Table 4.9 Summary of Capital Investment, Earnings, and Expense of Alberta Government Railways, 1921, 1925, and 1928 (in thousands of dollars)

	1921	1925	1928
ALBERTA AND GREAT WATERWAYS:			
Capital investment	7,450	7,450	10,935
Gross earnings	177	256	326
Operating expenses	430	305	264
Available for capital recovery and interest	0	0	62
EDMONTON, DUNVEGAN & BRITISH COLUMBIA:			
Capital investment	11,798	14,810	14,664
Gross earnings	1,116	941	1,728
Operating expenses	1,909	871	872
Available for capital recovery and interest	0	70	856
CENTRAL CANADA:			
Capital investment	3,084	3,840	4,376
Gross earnings	58	66	124
Operating expenses	184	151	148
Available for capital recovery and interest	0	0	0
LACOMBE AND NORTHWESTERN:			
Capital investment	Not	2,344	Sold
Gross earnings	operating	60	to
Operating expenses		62	C.P.R.,
Available for capital recovery and interest		0	1928

Source: *C.Y.B.*, 1923, 1927, and 1930.

DEBT CHARGES

The interest on public debt, direct and indirect, grew alarmingly during 1921 and 1922 (see Table 4.8). With the addition of further debt the total grew gradually throughout the decade and reached $6.2 million in 1929–30, about 24 per cent of total expenditure.

The interest on direct debenture debt and on temporary loans almost trebled between 1920 and 1930. In 1920 this item equalled $1,211,000; in 1929–30 it amounted to $3,554,000. Interest paid on indirect or guaranteed debentures rose from $462,000 in 1920 to a peak of $1,110,000 in 1924. Thereafter it declined as the railways were disposed of, but it still remained substantially high and in 1929–30 it amounted to $650,000.

Interest on the provincial savings certificates increased steadily from year to year from $100,000 in 1920 to $516,000 in 1929–30. In 1921, the 5 per cent compounded rate was amended to 5 per cent simple interest. In 1922 a further reduction to 4.5 per cent simple interest was made. These cuts were in line with the falling trend in interest rates after 1921. But withdrawals were heavy, especially in 1928–29 when they practically equalled receipts. It was a method of financing which was far from reliable in a community subject to great income instability.

The cost of management and foreign exchange reached a peak of $210,000 in 1921. It declined in the subsequent years. The telephone bond interest jumped from $570,000 in 1920 to $1,247,000 in 1922 and remained near this level until 1929–30 when it rose to almost $1,300,000.

The irreducibility of the debt charges was a constant source of irritation and complaint. The provincial treasurer indicated in budget speeches their inability to expand social and administrative services because of the straightjacket imposed by debt charges. Continued borrowing eased the current situation somewhat in each year but worsened the long-run outlook as long as revenue failed to increase materially. The economic recovery of 1926–28 and the sale of the railways brightened the situation, but sustained economic development on a much higher level than that attained in 1926–28 was required to provide the favourable fundamental conditions needed to remedy the debt situation. Such development was not to come until the 1940s.

THE DEVELOPMENT OF REVENUE

The revenue of the government almost doubled between 1921 and 1930.[30] Most of this increase was attributable to the imposition of new taxes and increasing the rates of old ones, to the growth of licence fee revenue, to the rise to prominence of liquor revenue, and to a substantial rise in the telephone revenue in the closing years of the decade (see Table 4.10). Revenue, too, came to form a larger proportion of total expenditure than in previous periods (see Table 4.11). In 1929–30 it exceeded expenditure for the first time since 1906; this, however, was due to proceeds from the sale of railways. Revenue as a percentage of provincial income increased from 4.5 per cent in 1921 to 6.9 per cent in 1928, the year before the sale of the railways. Thus it absorbed almost twice as many per cent of provincial income as in the pre-1920 era. One can readily understand why the opposition kept insisting taxes were too high. In terms of expenditure requirements and rate of debt growth, revenue was, of course, too low and it has been suggested that the government did not exploit to the full the recovery situation of 1926–28.[31] Additional revenue could no doubt have been collected during those years, but the order of magnitude would have been such that little fundamental change in the financial condition of the government would have ensued.

There was little change in the amount of the Dominion subsidy and it shrank to less than 10 per cent of total revenue by the end of the decade. Several grants-in-aid were received, but they failed to relieve the financial pressure upon the province. Indeed, they tended to increase such pressure because they required the province to match Dominion contributions with equivalent, and sometimes greater, expenditures.

The greater ease of tax collections and the imposition of additional taxes resulted in a gradual increase in tax revenues. Taxes on real property peaked in 1923. The most important of these taxes was the supplementary revenue tax, which had been imposed in 1918 for the first time. It was a very controversial tax because both rural and urban property owners felt they were discriminated against for various reasons.[32] The assessment board established in 1921 had almost insuperable difficulties in finding even acceptable criteria of "equalization." If the rate had been increased to three mills in 1926 another half million dollars could have been collected.

The wild lands tax was next in importance among real property taxes. It had been passed in 1914 to tax speculators in land. During the later 1920s more and more land, which had been alienated but abandoned, was occupied. As a result the tax base shrank. This tax therefore provided no hope for increasing revenues. A similar process reduced the collections from the educational tax, which fell from a high of $215,000 in 1923 to $93,000 in 1929–30. There simply was less alienated land outside school districts than before. The unearned increment tax yielded an unstable revenue, which fell

Table 4.10 Revenues of the Government of Alberta, 1921–1930
(in millions of dollars)

Fiscal year ending (a)	1921	1922	1923	1924	1925	1926	1928	1929	1930
Dom of Canada	1.9	1.9	1.9	1.8	2.0	2.2	3.4	1.8	1.7
Taxes	2.8	3.0	3.7	3.7	3.9	3.6	4.5	4.6	5.5
Lic. and fees	1.8	1.8	1.9	2.0	2.0	2.2	3.6	3.4	3.3
Public domain	0.3	0.4	0.4	0.3	0.4	0.4	0.2	0.1	0.1
School lands	0.6	0.6	0.5	0.6	0.6	0.7	0.8	0.7	0.8
Liquor control	0.3	0.9	1.1	1.7	1.6	1.9	2.8	2.9	2.6
Fines	0.2	0.2	0.2	0.2	0.1	0.1	0.1	0.1	0.2
Sales	0.9	0.9	0.6	0.3	0.4	0.5	0.6	0.7	0.7
Refunds	0.3	0.2	0.5	0.4	0.3	0.4	0.4	0.4	0.6
Interest	1.2	1.5	1.8	1.7	1.9	1.7	2.2	1.9	2.0
Repayments	0.2	0.2	0.4	0.7	0.7	1.0	1.5	3.5	7.6
Telephones	1.6	1.5	1.3	1.3	1.4	1.7	2.6	2.5	2.5
Total revenue	12.1	13.3	14.4	14.7	15.4	16.5	22.9	22.8	27.6

Source: Appendix B.
(a) December 31 for 1921 to 1926 respectively; the fifteen months ending March 31, 1928 for 1927–28; March 31 for subsequent years.

Table 4.11 Revenue of the Government of Alberta as a Per Cent of Provincial Income and as a Per Cent of its Own Expenditure, 1921–1929

Year[a]	1921	1922	1923	1924	1925	1926	1927	1928	1929
Per cent of provincial income	4.5	4.9	4.9	5.3	5.5	5.7	5.3	6.9	9.5
Per cent of expenditure	42	57	82	70	72	75	88	92	104

Source: Appendices A and B.
(a) Fiscal years of the province adjusted to the provincial income data which cover calendar years.

off after 1921 and then recovered briefly during the 1927–28 period. The total tax collected in 1929–30 was $133,000.

Corporation taxes furnished a steadily increasing revenue. After 1921 more railway branch lines became taxable and about $250,000 was collected annually from the railway tax. Various corporation taxes yielded about $707,000 in 1929–30, or about twice as much as in 1921. It is probable that another half million dollars could have been collected during the late 1920s if the government had been prepared to make corporation taxes the stiffest in Canada.[33]

Succession duties furnished a revenue that varied greatly from year to year. Again it was a dubious step to increase rates to the extent of getting greatly out of line with the other provinces. Amusement taxes provided revenue, which was quite income-elastic, and increases in rates were feasible. A 50 per cent increase in rates would probably have added about $150,000 to revenue annually after 1926.

A new and lucrative revenue source was the gasoline tax, imposed for the first time in 1922 at the rate of two cents per gallon. In 1927 the rate was increased to three cents and in 1929 to five cents. Collections grew rapidly from $185,000 in 1922 to $1,793,000 in 1929–30. The five-cent rate might well have been imposed in 1922; this would have more than doubled the yearly revenues from the tax. But it must be kept in mind that it was levied for the first time in 1922; there would have been much resistance to the tax initially at such a rate. Alberta, too, was the first province to levy a gasoline tax.

It appears, then, that the government might have been able to add about two million dollars annually to revenue by increasing the rates of existing taxes. Probably even a little more might have been collected. But to have increased the rates on such a scale would have met with much determined opposition, for there was a great deal of talk in the legislature about the "heavy burden of provincial taxes." Another two million dollars annually would have balanced the budgets of 1927–28 and 1928–29, but would have left nothing for the retirement of debt.

The revenue from licences and fees rose from $1.8 million in 1921 to $3.3 million in 1929–30. The outstanding development in this category was the rise of the revenue from motor vehicle licences, which trebled between 1921 and 1929–30, reaching more than $2 million annually between 1927 and 1929. Land title fees surged upward briefly during 1927 and 1928 and then tapered off. Probably another half million dollars could have been collected in licences and fees if rates had been increased, but again there would have been much public resistance.

Public domain revenue remained relatively unimportant. A tax on coal yielded between $200,000 and $300,000 million annually until 1927 when the Privy Council declared the tax to be unconstitutional. A fur tax provided a revenue of about $60,000 annually. Game licences also provided from $50,000 to $70,000 per year. The question of ownership of Public Domain lands has already been discussed.

Revenue from the sale of liquor increased rapidly until 1929–30 when this income-sensitive revenue fell in response to the decreases in personal incomes. A plebiscite in 1923 had put an end to prohibition, which had proved, both expensive and embarrassing to the government. The government subsequently channelled all legal sales of liquor through its stores. The rapid growth caused some opposition members to castigate the government for attempting to balance the budgets with liquor revenues.[34] Probably more could have been collected if the number of retail outlets had been increased, but a strong temperance movement resisted such extensions.

The telephone system continued to show an overall deficit until 1927, and for 1929–30 a deficit materialized again after surpluses in 1927–28 and 1928–29. Increased rates would have done much to put the system on a self-sustaining basis even if it was not possible to have repaid debt. But such a step was full of political pitfalls in a province dominated by rural legislative members.

School lands revenue did not increase substantially during the decade. Fines and penalties fell off after the abandonment of prohibition in 1923. The disposal of the government creameries after 1922 led to a sharp decline in sales of commodities. Refunds rose because of the rising contributions of municipalities for mothers' allowances, unemployment relief, seed grain, and because of increased charges made by the municipal affairs department for the administration of improvement districts.

Revenue from interest rose from $1.2 million in 1921 to $2.0 million in 1929–30. The major item was interest on the telephone debt, which was an offset to interest paid on the expenditure side. The major part of the interest on advances of various kinds was collected annually.

Repayments became a revenue category of importance in the second half of the 1920s. Repayments of advances to the government printer, public works, and the schoolbooks branch became recurrent items with the reorganization of the provincial accounts in 1924. These formed the core of the repayment category. The Lethbridge Northern Irrigation District began to make some repayments of advances after 1926. Repayments by school districts and normal school students exceeded $150,000 in most years. Some drought relief repayments were made, but here the government recovered relatively little of its advances; the same may be said with respect to the advances made to combat agricultural pests (chiefly grasshoppers) and to purchase livestock. The United Grain Growers Limited met its repayment obligations scrupulously. The largest item in the category at the end of the decade was from sale of the railways.[35]

How much more, then, might the government have raised its revenue during the 1926–29 period to bolster its position before the onslaught of the Depression? This question was not an issue at the time for the government did not foresee the depression, not to say its magnitude. But it may be useful to examine what might have been done. The following increases suggest themselves from the previous discussion:

Annual average increase, 1926–29 (millions)

Supplementary revenue tax	$0.6
Corporation tax	0.5
Amusement taxes	0.2
Succession duties	0.2
Licences and fees	0.2
Public domain (with provincial control)	0.4
Liquor control	0.1
Repayments	0.1
Telephones	0.5
Total increases	$2.8

These additional annual amounts would have balanced the overall budgets for the four years in question. On the other hand, these additional collections would have encouraged greater spending, especially if great frictions had attended the increases in rates. And great frictions there would have been in the light of the temper of the times. Governments, too, were tapping an appreciably higher percentage of personal incomes than in any previous era. Finally, the increased amounts would have been insufficient to retire more than about $2 million of debt during the later 1920s, assuming that expenditures had not increased.

THE FINANCIAL CONDITION OF THE PROVINCIAL
GOVERNMENT IN 1930

The province entered the depression with a direct debt excessive in terms of depression revenue. In 1921 the direct debt, aside from guaranteed loans, amounted to one-quarter of the provincial income. In 1929 it was one-third. Thus the debt position, despite attempts at retrenchment during the 1920s, was worse at the end of the decade than at the beginning. By 1930 income had fallen so rapidly and debt had risen to such an extent that direct debt equalled one-half of the provincial income, and by 1933 it exceeded the provincial income.

The growth in debt during the 1920s was in large measure attributable to the unfortunate policies and guarantees of the Liberal administration during the optimistic era preceding 1921. It was ironic that the U.F.A., which had plagued the Liberal administration for many years, had to cope with the consequences of its own pressures. There were many useless recriminatory charges during the 1920s among the rivals in the political arena. Only the Conservatives, who never took office, belaboured expenditure policies on any serious scale, but they, like the other parties, talked incessantly about the rising tax burden. The crux of the matter was that all parties and the electorate attached too great a significance to the functions of the provincial government. It was expected to perform functions clearly beyond its fiscal capacity and not foreseen by the founders of the Canadian federation. To the pioneer on the frontier the provincial capital seemed sufficiently far away to be surrounded by the mystery of finance. Did not the provincial government seem to find money to spend when the local municipal council was unable to borrow one cent? Perhaps the provincial government was able to create money! And in a sense the guarantee, that standby of hard-pressed provincial administrations was a method of creating new money for it enabled promoters to build railways and irrigation projects, municipalities to dispense seed grain and relief, and individuals to purchase cattle on bank notes backed by the provincial government.

The Alberta government entered the depression with a public debt that was altogether too large and a cash balance that was almost non-existent. It had managed to strip itself to a large extent of railway liabilities by a good stroke of fortune. If it had been able to get rid of the telephone and the irrigation systems it might have been able to weather the rough years ahead. In other words, if the government had confined itself to the rather humdrum and routine activities of providing justice, highways, public health, protection, and education it would have withstood the lean years with less strain. But in a capital-hungry region an organized institution like the provincial government which had a good credit rating in the capital market and, whose decisions were in the ultimate sense made by the citizens of the region, had inevitably to be used to obtain funds not otherwise obtainable for resource development. This process might have gone on until the interest charges on the debt would have exceeded the provincial revenue for, as pointed out, the debt grew faster than both government revenue and provincial income. The government would have been cut off from funds by the capital market at some point before debt charges exceeded revenue. Indeed, during the early 1930s this eventuality did take place; the depression hastened its occurrence.

The municipalities largely marked time in the 1920s. For many of them it was a period of continued retrenchment to meet debt burdens incurred in the previous period. The chief development was the rising importance of the rural municipalities, which began to impose higher taxes and to provide better services than before. Thus in 1921 the rural districts spent about 25 per cent of total municipal expenditure; in 1929 they spent about 33 per cent. In 1921 they imposed about 30 per cent of total municipal taxes; in 1929 they imposed about 40 per cent. In terms of total revenue this trend was not in evidence because utility revenues in the cities grew more rapidly than taxes.

Provincial grants-in-aid and shared revenues remained relatively unimportant during the 1920s. The various sums are laid out in Table 4.12. The municipalities had entertained great hopes of obtaining a considerable share of provincial liquor revenues after prohibition was repealed, and originally it was intended to distribute one-third of liquor profits among them. But the financial predicament of the provincial government precluded any such arrangement in the final analysis. While such distribution would have increased payments to the municipalities by almost $1 million per year by the end of the 1920s, it would have done little to ease the strain on municipal budgets. Total grants were less than 7 per cent of total municipal expenditures in the respective years. Another million dollars would have brought the proportion up to only about 10 per cent in 1929.

GOVERNMENT AND THE ECONOMY

The provincial government in 1921 deliberately set out to create income for provincial residents, motivated not by Keynesian theories (which are surprisingly old in some respects) but by a pending election. Net income-producing expenditures of all governments within the province reached almost $15 million in that year (see Table 4.13). Once the splurge of 1921 was over there were too many pipers to pay and governments, both provincial and municipal, tended

Table 4.12 Provincial Government Payments to Municipalities, 1921–1930 (in millions of dollars)

	1921	1922	1923	1924	1925	1926	1927	1928	1929
GRANTS-IN-AID:									
Schools	1.2	1.3	1.2	1.1	1.1	1.2	1.7	1.4	1.4
Highways	0.1	0.2	0.1	0.3	0.3	0.3	0.3	0.4	0.6
Hospital dists.	–	–	–	–	–	–	0.1	0.1	0.1
Total grants	1.3	1.5	1.3	1.4	1.4	1.5	2.1	1.8	2.1
OTHER:									
Mothers' allow	0.2	0.2	0.2	0.2	0.2	0.3	0.4	0.3	0.3
Misc.[a]	0.2	0.2	0.2	0.2	0.2	0.1	0.2	0.2	0.5
Total other	0.4	0.4	0.4	0.4	0.4	0.4	0.6	0.5	0.8
Total, all	1.8	1.9	1.7	1.8	1.8	1.9	2.6	2.3	2.9
PROVINCIAL CONTRIBUTION AS A PERCENTAGE OF TOTAL EXPENDITURE:									
Schools	14	13	13	12	12	12	14	12	12
Highways[b]	3	5	3	8	8	8	11	12	15
Hospital dists	10	10	10	10	10	10	10	10	11
Mothers' allow	71	67	59	67	59	63	61	59	58

Sources: See Appendices B and C. The 1927 figures are for fifteen months; the ones for 1928 and 1929 are for the fiscal years 1928–29 and 1929–30. The percentages for 1927 are adjusted on a 12-month basis.

(a) Includes tax collection commissions, liquor fines, indigent relief, and old age pensions (the latter for 1929 only).

(b) The percentages apply to the expenditures of municipal and improvement districts since urban units received practically no highway grants. Highway expenditures of the rural units in question were taken to equal 70 per cent of their total expenditure.

Table 4.13 Net Income-Producing Expenditures of the Provincial and Local Governments of Alberta, 1921–1929 (in millions of dollars)

Year	Dominion. Grants	School Lands Fund	Overall Deficits less Interest Payments	Miscellaneous	Total
1921	1.9	0.6	12.0	–	14.5
1922	1.9	0.6	1.6	–	4.1
1923	1.9	0.5	−6.8	–	−4.4
1924	1.8	0.6	−4.3	–	−1.9
1925	2.0	0.6	−5.0	–	−2.4
1926	2.2	0.7	−3.2	–	−0.3
1927	3.4	0.8	−9.5	0.2[a]	−5.1
1928	1.8	0.7	−6.2	2.4[a]	−1.3
1929	1.7	0.8	−9.6	6.4[a]	−0.7

Sources: Appendices B and C. The municipal data cover the calendar years; so do provincial government data until the end of 1926. For 1927, 1928, and 1929 the new fiscal years of the provincial government are assumed to coincide with the calendar year containing the longest portion of the fiscal year.

(a) From the sale of railways.

to exert considerable pressure upon the cash balances and incomes of Alberta residents. Examination of Table 4.13 reveals the trend. Interest payment began to exceed overall deficits and the two levels of government no longer played the role of income creators. The downward trend in overall deficits and the upward trend in interest charges can be seen from Table 4.14.

Taxation of both levels of government rose somewhat during the decade and absorbed about 7 to 8 per cent of the provincial income in each year. This was a level considerably higher than during the years preceding 1921 when taxes had seldom equalled more than 6 per cent of provincial income. Table 4.15 sets out the data.

Expenditures on public works by the provincial government fell to low levels after 1921. There was some increase after 1925, but the 1929 level of $6.4 million was far below the 1921 level of $11.0 million. The public debt was simply too high and prosperity was too short-lived to induce large-scale public works programs. Similar observations are pertinent to the municipalities.

Table 4.14 Overall Deficits and Interest Payments in Alberta, 1921–1929
(in millions of dollars)

	1921	1922	1923	1924	1925	1926	1927	1928	1929
Overall deficits	−19.5	−10.1	−2.1	−5.2	−4.4	−6.6	−2.0	−4.1	−0.9
Interest charges	7.5	8.5	8.9	9.5	9.4	9.6	11.5	10.3	10.5

Sources: Appendices A and B.

Table 4.15 Total Taxation of Alberta Governments, 1921–1929

	1921	1922	1923	1924	1925	1926	1927	1928	1929
Millions of dollars	21.3	20.4	21.9	21.6	21.1	??	23.0	23.8	25.3
Per cent of provincial income	8.0	7.5	7.4	7.8	7.5	??	6.6	7.3	8.7

Sources: Appendix A for income; Appendices A and B for taxes.
         ?? illegible in original document.

THE GREAT DEPRESSION, 1930–35

5

ECONOMIC DEVELOPMENT

Before World War I, the relative freedom of trade encouraged a relatively high degree of regional specialization in the production of agricultural commodities, and the Canadian prairies turned to the production of wheat. However, during the 1920's a number of European countries turned increasingly to a policy of self-sufficiency, which featured the subsidization of wheat production and the imposition of high tariffs on wheat imports as well as other agricultural products. Thus the structure of regional specialization that had developed previously was seriously undermined and the volume of world trade shrank. With the advent of the depression, residents of Alberta felt the impact both painfully and swiftly.[1]

The decline in the net income of farmers between 1927 and 1929 was drastic.[2] Such income fell further from $62 million in 1929 to $6 million in 1933 (see Table 5.1). Thus for the six successive years 1930–35, the net income per farmer was less than $400 annually. Under such conditions it became impossible for many farmers to make repayments of debts incurred in the 1920s, to meet the interest payments on such debt, or to pay municipal and provincial taxes. Many farmers, indeed, were unable to obtain enough cash to meet their much-reduced living and operating expenses and became recipients of government relief.

The decline in agricultural net income was attributable to great decreases in the prices of agricultural products, to relatively inflexible direct production costs and rigid overhead costs, and to below-average crop yields. In 1932, the price index of agricultural products for Alberta fell from 106 in 1929 to a low of 35,[3] and the yearly average price of wheat in Alberta fell from $1.02 in 1929 to $0.32 in 1932, a decline of 69 per cent (see Table 5.2). The price of No. 1 Northern wheat fell to less than $0.25 a bushel, oats by 73 per cent to $0.13, steers by 68 per cent, and hogs by 78 per cent between 1929 and 1932.[4] However, in the interval 1929–33 the price index of commodities and services purchased by farmers in Western Canada fell by only 22 per cent. Interest on

Table 5.1   Provincial Income, Net Value of Agricultural Production, Cash Income from Sale of Farm Products, and Net Income of Agriculture in Alberta, 1925–1935 (in millions of dollars)

Year	Provincial Income[a]	Net Value of Agriculture[b]	Cash Income, Farm Products[c]	Net Income, Agriculture[d]
1929	290	128	171	62
1930	259	86	95	47
1931	201	92	71	14
1932	169	100	69	15
1933	146	94	69	6
1934	183	109	95	36
1935	186	97	99	31

(a) See Appendix A.
(b) *C.Y.B.*, 1930–1937.
(c) D.B.S., *Quarterly Bulletin of Agricultural Statistics.*
(d) See Appendix A.

and repayments of debts contracted in the 1920s did not decline at all for they were contractual payments. Taxes payable to the provincial and local governments increased rather than decreased. Under these price and cost conditions, the agricultural net income was bound to be abnormally low.

Crop yields were relatively high in 1930, 1931, and 1932 and the crop acreage expanded (see Table 5.2). But in 1933, 1934, and 1935 there were serious droughts that reduced yields below the long-run average. A heavy frost in early August 1935 did much to reduce yields as well as quality in that year.[5] The incidence of drought and frost varied, however. The southeast suffered from drought from 1929 to 1935 except in 1932. For the 1931–35 period yields in this region were 43 per cent below those of the 1926–30 period.[6] Other regions were not hit by the drought on any significant scale until the 1933–35 period. On the other hand, the frost of 1935 did far more damage in the central, northern, and western parts of the province than in the south and southeast. Examining Table 5.3 reveals the uneven incidence of weather factors. The decline in yields in the southeast, coupled with low prices, made the inhabitants of this region destitute and necessitated heavy relief expenditures. The decline in the southwest was less drastic, but nevertheless led to serious problems of relief.

The decline in agricultural income in turn generated unemployment in the urban centres even though immigration fell off to a trickle and the rate of population increase fell below the rate of natural increase after 1931. Aggregate

Table 5.2   Wheat Yields, Wheat Prices, Field Crops, and Value of Field Crops in Alberta, 1929–1935

Year	Wheat Yield (bu. per acre)	Wheat Price (cents per bu.)	Field Crop Acreage (millions)	Value of Field Crops (millions of $)
1929	12.3	102	12.4	157
1930	20.5	45	12.6	110
1931	17.7	36	13.4	99
1932	20.0	32	14.0	96
1933	13.0	45	13.9	86
1934	15.0	58	12.9	111
1935	13.2	61	13.5	94

Source: *C.Y.B.*, 1930–38.

Table 5.3   Changes in Wheat Yields Per Acre for 1931–1935 as Against 1926–1930 and 1927–1928

Region	Percentage change in 1931–1935 yield average as against 1926–1930	Percentage change in 1931–1935 yield average as against 1927–1928
Southeast (A)	–43	–62
Southwest (B)	–23	–38
Centre (C)	–11	–17
Northeast (D)	–12	–18
Peace River (E)	–7	–12
North and west (F)	5	1
All Alberta	–18	–37

Source: Government of Alberta, Department of Agriculture, *Statistics of Principal Grain Crops of Census Divisions, 1921–1940 Inclusive* (Edmonton, April 1941).

Table 5.4   Net Value of Production of Industries in Alberta, 1929–1935
(in millions of dollars)

	1929	1930	1931	1932	1933	1934	1935
Agriculture	128.3	86.5	91.8	99.5	94.0	109.0	97.4
Forestry	7.7	7.2	5.4	3.2	3.0	3.4	3.1
Fishing	0.7	0.4	0.2	0.2	0.1	0.2	0.2
Trapping	2.3	1.0	1.0	0.6	0.8	1.1	1.1
Mining	34.7	30.6	23.6	21.2	19.7	14.7	16.7
Electric power	4.4	4.7	4.7	4.7	4.3	4.4	4.6
Construction	19.0	16.3	9.3	3.9	1.8	5.4	5.6
Custom and Repair	7.0	7.0	5.5	4.5	3.5	4.3	4.1
Manufacturing	44.1	40.7	32.3	26.9	23.8	27.6	23.8
Total	248.2	194.4	173.6	164.6	151.1	170.2	156.5
Less duplication	10.8	9.7	8.7	7.5	6.9	7.4	3.2
Total, net	237.5	184.7	164.9	157.0	144.2	162.8	153.3

Source: *C.Y.B.*, 1931–1937.

wages and salaries fell from $164 million in 1929 to a low of $96 million in 1933. Profits of individual enterprises decreased from $29 million in 1929 to $16 million in 1933. Investment income, which was partly dependent upon earnings of corporations outside Alberta, declined from a high of $29 million in 1930 to a low of $18 million in 1934; it was less adversely affected than other constituents of personal income.

On June 1, 1931, 24.0 per cent of all wage earners were unemployed, or a total of 27,846 persons.[7] Wage earners in mining were especially hard-hit with 57.4 per cent unemployed. The degree of unemployment increased until 1933, after which it declined somewhat. On June 1, 1936, however, 19.0 per cent of all wage earners were still unemployed.[8] Unemployment among trade union members increased from 6.4 per cent in 1929 to a peak of 22.6 per cent in 1932; it declined to 15.4 per cent in 1935.[9] In any event, the problem of unemployment was still very serious in 1935 and there were large relief expenditures throughout the whole decade of the 1930s.

All industries were affected by the general downward trend in prices and income. The value of output decreased materially until 1933 after which there was some recovery. Table 5.4 sets out the data of net values of production.

It is difficult to describe the full impact of the depression upon Alberta, and indeed the whole prairie region. The most adequate objective description is probably that given by George Britnell in *The Wheat Economy*.[10] The decline in real income was as to be almost unprecedented. Individuals were generally unable to pay debts that had been incurred before the depression struck. This problem was of such magnitude that special legislation was passed to cope with it all. And governments, of course, also had difficulties with their debts.

FISCAL DEVELOPMENT

CONTINUOUS BUDGET DEFICITS

By 1930 the provincial government had managed to put its finances in tolerable order and to get out of its railway ventures. It had also finally obtained control of the public domain. In 1929–30 it even had an overall surplus for the first time in twenty-four years. But when the depression struck early and hard, it found itself subjected to a variety of requests for financial assistance. It aligned itself with the other two Prairie Provinces to assist the wheat pool, which was in precarious financial straits as a result of large and rapid grain price decreases. It began to provide for unemployment relief in response to the distress that became more evident daily, especially in the urban centres. It set up a program of agricultural relief for farmers rendered destitute by drought and low prices. It attempted to increase grants to schools and to make grant advances, months ahead, to keep schools open in the southeast and on the northern and western fringes of settlement.

Nor was this all, for old ghosts walked again. The farmers in the irrigation districts whose bonds the government had guaranteed were given additional assistance when their incomes fell off with declining prices. The telephone system, which had overall surpluses during the 1927–29 period, rapidly became a financial liability. The resistance to provincial taxes grew and the revenue structure generally failed to produce the amounts expected, let alone needed.

The ultimate results in financial terms were a series of budget deficits in every year from 1930–31 to 1935–36, both on income account and on an overall basis (see Table 5.5). The deficits were especially large during the first two years of the depression when the government attempted to combat the problem of unemployment and agricultural distress by relief work, by agricultural measures, and by a highway program on a relatively large scale. As the depression deepened the government found it increasingly difficult to borrow from the money market, and after 1931 the Dominion government came to the rescue by purchasing provincial treasury bills. Only in 1933–34 did the deficit fall below $7 million.

Table 5.5 Revenue and Expenditure of the Government of Alberta, 1930–1935 (in millions of dollars)

Fiscal year	Overall basis[a]			Overall basis[b]			Income account[c]		
	R	E	S or D(–)	R	E	S or D(–)	R	E	S or D(–)
1930–31	20.7	31.1	–10.4	17.1	27.3	–10.2	15.7	18.0	–2.3
1931–32	19.0	35.5	–16.5	15.9	32.3	–16.4	13.5	18.6	–5.2
1932–33	19.7	27.6	–7.9	17.0	23.9	–6.9	15.4	17.5	–2.1
1933–34	24.0	25.3	–1.3	21.6	22.6	–1.0	15.2	17.1	–1.9
1934–35	20.6	27.7	–7.1	18.3	25.1	–6.9	15.7	17.4	–1.7
1935–36	22.3	30.7	–8.4	19.9	28.1	–8.2	16.6	18.2	–1.7

(a) Including telephones. For sources see Appendix B.
(b) Excluding telephones. For sources see Appendix B.
(c) *P.A., 1950–51*, Statement No. 18.

The low deficit of that year, about $1.3 million was attributable chiefly to the second instalment received by the government for the railways sold in 1929, an amount exceeding $5 million.

A remarkable feature of this deficit was that the government had budgeted for a deficit of only $0.4 million; it did not foresee the drastic fall in revenue that occurred; it hoped that the people who foresaw "prosperity around the corner" were right. The revenue estimated was $18.4 million; the actual amount collected was $13.5 million, a figure that was $2 million less than the actual amount collected in 1930–31. The imposition of new taxes, and of higher rates on old ones brought an increase in revenue of almost $2 million in 1932–33. But this fell short of the government's estimates by almost $3 million, for the government still retained some hope of more or less immediate economic recovery. On the expenditure side, however, there was a much smaller margin of error in forecasting, since expenditures were controllable to a greater degree than revenues. The government reduced its rate of spending in the latter part of each year when it became evident that revenues were not going to attain expected levels. Consequently actual expenditures fell somewhat below the estimates in each year. Deficits fell below the $2 million mark in the three years between 1933 and 1936. The government still continued to overestimate revenues, but the gap gradually diminished and in 1935–36 estimated revenues exceeded actual by only half a million dollars.

It was a trying period for the government, and yet the budget speeches reflected tinges of optimism. If anything, the budget speeches of the early 1920s make gloomier reading than those of the early 1930s. Perhaps the shock of finding out the limitations of the Alberta economy after the optimistic 1905–20 era was greater than the shock resulting from the frustrations of the 1930s. Nevertheless, it was an enervating experience and one suspects that it was a relief to turn over financial matters to a new administration in 1935, although this change did not occur without a great deal of bitter political and economic controversy.

DIFFICULTIES IN SECURING FUNDS

The provincial government encountered increasing difficulties in obtaining funds to meet its obligations, and it was forced to guard its cash balance very closely from day to day during the trying days of the 1930's.[11] The working balance was altogether too low for administrative ease in making payments and for granting any respite from the relentless need to go to the money market continuously and at unfavourable periods. Transfers of balances from one bank to another to meet payments of cheques as of any given time were of frequent occurrence. The treasury, too, tended to delay the issue of cheques wherever feasible until deposits could be made or revenues or other receipts came in to take care of the cheques. The total cash balance of the treasury seldom exceeded one million dollars, or about 2 per cent of annual payments. It was much too small to provide for the smooth operation of the system of payments, and any lag in receipts made the treasury very vulnerable to default on its obligations whether they were civil service salaries or debt interest.

In 1930–31 there was an overall deficit of more than $10 million to be met; savings certificates withdrawals exceeded new issues by almost $1 million; sinking fund contributions accounted for a further deficiency of more than $0.7 million, excluding the telephone sinking fund. Debentures and temporary loans amounting to about $9 million matured. The government issued debentures and treasury bills and secured temporary loans to meet its obligations. The debentures sold at a heavy discount, for while the coupon rates of all issues were 4.5 per cent, the yield rates to purchasers were nearly 5 per cent.[12] A five million dollar issue of six-month bills carrying interest at 4 per cent sold to yield 4.7 per cent. Only one issue, a temporary loan from the Bank of Montreal, carried a rate of less than 4 per cent. It happened to be negotiated at the end of 1930 when interest rates had generally fallen somewhat.

In 1931 the government, anticipating a large overall deficit and the maturing of a large volume of debt, appointed a fiscal agency to advise with respect to the terms and time of the flotation of loans.[13] It was a commendable move for the bond market was unsettled and the market analyses of experienced bond dealers would, in the ordinary course of events, be more reliable than those of treasury officials. Large issues of debentures were sold during the first half of 1931 when interest rates were fairly favourable. But the government was unable to build up a cash balance that sufficed to meet obligations even a month ahead, and the fiscal agency failed to foresee, like so many investors at the time, the sharp increase in interest rates that occurred toward the end of 1931 when the European financial crisis culminated in the abandonment of the gold standard by Great Britain. Consequently, the government had to go to the money market at very unfavourable times. It had to sell treasury bills at rates of 5.25 to 5.5 per cent to the Imperial Bank of Canada.[14] A million dollar issue of treasury bills was sold at 6 per cent in December 1931, to the Bank of Manhattan Trust Company, New York. An issue of twelve-month treasury bills amounting to $500,000 was sold to C. Woodward Stores, a concern with a large department store in Edmonton, at the relatively low rate of 5 per cent in the same month. The Dominion government, too, purchased a $500,000 issue of twelve-month treasury bills in December 1931, to enable the province to finance unemployment relief and a $320,000 issue to assist the province to meet debt interest. The Dominion charged 5.25 per cent and 5.375 per cent, somewhat more than the local business firm. All in all, the last month of 1931 was one of financial stress and there were days on which treasury officials were uncertain whether obligations were going to be met on time.

The shortage of funds persisted into 1932 as the overall deficit mounted rapidly, repayment dates of debentures and temporary loans kept on coming up, and savings certificate withdrawals continued to exceed the issue of new certificates. Revenue collections proved disappointing. Finally, depreciation of the Canadian dollar in relation to the American imposed a heavy drain because of debt maturities and interest payments, which had to be made in New York. The banks were unwilling to extend further credit and the bond market was unreceptive. The Dominion government again acted as a lender of last resort by purchasing provincial treasury bills carrying 5.375 per cent to enable the province to meet debt maturities and interest amounting to $2,822,000 in January, 1932, and to meet unemployment relief expenses to the extent of $500,000 in February, 1932. These amounts proved insufficient, however, and the government reluctantly but desperately set a coupon rate of 6 per cent on a $5 million fifteen-year debenture issue dated March 1, 1932. Even this rate proved too low, for it finally sold at a discount that yielded 6.78 per cent to purchasers.[15]

After two years of depression the government finally made a determined effort to reduce expenditures and to increase revenue. The treasurer in the budget speech of February 25, 1932, outlined proposals accordingly. The motor vehicle licence fees, which had been reduced in the previous year, were increased to their former level. A personal income tax was imposed for the first time. Corporation taxes were increased. Amusement tax rates, which had been reduced previously, were increased. Relief expenditure estimates were cut, and the public works program for the year was scaled down drastically. Reductions were proposed in all spheres of expenditure. The debate on the budget was short for cabinet ministers refused to make any replies to the speeches of the opposition members who, in the main, struck hard at the increased taxes and called for even greater expenditure economies. Mr. Howson, the Liberal leader, expressed alarm at the growth in the public debt and concern over increased taxes. Mr. Duggan, the Conservative leader, asked for an investigation to devise ways and means of balancing the budget without increased taxation.[16] But the financial situation had deteriorated too much to permit a balanced budget without increased taxes and the cabinet knew it.

There was another large deficit for the fiscal year 1932–33. Unemployment and agricultural relief made it unavoidable, and the American exchange situation forced the province to pay more than $600,000 over and above its U.S. dollar obligations in New York. Treasury bills issued in the previous year came due and had to be renewed. For the first time since before World War I the government marketed a £1,000,000 debenture issue in London in June 1932. It was a costly venture for it sold finally to yield 6.72 per cent, 1.72 per cent above the 5 per cent coupon rate. A $250,000 Treasury bill issue was sold to Woodward Stores at 5 per cent in June. Otherwise the province came to lean more and more heavily on the Dominion government, which advanced $2,168,000 on the basis of treasury bills throughout the fiscal year 1932–33. These advances were made for the purpose of unemployment relief and to meet a subsidy overpayment in a previous year.

There was little improvement in the fiscal year 1933–34, the chief relieving feature being the receipt of the second instalment on the sale of the railways, an amount exceeding $5 million. Further expenditure reductions were made in the budget, and the provincial government stated that it was attempting to balance the budget by "drastic economies" rather than by increasing the tax rates substantially and the imposition of widely based new taxes.[17] The fuel oil tax was increased from 5 cents to 6 cents per gallon, but motor vehicle licence fees were reduced somewhat. One new tax, a levy on pipelines, was proposed. The government almost succeeded in balancing the budget on an overall basis in 1933–34, falling short by about one million dollars.

A large amount of debt maturities forced it to borrow continually. Two debenture issues were sold in Canada at a high cost: a $1,000,000 twenty-year 4 per cent issue in July, 1933 at 80.25 to yield 5.66 per cent,[18] and a $1,218,000 twenty-two year 5 per cent issue in September, 1933 at 93.37 to yield 5.525 per cent.[19] The government did not venture into the New York market for the cost there would have been prohibitive because of the discounted value of the Canadian dollar. Foreign exchange discount on the obligations payable in New York continued to be a heavy drain on the treasury throughout the year.[20] Treasury bills amounting to more than one million dollars were sold to the commercial banks at rates varying from 5 to 6 per cent. The Dominion government extended maturing treasury bills amounting to $6 million for another twelve months and lowered the interest rate to 5 per cent to finance unemployment relief. The net result of all transactions was an overdraft of nearly $200,000 at the end of the fiscal year.

There was a large overall deficit and a large volume of debt maturities to be financed in 1934–35, and further heavy borrowings. The cost of borrowing declined to less than 4.5 per cent in the case of debentures and the Dominion government reduced its rate on renewed and new treasury bills to 4.5 per cent. The latter government continued to make large advances for unemployment relief, agricultural relief, highways, loans to cities, and debt maturities, and the total for the year amounted to $7,711,000.[21] The discount on American exchange fortunately ceased to be a significant expenditure item. Nevertheless, the provincial government operated with a precariously low cash balance throughout the year.

During the following year the government relied almost exclusively upon loans from the Dominion government to finance an overall deficit of more than $8 million, as well as debt maturities. The bond market was not receptive enough to permit the government to issue debentures on a large scale, which would have been required. The Dominion government scaled down the interest rate on treasury bills outstanding and on new bills to 4 per cent. Debenture issues could not have been sold in terms of the amounts involved at such a rate. During the year 1935–36 the Dominion government purchased provincial treasury bills amounting to $9,259,000.[22]

In August 1935, the U.F.A. government, tired out by the magnitude of financial problems that had confronted it for years, turned over the reins of office and an empty treasury to the new Social Credit administration. The new premier, William Aberhart, complained bitterly when he found out that there were practically no funds at hand; he had apparently not realized the kind of struggle the previous administration had in making ends meet from day to day. But like other reformers given the responsibility of office, he and his cabinet soon learned the hard lessons of making ends meet and of resistance to pressures to spend that must be mastered by responsible cabinet ministers.

THE INCREASE IN THE PUBLIC DEBT

Table 5.6 sets out the assets and liabilities of the province at the end of the fiscal years 1929–30 and 1935–36. The total outstanding debt increased by almost $45 million during the six-year period. Almost $14 million was obtained by the sale of debentures; the Dominion government supplied more than $25 million; the floating debt went up by more than $5 million. On the assets side, the major items accounting for the increase in debt were public works (nearly $19 million), current deficits (more than $13 million), capital losses arising chiefly from the writing down of the telephone assets (more than $11 million), direct relief (nearly $7 million), and an advance to the Alberta Wheat Pool ($5 million). An examination of Table 5.6 reveals a number of minor items that need not be mentioned here. There were also a number of offsetting items such as the decrease of $7 million in the investment fund, of $5 million in the balance due on the sale of railways, and of almost $5 million in the sinking fund reserve.

PROPOSALS TO REORGANIZE THE DEBT

The increase in the debt became alarming to many observers because of the annual recurrence of deficits on income account and because of the relative as well as absolute growth of the annual interest payments. In the 1930–35 period, Alberta's net debt charges relative to current revenue continued to be the highest on the average among the provinces for the whole period, although there were some other provinces which did exceed the Alberta level in some years. Table 5.7 sets out comparative data of net interest charges. Throughout the six-year period the net interest charges in Alberta absorbed from one-third to more than half of current revenue annually. These were dangerously high proportions.

Table 5.8 provides a summary of the relationship between the net interest charges and the provincial income of the various provinces. Alberta ranked second highest, Saskatchewan ranking first, during the early 1930s with respect to the percentage of income absorbed by net interest charges. The Alberta percentage, too, was almost twice the average percentage for all the provinces in every year from 1930 to 1935.

Table 5.6   Assets and Liabilities of the Government of Alberta, March 31, 1930 and March 31, 1936 (in millions of dollars)

	March 31, 1930	March 31, 1936	Net change
ASSETS			
Cash	1.3	1.9	0.6
Taxes Receivable, Inventories, etc.	4.4	5.1	0.7
Due from the Dominion of Canada:			
(a) Relief accounts	0.0	0.2	0.2
(b) Old age pensions accounts	0.1	0.3	0.2
(c) Other accounts	–	–	–
Investment Funds, securities	8.5	1.5	–7.0
Debenture Discount, unamortized	2.9	4.2	1.3
Advances and Accounts Receivable, on which contractual interest has always been paid:			
(a) Relief accounts	0.0	2.7	2.7
(b) Other accounts			
i) Balance due on sale of railways	10.6	5.6	–5.0
ii) Alberta Wheat Pool	0.0	5.0	5.0
iii) Miscellaneous	1.0	0.6	–0.4
Working Funds, net assets	1.1	0.5	–0.6
Subtotal	29.8	27.6	–2.2
INVESTMENT IN GOVERNMENT UTILITIES:			
(a) Railways	11.4	11.4	
of which transferred to capital losses	–11.4	–11.4	0.0
(b) Telephones	21.9	25.2	
of which transferred to capital losses	0.0	–9.0	–5.7
Subtotal	21.9	16.2	–5.7
PUBLIC WORKS:			
(a) Public buildings	15.2	18.2	3.0
(b) University of Alberta	4.5	4.7	0.2
(c) Highways, bridges, and ferries	23.5	32.6	9.1
(d) Relief work: highways and bridges	0.0	2.8	2.8
(e) Relief work: other	0.0	0.1	0.1
(f) Irrigation and drainage districts	9.3	12.0	2.7
(g) Other public works	0.9	1.8	0.9
Subtotal	53.4	72.3	18.9

Table 5.6   (continued)

ADVANCES AND INVESTMENTS, ON WHICH PARTIAL OR NO INTEREST HAS BEEN PAID:

(a) Relief accounts	0.0	0.7	0.7
(b) Other accounts			
i) Seed grain and relief (old)	3.8	2.4	−1.4
ii) Other	3.8	7.4	3.6
Exchange, capitalized	0.0	1.4	1.4
Direct Relief, capitalized	0.0	6.8	6.8
Relief Works, of municipal and other authorities, provincial contribution capitalized	0.0	1.5	1.5
Other Expenditures, capitalized	2.6	3.9	1.3
Subtotal	10.3	24.5	14.2
Capital Losses	12.1	23.3	11.2
Current Deficit	1.9	15.3	13.4
Debenture Discount Amortized, not included in current deficit	1.0	2.1	1.1
Sinking Fund Reserve		−2.6	−7.5
Capital Surplus Account	−0.9	−1.2	−0.3
Deferred Revenue	0.0	−0.8	−0.8
TOTAL represented by outstanding debt	126.9	171.8	44.9

LIABILITIES

Funded Debt

Direct Bonds, Debentures, and Stock	106.9	128.1	
Less sinking funds	−4.5	−10.6	15.1
Guaranteed Bonds and Debentures	7.2	7.0	
Less sinking funds	−0.2	−1.4	−1.3
Treasury Bills:			
(a) Held by Dominion of Canada	0.0	25.2	25.2
(b) Held by banks and others	0.0	0.2	0.2
Subtotal	109.4	148.6	39.2
Floating Debt			
Temporary Loans	–	5.7	5.7
Savings Certificates	11.8	9.3	−2.5
Superannuation Fund	1.0	2.2	1.2
Other	1.8	2.8	1.0
Subtotal	14.6	19.9	5.3
Contingent Liabilities	2.9	3.3	0.4
Total Outstanding Debt	126.9	171.8	44.9

Table 5.7 Net Interest Charges as a Percentage of Current Revenue, Alberta, New Brunswick, Manitoba, Saskatchewan, and All Provinces, 1930–1935

	1930	1931	1932	1933	1934	1935
Alberta	31	55	47	48	44	33
Saskatchewan	21	44	44	42	50	47
Manitoba	16	33	48	37	31	30
New Brunswick	32	38	46	55	49	42
All provinces	17	24	31	33	32	28

Source: *Sirois Report,* Public Accounts Inquiry, *Dominion of Canada and Canadian National Railways and Provincial Governments,* Comparative Statistics of Public Finance, Appendix I (Ottawa, 1939), Statement No. 38, 95.

Table 5.8 Net Interest Charges of the Canadian Provinces as a Percentage of Income Paid Out to Individuals, 1930–1935

	1930	1931	1932	1933	1934	1935
Prince Edward Island	0.5	0.8	1.1	1.3	1.3	1.3
Nova Scotia	1.0	1.2	1.8	2.0	1.9	2.1
New Brunswick	1.7	2.2	3.1	3.7	3.2	2.9
Quebec	0.2	0.4	0.6	0.8	0.8	0.8
Ontario	0.6	0.8	1.4	1.6	1.7	1.5
Manitoba	0.7	1.4	2.8	2.6	2.1	2.0
Saskatchewan	1.2	2.7	3.9	4.0	3.6	3.6
Alberta	1.7	3.1	3.5	3.8	3.3	3.0
British Columbia	1.4	2.1	2.8	2.9	2.7	2.6
All Provinces	0.7	1.1	1.7	1.9	1.9	1.7

Source: Data on income paid out to individuals for each province were obtained from *Sirois Report,* W.A. Mackintosh, *The Economic Background of Dominion–Provincial Relations,* Appendix 3 (Ottawa, 1939), 63–66. Data on net interest charges were obtained from the same source as those from which Table 5.7 was derived.

The government adopted a policy of maintaining the credit of the province and met its interest and repayment obligations punctiliously. This was not done, of course, without a great deal of strain on the treasury cash balance and without Dominion government advances made by purchasing treasury bills in response to provincial appeals. The large foreign exchange premiums of the 1931–33 period proved to be very embarrassing to the government and only aid from the Dominion enabled the province to meet its obligations.

Both the opposition parties in the legislature criticized the growth of debt. The Conservatives called for reduction in expenditure from year to year, and advocated an investigation of the whole revenue structure before taxes be raised. The Conservative leader, Mr. Duggan, was emphatic in declaring, "that default (on debt) must not be considered until we have exhausted every conceivable means to pay our way."[23] In the session of 1934, Mr. Howson, the Liberal leader, suggested that the holders of Alberta bonds should be asked to reduce their interest rate by one-half. Perren Baker, the Minister of Education, in defending the government's record on February 13, 1934 pointed out how difficult it would be to assemble sufficient bondholders scattered through Canada, United States, and Europe, to begin to negotiate along the lines of interest reduction.[24]

Nevertheless, as market interest rates declined generally in 1934 and continued to do so, the government began to give serious thought to debt reorganization involving the refunding of outstanding securities by the substitution of bonds and debentures carrying rates more in alignment with market rates than existing coupon rates on the Alberta debt.[25] This, it was suggested, was to be done by negotiations with representatives of bondholders and with the Dominion government assistance. J.R. Love, who had been appointed treasurer when R.G. Reid succeeded J.E. Brownlee as premier in 1934, announced a tentative refunding plan in the budget speech of March 8, 1935.[26] It was suggested that the amount of debt to which a refunding plan should apply would be $131,000,000 after excluding savings certificates, sinking funds, the special investment fund, cash in hand, and sterling issues. It was a reasonable enough proposal but nothing came of it. Negotiations with the bondholders would have been long and protracted. The Dominion government was not receptive to such suggestions at the time. It was in the throes of an election year and was subjected to requests for financial aid by all the provinces.

The Alberta administration was on its last legs; it had failed to solve the economic and financial problems of the provincial economy in the minds of the electors; it had lost much prestige because of the involvement of the premier in a seduction case and of the public works minister in a divorce litigation case. The new Social Credit administration took over in August 1935. It presented a plan to bond dealers by which the rate of interest on the Alberta debt might be cut from the current 5 per cent average to an average of 2.75 per cent. Nothing came of this proposal either. In the meantime the new Dominion administration continued to provide funds to enable Alberta to meet debt repayments and interest. Thus a loan of $2,000,000 was made on January 15, 1936 for this purpose.

At the Dominion-provincial conference in December 1935, a proposal had been approved for a loan council, consisting of representatives of the Dominion of Canada, the provinces, and the Bank of Canada, to supervise the borrowings of provinces requiring financial assistance from the Dominion. The Alberta government applied to the Dominion for a loan of $3,200,000 to meet a debt obligation maturing on April 1, 1936. Premier Aberhart, however, objected to the loan council principle on the grounds that it would mean giving up the autonomy of the province. As a result the Dominion government refused the loan. The Alberta government lacked sufficient funds to make the required bond repayments and the province defaulted. Finally, in May 1936, the provincial government reduced the rate of interest payable on Alberta securities to one-half of the contractual rate. But this is a story to be examined in the next chapter.

SPECIFIC MAJOR ISSUES

The general problem of public debt permeated all public finance issues to a greater or lesser degree. But the growth of public debt and interest payments stemmed from such specific problems as unemployment and agricultural relief which became of major importance during the 1930s, from the wheat pool guarantee, from the financial collapse of the telephone system, and from the failure to collect revenue adequate even to meet deficits on income account. Finally, out of the collapse of the provincial economy and the inability of the provincial government to cushion the shocks and to alleviate the sufferings, there emerged a steadily growing stream of criticism of the monetary system and of demands for monetary reform. It was not a new rivulet for it had been swollen before during the 1913–15 and 1921 depressions, and at all times there had been a continuous flow of diatribes against creditors and of proposals to reorganize the existing monetary system. By 1935 it became a veritable river flooding its banks. Consequently, some of the tributaries that emptied into this river are examined here.

UNEMPLOYMENT AND AGRICULTURAL RELIEF

The volume of unemployment, the drastic fall in agricultural prices, and the decrease in average crop yields during the first half of the 1930s have been indicated in the discussion of economic development. A heavy financial burden had to be assumed by the provincial government, which was constitutionally responsible for relief in the first instance, and by the municipalities, which were generally regarded as primarily responsible by provincial delegation of powers. The municipalities somehow weathered the storm, but the mortality rate among them was high in the southeast. The whole relief problem grew to such proportions that the Dominion government came to render assistance from the beginning of the depression. The revenues of the province and of the individual municipalities were quite inadequate to provide sufficient relief. Nevertheless, the relief burden in Alberta proved to be smaller than in the other two Prairie Provinces, and it was approximately equal to that of the average for all the Canadian provinces.[27] The total area affected by crop failures was smaller and mixed farming prevailed to a greater extent than in Saskatchewan. The unemployment problem in Alberta cities was less severe than that of, for example, Winnipeg.

The province and the municipalities spent more than $2.2 million on relief in 1930–31 while the Dominion contributed less than $0.2 million (see Table 5.9). About two-thirds of the amount spent was devoted to relief works, both provincial and municipal; direct relief absorbed almost one-third; and agricultural relief was only 2.5 per cent. The Dominion participated to a greater degree after the passage of The Dominion Unemployment Relief Act of 1930, which provided funds principally for providing work for the unemployed. For works projects undertaken by municipalities, the Dominion assumed 25 per cent of the cost. The province undertook to pay 25 per cent also. The Dominion and the province shared provincial works equally.[28] Direct relief in the form of food, clothing, fuel, and shelter was to be shared equally by all three levels of government. The Dominion appropriation for this purpose was small at first.

Under The Unemployment and Relief Act of 1931 and The Continuance Act of 1932, the Dominion share of expenses rose. It assumed 50 per cent of provincial expenditures on relief works, and half the cost of municipal undertakings in regards to relief works and transients in the western provinces.[29] If municipalities could not afford this much, the Dominion would pay a greater share. The Dominion also agreed with the provinces to split the costs of drought relief.

In 1932 there was less emphasis upon public works to provide employment as it became evident that unemployment was going to persist longer than

Table 5.9   Relief Expenditures of Provincial–Municipal Agencies in Alberta, April 1, 1930 to March 31, 1936 (in thousands of dollars)

Fiscal years	1930 -31	1931 -32	1932 -33	1933 -34	1934 -35	1935 -36
DIRECT AND MISC. RELIEF:						
Dominion share	12	622	1,415	1,411	1,577	1,688
Provincial share	373	793	1,224	1,783	1,794	2,286
Municipal share	300	607	869	1,102	1,106	1,375
Subtotal	685	2,022	3,508	4,296	4,477	5,349
RELIEF WORKS:						
Dom. share of prov. works	79	1,079	534	28	60	117
Dom. share of munic. works	96	865	638	13	5	0
Prov. share of prov. works	660	1,043	608	32	293	277
Prov. share of munic. works	345	588	245	11	340	0
Munic. share of mun. works	500	708	151	10	0	0
Subtotal	1,680	4,283	2,176	94	698	394
AGRICULTURAL AID:						
Dom. grant to provinces	0	0	18	0	3	0
Prov. expenditures	60	382	160	461	776	1,278
Munic. expenditures	0	0	6	45	43	18
Subtotal	60	382	184	506	822	1,296
Total	2,425	6,687	5,868	4,896	5,997	7,039
SUMMARY:						
Dominion share	187	2,566	2,605	1,452	1,645	1,805
Provincial share	1,438	2,806	2,237	2,287	3,203	3,841
Municipal share	800	1,315	1,026	1,157	1,149	1,393

Source: *Sirois Report*, Book 3, Table 41, 112–13.

contemplated. A larger amount was appropriated for direct relief, with the three levels of government sharing costs equally except in cases where the municipality was unable to contribute one-third. In the drought areas, the Dominion government assumed 100 per cent of relief costs and 50 per cent of other measures, the province paying any residual. A scheme for settling families on the land and of moving farm families was begun, and the relief of single homeless men was dealt with. In each case the province and the Dominion worked out a basis to share the costs.

There were no substantial changes in 1933 except that the provinces requested the Dominion government to spend more money upon public works again. In Alberta, however, little was spent on relief works in the fiscal year 1933–34; direct relief absorbed more than 80 per cent of the total provincial-municipal expenditures in that year. In 1934–35 there was some increase in relief works expenditure. In that year, too, the Dominion began to undertake work of its own in various parts of the Dominion under The Public Works Construction Act of 1934.

A major change in the basis of the Dominion contribution toward direct relief was made in 1934. The Dominion abandoned the percentage basis and announced a policy of making monthly grants-in-aid, the amounts to be determined on the basis of need and the ability of the province to deal with direct relief. Thus contributions were put on an *ad hoc* basis, which was more flexible than the previous system. Minor changes were made in other relief measures, most of them involving some increases in rates and percentages contributed by the Dominion. The 1934 provisions were not materially altered in 1935.

No permanent solution to the problem of relief had been found in 1936. Dominion aid was still on an emergency basis. Total expenditure mounted yearly (see Table 5.9), and all levels of government contributed increasing amounts. Relief, in short, had become "institutionalized" and showed signs of demanding ever-increasing expenditures as economic recovery on any significant scale failed to materialize and as more and more individuals overcame their pride and requested assistance.[30] These people often felt that the financial system was working against them, and this led to agitation for monetary reform.

DIFFICULTIES OF THE TELEPHONE SYSTEM

The Alberta Government Telephones encountered serious difficulties after the relatively prosperous years of 1927–29. Small overall surpluses had been realized in those years, but in the 1930s overall deficits reappeared again despite the almost complete cessation of capital expenditure on the system. See Table 5.10 for a summary of the development of the system. It shows that there

Table 5.10 Revenue and Expenditure of the Alberta Government Telephones, April 1, 1928 to March 31, 1936 (in millions of dollars)

Fiscal year ending March 31	1929	1930	1931	1932	1933	1934	1935	1936
Expenditure:								
Maintenance	0.4	0.4	0.4	0.4	0.4	0.3	0.3	0.3
Operation	1.0	1.1	1.1	1.0	1.0	0.8	0.8	0.7
Operating cost	1.4	1.4	1.5	1.4	1.4	1.1	1.1	1.0
Interest	1.2	1.3	1.3	1.4	1.4	1.4	1.4	1.4
Total current expenditure	2.6	2.8	2.8	2.8	2.8	2.5	2.5	2.5
Construction and placements	0.9	1.5	1.0	0.2	0.7	0.1	0.1	0.1
Total expenditure	3.6	4.4	3.8	3.2	3.6	2.7	2.6	2.6
Revenue:	3.7	3.8	3.6	3.0	2.7	2.4	2.4	2.4
Current surplus or deficit (–)	1.1	1.0	0.8	0.3	–0.1	–0.1	–0.1	–0.1
Overall surplus or deficit (–)	0.2	–0.6	–0.2	–0.2	–0.9	–0.3	–0.2	–0.2

Source: *P.A., 1927–1936*, as per Appendix B.

were deficits after excluding capital expenditures and there was nothing left for replacement or for depreciation.

The telephone system imposed a cash drain on the treasury after 1929, which aggregated more than $2.5 million for the seven years from 1929–36. If depreciation were taken into account on a 25-year basis, the deficits would be greater by about one million dollars in each year. As it was, it became increasingly difficult to finance replacements where the demand for service continued to be existent. On the other hand, the number of telephones in use in Alberta, including the Edmonton Telephone System, fell from 80,300 in 1929 to 57,400 in 1933.[31] In some rural communities there were hardly any subscribers. Finally, many miles of line needed to be replaced in areas where services were demanded.

In 1934 the government invited H. Barker, a consulting engineer, to investigate the telephone system. He reported that a large part of the rural system would have to be rebuilt at a cost of about $4.5 million, or else abandoned. He recommended that the rural properties be sold at scrap value to non-profit making companies that could operate the service at whatever standards they decided upon. The government adopted his recommendations and gradually disposed of rural lines to small rural companies in succeeding years. The as-set value of the telephone system was written down from $25 million to $16 million (see Table 5.6). In effect, another expensive chapter in the province's financial history was closed. Between the inception of the system in 1906 and March 31, 1936, the telephone system had brought in a revenue of $56.0 million and had caused a total expenditure, including interest charges, of $79.6 million.[32] Thus there had been a cash drain of almost $24 million on the provincial treasury throughout the thirty-year period. In addition, there was an accumulation of bond discount amounting to more than one million dollars. In the years immediately following 1936, by virtue of operation in and between urban centres only and of the urban reduction in interest rates, the telephone system showed a surplus. Improvements in economic conditions in the 1940s have augmented revenues to such an extent that today the system is self-liquidating to the extent of covering all costs including depreciation.[33] However, the less successful years had reinforced people's impressions that the financial system worked against the provision of basic services.

THE ALBERTA WHEAT POOL GUARANTEE

The provincial government had given financial assistance to the Farmers' Cooperative Elevator Company in 1913. This company, after some initial difficulties, became financially stable in time and was able to repay instalments and to pay interest on the government loans. In 1917 the company amalgamated with the Grain Growers' Grain Company to form the United Grain Growers' Limited. The latter company continued to fulfil the obligations of the former Alberta company. In short, the Alberta government had suffered no financial loss by its aid to the grain company of 1913.

By 1924, provincial pool movements had been established in all three Prairie Provinces and they co-operated to form a central sales agency, Canadian Co-operative Wheat Producers Limited. Pool members signed contracts stipulating that they would sell their grain through the pool for the next five years. The pool acted as sales agent for the grower and bought no wheat outright. It made an initial payment on delivery and paid the balance at a later date when wheat had been marketed. The average cost of selling and certain reserves were deducted in determining the final price. The business of the three provincial pools grew rapidly, and in 1926, 70 per cent of the wheat in the Prairie Provinces was under pool contract. The relative acreage declined to about 50 per cent in the next few years.[34] The pools also began to build and operate their own elevators to an increasing degree. The pools did much to solve the marketing problems of farmers although they fell short of stabilizing the price of wheat.[35]

After 1926 the trend of wheat prices was downward. In addition, the world crop, as well as the Canadian one, was of record size in 1928. Carryover of wheat from year to year increased beginning in 1926. Grain also came to be held back in the hope of obtaining higher prices.[36] The pools held an increasing amount of grain and entered the 1929 crop year with a carryover of 52 million bushels. At the same time the private grain trade had reduced its carryover. There seemed to be no cause for alarm as the carryover of the wheat pool was less than 10 per cent of the Canadian wheat crop in 1928 and the pool also correctly forecast a light Canadian crop in 1929. But world events took a hand in the situation. Carryovers in the United States and Argentina had increased more rapidly than in Canada; the world wheat crop in 1929–30 was greater than had been estimated. Canadian wheat exports declined accordingly and the price of wheat fell disastrously. The initial price paid by the wheat pool in 1929 had looked quite safe at the time for it was less than two-thirds of the current price of wheat at the time it was determined, but it turned out to be too high in the face of severe and rapid market price declines.

The wheat pool was heavily indebted to the commercial banks for loans to enable it to make initial payments to growers. Now it was unable to repay these loans and it requested assistance from the three provincial governments. The three governments, including Alberta, made the requested guarantees in February 1930. In the meantime the price of wheat fell from $1.40 at the beginning of 1930 to $0.50 at the end of the year. The pool was unable to repay its bank loans in 1931, and the provincial governments made good the guarantees to the extent of $22 million. Of this amount the Alberta government supplied $5,561,000 in the fiscal year 1931–32. The initial price of 60 cents set in 1930 proved to be altogether too high. The Dominion government now stepped in to protect the banks, and took official charge of the wheat pool. It appointed a manager to liquidate the existing stocks of wheat and the central selling agency of the pool ceased to function. The three provincial pool elevator companies undertook independent selling and pooling was continued on a voluntary, non-contract basis only.

The implementation of the wheat pool guarantee struck the provincial treasury a staggering blow at a time when it was almost overcome by the buffetings of relief, American exchange premiums, debt repayments of its own, and an unprofitable telephone system. Yet, it is difficult to censure the government for its role in the wheat pool incident of 1930; there was practically speaking no other alternative. At that time there was still hope that the depression was only temporary and the welfare of the majority of Alberta farmers was involved. Between 1931 and 1948 the provincial government recouped all of the money extended to the pool.

PRIVATE DEBT AND THE DEMAND FOR MONETARY REFORM

A writer on Alberta once said:

> Comparatively few of the residents of Alberta have been able to finance their highly capitalistic methods of production from their own resources. J.S. Mill may have thought that capital is the result of saving. An Albertan, however, knows better. For him, capital is the result of borrowing. In Alberta, broadly speaking, happiness means credit. The seeds of Social Credit, therefore, have found a friendly soil.[37]

Although this quotation borders on the facetious, it is expressive in its indication of the debt problem that faced Albertans after 1929. They had borrowed heavily to finance increases in productive capacity, and their provincial government, as well as municipal ones, had utilized their credit standing to a high degree before 1930. The Commission on Dominion-Provincial Relations has summarized the situation both adequately and aptly:

> The incidence of ruinously low prices, however, was perhaps more severe than elsewhere. Owing to the more recent development of Alberta fixed debt charges were relatively higher than in any other province. In addition, farmers had no time to become well established. Under these circumstances, the drastic fall in prices of agricultural products produced a relatively greater strain on the farming industry and on governments. Alberta's depression problem was more one of debt and high overhead costs than one of widespread destitution.[38]

The drastic drop in prices has already been indicated in quantitative terms. The mixed farming techniques in use throughout large parts of the province enabled most farmers to eke out a subsistence in terms of food, shelter, and fuel. In southeast Alberta, however, droughts were too severe to permit much raising of livestock. Even if farmers in this area attempted to do so, they found it difficult to borrow the cash required.

Large areas of the province had been newly settled, and as a result of having borrowed to make the initial purchase, many farmers had a heavy debt load at the beginning of the depression. Many farmers who had been established on their farms since an earlier era had been hard-hit by the winter of 1919–20 during which they had become heavily indebted for feed only to see cattle prices fall disastrously in the spring. It took many of them years to recover financially. The improved price-cost relationships in agriculture during the second half of the 1920s encouraged farmers generally to borrow in order to purchase more land and machinery. New farmers, such as those in the Peace River and on the fringes had to borrow to get started at all in farming. Finally, the trend toward mechanization in farming was accompanied by growth in debt incurred to purchase machinery. The Alberta farmer certainly entered the depression ill-prepared. The vulnerable position of the farmer is well summarized in the following metaphorical quotation:

> Tempted by the ease with which larger and yet larger areas could
> be cultivated and harvested by means of machinery, the farmers
> doubled and even trebled their estates and added to their debts.
> The result was that the world depression, which began in 1930,
> came as a surprise and brought despair. The farmers' ship loaded to
> the decks, with all sails set, and a deck load of debts, was suddenly
> struck by a hurricane. The problem of the coming years is not how
> to unload the debts, and save the cargo, but how to save the ship
> and the crew.[39]

There are various estimates as to the amount of farm debt in Alberta and on the Canadian prairies as a whole in 1930, ranging from a census figure of $107.5 million to an independent estimate of $400 million.[40] An estimate of total farm debt in 1931 is presented in *The Case for Alberta*, a document of the Government of Alberta published in 1938. It was made on the basis of the census figures for mortgage debt in 1931, of Professor Allen's (the document's author's) estimates of debt incurred under agreement of sale in Saskatchewan,[41] of figures quoted by a representative of farm implement companies in testifying before the Agricultural Committee of the Alberta Legislature in 1931, of estimates of the Retail Merchants' Association in 1931 with respect to store credit, and of surveys of the Canadian Pioneer Problems Committee. The results are set out in Table 5.11.

Table 5.11 Estimated Debt of Farmers in Alberta in 1931 (in millions of dollars)

Mortgage	162.0
Agreement for sale	90.0
Implements	21.0
Banks	16.5
Stores	10.0
Miscellaneous	18.3
Total	317.8

Source: Government of Alberta, *The Case for Alberta* (Edmonton, 1938), 118.

The total figure for 1931, namely, $317.8 million is equivalent to more than $3,000 per farm. It is approximately equal to the net income received by farmers in Alberta during the eight years of 1930 to 1937 inclusive.[42] It is somewhat more than the cash income received from the sale of farm products in Alberta during the four years of 1930 to 1933 inclusive. Farm debt continued to grow during the early years of the 1930s. Table 5.12 sets out an estimate of farm debt in Alberta in 1936 made by the Alberta Debt Adjustment Board.

Interest rates were high, an inheritance of the 1920s when interest rates throughout the western world were the highest since the beginning of the industrial revolution, and a consequence of the risk differential on investments in Western Canada. The usual rate on farm mortgages was 8 per cent, and rates of 9 and 10 per cent were not uncommon. The rate on bank loans ran at 7 per cent and up. Even if the debt estimates presented are discounted somewhat, interest charges on farm debt would exceed $20 million per annum, a figure which is greater than the annual net income of farmers in Alberta in each of the years 1931–33 inclusive. It is approximately one-third of the cash income derived from the sale of farm products in each of the years 1931 to 1933 inclusive.

The tax collections of the provincial and municipal governments suffered accordingly while at the same time there was an increased need for expenditure on agricultural relief. In addition, the demand for legislation affording relief from pressing creditors increased. The basis for such legislation had been laid many years before, and a series of new legislations followed. The Exemption Act of 1898 provided exemptions intended to prevent the resident of a farm from being deprived of means of livelihood, and the list of exemptions grew over the years. The Extra Judicial Seizure Act of 1914 provided that all extra judicial seizures must be made by the sheriff or person authorized by him, and that no sale of seized items should be held except upon an order of a judge.[43]

Table 5.12 Estimated Debt of Farmers in Alberta in 1936 (in millions of dollars)

Mortgages, members of the Mortgage Loans Association	45.0
Canadian Farm Loan Board	6.5
Soldier Settlement Board	8.0
School lands contracts	4.5
Organized vendors of land (C.P.R.,Hudson's Bay Company, etc.)	21.0
Private parties, mortgagees, and vendors of land	65.0
Banks	35.0
Implement dealers	50.0
Retail merchants	40.0
Oil companies	15.0
Finance corporations	15.0
Governments, seed grain and relief	15.0
Taxing authorities, arrears	20.0
Sundry creditors	55.0
Total	395.0

Source: Government of Alberta, *The Case for Alberta* (Edmonton, 1938), 118.

In 1922, the provincial government passed The Drought Area Relief Act, which provided that those located in designated dry areas should be permitted to retain, out of the 1922 crop, sufficient proceeds of the crop to enable them to maintain themselves. The Debt Adjustment Act of 1923 replaced the Act of 1922. This Act was designed to permit farmers in "dry areas" to keep their land and equipment in order to enable them, if possible, to pay their debts in the long run. A farmer could apply to the Debt Adjustment Board for a certificate to stay seizures. A creditor, however, could contest this certificate, in a district court. Thus much discretion was left in the hands of the judges of such courts.[44]

The act of 1923 was broadened in 1931 to include all resident farmers in the province. In 1932 it was extended to include all persons who had retired from farm operations and had either leased or sold their property under agreement for sale or under mortgage. In 1933, amendments provided that a creditor may apply to the board for a permit to take proceedings for any debt. More drastic steps were taken after 1935. In 1936, The Reduction and Settlement of Debts Act was passed, restricting interest rates, interest collection, and method of interest payment.[45] This act was declared *ultra vires* by the Alberta courts. Consequently, the government passed The Postponement of Debts Act in 1937, which enabled the provincial government to declare a moratorium at any time or for any period. This provision was made effective with respect to certain debts. Finally, The Local Tax Arrears Consolidation Act was passed in 1931 to provide for the consolidation of tax arrears over a five-year period. This measure enabled farmers to spread the payment of tax arrears over a period of five years and provided for extensions in the event of a crop failure. Thus they were, in effect, protected from municipal authorities that might want to seize their land for tax delinquency.

The whole topic of debt legislation is too large to explore thoroughly here. Mortgage companies and financial institutions subjected the moratorium, declared in 1937 for many types of debt, too much criticism. Coupled with the provincial government default of 1936, it did much to restrict credit facilities available to Alberta citizens and governments in succeeding years. Thus, for example, loans under the federal National Housing Act were not made in Alberta until after World War II.

Despite these legislative efforts to help farmers deal with their financial situation, farmers shackled by debt grew increasingly antagonistic toward credit-granting institutions. They became more and more critical of the existing monetary framework. Theories of monetary reform which had lain dormant in the 1920s attracted attention and support on a widespread scale in rural communities. When a strong leader of the Social Credit monetary reform movement, Mr. William Aberhart, emerged in 1933, his proposals found eager adherents, not only in the rural areas of the province but also in the urban centres. The emphasis of the new movement upon the iniquity of the debt situation and upon the inability of the economic system to provide work for all was well placed. The Social Credit party was organized and won a landslide victory at the polls in 1935.

THE ELECTION OF 1935

The rise of the Social Credit party is a complex matter and it was a phenomenon that seemed inexplicable to inhabitants of communities older than Alberta. Yet the matter is simple enough to the contemporary observer of and participant in the events of the 1930s in Alberta. To him, it is a source of wonder that organized protests against existing conditions did not become effective before 1935. But when the strength of the leadership of the Social Credit movement became apparent, the distances were conquered and the U.F.A. organization fell apart. Alberta was a region that had not enjoyed even the modicum of stability that most Occidental communities possessed. The specialized economic institutions of Western civilization appeared to have let the farmer down even before the 1930s, and he had acquired a deep distrust of them. They certainly did not represent to the farmer requisites deemed necessary for the survival of an agricultural economy. "Conspiracy" explanations of the plight of the farmers and unemployed were rampant; the depression was a device of the financial magnates of Eastern Canada, the United States, and Europe, to reduce the farmers to the status of peasants and the urban workers to the status of docile labourers. The remoteness of the region from other, more populated areas of the world, where tertiary occupations are readily seen and admitted, and where specialized economic institutions have been taken for granted to a greater degree than in Western Canada, made "conspiracy" theories plausible to the inhabitants. It also appeared anomalous to many Albertans that the abundant physical resources of their province should lie dormant, especially at a time of unemployment. The failure to develop these resources coupled with the surplus of grain and agricultural commodities produced even in drought years led to the ready acceptance of "underconsumption" economic theories. The whole economic system was believed to be capable of producing a sufficiency for all at such a level that the economic problems of individuals could be solved once and for all.

The Social Credit principles expounded in Alberta were a mixture of all the above ideas and met ready acceptance. The basic facts on which any interpretation of the rise of the Social Credit movement must rest are, of course, the extremely low incomes of the majority of Albertans and the loss of personal dignity and self-respect engendered by the inability of many individuals to support themselves. Residents outside the western prairies, both Canadians and Americans, have displayed an utter lack of understanding of the suffering and humiliation to which so many westerners were subjected in the 1930s. At the same time, such outsiders fail to understand the "splurges" of westerners when a few wet years coupled with rising agricultural prices came along. It is doubtful whether the Canadian federation would stand the strain of another depression of the magnitude of the 1930s.[46]

The Social Credit election platform called for the cessation of external borrowing by governments and individuals and the creation of provincial credit; the distribution of purchasing power by means of "basic dividends" for all men and women in the province; the establishment of a "just price" on all goods and services; the regulation of price spreads between the primary producer and consumer; an amendment to the Alberta debt adjustment legislation extending the provisions to all classes of debtors and preventing hasty foreclosures; loans to be made to all who needed funds for productive enterprises; the development of markets for agricultural products and a definite policy for the drought areas; the establishment in the province of more manufacturing industries producing "essential goods"; and the right of recall of legislative members.[47]

In the meantime, the U.F.A. government had engaged the services of Major Douglas, the original founder of the Social Credit movement, to come to Alberta to report on the feasibility of introducing Social Credit. Major Douglas visited the province in May 1935, and published a report. He stated that every step taken by the province to institute Social Credit would be opposed by the Bank of Canada acting for the international bankers.[48] He recommended that the provincial government set up a news circulation system to combat propaganda of financial authorities; the organization of a credit institution under the Dominion Bank Act or otherwise "which will give access to the creation of effective demand through the credit system"; and, the accumulation of foreign exchange to solve the problem of paying for imports in the probable event that areas outside Alberta should refuse to accept Alberta currency.[49]

The U.F.A. government found the recommendations to be unsuitable. In a letter to the public, Mr. Lymburn, the Attorney-General, indicated that the Douglas Social Credit plan was based on the power of the government to issue money. The provincial government, he said, lacked this power. Furthermore, he pointed out, the idea that every province should have such power was not in harmony with the whole conception of confederation.[50] The U.F.A. government, then, in effect, rejected monetary reform based upon Social Credit.

The Liberal party included some monetary reform proposals in its platform. It advocated the reduction of debt charges, both governmental and individual; it plumped for public ownership of the Central Bank of Canada; and it pledged itself, if returned to office, to employ three expert advocates of Social Credit to investigate proposed schemes and to prepare a Social Credit plan to be submitted to the legislature.[51]

Only the Conservative party expressed "unequivocal opposition" to Social Credit. In the main, it advocated the refunding of provincial and municipal debt at lower rates of interest; the readjustment of responsibilities and powers of the Dominion and the province; and a balanced budget.[52]

The results of the election are well known. The Social Credit party captured 56 seats out of a total of 63. The Liberals elected five members and the Conservatives two. The U.F.A. failed to return a single supporter. The Social Creditors met in caucus in the assembly hall of the Prophetic Bible Institute in Calgary, an institution founded by Mr. Aberhart and from which he had broadcast religious addresses by radio for many years. They invited Mr. Aberhart, who had not been a candidate in the election, to become premier of the province. He accepted, and on August 30, 1935, formed a Social Credit cabinet.

THE TAXATION REPORT OF 1935

It perhaps constitutes an anticlimax to mention the report of the Alberta Tax Inquiry Board tabled in November 1935. This report proposed remedies in the taxation field, which were very prosaic, compared to the heady medicines desired by the electorate of the province. The board had been appointed in December 1933, and was headed by Mr. J.F. Percival, Deputy Provincial Treasurer.[53] The report stressed that changed social and economic conditions had strained the tax structure of the urban municipalities to the breaking point and that the provincial tax structure was inadequate to provide sufficient revenue relatively to provincial expenditures.

It made recommendations in regards to broadening the revenue base of the province by various tax measures, and found many problems with the municipal tax system, Some of these issues were beyond the ability of the province to address, but they were taken up by a 1937 Royal Commission on Dominion–Provincial Relations. Of the recommendations that were within provincial jurisdiction, Alberta only acted on those suggesting an increase in tax rates and the formation of larger school administration units. The drafting and passage of legislation designed to implement Social Credit absorbed most of the energies of the new administration during the first few years of office. Like so many other taxation inquiries, the Alberta one of 1935 was quietly shelved if not forgotten entirely.

LEVELS OF PROVINCIAL EXPENDITURE

The major financial problems of the Alberta government have already been dealt with in considerable detail. Consequently, the discussion of the magnitudes of specific expenditures can be shortened here.

GENERAL GOVERNMENT

Expenditure on general government fell from $4.4 million in 1930–31 to $2.5 million in 1934–35 (see Table 5.13). In 1935–36 the total rose to $2.7 million, chiefly because of general election expenses. Most of the decline after 1931 was attributable to the virtual cessation of construction projects, to cuts in the salaries of civil servants, and to the dissolution of the provincial police force when the services of the Royal Canadian Mounted Police were again secured after 1931. In other administrative spheres there were attempts to reduce expenditures, but the economies secured were minor in magnitude because a reduction

Table 5.13 Expenditures of the Government of Alberta, 1930–1936, According to Functions (in millions of dollars)

Fiscal year	General Government				Social Expenditure				Economic Expenditure					Debt int.	Other	Total
	Leg.	Adm.	Just.	Total	Educ.	P.H.	P.Wel	Total	Agr.	P.D.	Hwys	Tel.	Total			
1930–31	0.4	2.4	1.6	4.4	4.1	2.3	2.2	8.5	0.7	1.3	6.3	2.5	10.7	6.2	1.3	31.1
1931–32	0.2	1.9	1.3	3.4	3.2	1.9	2.3	7.4	6.6	1.6	6.3	1.6	16.1	7.6	1.0	35.5
1932–33	0.2	1.6	0.8	2.6	3.0	1.7	4.2	8.9	0.7	1.7	2.6	2.1	7.1	8.0	1.0	27.6
1933–34	0.2	1.4	0.8	2.4	2.8	1.6	4.9	9.3	1.6	1.1	1.0	1.2	4.9	8.0	0.7	25.3
1934–35	0.2	1.5	0.8	2.5	2.7	1.7	6.2	10.6	1.8	1.1	2.1	1.2	6.2	7.7	0.8	27.7
1935–36	0.4	1.6	0.8	2.7	2.9	1.8	6.9	11.6	2.9	1.1	2.6	1.2	7.8	7.8	0.8	30.7

Source: See Appendix B.

of, say, one-third in administrative expenditures, would have meant only a three per cent reduction in total expenditure.

SOCIAL EXPENDITURE

Social expenditure increased both absolutely and relatively in this period. In 1930–31, it amounted to $8.5 million and 27 per cent of total provincial expenditure; in 1935–36, the total had increased to $11.6 million and absorbed 37 per cent of total expenditure. The increase was, however, chiefly confined to the public welfare category.

Expenditures on all levels of schools were reduced, and the construction of educational buildings was brought to a standstill. The policy of making loans to normal school students was discontinued as well, for a surplus of teachers materialized. Expenditure on public health was likewise reduced, and there were reductions in general public health services provided. Hospital grants, however, remained at about the same level throughout the six-year period, and expenditure on mental institutions remained fairly constant. In contrast to these reductions, expenditure on public welfare rose, chiefly in the areas of unemployment relief outlays and old age pensions.

ECONOMIC EXPENDITURE

Economic expenditure shrank in dollar terms as well as relatively between 1930 and 1935. Despite this trend, the government's expenditure on agricultural relief grew rapidly after 1933, and the 1931–32 wheat pool guarantee was a major expenditure. The chief expenditure item in public domain expenditure were drainage and irrigation outlays, although there were also new found costs in the administration of lands following the 1930 transfer of natural resources to the province. At the beginning of the depression, a highway construction program involved serious spending, but it was curtailed as it proved to be ineffective in coping with unemployment, and as the government found it increasingly difficult to obtain funds. Grants to municipalities for the maintenance and construction of roads were also virtually eliminated. The telephone question has already been discussed. Expenditures on this item, exclusive of interest payments, fell from $2.5 million in 1930–31 to $1.2 million in 1935–36.

Table 5.14 Revenues of the Government of Alberta, 1930–1936
(in millions of dollars)

Fiscal year	1930 –31	1931 –32	1932 –33	1933 –34	1934 –35	1935 –36
Dom. of Canada	2.1	2.3	2.9	2.7	2.8	4.6
Taxes	4.9	3.9	5.0	4.7	5.0	5.4
Licences and fees	3.0	2.5	2.5	2.6	2.6	2.4
Public domain	0.7	0.9	0.7	0.9	2.0	1.1
School lands	0.9	0.6	0.7	0.7	0.8	0.7
Liquor control	1.9	1.4	1.4	1.3	1.5	1.8
Fines	0.4	0.1	0.1	0.1	0.1	0.1
Sales	0.6	0.6	0.6	0.5	0.5	0.5
Refunds	0.4	0.5	0.6	0.9	1.0	1.0
Interest	2.4	2.3	2.6	2.7	2.2	2.3
Repayments	1.3	2.3	1.3	6.1	2.2	1.4
Miscellaneous	0.1	0.1	0.1	0.1	0.1	0.1
Telephones	2.3	1.7	1.2	1.0	0.9	0.9
Total revenue	20.7	19.0	19.7	24.0	20.6	22.3

Source: See Appendix B.

DEBT CHARGES

Debt charges constituted a rigid item that proved to be of increasing embarrassment to the government. Dominion loans were obtained from time to time to facilitate the payment of interest. Total expenditure on this item equalled 20 per cent of total expenditure in 1930–31 and 25 per cent in 1935–36. In terms of total revenue, including telephones, it absorbed 30 per cent in 1930–31 and 35 per cent in 1935–36.

REVENUE DEVELOPMENTS

Total revenue fluctuated between $19 million and $24 million annually between 1930 and 1936. There was relatively little decline below the levels of the late 1920s because of the increased grants from the Dominion, growing collections from public domain, and the imposition of new taxes. A detailed examination of revenue bears out this observation (see Table 5.14).

The amount of revenue from a number of sources increased in this period. In terms of funds received from the senior government, the increase was attributable to growing grants-in-aid, of which the chief item was the Dominion grant for public welfare. Tax revenue initially declined, but the imposition of income taxes on persons and corporations in 1932 and increased yields from the gasoline tax led to a recovery of tax revenues in succeeding years. Revenue from public domain jumped up as royalties and fees from coal, petroleum, and natural gas production were collected. Timberlands also brought substantial revenue in the form of fees and rentals. The increase in revenue from refunds resulted chiefly from increased municipal contributions as the number of application for pensions and relief increased

In other areas, however, revenue fell. The revenue from licenses and fees declined rapidly after 1929–30, mainly because of the fall in motor vehicle licence revenue and in land title fees. Less and less revenue from school lands, liquor control, telephones, and from the sales of commodities and services, was obtained during this period. Revenue from interest remained fairly constant, although interest on investments declined as the government divested itself of its holdings of bonds in order to obtain cash. Revenue from repayments fluctuated considerably due to annual differences in repayment of relief advances and the receipt of the second railway sale instalment in 1933–34.

The municipalities of Alberta were also hard-pressed by the depression. Somehow they weathered the storm, but the mortality rate among them was high in the southeast. Table 5.15 shows payments made to the municipalities exclusive of unemployment relief assistance. The only provincial-municipal expenditure, which increased substantially, was that of old age pensions. Further, the Dominion government financed the bulk of this outlay.

GOVERNMENT AND THE ECONOMY

The governments of Alberta exerted a positive influence during the first years of the depression (see Table 5.16). This was almost solely the result of the provincial government expenditure policy of 1930 and 1931, which led to large overall deficits. After 1931 borrowed funds became more difficult to obtain than before, and overall deficits diminished. At the same time, interest costs of public debts rose yearly. Consequently, the community's flow of income tended to be diminished rather than enlarged by provincial and municipal fiscal policies.

The burden of provincial and local taxation upon the economy rose rapidly after 1930. During 1932 and 1933 such taxes absorbed about one-seventh of provincial income, but this figure does not show the uneven incidence of taxation upon economic groups or individuals. Since the income of the rural

Table 5.15 Provincial Government Payments to Municipalities, 1930–1936
(in millions of dollars)

Fiscal year ending March 31	1931	1932	1933	1934	1935	1936
Grants-in-aid:						
Schools	1.8	1.4	1.4	1.5	1.4	1.4
Highways	0.6	0.5	–	–	0.1	0.2
Hospital districts	0.1	0.1	0.1	0.1	0.1	0.1
Total grants	2.5	1.9	1.5	1.6	1.6	1.7
Other:						
Mothers' allowances	0.4	0.4	0.3	0.4	0.3	0.4
Old age pensions	0.7	0.9	1.1	1.2	1.3	1.6
Miscellaneous[a]	0.2	0.2	0.3	0.3	0.3	0.3
Total other	1.3	1.5	1.7	1.9	1.9	2.3
Total	3.7	3.4	3.2	3.4	3.5	4.0

Provincial contribution as a percentage of total expenditure:

Schools	15	13	15	18	16	16
Hospital districts	11	12	12	13	15	14
Highways[b]	19	15	2	1	2	7
Mothers' allowances	63	63	60	67	63	66
Old age pensions	94	5	93	94	92	94
Dominion government contribution to old age pensions and included in the provincial share (in millions of dollars):	0.4	0.5	0.9	0.9	1.0	1.2

Source: See Appendix B.
  (a) Includes tax collection commissions, liquor fines, payments to cities in lieu of "service tax" after the province imposed an income tax in 1932, indigent relief.
  (b) Estimated from the total expenditure of municipal and improvement districts. Highway expenditures of these units were taken to equal 70 per cent of total expenditure.

Table 5.16 Net Income-Producing Expenditures of the Provincial Government and the Local Governments in Alberta, 1930–1935 (in millions of dollars)

Year	Dominion grants	School lands fund	Overall deficits less Interest Payments	Misc.	Total
1930	2.1	0.9	3.1	0.0	6.1
1931	2.3	0.6	5.3	0.0	8.2
1932	2.9	0.7	−5.1	0.0	−1.5
1933	2.7	0.7	−10.9	5.0[a]	−2.5
1934	2.8	0.8	−3.2	0.0	0.4
1935	4.6	0.7	−4.4	0.0	0.9

(a) Railway sale instalment received by the provincial government.

community fell by a greater percentage than that of the urban one, and since both rural and urban tax levies fell very little, it is safe to say that the tax burden increased to a greater extent in rural areas than in urban centres. In any event, tax arrears mounted in both types of communities, and property owners, whether rural or urban, were particularly hard pressed.

DEFAULT, RECOVERY AND PROSPERITY, 1936–50

6

ECONOMIC DEVELOPMENT

AGRICULTURE AND PRICES

Recovery came slowly and hesitantly between 1935 and 1939. The prices of agricultural products in Alberta turned upward during 1935–37 but then declined to 1935 levels in 1939 (see Table 6.1). Hence, in 1939 prices were still far below 1929 levels. Table 6.2 below reveals the magnitudes. There had been a favourable cost-price relationship in 1936 and 1937, but farmers were unable to benefit from this because a province-wide drought reduced yields to the lowest levels since 1919. After 1937, the cost-price relationship ceased to be so favourable because of a recession in agricultural prices, and thus farmers could not capitalize on their increased yields. In short, agriculture in Alberta was far from prosperous in the immediate pre-war years.

Fortunately, an upturn in agricultural economic conditions came rapidly after 1939. Farm costs rose slowly while the prices of agricultural products more than doubled between 1940 and 1945 (see Table 6.1). The value of field crops rose and, with some fluctuation, so did crop yields (see Table 6.3). There was also a sudden favorable change in the cost-price relationship for agriculture. Between 1946 and 1950, the yearly average wholesale price index rose, as did the Canadian urban cost-of-living index and the index of the cost of farm purchases in Western Canada. The prices of agricultural products, however, rose less rapidly (see Table 6.1). This lag is largely attributable to the federal government stabilization policy as applied to wheat. The prices of other grains, and of steers and hogs, all rose during this period. But since wheat carries the greatest weight in the index of agricultural prices, the overall increase shown by the index was much less than the increases of most of the product prices that were not subject to any significant measure of government control.[1]

The agricultural industry, however, continued to prosper; it was largely a question of how much more agricultural income would have risen if wheat had been sold at world market prices. Wheat yields were about average for the

Table 6.1   Selected Price Indicators, Canada and Alberta, 1936–1950

Year	Wholesale, Canada[a]	Agricultural products, Alberta[b]	Cost of Living Index, Canada[c]	Cost of Farm Purchases, Western Canada[d]
1936	75	94	98	98
1937	85	131	101	103
1938	79	106	102	102
1939	75	85	101	100
1940	83	91	106	107
1941	90	103	112	116
1942	96	122	117	125
1943	100	150	118	133
1944	103	177	119	140
1945	104	196	119	142
1946	109	220	124	148
1947	129	232	136	164
1948	153	263	155	187
1949	157	266	161	192
1950	166	265	166	203

(a) 1926 is 100. From D.B.S., *Prices and Price Indexes, 1944–1947*, and *C.Y.B.*, 1951, 961.
(b) 1935–39 is 100. From D.B.S., *Quarterly Bulletin of Agricultural Statistics*, Jan. 1937, 29; Oct.–Dec. 1946, 174–79; and Jan.–March 1951, 8–9. The above series is not strictly comparable to the pre-1936 series.
(c) 1935–39 is 100. From Government of Canada, Department of Labour, *Labour Gazette* (Ottawa, June 1950), 967, and from *C.Y.B.*, 1951, 966.
(d) 1935–39 is 100. From D.B.S., *Price Index Numbers of Commodities and Services Used by Farmers, 1913 to 1948* (Ottawa, July 21, 1948), 7; April 1950; and April 1951. The indexes are for August of each given year, the last month of each year for which the data is computed.

Table 6.2 Average Prices of Selected Agricultural Products in Alberta, 1926–29, 1930–34, and 1935–39

	1926–29	1930–34	1935–39
Wheat, per bushel	$1.20	$0.43	$0.72
Oats, per bushel	0.34	0.18	0.24
Steers, per cwt.[a]	7.74	3.92	4.50
Hogs, per cwt.[a]	10.81	6.10	7.98

Source: *C.Y.B.*, 1927–41.
  (a) Edmonton prices.

1946–50 period; only in 1949 were yields lighter than average (see Table 6.3). Field crop acreage expanded little during this period for the number of farms in the province decreased and new agricultural settlements were not established on any substantial scale. The value of field crops rose to an all-time high in the years 1946 to 1948 inclusive; low yields led to a decline in 1949 and the low quality of the 1950 crop kept the value of field crops in that year below the annual values of 1946–48 (see Table 6.3).

Despite the yearly fluctuations in crop yields and quality, the agricultural prosperity between 1942 and 1950 was unprecedented in the economic history of Alberta. Never before had Alberta farmers enjoyed a period of prosperity exceeding three years in length. This fact must not be overlooked by anyone who attempts to explain the rising prosperity of the Albertan economy during the last decade.

POPULATION TRENDS

The prosperity period of the 1940s, unlike the period before World War I and the 1926–29 period, was unaccompanied by any new agricultural settlement boom. Instead the trend was one of migration to the urban centres with their employment (and money-making) opportunities. Social reasons were operative also, for many people considered that urban centres offered a more convenient and attractive life than rural areas. When urban employment opportunities presented themselves after 1940, rural inhabitants moved in large numbers.

From 1931 to 1941, rural population continued to increase, but the rate of increase became almost zero by the end of the decade. The 1941–46 period saw a sharp downturn in rural population and only a very small absolute gain

Table 6.3   Wheat Yields, Wheat Prices, Field Crop Acreage, and Value of Field
Crops in Alberta, 1936–1950

Year	Wheat Yield (bu per acre)[a]	Wheat Price (cents per bu.)[b]	Field Crop Acreage (millions)[c]	Value of field crops (millions)[d]
1936	8.8	87	12.7	$104
1937	9.7	102	13.4	134
1938	18.6	58	13.6	122
1939	19.3	52	13.9	127
1940	20.8	49	14.2	147
1941	15.1	50	12.9	112
1942	26.8	66	13.6	253
1943	17.1	110	13.1	235
1944	14.7	123	14.0	254
1945	12.9	154	14.5	231
1946	18.2	151	13.6	326
1947	15.8	153	14.0	339
1948	18.4	153	13.5	340
1949	13.0	249	14.4	276
1950	16.1	127	14.4	295

(a) From *C.Y.B.*, 1938–47, and D.B.S., *Quarterly Bulletin of Agricultural Statistics*, Jan.–March 1951, 43.
(b) From *C.Y.B.*, ibid., and D.B.S., ibid., respectively.
(c) From *C.Y.B.*, ibid., and D.B.S., ibid., respectively.
(d) From *C.Y.B.*, ibid., and D.B.S., ibid., respectively.

during the 1946–51 period. The urban population increased slowly during the
1930s and rapidly between 1941 and 1951. A notable fact is that the census of
1951 indicates that the urban population has finally exceeded the rural. The
greatest urban population gains were made by the southwest, which contains
the city of Calgary, and the centre, which contains the city of Edmonton.

URBAN ECONOMIC ACTIVITY

Urban economic activity and investment showed little gain during the 1935–39
period, and the recession of 1937 set back what little recovery there had been
before that year. Bank clearings remained almost constant for 1936–40 inclusive (see Table 6.4). Building activity remained at a very low level until war

construction contracts increased it after 1939. In 1939, the index of employment reached the 1926 level, certainly not a high level when one considers that the population had increased by about 30 per cent during the intervening thirteen years.

Investment and business activity were stimulated by wartime demands. Bank clearings more than doubled between 1940 and 1944. Building activity remained at a level approximating that of 1940, and far above the 1936–39 levels. The increase in employment was spectacular, for the index rose from 100 in 1939 to 159 in 1944. Provincial income doubled between 1939 and 1944. The year 1945 saw some decline in employment and income, the former partly attributable to the cessation of hostilities, while the latter was a composite effect of declining employment, and more importantly, of a poor crop year.

Alberta took the conversion from wartime to peacetime conditions in its stride. Prosperous conditions continued to prevail after a brief pause in late 1945, and this pause was only momentary. Business activity, fed by wartime accumulations of cash and bonds, climbed upward in 1946 with the post-war increase in the demand for durable goods and housing. The world demand for agricultural products continued to be strong, thus maintaining, and even increasing, agricultural income in the province. The federal government, too, by feeding significantly large transfer payments into the income stream, added fuel to the inflationary fire of the post-war years. Finally, in 1947 new oil discoveries were made near Edmonton; this set off an investment boom that finds precedent only in the 1906–13 era.

Urban economic activity rose to new peaks. Table 6.4 provides the details of this boom period wherein the 1912 record, in real terms, was almost reached; in money terms, of course, the 1950 level was much higher than the 1912 level. The population of the province also began to increase, and immigration began to become significant again, although it did not reach the proportions attained during the late 1920s. Much of the upsurge in economic activity and investment after 1946 is attributable to the most dramatic economic event of the post-war years, namely, the discovery of oil fields in Leduc, south-west of Edmonton, which is now the largest producer in Alberta. Yet, the sustained agricultural prosperity of the period was even more important quantitatively in maintaining business activity at high levels.

Table 6.4   Selected Indicators of Investment Activity in Alberta, 1936–1950

Year	(a)	(b)	(c)	(d)	(e)	(f)
1936	502	0.8	1.7	6	8	n.a.
1937	513	0.9	1.5	5	3	n.a.
1938	501	1.2	3.7	8	5	95
1939	492	1.7	2.7	5	5	100
1940	507	1.6	5.3	24	4	106
1941	608	0.4	6.1	16	6	120
1942	685	0.3	6.7	14	−20	141
1943	887	0.3	8.7	19	16	148
1944	1,064	0.8	9.6	20	26	159
1945	1,115	2.2	15.3	33	8	153
1946	1,340	5.3	26.8	39	−23	160
1947	1,518	3.9	23.7	47	19	171
1948	1,795	9.7	41.1	74	24	177
1949	2,107	8.5	61.9	104	25	192
1950	2,423	6.4	72.0	135	24	198

(a)   Bank Clearings, Edmonton and Calgary, in millions of dollars. From *Facts and Figures*, 352, for 1936–48 inclusive, and from information supplied by Government of Alberta, Department of Industries and Labour, Bureau of Statistics, for 1949 and 1950.

(b)   Immigration, in thousands. From *Facts and Figures*, 51, for 1936–47 inclusive; from *C.Y.B.*, 1950, 192, for 1948; from *C.Y.B.*, 1951, 149, for 1949; from preliminary figures for 1950.

(c)   Building Permits, Edmonton and Calgary, in millions of dollars. From *Facts and Figures*, 274, for 1936–48 inclusive. The figures for 1949 and 1950 were obtained from the Bureau of Statistics for the Government of Alberta.

(d)   Construction Contracts Awarded, in millions of dollars. From *C.Y.B.*, 1938–51, and the Bureau of Statistics of the Government of Alberta.

(e)   Annual Population Change, in thousands. From intercensal estimates of the D.B.S. as published in *C.Y.B.*, 1946, 127, and in D.B.S., *Canadian Statistical Review*, 1949–51.

(f)   Index of Employment, 1926 is 100. From Government of Canada, Department of Labour, *Labour Gazette* (Ottawa, June 1950), 946. The index is for March 1 in each year.

INDUSTRIAL DEVELOPMENT

The indifferent recovery of the late 1930s and the accelerating rise in economic activity during the 1940s may be shown in terms of net values produced in primary and secondary industries.[2]

The net value of agriculture fluctuated between $100 million and $140 million during the 1936–40 period, between about $120 million and $260 million during 1941–45, and between $250 million and $390 million during 1946–49. Thus the levels attained were approximately three times the pre-war levels.

The net value of mining increased steadily from year to year in contrast to agriculture, which fluctuated annually. In 1950, the net value of mining was almost five times that of 1936, more than three times that of 1940, and more than twice that of 1945. The rise during the pre-war years came mainly from the great increase in the production of petroleum and natural gas after 1936. Deeper drilling resulted in important petroleum discoveries in the Turner Valley field, and production for Alberta rose from 1.3 million barrels in 1936 to a high of 10.1 million barrels in 1942. After 1942 there were declines in each year, and a low of 6.8 million barrels was reached in 1947. Production from newly discovered fields led to a rapid increase after that year, and 27.2 million barrels were produced in 1950.[3] The production of natural gas rose from 19.2 billion cubic feet in 1936 to 75.6 billion cubic feet in 1950, with only minor setbacks in 1939 and 1946. Coal production remained at a level of about 5.5 million tons before the war. During the war years, annual production was almost 7.5 million tons in each year. There was a further increase to more than 8 million tons annually after 1945. In value terms, petroleum production rose from $3 million in 1936 to $82 million in 1950; in 1949, it exceeded the value of coal produced for the first time in the history of the province. The value of natural gas produced rose from about $4 million in 1936 to about $10 million in 1950. Finally, the value of coal produced rose from about $15 million in 1936 to about $41 million in 1950.

The value of manufacturing showed steady gains until 1940; after that date it rose impressively, and by 1945 it was more than three times the 1936 level. Further gains were made during the post-war years in money terms, if not in real terms. The construction industry revived during the war years and made tremendous strides during the post-war years. Secondary industry in general became more important relatively; between 1936 and 1945 it made almost a three-fold gain while primary industries expanded only somewhat more than twofold. Even in the post-war period the secondary industries expanded more rapidly than primary industries despite the increasing importance of petroleum production. It should be noted, however, that much construction activity was generated by the intensive search for oil that began after the initial discoveries of 1947.

CHANGES IN PERSONAL INCOME

The personal income of Alberta residents is illustrated in Table 6.5. The war years showed the greatest relative gains while the post-war years brought the greatest absolute gains. The fact that personal income in 1950 was more than three times that of 1939 is a striking one. Governments have found that their revenue bases have expanded accordingly.

The largest component of income, wages and salaries, rose almost without interruption between 1936 and 1950. This rise was attributable to defence construction projects undertaken in Alberta, to increases in the number of employees in tertiary industries, and to increases in military pay and allowances. The post-war period brought further gains in employment and substantial increases in rates of pay. In 1950 salaries and wages were almost 50 per cent above the 1945 level.

The net income of agricultural enterprises, the second largest component of provincial income, is outlined in Table 6.6. It should be kept in mind that there were *more* farmers in Alberta in each year between 1926 and 1940 than after the latter year, and that the number of farmers was greatest during the 1930s.

SOCIAL CREDIT LEGISLATION

Some attention to the attempts of the new government to implement Social Credit will help provide the background for explaining legislation and events having a direct impact upon the treasury. Much of the legislation would have made the government a money-issuing institution if the statutes had been ruled constitutional. Presumably the government could then have used its own currency to meet treasury obligations. What the economic and financial effects of this would have been are not easy to assess. Nevertheless, the experiences of the "scrip" issue of 1936 indicated the difficulties of persuading people to accept what was, in effect, a provincial currency.[4] This reluctance had its roots in the high proportion of payments for goods that had to be made to non-Albertans; Alberta was both a heavy importer and exporter of goods. Consequently, the success of a provincial currency would, in the end, have hinged upon the occurrence of an increase in the demand for Alberta exports, an increase that did not materialize until the 1940s. When the increase did come, economic recovery necessarily followed without any issue of Alberta currency. As economic activity rose to higher and higher levels, too, attempts to initiate a Social Credit system of whatever degree and complexion diminished in number and intensity. The government retained much of its basic philosophy underlying the doctrines of

Table 6.5 Personal Income of Residents of Alberta by Sources of Income, 1936–1950 (in millions of dollars)

Year	Wages and Salaries[a]	Agriculture	Unincorporated Business	Investments[b]	Transfer Payments	Total
1936	117	20	19	19	12	188
1937	130	67	20	22	14	252
1938	127	81	24	25	13	268
1939	132	68	24	26	12	262
1940	151	89	28	29	13	310
1941	182	72	30	29	11	324
1942	209	209	34	40	20	512
1943	242	110	40	42	13	447
1944	273	207	45	46	18	589
1945	287	141	49	47	40	564
1946	285	182	61	55	83	666
1947	307	206	76	61	59	709
1948	362	306	80	64	58	870
1949	403	279	85	68	63	896
1950	430	245	90	75	69	907

Sources: See Appendix A.
(a) Includes military pay and allowances.
(b) Consists of income from interest, dividends, and net rentals.

Table 6.6 Annual Average Net Income of Farmers in Alberta, 1926–29 and Subsequent Five-Year Periods (in millions of dollars)

Period	1926–29	1930–35	1936–40	1941–45	1946–50
Current $	106	25	65	148	244
Constant $ (a)	85	25	64	113	136

Sources: See Appendix A.
(a) 1935–39 dollars. The price index of commodities and services purchased by farmers in western Canada was used in "deflating" the current dollar figures.

Social Credit, but during the 1940s it began to express with increasing emphasis its desire to provide the opportunities of a free enterprise economy, to encourage private investment in the province, to pursue policies designed to provide government services efficiently, and to manage the financial affairs of the provincial treasury so as to minimize the growth of debt and taxation. Aided by economic recovery, the government has found its expressed desires largely fulfilled. Thus the policies of the 1940s have been followed by tangible results, while the Social Credit policies attempted during the late 1930s proved to be abortive.

The government had been elected in 1935 on the basis of its promises to usher in a "new economic order." The money incomes of the citizens of Alberta were to be augmented by the introduction of a social credit system in order to bring consumption into equilibrium with production, it being asserted that the latter had outstripped the former.[5] To this end the government passed many statutes between 1935 and 1938. Much of this legislation was disallowed by the Dominion government and/or declared *ultra vires* by the courts.[6] More concretely, this legislation was designed to increase the level of income of Albertans, to provide debt relief, and to decrease urban unemployment and agricultural distress.

In the first session of 1936, the government passed the Social Credit Measures Act[7] which aimed to "put into operation any measure designed to facilitate the exchange of goods and services or any other proposal / calculated to bring about the equation of consumption and production" and consequently provide the people of the province with "the full benefit of the increment arising from their association." A board was appointed to make recommendations on this matter.[8] In the second 1936 session, the Albert Credit House Act was passed[9] which provided for the establishment of credit houses in Alberta. No immediate steps were taken to put either legislation into effect.

Meanwhile, rifts began to appear among members of the cabinet and of the legislative assembly. The premier was under pressure to produce results in terms of "social credit"; he was also beset by the everyday problems of governmental administration and finance. The urgency of dealing with the latter is seldom realized by backbenchers of a reform or protest party, but it bore heavily upon the premier. He was becoming increasingly concerned with the operation of the administrative and financial machinery of his government, a not unusual experience of leaders of reform parties that attain power. The first budget of the new government was presented along traditional lines and principles with only a casual reference to Social Credit aims.[10] The second budget, presented in February 1937, was thoroughly "orthodox," especially in the insistence upon the desirability of balancing revenue and expenditures at the earliest possible moment. This was too much for a number of backbenchers to take, and these "insurgents," as they were called at the time, were numerous enough to secure the passage of a motion to adjourn the budget debate on March 25, 1937, by a vote of 27 to 25. The "insurgents," who have also been labelled the "Douglasite" wing of the party as against the "Aberhart" wing, insisted upon the implementation of social credit measures.[11] The government secured the passage of temporary estimates covering the first three months of the fiscal year, dispatched representatives to England to confer with Major Douglas and to induce the latter to come to Alberta to act as advisor, and drafted a number of new Social Credit statutes, which were designed to secure the implementation of a social credit system. The "insurgents" were appeased, and on June 14, 1937, the budget debate was resumed, the budget approved, and the yearly estimates passed.

The details of the new legislation cannot be given here.[12] The Alberta Social Credit Act set up elaborate administrative machinery for the implementation of social credit aims.[13] It was subsequently declared *ultra vires* of the province by the Supreme Court of Canada on the ground that it set up, in effect, a provincial banking system, and thus conflicted with the intent of Section 91 of the B.N.A. Act.[14]

Foiled in this attempt to set up a provincial credit system, the government enacted legislation during the fall of 1937 designed to regulate the chartered banks, to control the press, to study ways and means of implementing social credit, and to set up an "interim plan" to induce economic recovery in Alberta. The Credit of Alberta Regulations Act emphasized the dependence of the enjoyment of property and civil rights in the province upon "principles governing the monetization of credit" and provides for the licensing of banks and bank employees in the province.[15] The Bank Employees Civil Rights Act provided for the deprivation of civil rights of bankers who refused to become licensed under the previous act.[16] These two bills were disallowed by the Dominion government, along with The Judicature Amendment Act[17], which prohibited action or proceedings to question the constitutionality of any act of the provincial legislature without the permission of the government.[18] This action was taken after the Dominion Prime Minister, Mr. Mackenzie King, had requested the provincial premier to take no measures under the acts while they were referred to the Supreme Court of Canada.

A third session of the legislature was called to deal with disallowed legislation. The Bank Taxation Act was passed imposing additional taxes on banks.[19] First, banks doing business in the province were to pay one-half of one per cent on their paid-up capital, and secondly, they were to pay one percent on their reserve funds and undivided profits. The Credit of Alberta Regulation

Act was re-enacted after omitting all references to banks, bankers, and banking and substituting such terms as "credit institutions" and "the business of dealing in credit." The Accurate News and Information Act provided for the regulation of newspapers so that "the newspapers published in the province should furnish to the people of the province statements made by the authority of the government of the province as to the true and exact objects of the policy of the government and as to hindrances to or difficulties in achieving such objects, to the end that people may be informed with respect thereto."[20] This Act naturally created a great furore not only among the provincial pressmen, but also among those of the whole continent. All three bills were reserved by the Lieutenant Governor of the province for the signification of the pleasure of the Dominion government. The provincial government thus found that Section 92(13) of the B.N.A. Act[21] on which it had based the drafts of the legislation was a weak constitutional vessel.

One fragment remained. This was the Social Credit Board, set up by the Alberta Social Credit Act. According to Section 3 of the 1937 Act, this body was to consist of five members who were empowered to appoint social credit technical experts, to recommend social credit legislation, and to record and study economic conditions in the province. This body remained active after 1938 and made various proposals from time to time to "devise ways and means for the evaluation, conservation, enhancement, advancement and realisation of the social credit of the province."[22] The legislature appropriated $100,000 annually to support the activities of the board, beginning in 1938.

The main proposal of this board, which received legislative sanction, was the initiation of an "interim plan" which, it was asserted was to prepare the way for the implementation of social credit. The Treasury Branches Act was passed to authorize the provincial treasurer to establish "treasury branches" throughout the province.[23] These branches were empowered to receive deposits of currency and bank checks and to use the proceeds to purchase securities or to purchase goods for resale. Debts due to the provincial government could be paid by orders drawn upon treasury branch deposits. The provincial treasurer could also issue orders on the treasury's account with its branches to meet "any expenditure of the Province." All earnings of the branches were to be deposited in and to form a part of the general revenue fund of the government; expenditures were to be met out of legislative appropriations.

The ultimate objectives of the treasury branches were two. They were to "provide the people / with alternative facilities for gaining access to their credit resources" and to place at the disposal of the people "an institution under their own control so that they / could release themselves from the domination of the private money monopoly."[24] More immediately, the "interim program," through the institutions set up, was to give impetus to the recovery of the Alberta economy and to increase the purchasing power of consumers.

The drafters of the program envisioned a provincial system of bookkeeping, which it was hoped, would ultimately come to embrace all transactions in the province and provide a substitute for Dominion currency and commercial bank credit. Participation in the system by individuals and businesses was to be voluntary, and it was hoped that general use of the system could be promoted by the compulsory issue of bookkeeping credits to people dealing with the provincial government, by the overlapping effects of another medium of exchange, and by a scheme of bonuses and penalties (the latter to be applied to withdrawals of national money). Ultimately, by the inclusion of almost all transactions in the provincial economy, it was considered possible that "basic dividends" could be issued to Alberta citizens in the form of bookkeeping credits. [25]

The main device used initially to give the program a start was the "consumers' bonus." This bonus was in the form of a rebate to consumers who purchased Alberta goods through the Alberta credit system. It was to furnish an incentive to use the system and at the same time represented a kind of dividend.

The *modus operandi* of the system was based upon the transfer of claims from one account to another one in the books of the treasury branches when transactions were settled among individuals and firms. Individuals and firms wishing to participate in the system had to make an initial deposit of currency or claims on currency into a treasury branch account. These deposits were to constitute a reserve to meet demands for cash in transactions with individuals and firms, which did not have accounts with the branches. The instruments issued to make the internal transfers were called "non-negotiable transfer vouchers." To induce people to make use of the facilities of the branches, a bonus of up to 3 per cent of the sale was to be paid to purchasers of consumer goods by merchants if the purchaser used transfer vouchers. The bonus was to be paid in voucher credit, and not in cash; its size varied according to the proportion of Alberta-made goods included in the transaction; the maximum bonus of 3 per cent was to be paid when one-third of the goods were Alberta-made.

It is not possible to describe here, even briefly, the complexity of regulations governing the system, or to analyse its effects. [26] The operation of the system is a case study, which illustrates that the advantages of a uniform currency are all too often taken for granted, even in elementary money and banking classes. With the realization that the system was far from supplanting Dominion currency and bank credit and with the rapidity of economic recovery after 1939, most of the original social credit features of the program, including the consumers' bonus, were dropped by 1943. Instead, the treasury branches turned to a policy of performing banking services designed to compete with the chartered banks. In 1949, there were 108 branches with total deposits of more than $32 million.[27] Many of them perform a useful service in communities that lack commercial bank branches; this is perhaps their chief economic function today. Since the branches have failed to meet operating costs until recent years, the questions of subsidization of sparsely-populated (and hence uneconomic) areas and of overlapping bank services in areas where the chartered banks have established branches (presumably profitable territories) were prominent political issues during the early 1940s.

During the war there was a respite in new Social Credit legislation. The government played down social credit issues in the 1944 election and emphasized instead its support of a private enterprise economy. To meet the threat of the C.C.F. (Cooperative Commonwealth Federation), it attacked socialism vehemently. A new premier, Mr. Ernest C. Manning came to the helm. He was a less controversial figure than William Aberhart who died in 1943, and he was respected and trusted by people in all walks of life, including those in the business world. Nevertheless, there were still many social creditors, especially from the rural constituencies in which social credit doctrines still find the most ready support, who felt that a renewed attempt should be made to implement social credit measures. The demand for measures to curb the "financial interests" and to distribute dividends grew so strong that in 1946 the government gave in and passed The Alberta Bill of Rights.[28]

The effective part of the act consisted of two parts: the first outlined the rights and responsibilities of Alberta citizens, and the second outlined the administrative bodies to be set up and the functions and administrative techniques they would use to implement social credit measures. The details cannot be set out here.[29] One detail, however, may be mentioned: a section stated that the provisions of the Act were not to be put into effect until the courts had tested the validity of the act. It seemed as if the government expected the act to be declared *ultra vires*, as did the opposition parties, which maintained what was probably a studied indifference. The Alberta Supreme Court declared the part of the Act that authorized the setting up of administrative machinery to be *ultra vires*. The Judicial Committee upheld this decision in 1947. Since that time, the government has introduced no further direct Social Credit legislation; it has instead tended to emphasize to the electorate its willingness to stand or fall on the basis of its record as a provider of conventional government services and as an administrator of public funds.[30] But the premier has preached a sermon on the Social Credit solutions for the world's ills at the end of each budget speech since 1945. Thus the basic philosophy and doctrines of the party are given periodic expression.

THE PUBLIC DEBT DEFAULT, 1936–45

INTRODUCTION

The most controversial fiscal event of the period was the debt default of 1936.[31] It was followed by protracted negotiations and disputes between the government and the bondholders, culminating with a debt reorganization program in 1945.

The issue of refunding the provincial debt at lower interest rates was very much in the foreground in the provincial arena between 1933 and 1935, and has already been discussed. The burden of debt charges was a heavy one, and the decline of about 25 per cent in interest rates between 1932 and 1935 made the burden even less bearable. Much was made of the Australian and New Zealand "voluntary" refunding of their internally held government debts.[32] The exposition of social credit principles added fuel to the fire for, in essence, the social credit doctrine with respect to debt was that it was a device of "world plotters" to perpetuate the existing financial system. Social creditors argued that the existing financial system was inherently defective because of its failure to distribute to consumers sufficient purchasing power to enable them to buy the goods and services that the economy was capable of producing. Only the creation of debt, which made future income effective in the present, partially offset the deficiency in income received by consumers. But for this debt creation process, the financial system would have broken down long ago. The social credit remedy was to substitute the payment of "dividends" to consumers for the creation of debt so that the financial system could become truly "self-liquidating."

This doctrine, coupled with the existence of an almost empty treasury, does much to account for the two outstanding fiscal policies adopted in 1936: the debt default and the pay-as-you-go policy in provincial financing. Failure to pay one's debts is usually viewed as a sin of the first order. Balancing one's budget is usually considered a virtue of the same order. The provincial budget, however, could not have approached balance without the arbitrary reduction in interest rates that took place.

In December 1935, the new government appealed to the bond dealers for co-operation in dealing with its proposal to reduce the interest on the debt from

5 per cent (the average rate on the funded debt outstanding) to 2.75 per cent. The proposal got little response and nothing was accomplished.

THE LOAN COUNCIL PRINCIPLE

In the meantime, a Dominion-provincial conference was in progress in Ottawa, and one of the main items on the agenda was the financial position of the provinces, including the four western ones, whose credit had been maintained during the previous years by financial support from the Dominion. A continuing committee on financial questions was set up. This committee met in January 1936, to discuss methods of dealing with the seemingly chronic inability of the provinces concerned to stand on their own feet. The committee, consisting chiefly of the treasurers of the governments concerned, agreed unanimously that steps should be taken to initiate an amendment to the B.N.A. Act which would give the provinces the power to levy taxes on retail sales, enable the Dominion to guarantee debts of a province, and enable a province to pledge as security to the Dominion its Dominion subsidies. The principle of a loan council was accepted unanimously; such a council was to approve or disapprove of guarantees of provincial bonds made by the Dominion.[33] The provincial treasurer of Alberta, Mr. Charles Cockcroft, was Alberta's representative at the meeting of the continuing committee.

Mr. Magor, a financial expert from Montreal who had been retained by the Alberta government to assist in drafting the first budget and in advising it on fiscal policy, advised Premier Aberhart by telegram on January 11 to advise Ottawa that he (Aberhart) was ready to co-operate with respect to the loan council.[34] Magor argued that this step was preliminary to possible refunding and to a balanced budget and that it would strengthen the credit standing of the Alberta government. The premier did not act upon this advice. At about the same time, Major Douglas of London, the founder of the Social Credit theory and also an adviser retained by the government, transmitted a letter to Premier Aberhart in which he advised strongly against the acceptance of the loan council principle.[35] Evidently, in view of subsequent debt default, the government followed the advice of the originator of its formal political and economic doctrines rather than that of the "financier" who, strangely enough, had been retained by it. This course of action was natural enough.

MR. DUGGAN URGES AGREEMENT WITH THE DOMINION

There was much debate on the part of the opposition members in the legislature in February and March as to what the government was going to do to meet its debt obligations during 1936. The budget presented on March 2 provided for the full payment of interest, but the following remarks at the end of the budget speech presented by Charles Cockcroft foreshadowed the government's decision in April:

> In increasing taxation to the extent we propose, we are more firmly convinced that the refunding of our debenture debt must be accomplished. When it is realised that nearly 50 per cent of our total revenue is expended in debt charges, the greater portion of which is withdrawn from the Province, and from which our people receive no benefit, it becomes painfully clear that this crushing burden is rapidly draining the resources of our people. The progress of the province is being seriously impeded, and our people are unable to move forward into the realisation of the things which by common heritage should be theirs, until they are relieved of a substantial portion of the burden of these interest charges. When this is accomplished, we shall be able to balance our budget.
>
> It would seem evident, therefore, that this government will be compelled to call upon the bondholders to accept the lower rate of interest as already proposed to them some months ago.[36]

The Conservative leader in the legislature, D.M. Duggan, one of the ablest legislators the province has ever had, urged the government on March 5 to come to an agreement with the Dominion government in respect of the loan council.[37] He suggested that it was the only way out of the existing problem facing the provincial government. Further, he refused to take a pessimistic view of the long-run prospects of the provincial economy; he had hopes that the existing predicament was but a passing phase and that in time, the Alberta economy would revive and develop sufficiently to enable the government to meet its obligations. The passage of time has proved him to be right in his views. As to the debt-refunding scheme proposed by the government, Duggan suggested that it was presumptuous for one province to hope that bondholders would accept voluntarily a rate of 2.75 per cent when the average rate paid by the other provinces varied from 3.97 per cent (Quebec) to 5.18 per cent (Saskatchewan). In addition, there would be difficulties in securing the consent of bondholders in view of the widespread domicile of the debt, about one-third of it being held in Canada, and the balance chiefly in England and the United States.

Duggan's remarks went unheeded. Premier Aberhart, had he wished to accept the loan council principle (and this one does not know) could hardly have done so. First, a majority of the electors and legislative members desired to see the debt refunding scheme at reduced interest rates implemented; they had, by and large, little conception of all the implications of such a move, implications which the premier probably saw in the light of his few months of experience in office. Yet, the premier had already been embarrassed more than once by demands for the immediate implementation of social credit measures. Electors and legislators were in no mood to tolerate an agreement with the Dominion government, which might possibly make the implementation of social credit even more difficult. Secondly, Major Douglas had expressed opposition to the loan council principle. Third, and probably most important, some tangible relief was sought from the heavy burden of debt, and the refunding proposal seemed to be an obvious way of obtaining it. Such an attitude is not strange among people who have nothing to lose by suggested financial measures that provide short-run relief. And in the Alberta of 1936 there were thousands upon thousands of people who had "nothing to lose" in the short-run.

FINAL NEGOTIATIONS WITH THE DOMINION

Premier Aberhart continued to try to obtain a loan from the Dominion government without acceptance of the loan council principle. At the same time he expressed the intention of his government to effect compulsory conversion of part of Alberta's bonded indebtedness. On March 27 he wired Mr. C.A. Dunning, the Dominion Minister of Finance, expressing his unwillingness to accept the loan council principle and requesting financial assistance to meet the $3,200,000 debenture issue maturing on April 1.[38] Mr. Dunning replied as follows by wire on March 30:

> Your wire 27 has been considered by Government. You state that you cannot agree to accept Loan Council arrangement. Regret very much that your decision makes it impossible for the Dominion to assist you on April 1. Nor can Dominion Government agree to ask Parliament for authority to given Dominion guarantee to your proposed partial refunding programme under conditions outlined in your wires.[39]

Premier Aberhart sent a wire on the same day, crossing the one that Mr. Dunning sent, in which he proposed the following:

> Further to our wire 27th, if you assist us as requested to meet maturity we would agree to reimburse you to full amount from natural resources settlement as and when agreed upon. On this basis we would owe the Dominion less than any Western Province. If you accept our proposal we are confident refunding plan can be carried out.[40]

Mr. Dunning replied on March 30, the same day, as follows:

> Your wire 30th reached me in the House after my wire giving Government decision had been dispatched. Your suggestion that natural resources settlement amounting to five million dollars and interest should be offset against new loan was made to me in January by your Provincial Treasurer. I pointed out to him that as in the case of Saskatchewan the natural resources award would have to be offset against debts already owing by the provinces to the Dominion amounting in Alberta's case to twenty-four million seven hundred and forty-nine thousand dollars.[41]

This was the last communication pursuant to the issue dispatched by either party. Mr. Dunning made no formal statement to the House of Commons, but later told the press that he was chiefly concerned with preserving the credit of the Dominion and that there were no political considerations in the incident. He also emphasized that the Dominion government would continue to contribute its share to unemployment and agricultural relief in Alberta on the same basis as the contributions made to the other provinces.[42]

THE PROVINCE DEFAULTS

Premier Aberhart and his cabinet waited in vain for a last-minute reversal of the Dominion decision on March 31. Lacking sufficient immediate cash, the government cancelled the part of the issue held by the sinking fund ($354,000), and defaulted on the balance, an amount of $2,846,000. In addition, it paid only a portion of the interest charges.

The government followed up this action by passing The Provincial Loans Refunding Act, which provided for the compulsory refunding of provincial debt at lower rates.[43] The act was not to be operative, however, until proclaimed by the Lieutenant-Governor-in-Council. No action was ever taken under the terms of the act; necessary Dominion co-operation could not be obtained without provincial assent to the loan council principle. Instead, an order-in-council was passed on May 30, 1936, under The Treasury Act, which ordered the reduction of the rate of interest on all Alberta government bonds by one-half with a minimum of 2 per cent except on the Alberta and Great Waterways issue of $7,400,000 of 5 per cent bonds maturing on January 1, 1959 and callable in 1947.[44] The order-in-council was to take effect on June 1. The government emphasized that its action was forced upon it because of the depressed level of the incomes of Albertans, and that it was not to be regarded as a repudiation of the government's bonded debt.

NEGOTIATIONS WITH THE BONDHOLDERS

The Alberta Bondholders Protective Committee was formed in June 1936, including representatives of Canadian and American life insurance companies, certain cities in Western Canada, mortgage companies, and the United Church of Canada. Some bond dealers advised their clients not to accept the reduced interest payments in order to protect their legal rights. Representatives of the bondholders' committee met with the Alberta cabinet on June 11 and tried unsuccessfully to dissuade the government from continuing to follow its chosen course of action. The committee then engaged the services of J. Courtland Elliott and J.A. Walker, two financial authorities, and James C. Thompson, former provincial auditor of the Alberta government and head of a Montreal firm of chartered accountants at the time, to prepare a report on the economic condition of Alberta and the fiscal position of its government.[45]

These individuals completed a report in July 1936, within thirty days of being given their assignment, for consideration by the bondholders' committee. On October 2, 1936, representatives of the committee called upon Premier Aberhart at his office in the legislative buildings. The delegation read to the premier a summary of the report and then retired.[46] Premier Aberhart called a special cabinet meeting to consider the report, but no statement was made as to conclusions reached by the cabinet.

The gist of the report was that the government was quite able to meet its debt obligations. It asserted, among other things, that the income of Alberta citizens in 1934, the last year for which detailed data were available, was $90 million in excess of living costs. It also asserted that a budget adjustment could be made to enable the government to pay debt obligations in full. Funds for the

Default, Recovery and Prosperity, 1936–50

177

redemption of maturing securities, however, would have to be obtained from the Dominion government. The delegation asked that the whole question of default be submitted to an impartial commission in the event that the government refused to accept the findings of Elliott, Walker, and Thompson. The assertions made with respect to provincial income and government budget adjustments were not accepted by the government; they were also questioned by at least two economists who reviewed the report.[47] In any event, the income estimates made by Messrs. Elliott and Walker have proved to be altogether too high in the light of subsequent statistical data made available. These estimates constituted the weakest part of the bondholders' argument, while their suggested budget adjustments were quite sensible. But no matter how the budget items had been juggled, money would have to have been found somehow, presumably from the Dominion government, to finance maturing debt. And that involved the loan council principle which the Alberta government and much of the electorate opposed so stubbornly.

The Alberta government and its bondholders opened up and closed negotiations from time to time in attempts to secure a mutually satisfactory refunding plan. Negotiations in 1941 and 1942 broke down because of lack of agreement and compromise on fundamental points. The bondholders proposed a 4 per cent basic rate of interest; the government offered 3.5 per cent. The bondholders also requested recognition of all unpaid interest from June 1, 1936, and provision for differentials in coupon rates on all outstanding bonds to their maturities.[48] The government did not accept these principles in full, and there the matter stood until 1945.

FURTHER PUBLIC DEBT LEGISLATION

A special session of the legislature took place between August 25 and September 1, 1936. During this session The Provincial Securities Interest Act was passed,[49] ratifying and validating the order-in-council of May 30. The Municipal Securities Act was also passed providing for a maximum interest rate of 3 per cent on any municipal security.[50] The Independent Order of Foresters (IOOF) took action regarding Lethbridge Northern Irrigation District bonds, challenging the Provincial Securities Interest Act. The Supreme Court of Alberta declared the Act unconstitutional, and the Order was allowed a claim for full interest payments. It failed, however, to collect.

Some minor amendments were passed with respect to The Provincial Securities Interest Act in 1937. The Provincial Guaranteed Securities Proceedings Act was passed, prohibiting all actions and proceedings regarding interest rate reductions without the consent of the government.[51] The Provincial Guaranteed Securities Interest Act was passed to define the interest payable on the various securities guaranteed by the province.[52] The IOOF took action again to test the two new acts. The Alberta Supreme Court, in a judgement handed down on October 9, 1937, held The Provincial Guaranteed Securities Interest Act to be *ultra vires* and the Provincial Guaranteed Securities Proceedings Act to be invalid as it affected the case on which judgement was given. The court granted a writ of execution for the collection of interest from the irrigation district. The government appealed to the Appellate Division, which upheld the Supreme Court's decision, and in turn to the Judicial Committee, which also upheld the decision. Nevertheless, the Order failed to collect; it is not easy to seize irrigation ditches and dams or other works.

DOMINION–PROVINCIAL DEVELOPMENTS

In December, 1936, at a meeting of the National Finance Committee, attended by all Canadian provincial premiers except Mr. Hepburn of Ontario, several provinces, including Alberta, requested the Dominion government to appoint a Royal Commission to investigate the broad question of the economic and financial basis of confederation, including the system of Dominion and provincial taxation. A request was also made by the Prairie Provinces for an interim investigation of their financial conditions by the Bank of Canada. The Dominion government appointed the now famous Rowell-Sirois Commission to inquire into Dominion-provincial relations, and it delegated the Bank of Canada to make a study of the financial condition of the three Prairie Provinces.

The Bank of Canada issued its report in 1937. It recommended that Manitoba and Saskatchewan be paid annual fiscal need subsidies but that none be paid to Alberta because its government was securing budget balance by the arbitrary reduction in interest rates. It found that if Alberta had not defaulted, the condition of its treasury would have been somewhat better than that of Saskatchewan's and somewhat worse than that of Manitoba's. Presumably a fiscal need subsidy would have been recommended for Alberta also if debt default had not occurred.

While the Alberta government had been one of those, which had requested the Royal Commission on Dominion-provincial relations, it soon registered a strong protest against the selection of the personnel of the commission and against the terms of reference. The provincial government stated that the members of the commission were "bound by orthodoxy" and that the terms of reference were altogether too narrow. It refused to present a submission, and instead prepared a monograph entitled *The Case for Alberta*, which was distributed throughout the Dominion.

The Royal Commission reported in 1940; the recommendations were many and detailed. A significant one in this context was that with respect to national adjustment grants. On the basis of its computations, the commission recommended payment of such grants to six provinces while Alberta, British Columbia, and Ontario were left out in the cold. It was also the premiers of these provinces who opposed proceeding on the basis of the report at the Dominion-provincial conference in January 1941.

Both the Bank of Canada Report and the Sirois Report failed to make any special concessions to Alberta. The end result was further impairment of the already strained relations between Alberta and the Dominion.[53] A rapprochement between the two governments to settle the debt default question was accordingly out of the question in 1941.

THE PROVINCIAL DEBT REORGANIZATION PROPOSAL OF 1945

By 1945, the provincial government, embarrassed by the legal complications growing out of default on bond maturities and interest and by recurrent budget surpluses, became seriously concerned with securing a settlement. There were conferences with members of the bondholders' committee, with various financial executives and consultants, and with officials of the Dominion Treasury and the Bank of Canada. On March 9, 1945, Premier Manning outlined the government's conclusion with respect to the debt situation.

He emphasized that, with more than $34 million of bonds in default and disputed unpaid interest in excess of $25 million, the province was "faced with increasingly difficult legal complications" which would grow with the passage of time.[54] He indicated that the Dominion government was prepared to support a refunding arrangement and to assist the province financially in its implementation only if all the unpaid interest were recognized and paid together with differentials on all immature bonds. The Alberta government, he said, was not prepared "under any circumstances" to agree to such an arrangement. The province accordingly made its own proposal wherein the total amount of adjustable payments would be $8.4 million if all bonds were exchanged; this represented about one-third of the $25 million disputed unpaid interest. This was to be financed from the cash on hand accumulated through surpluses of previous years. In addition, the government proposed to provide at least $2 million per year for debt retirement by purchase or call of the new bonds issued, and it was hoped that a "satisfactory call feature" could be included to enable the province to refund at still lower rates at later dates.

One finds it difficult to consider the proposal as generous in the light of the government's expressed desire to be fair and equitable and its implicit desire to encourage public and private investment in Alberta during the post-war years to come. It was considered to be far from satisfactory by the Dominion government, which had already expressed its views to Premier Manning in a letter written by Dominion Finance Minister Ilsley and dated March 3, 1945. The senior government offered financial aid on condition that all unpaid interest be recognized. Mr. Ilsley said that this was necessary if parliament was to consider retroactive amendments proposed to the taxation agreement of 1942 between the Dominion and Alberta. He also declared that the Dominion government could not endorse a debt reorganization plan that did not observe the law and the constitution. The Finance Minister stipulated, too, that coupon rate differentials should be recognized in refunding. Finally, he proposed a full tax on any speculative profits in Alberta bonds after negotiations were undertaken. He showed that, if the province accepted the Dominion proposals, there would be little additional cost to the province. He concluded by pointing out the desirability of an equitable settlement to restore Alberta's credit standing and to maintain that of all the governments in Canada.[55] The Alberta government, after further negotiations with the Dominion government, swung over to Ilsley's proposal. A detailed plan was worked out and agreed to by the Alberta bondholders' committee; the plan was to become operative when at least 75 per cent of the outstanding debentures and registered stock was deposited with letters of acceptance by the individual holders, and when the sale of new debentures totalling $29,565,000 had been negotiated. By October 6, 1945, the required amount had been deposited, and on October 24 the program was declared operative.[56]

THE DEBT REORGANIZATION PROGRAM OF 1945

In his budget speech of March 4, 1946, Premier Manning reported that 95.28 per cent of the total had been deposited and the adjusting payments and the exchange of debentures involved were practically complete. Having worked out the details of the program with the Dominion government, they were presented by the premier as follows:

(1) Alberta debentures held in the sinking funds and the special investment fund, totalling $13,846,000, were cancelled, reducing

the gross debenture debt by that amount. This left a net total of $113,253,000 to be dealt with under the refunding plan. This procedure involved no change from the provincial proposal of the previous year.

(2) The adjustments on unpaid interest, together with the premium adjustments for immature bonds, required a cash settlement of $17,565,000 of which amount $9,388,000 was provided by the Dominion government under an amendment to the wartime tax transfer agreement and by a fiscal need subsidy. The retroactive amendment of the tax transfer agreement by the Dominion parliament enabled the province to substitute the debt option for the tax option provision of the agreement; the aggregate amount by which the former exceeded the latter for the period April 1, 1941, to March 31, 1945, was $6,988,000.[57] The fiscal need subsidy was computed to equal $600,000 per annum for each of the years 1937 to 1940 inclusive, thus aggregating $2,400,000. The Bank of Canada recommended the subsidy in 1937 in its report on the three Prairie Provinces (Alberta did not qualify for it at the time because she was not paying full interest on her bonds). The balance of $8,177,000 was to be paid by the province. This was over $200,000 less than the $8,400,000 adjustment payment under the original provincial proposal.

(3) A further sum of $10,827,000 for unpaid interest and premium adjustments was to be provided over the next five years without the payment of interest therein during the period. Special talons or coupons were attached to the new 3.5 per cent debentures equalling $10,827,000. Of this amount, the Dominion government was to provide $3,494,000 representing two increased annual payments under the amended tax transfer agreement already referred to. The provincial premier expressed the hope that new tax agreements with the Dominion would provide a substantially increased grant to the province, thus implying that such an increase would take care of the difference between $10,827,000 and $3,494,000. Thus the total unpaid interest adjustments aggregated $28,392,000 as against the $8,400,000 originally proposed by the province.

(4) The new program called for the retirement of the entire debt in 35 years at interest rates varying from 2 per cent to 3.5 per cent

and requiring an annual debt service charge of $5,841,000. Thus the debt service charge under the implemented proposal was $26,000 less per year for the first fifteen years under the original proposal, and it was $332,000 less per year for the last 20 years.

(5) To provide cash for the redemption of matured bonds in default, two new debenture issues were floated. An issue of $3,472,000 payable in Canada only, maturing in one to five years, and bearing interest at 2 to 2.5 per cent, was sold at $99.75 and accrued interest, or at a cost of approximately 2.20 per cent. Another issue of $26,093,000 serial bonds maturing in 1951 to 1960, carrying interest at 2.75 per cent, an average coupon rate of 3.09 per cent and payable optionally in Canada or the United States, was sold at $96.25 and accrued interest in United States dollars. This transaction, consummated in the United States, eliminated the necessity for paying on matured debentures payable in the United States the 10 per cent differential obtaining between American and Canadian dollars at the time. It enabled the province to await a more favourable exchange rate than that of 1945. The sale of these two issues at rates below 3.5 per cent accounts for the interest savings of the implemented plan *vis-à-vis* the original plan which had provided for the redemption of matured bonds in default over 33 years instead of the flotation of new bonds.

(6) Approximately $4,000,000 of cash and securities other than those of the province were released from the sinking fund of the province. This brought assets of the sinking fund down to almost nothing.

(7) All the new 3.5 per cent debentures, totalling $79,000,000 were callable at par at the option of the province in advance of maturity on any interest date on or after June 1, 1950. The new bonds, too, were not exempt from income taxes and succession duties imposed by the province; this was in contrast to the provisions under which most of the replaced bonds had been sold.

The transactions involved in the program are summarized in Table 6.7. The bondholders received all unpaid interest in full and defaulted bonds were redeemed. This statement, of course, does not apply to those who had sold their bonds before the debt reorganization program was implemented; they lost heavily by the Alberta default. The Dominion government, to prevent speculation in Alberta bonds during the negotiations, imposed a 100 per cent tax on the profits made from the bonds purchased between January 31, 1945, and August 7, 1945.[58]

The settlement was rendered possible by the pressure exerted by the Dominion government upon the provincial government and its willingness to interpret to the most liberal point the provisions of provincial subsidy and tax agreements, past and present. And when actual money savings became apparent to the provincial government by adopting the Dominion proposals, pressure was hardly needed to persuade the former to agree. The end result of the settlement was that the provincial government provided about $12 million more than it had paid at reduced interest rates from 1936 to 1945; it secured a reorganization of its debt at an average coupon rate of 3.40 per cent, the lowest of any province; it also became the first provincial government to serialize its indebtedness.

PROVINCIAL BUDGETS, 1936–51

The story of Alberta budgets between 1937 and 1951 is one of realized and growing annual surpluses. The first treasurer of the Social Credit government emphasized in the course of his budget speech of March 2, 1936, the desire of the government to balance the budget:

> The government has given careful consideration to expenditures, both on capital and income account. We have placed in income account the estimated expenditure for direct relief and other items formerly charged to capital, which should be met from revenue. The methods by which we hope to place this province on a sound financial basis we feel sure will appeal to all who understand the situation. Be that as it may, Mr. Speaker, we are firmly convinced we cannot continue to allow the debt of the province to increase as it has done in the past. If we do not take immediate action recovery may be impossible, and we would be remiss in our duty to the people of this province. Briefly, we must see to it that our expenditures are brought into balance with our receipts.[59]

The interpretation of the words "surplus," "deficit," and "balanced budget" was also meaningful in this instance. Previous provincial treasurers had had occasion to announce surpluses of various kinds while the government was

Table 6.7   Summary of Transactions under the Debt Reorganization Program,
Government of Alberta, April 1, 1945 to March 31, 1946

Sources of Funds
1. Dominion of Canada
    a) Fiscal need subsidy, 1937–38 to 1940–41   2,400
    b) Tax suspension agreement, excess of debt   6,988
       option over taxation for the years 1941–42
       to 1944–45
       April 1 to June 1, 1945   291   9,679

2. Reimbursements
    a) Interest and adjustments
       Alberta Government Telephones   3,646
       Alberta Wheat Pool   793
       Drainage districts   65
       Irrigation districts   1,256   5,759
       Less: Portion deferred,
       payable by special adjustment
       coupons on June 1, 1946 to 1950   3,007   2,752
    b) Expenses   8   2,760

3. Capital account
    a) Proceeds of new debentures   28,578
    b) Provincial sinking fund applied on debt   14,491
    c) Irrigation and drainage districts
       Guaranteed debentures surrendered in   3,790
       exchange for direct issues
       Sinking fund applied on advances   2,611
    d) Alberta Wheat Pool Loan
       Sinking fund applied   2,999
       Reimbursement   350
    e) Profit on redemption of stock issues   236
TOTAL   65,492

Uses of Funds
1. Interest adjustments on direct and guaranteed debentures   17,625
2. Debt reorganization expenses   272
3. Interest adjustments on savings certificates   950
4. Redemption of debt
    a) Matured debentures
       Redeemed for cash   32,340
       Cash provided for redemption in full   1,021
    b) Debentures and treasury bills   14,802

Table 6.7 (continued)

c) Province's share of drainage district debentures assumed under Chap. 51, 1925, and Chap. 75, 1931	213
d) Commuted rates funds repaid to the irrigation and drainage districts	25
5. Advances to irrigation and drainage districts	
a) Districts' funded debt surrendered in exchange for Province of Alberta debentures	6,255
b) Interest adjustment on funded debt	1,321
6. Advance to Alberta Government Telephones toward share of interest on funded debt	3,000
Total	77,824
Deficit, 1945–46	12,332

Source: *P.A., 1945–46*, Statements No. 29 and 1931.

increasing its debt at the same time; the new government definitely tied the concept of a balanced budget to changes in debt. Provincial treasurers adopted the practice of announcing surpluses (or deficits) in overall terms and tended to place less emphasis on end results on income account.

The financial results of budgets are set out in Table 6.8 in terms of, the accounting methods employed by the provincial accountants in preparing the public accounts, and in terms of budget speech estimates.[60] In every year of the fifteen-year period surveyed, the government had a surplus on income account, and there is a rapid growth in the size of these surpluses. It should be kept in mind here that direct relief expenditures are included in expenditures on income account in contrast to the procedure used before 1936. On an overall basis, the government had a surplus in every year except 1936–37; these surpluses also grew in size, though somewhat less rapidly, than those on income account.

Three main factors account for the appearance of surpluses on income account and on the overall basis after 1937. The first and most obvious was the reduction in the interest rate on the public debt and the cessation of sinking fund contributions.[61] The second factor was the rising level of revenue, but by and large, increasing revenues were the result of external factors. Table 6.9 sets out the absolute figures. The third factor was the adoption by the government of cautious expenditure policies. There was a determination to secure balanced budgets and even to "put something by." This philosophy is well exemplified in the pay-as-you-go policy that the government adopted early on.

The pay-as-you-go policy grew out of the antagonism against the debt burden, which became so onerous in the 1930s, and its adoption was given impetus by the social credit doctrine on debt. The purpose of the policy was not merely to balance the budget, but also to reduce the debt. Such reduction has been secured throughout most of the 1936–51 period. The policy has also found support among traditionalists who feel that the budget should be balanced annually, if possible. Large surpluses are hardly consistent with this train of thinking, but the surpluses that were achieved by the Alberta government have mainly come from fortuitous or extraordinary sources so that there can be little quarrel with the size of the surpluses even on logical grounds.[62] And after all, debt reductions are very respectable and venerable phenomena!

Judged on counter-cyclical grounds, the pay-as-you-go policy meant revenue rate increases and expenditure reductions during the late 1930s. These were hardly conducive to economic recovery. During the war period, the policy was attuned to the need for reducing expenditures, especially capital ones, in the national interest. During the post-war boom, the pay-as-you-go policy appears to be one that should be largely neutral in its influence upon the income stream of the economy. But the nature of the Alberta revenue structure makes any such generalization invalid. Such a large portion of Alberta's revenue during this period has been obtained without reducing the cash balances of Alberta residents that the net effect of provincial fiscal policy has been inflationary.

An interesting commentary on the care exercised with respect to expenditure estimates and the consistent tendency to underestimate the revenues can be made by examining Table 6.8. The record is one of which British fiscal officers, with their close estimates, would be contemptuous.[63] At the same time it is a record which would secretly please even the most meticulous chancellor of the exchequer, for few treasurers are disappointed if a surplus turns up when they expected a deficit. On an overall basis, there were twelve predictions of deficits made in budget speeches, and four predictions of modest surpluses (see the last column of Table 6.8). The overall figures for the eight years from 1937–38 to 1944–45 are somewhat peculiar, however, for they include what were called statutory payments which, in essence, were not expenditures: they consisted chiefly of repayments of unfunded debt. By excluding these payments, the overall estimates in the sixth column of the table are obtained; this yields consistency in the accounting procedure for the period. On this basis, these were still ten deficit predictions and six surplus ones. Actually, there were surpluses

Table 6.8   Actual and Estimated Surpluses and Deficits (–), Government of Alberta, April 1, 1936 to March 31, 1951 (in thousands of dollars)

Fiscal year ending March 31	Income account			Overall basis			Overall Budget Speech Estimate
	Actual	Estimated	Actual less Estimated	Actual	Estimated mated	Actual less Estimated	
1937	78	–266	344	–1,640	–2,549	909	–2,549
1938	2,768	1,966	802	1,083	–62	1,145	–1,228[a]
1939	3,027	950	2,077	1,366	–483	1,849	–1,568[a]
1940	2,488	1,198	1,290	5,917	5,311	606	–1,151[a]
1941	4,351	1,151	3,200	2,271	–503	2,774	–1,170[a]
1942	7,248	2,025	5,223	4,596	637	3,959	11[a]
1943	6,373	3,500	2,873	4,878	937	3,947	230[a]
1944	6,691	1,762	4,929	4,853	856	3,997	–292[a]
1945	5,886	1,829	4,057	3,375	–314	3,689	–839[a]
1946	11,647	800	10,847	10,311	–702	11,013	–702
1947	10,649	1,061	9,588	6,028	–3,658	9,686	–3,658
1948	17,189	11,447	5,742	6,740	–633	7,373	–633
1949	24,951	8,772	16,179	7,528	–6,307	13,835	–6,307
1950	46,544	13,247	33,297	29,838	–2,427	32,265	–2,427
1951	56,348	23,771	32,577	24,102	2,536	21,566	2,536
1952	n.a.	27,575	n.a.	n.a.	253	n.a.	

Sources: *P.A., 1936–51*, for actual figures, and Budget Speeches, 1936–51, for estimates. Telephone revenues and expenditures are not included; advances and repayments involving the telephone system do not enter into the accounts in some years.

(a) Includes certain statutory payments such as repayments of savings certificates. It is not entirely clear why these repayments were included in the expenditures for the purpose of arriving at overall surplus or deficit estimates between 1936 and 1944.

Table 6.9 Revenue and Expenditure of the Government of Alberta, 1936–1951 (in millions of dollars)

Fiscal Year Ending Mar. 31	Overall basis Including Telephones[a]			Overall Basis Excluding Telephones[a]			Income Account Excludes Telephones[b]		
	Revenue	Expend.	Surplus	Revenue	Expend.	Surplus	Revenue	Expend.	Surplus
1937	26.0	27.4	−1.4	23.6	25.5	−1.9	20.7	20.7	0.1
1938	29.0	27.8	1.2	26.6	25.9	0.7	24.1	21.4	2.8
1939	29.3	27.9	1.5	26.9	25.8	1.1	24.3	21.2	3.0
1940	35.0	28.9	6.1	32.4	26.7	5.7	24.4	21.9	2.5
1941	29.9	27.1	2.7	27.1	24.9	2.2	24.9	20.6	4.4
1942	32.4	26.9	5.5	29.5	24.9	4.6	27.2	20.0	7.2
1943	33.8	27.9	5.9	30.6	25.7	4.9	28.0	21.6	6.4
1944	36.1	29.7	6.4	32.3	27.5	4.9	29.8	23.1	6.7
1945	38.6	33.4	5.2	34.5	31.2	3.4	31.8	26.0	5.9
1946	60.3	59.8	0.5	54.6	54.2	0.4	40.9	29.3	11.6
1947	50.8	44.1	6.7	45.7	41.5	4.2	42.6	31.9	10.6
1948	79.2[c]	58.1	21.1	73.1[c]	54.2	18.9	57.2	40.0	17.2
1949	80.7	74.5	6.2	74.2	69.2	5.0	70.4	45.5	25.0
1950	111.7	84.2	27.5	104.4	77.1	27.3	99.6	53.0	46.5
1951	134.7	107.9	26.8	126.3	100.3	26.0	118.2	61.8	56.3

(a) See Appendix B for sources and classifications.
(b) *P.A., 1936–51*, Statement No. 18.
(c) Includes the natural resources award of $8.0 million and cancellation by the Dominion government of $5.3 million of borrowings for unemployment and agricultural relief. These transactions are listed under transactions relating to funded debt in *P.A., 1947–48*, 67, and are not included in the revenue statements of the same.

in every year except the first one, and the actual figures easily exceeded the estimated in every year.

The Social Credit government tended to have orthodox budgets despite its somewhat unorthodox ideology. Its first budget, that of 1936, was the only one to result in a deficit. Despite the introduction of a (short-lived) retail sales tax and various increases in tax rates, the government was unable to avoid the default, which has already been discussed at length. One of the unusual changes in revenue this fiscal year was the loss of $0.6 million when the licence year for motor vehicles was changed. Although this loss of funds was untimely, an extra $0.6 million could not have stopped the default. In 1937, another traditional budget focused on balancing the budget was presented and, as previously mentioned, this was more than many Social Credit members could stand. But the government weathered this bout of discontent among its own supporters, and thus a tradition of cautious, orthodox budgets was begun. A key feature of Social Credit budgets during the following years was a tendency to overestimate expenditures and underestimate revenues. The result was a series of pessimistic predictions and actual surpluses. Table 6.8 reveals the magnitudes.

During the war years the treasurer, Mr. Low, was reluctant to admit that the wartime prosperity of industrial Canada would make it to the agricultural west, and so revenues were unduly expected to be low. He also stated:

That non-essential expenditures should be deferred wherever possible in order that the full resources of Canada should be available for the prosecution of the war.[64]

This mode of thinking continued even when liquor profits showed a gain of $2 million above the estimates, a not surprising result in view of the allocation of large defence projects in Alberta and the Northwest Territories by the U.S. government. In 1945, Premier Manning assumed the treasury portfolio after Mr. Low left the cabinet to become the national leader of the Social Credit party. The 1945 budget speech was notable because it outlined the government's debt refunding proposal.[65] This budget was also the first extended reference to the basic philosophy and objectives of the government in a budget speech since it had attained power, with the exception of Premier Low's remarks in the 1938 speech. Yet the premier did not break with the tradition of making unwarrantedly gloomy budget predictions.

In the March 1947 budget speech, Mr. Manning announced the treasury bill settlement reached with the Dominion government, and the post-war tax agreements with the Dominion government. Although the Social Credit government had learned the lessons of the past well and had acquired the ability to stand off expenditure pressure, in the late 1940's there were substantial increases for education, social services, and in grants to the municipalities, the latter following from implementation of recommendations of the provincial Royal Commission on Taxation appointed in 1947 (the Judge Commission). 1950 was notable because the premier predicted a surplus for the first time in seven years, albeit a smaller one than actually occurred.

Several broad policies emerge as being rather consistently adhered to throughout the period: the desire to accumulate liquid funds in order to have a "cushion" in the event of a recession; the emphasis put upon debt reduction and savings in interest payments; the attempts to retard the growth in expenditure on income account; the accompanying tendency to underestimate the growth in revenue; the shrewd bargaining with the Dominion government; the increasing emphasis upon assistance to local governments; the intention to gear capital expenditures to the rate at which revenue from all development came into the treasury; and the intention to develop the public domain on an orderly, long-term basis. Various expenditure policies and administrative techniques of a more specific nature are, of course, also in evidence, but any lengthy consideration to these cannot be given in this treatise.

FISCAL POLICIES AND TRANSACTIONS, 1936–51

7

The previous chapter engaged in a discussion of the general economic and po-litical conditions of Alberta from 1936 to 1950. This chapter refines the ideas brought up in Chapter 6 with an examination of the specific fiscal develop-ments that occurred during this time period.

EXPENDITURE TRENDS

An examination of the total expenditure column in Table 7.1 reveals a remark-able stability of annual provincial expenditures until 1944–45. The reasons for this have been discussed. Increased appropriations for social expenditures and for the Post-War Reconstruction Fund led to a considerable rise in 1944–45. The large increase for 1945–46 is accounted for by the debt reorganization in-terest payments. If the latter are subtracted, the 1945–46 level would be about $34 million or a little higher than the 1944–45 level. Since that date there have been very large increases in expenditure in each year. Thus in 1950–51 the gov-ernment was spending more than three times as much as in 1944–45. Many of the recent increases have been pursuant to the 1948 Royal Commission on Taxation (the Judge Commission), which recommended various increases in provincial grants to the municipalities and in shared payments.[1] Nearly all of these recommendations have been implemented.

GENERAL GOVERNMENT

Expenditure on general government rose slowly until 1945, but has risen rapidly since then so that in real terms 1950–51 expenditures are somewhat less than two times the 1936–37 level.[2] Yet in relative terms administrative expenditure actually declined from 9.9 per cent of total expenditure in 1936–37 to 8.6 per cent in 1950–51.

Expenditure on legislation has continued to be very stable except for the rhythmic rise in election years (see Table 7.1). Notable changes were the 1938 closure of lieutenant-governor's residence (for only a very small savings), and

Table 7.1 Expenditures of the Government of Alberta, 1936–1951, According to Functions (in millions of dollars)

Fiscal year ending Mar. 31	General government				Social expenditure				Economic expenditure						Debt Interest	Other	Total
	Leg.	Admn.	Just.	Total	Educ.	P.H.	P.Wel.	Total	Agr.	P.D.	Hws.	Tel.	T.B.	Total			
1937	0.2	1.8	0.8	2.7	3.4	1.8	7.0	12.3	1.8	0.9	2.4	1.1	0.0	6.3	5.2	1.0	27.4
1938	0.2	1.9	0.8	2.9	2.9	2.1	7.5	12.6	1.4	0.8	2.8	1.2	0.0	6.2	4.6	1.6	27.8
1939	0.2	2.1	0.8	3.1	3.2	2.2	6.8	12.1	1.3	1.0	2.9	1.4	0.0	6.5	4.6	1.6	27.9
1940	0.4	2.2	0.8	3.3	3.6	2.3	6.4	12.2	0.9	0.9	3.3	1.5	0.4	7.1	4.5	1.8	28.9
1941	0.2	2.0	0.8	2.9	3.6	2.5	5.2	11.3	1.2	1.0	2.6	1.5	0.4	6.8	4.4	1.7	27.1
1942	0.2	2.1	0.8	3.1	3.7	2.6	4.1	10.4	1.6	1.1	2.8	1.3	0.3	7.1	4.4	1.8	26.9
1943	0.2	2.1	0.8	3.1	3.6	2.8	4.5	11.0	0.8	1.1	2.8	1.5	0.4	6.6	4.5	2.8	27.9
1944	0.2	2.5	0.8	3.4	3.9	2.8	4.9	11.5	0.9	1.2	3.0	1.5	0.7	7.4	4.5	2.9	29.7
1945	0.4	2.5	0.8	3.7	4.6	3.6	5.4	13.6	1.2	1.3	3.5	1.5	0.6	8.1	4.5	3.6	33.4
1946	0.2	2.6	0.8	3.6	5.4	3.6	5.6	14.6	1.1	6.4	3.5	1.9	0.8	13.6	24.4	3.6	59.8
1947	0.2	3.0	0.8	4.1	6.3	4.3	6.2	16.8	1.3	1.4	7.0	2.6	0.8	13.1	7.3	2.8	44.1
1948	0.2	3.6	1.0	4.8	8.8	6.1	7.7	22.6	1.3	1.9	13.0	3.9	0.9	20.9	6.4	3.4	58.1
1949	0.6	5.1	1.1	6.8	12.8	8.4	8.9	30.2	1.5	2.5	17.2	5.4	1.0	27.6	6.1	3.8	74.5
1950	0.3	5.0	1.3	6.6	13.0	11.8	11.8	36.7	1.5	3.7	16.9	7.1	1.1	30.3	6.4	4.2	84.2
1951	0.3	6.2	1.6	8.1	17.1	14.5	13.9	45.5	1.4	5.7	22.4	7.5	1.2	38.2	6.0	10.1	107.9

Source: Appendix B.
Abbrev.: T.B. under "economic expenditure" is "treasury branches."

two increases in sessional indemnities. Salary increase also played a role in the increase of general administration expenditure, for the 1931 civil service salary cuts were restored, and salary increases were required in 1946 to meet the increasingly competitive labour market. Other increases were due to the introduction and expansion of agencies, construction of new buildings, and the annual $100 000 appropriation for the Social Credit Board. Expenditures on justice administration rose after 1947 in response to an increased need for law enforcement, and due to salary increases.

SOCIAL EXPENDITURE

Social expenditure fluctuated during this period in response to a variety of factors. Falling unemployment relief expenditures were responsible for the decline until 1941–42. After that date, rising appropriations for old age pensions, public health services, and education grants were the main factors leading to increases. The government was extremely chary and careful with respect to expenditure on this category before 1944–45, with the exception of public health. Education bore the brunt of the government's economizing in the sphere of expenditures. After 1944–45 there were substantial increases for all three categories.

Education: Expenditure on education rose from $2.9 million in 1935–36 to $3.4 million in 1936–37 because of a queer twist of fate. In the critical year of 1936–37 the government had to advance to the University of Alberta $450,000 to enable the latter to meet a most ill-timed 6.5 per cent debenture issue, due on July 1, 1936. In addition, there was the usual $150,000 for interest payments on the university bonds assumed in 1924. After this stroke of bad luck, the government's expenditure on education fell to $2.9 million again in 1937–38.

Grants to schools rose slowly until 1941–42, and then fell again in 1942–43. At the same time, important curriculum changes were introduced, large administrative units were organized, and a teacher shortage developed. Thus while the education department was attempting to improve educational standards and organization, the treasury was hardly keeping pace, and the government was exposed to considerable criticism from educators and others. Since 1942–43 there have been substantial increases yearly in grants to schools. Partly in response to too much pressure on the government by various groups interested in education, appropriations increased rapidly after 1944, indicating the government's willingness and ability to make amends for the seven lean years (see Table 7.1).

The present grants system for schools was instituted during the 1940s; it replaced one that was a modification of the original system adopted before

World War I. Many grants, too, had been made on an *ad hoc* basis to meet the emergencies of the 1930s. The new system may be set out as follows:

(1) A basic grant of X dollars per room is paid, the value of X varying directly with the size of the annual legislative appropriation for school grants, and level of schooling. Special grants are paid where special instruction is given to subnormal, blind, and deaf children.

(2) An equalization grant is paid on the basis of a differentiated schedule of property assessment per room. Consolidated and village school districts receive somewhat smaller equalization grants, and cities and towns the smallest of all. The result of this differentiation has been to eliminate equalization grants to some towns and cities, while others receive up to 80 per cent of their total expenditures, this percentage being the maximum proposition the province contributes even if the various formulae produce a higher percentage.

(3) Grants are paid to assist school districts in financing transportation; these have become important because of the increase in the centralization of schools in rural areas.

(4) Additional grants are paid for the upkeep of dormitories, the provision of vocational instruction, equipment, night school, mission schools, emergencies, buildings, and isolation bonuses for teachers in remote areas.

The rural bias inherent in the system is evident from the following figures for 1949:

Provincial grants as per cent of revenue of school districts:

Urban school districts	13.0
Rural school districts	33.0
All districts	25.2

This bias is certainly a desirable enough feature because it ensures the provision of minimum educational service not much below the provincial average in areas with low fiscal capacity. But in view of the present pressures upon school facilities of cities some modification may be called for. The Judge Commission on Taxation recommended that most of the increased grants be distributed on a per pupil basis has not been implemented. Such a modification would have favoured the urban rather than the rural districts; indeed, this was the intent of the recommendation.

In 1950 the province began to make capital expenditure grants and loans in order to enable school districts to meet rapidly expanding building needs and to prevent the sale of school debentures at high rates of interest in the capital market. This sensible and practical measure was adopted; there is little point in the reduction of provincial debt carrying low interest rates if the local governments are being forced to borrow at rising interest rates.

Public Health: Public health expenditures have had high priority in provincial budgets for two decades. After 1935 there was a gradual increase in the provision of free health services, such as tuberculosis treatment, cancer treatment and prevention, distribution of vaccines and sera, social and mental hygiene, polio treatment and prevention, and maternity benefits. After the war there was a sharp increase in expenditure to a high of $14.5 million in 1950–51, or four times the 1945–46 level. Construction accounted for $4.1 million of this.

Two new outlays involved large sums. One was the introduction of free hospitalization for all maternity cases in the province, regardless of financial need.[3] The second was the inauguration of free medical treatment and hospitalization for old age and blind pensioners, and mothers' allowance recipients and their dependants.

Also of note is the new system of hospital grants. The province pays a *per diem* grant yearly to all hospitals in the province, including those operated by churches and charitable institutions. Considerable increases have been put into effect during recent years. Further, in 1949 special and construction grants were introduced; these account for the substantial increases in 1949 and 1950. Following the recommendations of the Judge Commission, the province also pays for the medical care of old age pension recipients, insane persons, and tuberculosis patients.[4]

Public Welfare: The fall in unemployment relief expenditure after 1937–38 was the main factor responsible for the general decline in public welfare expenditure. The decline in direct relief was, of course, a major factor in improving the condition of the treasury during the first ten years of the period.

The other major item under public welfare is the expenditure on old age pensions. However, it should be kept in mind that the Dominion government has financed an increasing proportion of the total along with a percentage contribution by the municipalities. After April 1, 1950, the province will relieve municipalities of their ten per cent contribution towards basic old age pensions and of the municipal share of hospitalization and medical care of old age pensioners.

Beginning on January 1, 1952, the Dominion government pays $40 per month to every Canadian aged 70 and over without a means test. The province has decided to continue to pay the $10 supplementary allowance plus medical and hospital benefits with a means test. A means test scheme has been set up with respect to persons between the ages of 65 and 70, financed by both levels of government. The provincial government has been keen to make extensions in this sphere of expenditures; its total benefits are the highest in Canada, with the exception of British Columbia, which has equivalent, but certainly no higher, benefits.

Other changes in the provincial share of public welfare costs are an increased portion of the Mother's Allowance and contributing 60 per cent of the cost of child welfare services and indigent relief, which were both formerly municipal responsibilities.[5]

ECONOMIC EXPENDITURE

Economic expenditures remained between $6 million and $7 million annually until 1945–46 when the province assumed direct liability for $4 million of irrigation and drainage district bonds. There has been a resurgence of this category during the post-war years with the inception of an ambitious highway program, telephone construction, and new irrigation projects.

Expenditure on agriculture fluctuated a great deal from year to year, but the general level has not risen since 1936 (see Table 7.1), and agricultural relief expenditure has fallen to practically nothing in recent years (see Appendix B).

Public domain expenditure increases were due to the irrigation and drainage district boards, and forest administration. More recently, capital expenditures on a Dominion-provincial irrigation project, on water supply projects, land settlement and land breaking, aerial photography and forest inventory have become important.

Highway expenditure rose rapidly after the war, but the government has still been hampered by difficulties in getting men and materials and by the weather in bad seasons. Grants to the municipalities for the construction of local market roads are included in the totals, and have recently become important items. Highway grants are conditional items paid on a percentage basis. Before 1951 the province paid 60 per cent of the cost of construction of secondary highways. The Judge Commission recommended that this percentage be increased, and in 1951 the province assumed 75 per cent of the cost. The province maintains such roads. The municipalities wholly finance construction and maintenance of district and local roads. Special agreements provide for provincial contributions to meet the cost of maintaining highways running through urban centres. The overwhelming share of the total annual appropriations are paid to the rural local units; thus urban centres are again largely left to their own devices in this respect. The Judge Commission also recommended that 25 per cent of the revenue derived from the gasoline tax and motor vehicle licenses be paid to municipal and improvement districts as grants for roads. In implementing this, the government did not confine itself to a specific percentage of revenue sources.

DEBT CHARGES

Debt charges need be given only brief mention here for they are discussed at length elsewhere. They remained almost constant until 1945–46 when an extraordinary sum was paid out to settle interest arrears. During the post-war period, they have been at a level exceeding the pre-1945 one by a considerable amount (see Table 7.1).

PROVINCIAL REVENUE DEVELOPMENT AND TRENDS

Changes in revenue components are set out in Table 7.2. As to totals, it is seen that revenue rose by about 50 per cent between 1936 and 1946, and then attained a level five times that of 1936–37 in 1950–51.

DOMINION OF CANADA REVENUE

Revenue from the Dominion of Canada was more than five times as large in 1950–51 as in 1936–37. Further, there were important transformations in the components of such revenue. Table 7.3 provides a summary.

Natural Resources Award: Alberta and Saskatchewan were initially granted the sum of $5 million each as a Natural Resources award. Neither province was happy with this, and subsequent agreements brought the amount to $8.0 million in the case of Alberta.[6]

The 1942 Tax Agreement: Under the pressure of wartime conditions, the Dominion government proposed to the provincial governments that they should suspend the imposition of income taxes and corporation taxes for the duration of the war and one year after, and be reimbursed by the Dominion on the basis of the 1940 revenues of the particular province from these sources, or the current amount of that province's net debt services less succession duty collections

Table 7.2 Revenues of the Government of Alberta, 1936–1951 (in millions of dollars)

Fiscal year ending March 31	1937	1938	1939	1940	1941	1942	1943	1944	1945	1946	1947	1948	1949	1950	1951
Dom. of Canada	5.0	5.9	5.8	5.1	4.7	4.0	7.4	7.7	8.3	21.9	10.6	32.5	20.7	24.2	27.9
Taxes	7.3	8.7	8.2	8.5	8.9	10.2	6.1	6.6	6.7	7.5	8.2	9.2	9.8	12.4	14.1
Licences and fees	2.2	3.1	3.4	3.7	3.9	4.2	4.3	4.6	4.6	4.9	5.5	6.3	6.9	8.0	8.9
Public domain	1.3	1.5	1.7	1.8	1.9	2.2	2.4	2.4	3.0	3.0	3.5	4.5	16.2	36.5	46.6
School lands	0.7	0.6	0.8	0.8	0.7	0.8	0.7	0.8	0.8	0.8	0.8	0.8	1.3	1.6	3.0
Liquor control	2.4	2.6	2.8	2.9	3.1	3.9	5.0	5.4	5.9	8.1	9.7	9.9	11.0	12.0	12.0
Fines	0.1	0.1	0.1	0.1	0.1	0.1	0.1	0.1	0.1	0.2	0.2	0.2	0.2	0.3	0.3
Sales	0.5	0.5	0.5	0.5	0.6	0.6	0.7	0.8	1.0	1.5	1.7	2.1	2.4	2.4	2.8
Refunds	1.0	1.1	0.8	0.9	0.9	0.9	1.1	1.1	1.0	1.0	1.3	1.1	1.2	1.2	1.4
Interest	1.6	1.3	1.3	1.3	1.1	1.2	1.2	1.2	1.2	4.6	1.7	2.1	1.6	2.0	5.4
Repayments	2.3	2.2	2.3	7.6	1.9	2.0	2.2	2.2	2.6	3.2	3.6	5.4	3.7	4.8	4.9
Miscellaneous	–	–	0.1	0.1	0.1	0.1	0.1	0.1	0.1	0.1	0.1	0.1	0.1	0.1	0.1
Telephones	1.6	1.7	1.8	1.9	2.0	2.2	2.5	3.1	3.5	3.6	4.0	4.6	5.4	6.3	7.4
Total	26.0	29.0	29.3	35.0	29.9	32.4	33.8	36.1	38.6	60.3	50.8	79.2	80.7	111.7	134.7

Source: Appendix B.

in 1940.[7] The former basis was known as the "tax option" and the latter as the "debt option." In view of the reduced interest payments of the Alberta government, it chose to accept payments under the tax option.[8] In addition, the Dominion government offered to guarantee provincial gasoline tax revenues at the 1940 level because of its intention to ration gasoline.

Retroactive 1942 Agreement: When the provincial government adopted the debt reorganization program and provided for payments of deficiencies of interest arising from the 50 per cent reduction in 1936, the Dominion government agreed to permit Alberta to adopt the debt option retroactively, and payments were adjusted

The Retroactive Fiscal Need Subsidy: This is the aforementioned subsidy (see *ante*. VII, 20) in which the Bank of Canada left Alberta out as a result of the debt default. Alberta eventually received its share in connection with the debt reorganization program.

The 1947 Tax Agreement: This arose out of the dominion-provincial conferences of 1945 regarding intergovernmental fiscal relations. After some bargaining, the provinces were given the choice of the following formulae for determining their guaranteed annual payments: (1) a combination of $12.75 per capita of the 1942 population, plus 50 per cent of provincial income and corporation tax receipts in 1940, plus the statutory subsidies; or (2) $15.00 per capita of the 1942 population plus the statutory subsidies. Prince Edward Island was given an irreducible minimum of $2.1 million. Upward revisions in amounts were to depend upon increases in provincial population over 1942 and upon increase in the gross national product of Canada.

Alberta chose the first formula under which the irreducible minimum amounted to $14,277,000 and on this basis a five-year tax rental agreement was arrived at. The province suspended the acts under which it collected personal income taxes, corporation taxes, and succession duties until March 31, 1952, the end of the term of agreement. The provincial premier emphasized that the agreement was transitional on the grounds that it represented no solution of Dominion-provincial relations. He said:

> The proposed agreements do nothing more than provide for a
> redistribution of certain tax revenues under a formula which is nei-
> ther scientific or related in any way to the actual financial needs of
> the respective provinces measured in terms of human needs and the
> potential physical resources available to meet those needs. It leaves
> unsettled the whole question of constitutional reforms which are
> necessary in the light of modern circumstances and does nothing

> to clarify the ambiguity that exists as to the lines of demarcation
> between Dominion and provincial jurisdiction and responsibil-
> ity. The agreements will centralise in Ottawa control over the rates
> imposed in two of the major fields of taxation, namely; personal
> income tax and corporation tax...Furthermore, it should be borne
> in mind that the formulae approved by the Dominion government,
> and the procedure followed thus far in the endeavour to obtain
> agreements based on those formulae, has not been successful on a
> Dominion-wide scale.[9]

Incorporated in the agreement was the reintroduction of a provincial corporation income tax. This was to equal 5 per cent on net corporate income within
the province to be collected by the Dominion government as agent for the province. The proceeds from this tax would be deducted from the annual subsidy.

Because of increasing provincial population and increasing amounts under
the 1947 agreements (see Table 7.3), in 1950–51 the total amounted to $19.4
million of which the old subsidies equalled $2.1 million.

Public Health Grants: The only pre-war grant-in-aid under this category was a contribution toward the maintenance charges for Indian patients in
provincial tuberculosis wards. With the inception of the National Health Grant
Program of the Dominion government in May 1948, more than $30 million
was available annually for grants to the provinces.[10]

The program consists of three parts. First, there is a one-time survey grant
to assist the provinces in assessing their needs and the priority with which they
should be met. Second is a group of eight annual grants designed to assist in the
extension and development of provincial health services in these areas: general
public health, tuberculosis control, mental health, venereal disease control, crippled children, professional training, public health research, and cancer control.
The third part of this program is a hospital construction grant. All the grants,
except those for health survey and cancer control, are conditional upon the
provinces maintaining their own funds, and at least the pre-existing standard
of service in the field of each grant. The total amounts received by Alberta are
indicated in Table 7.3; the province has received grants from nearly all the
sources established by the Dominion government.

Education: During the war years the provinces each received a grant
under the Dominion youth training program designed to provide general and
specialized courses for rural young people in agriculture, rural home craft and
handicrafts and other related subjects, and for post-secondary training in selected subjects. Under the Canadian Vocational Training Program set up by

Table 7.3   Revenue Received from the Dominion of Canada by the Province of Alberta, 1936–37, 1940–41, and 1944–51 (in millions of dollars)

Fiscal year ending March 31	1937	1941	1945	1946	1947	1948	1949	1950	1951
SUBSIDIES AND RENTALS:									
Statutory subsidies	1.8	1.8	1.9	1.8	1.8	2.2	2.0	2.1	2.1
Natural resources award	0.0	0.0	0.0	0.0	0.0	8.0	0.0	0.0	0.0
1942 Tax Agreement	0.0	0.0	3.7	6.1	4.1	3.3	0.0	0.0	0.0
Retroactive 1942 agreement	0.0	0.0	0.0	8.7	1.7	0.0	0.0	0.0	0.0
Retroac. fiscal need subsidy	0.0	0.0	0.0	2.4	0.0	0.0	0.0	0.0	0.0
1947 Tax Agreement	0.0	0.0	0.0	0.0	0.0	9.9	14.0	15.3	17.3
Subtotal	1.8	1.8	5.6	19.1	7.6	23.4	16.0	17.4	19.4
GRANTS-IN-AID AND SUBVENTIONS:									
Agriculture	–	–	0.2	0.1	0.1	–	–	–	–
Public health	0.0	–	0.1	0.1	0.1	–	0.1	1.3	1.6
Public welfare:									
Unemployment relief	1.5	0.9	0.0	0.0	0.0	5.3	0.0	0.0	0.0
Old age pensions	1.4	1.8	2.4	2.5	2.7	3.3	3.9	4.9	5.9
Other	–	–	0.0	0.0	0.0	0.0	–	–	–
Education	0.0	0.0	–	–	0.1	0.4	0.5	0.5	0.6
Public works	0.4	0.2	0.0	–	–	0.0	0.1	–	0.3
Subtotal	3.2	3.0	2.7	2.8	3.0	9.0	4.7	6.8	8.5
Grand Total	5.0	4.7	8.3	21.9	10.6	32.5	20.7	24.2	27.9

Source: See Appendix B.

the Dominion government after the war, the youth training program was continued, and additional programs initiated.[11] In 1945 a ten-year agreement for vocational school assistance was signed with the nine provinces, Newfoundland making an agreement when it entered confederation.

Public Works: The Dominion contributions toward public works were chiefly for relief projects such as tourist roads, the Trans-Canada highway, and mining area roads. These payments stopped during the war, but a variety of contributions were again received after 1945. Agreements have been reached with respect to Forestry Conservation, the Trans-Canada highway,[12] and the St. Mary's Irrigation Project.

Other Grants: There were also a number of smaller grants from the Dominion to the province. Except for the 1944–45 and 1945–46 wool bonuses, agricultural grants were negligible, and were entirely discontinued after the war. Statutory subsidies decreased in both amount and importance to the point that they are now considered historical relics. Dominion grants for unemployment relief and blind pensions have declined. Except for a small grant for assistance to internees and evacuees, the old age pension contribution is now the only public welfare grant received from the Dominion.

Summary: The above outline of Dominion-provincial arrangements indicates that the Dominion contributions to the provincial treasury are growing both in terms of dollars and in number. The new tax agreement will provide for a substantial increase in the irreducible minimum of the tax rental payments since the Dominion proposed a 1948 basis instead of 1942 during the Dominion-provincial conference of December 1950. Increases in gross national product at factor cost and provincial population would augment the annual payments. The public health grants are increasing annually, but are subject to a reduction in the hospital grant after 1953. The old age pension payments under the new scheme will swell provincial expenditures by an as yet unknown sum; the provincial government will, however, pay a smaller proportion of the total cost than before. The education grants-in-aid show an upward trend and finally, highway and other public works grants are just beginning to be received. In general, then, Dominion payments show signs of becoming the largest revenue source of the province as well as the one least likely to fall off to any significant degree.[13]

TAXES

The details of the tax trends are shown in Table 7.4. The first notable point is the $2 million increase in tax revenue in 1936–37 over 1935–36; this was chiefly the result of increased rates and the imposition of a sales tax. Secondly,

Table 7.4   Tax Revenues of the Province of Alberta, 1936–1951
(in thousands of dollars)

Fiscal year ending Mar. 31	Real Property	Corporation non-income	Amusement	Income	Succession duties	Gasoline	Retail sales	Total
1936	1,001	1,090	158	683	271	2,221	0	5,422
1937	1,238	1,125	158	1,065	343	2,455	947	7,331
1938	1,233	1,532	164	1,190	1,326	2,610	601	8,657
1939	1,487	1,644	185	1,467	372	2,953	68	8,175
1940	1,339	1,666	204	1,795	375	3,097	1	8,477
1941	1,249	1,614	208	2,205	415	3,222	–	8,914
1942	1,359	1,518	219	2,241	673	4,212	–	10,221
1943	1,420	6	254	426	459	3,526	–	6,092
1944	1,596	2	317	318	686	3,646	0	6,566
1945	1,397	1	368	240	903	3,808	0	6,718
1946	1,437	1	405	20	1,130	4,463	0	7,455
1947	1,493	2	434	29	855	5,404	0	8,218
1948	417	–	466	3	652	7,658	0	9,197
1949	462	–	554	14	149	8,578	0	9,757
1950	788	–	774	432	98	10,365	0	12,457
1951	758	2	835	773	101	11,609	0	14,078

Source: *P.A., 1936–51.*

there was a marked increase in 1940–41 and 1941–42 as provincial income began to rise above depression levels. Third, there is a decline following the tax agreements and then subsequent annual increases to new high levels in collections in 1949–50 and 1950–51. Fourth, the present overwhelming importance of the gasoline tax is apparent.

There have been a variety of real property taxes, but after trying out a social service tax, a supplementary revenue tax, an educational tax, and the Wild Lands Tax and having found them all inadequate, the only property tax of consequence now is the unearned increment tax, although it previously yielded very small amounts. The Corporation Non-Income Taxes rose in accordance with the expansion of business until 1942, after which they ceased to be levied in accordance with the Dominion tax agreement of that year. Amusement taxes were levied on entrance charges and pari-mutuel betting, and they proved to be quite income-elastic. Income Taxes included those levied upon both persons and corporations,[14] but were suspended after the 1942 Tax Agreement; the collection figures for subsequent years indicate realized arrears. In 1949–50 the province began to receive half of the utility corporation income taxes collected by the Dominion government. An interesting note in the history of succession duties is that in 1937 Alberta cancelled its reciprocal agreements with other provinces and collected an abnormally high amount in 1937–38 before the other provinces retaliated. Succession duties ceased to be levied after the signing of the 1947 tax agreement; figures for subsequent years indicate collections from estates levied before 1947. The Gasoline Tax is now by far the most important tax revenue. The Retail Sales Tax was a 3 per cent tax on ultimate purchases first imposed in 1936. Continuous protests by various groups and administrative difficulties influenced the government sufficiently to lead to the suspension of the tax in August 1937. It could have become a large revenue producer in time.

LICENCES AND FEES

Revenue from licences and fees increased during the fifteen years approximately at the same rate as provincial income (see Table 7.2). Motor vehicle licences contributed the bulk of the revenue in this category (over 70 per cent in 1950–51).

PUBLIC DOMAIN

The dramatic change in both the size and composition of revenue received from the Dominion government has been almost completely over-shadowed by the phenomenal rise in public domain revenue. But whereas Dominion revenue is likely to remain at constant levels, the public domain levels of recent years are not likely to be maintained.

The chief levy on petroleum is an *ad valorem* royalty on the gross output of oil wells on Crown lands. At present the rates vary from 5 per cent on a monthly production of 600 barrels or less to 16 per cent on 4.050 barrels or more. The natural gas royalty is 15 per cent of the value of output with a minimum of 75 cents per thousand cubic feet. Following the Turner valley discoveries of 1936 and until recent years, royalties provided more than half of total petroleum and natural gas revenue annually. But there has been a relative decline due to the sudden emergence of other revenues from the same source (see Table 7.5).

The most important addition to oil and gas revenue during the 1948–51 period was that collected from the sale of petroleum and natural gas leases. When a new producing field has been proven, the discoverer is required to return

Table 7.5 Public Domain Revenues of the Government of Alberta for Selected Years (in thousands of dollars)

Fiscal year ending March 31	1937	1942	1947	1951
Petroleum and natural gas	456	760	809	41,915
Coal	291	298	394	757
Other mining	9	91	400	834
Forests	340	733	1,260	2,215
Grazing	74	120	215	338
Land	30	20	52	125
Furs	61	78	106	103
Fish	23	22	66	76
Game	56	75	154	213
Hay	3	4	6	10
Total	1,342	2,200	3,462	46,586
Petroleum and natural gas:				
Royalties	108	571	536	4,761
Fees and rentals	348	189	273	9,035
Leases	0	0	0	28,008
Miscellaneous	0	0	0	112

Source: *P.A., 1936–51.*

approximately one-half of the area he leased originally from the province.[15] The government then subdivides the tract, which is laid out in checkerboard fashion, and calls for competitive tenders for the right to work the properties. In addition, the royalties on production on the properties are still payable. Revenue from the sale of leases, however, is unstable; there are indications that it may fall in 1951–52 unless a large new productive field is discovered before the end of the fiscal year. Eventually it will fall to almost nothing; that time has not yet arrived for the area to be explored in Alberta is large.

Another lucrative but unstable revenue is that derived from rentals and fees paid to acquire the petroleum and natural gas rights of a property.[16] In addition, petroleum and natural gas rights may be reserved by applicants who wish to conduct geological and geophysical examinations of tracts of land, for which privilege there is a scale of fees on an acreage basis.[17] These rentals and fees have risen to prominence as revenue-producers since 1947, and in 1950–51 they provided twice as much revenue as royalties. Practically the entire province, except the northeast, is now subject to search for petroleum and natural gas by hundreds of geophysical and geological crews. Consequently, annual increases in rentals are not apt to rise greatly in the future; indeed, the present level may not be maintained for very many years.

Revenue from petroleum and natural gas may have reached its peak in 1950–51, and once new discoveries become less frequent, total revenue from this source will fall considerably below the 1950–51 level. The revenue from the sale of leases will then fall off greatly; fees and rentals will fall off considerably as geophysical and geological search is discontinued. Revenue from royalties, however, will rise through the years with production increases from more and more wells.[18]

Revenue has also been collected from royalties, fees and rentals on coal and other minerals (especially under the 1937 Mineral Taxation Act which taxed owners of mineral lands), as well as from timber leases and severance dues in Forestry. See Table 7.5 for the magnitudes.

OTHER REVENUES

An examination of Table 7.2 reveals the magnitude of other revenues. Since 1948–49, school lands have provided increasing royalties on production of petroleum and natural gas, and increasing revenue in terms of fees, rentals, and the sale of leases. Revenue from liquor control continues to be lucrative, although its relative importance has declined in face of the public domain bonanza. Fines are of little significance as revenue producers although there has been a steady upward trend since 1935. Revenue from the sale of commodities and services has increased materially because of the inclusion of the gross revenue of the treasury branches in this category. Refunds of expenditure have not responded to income increases in an upward direction to any significant degree; the nature of several items in this category is such that there are eventually declines after a period of a high-sustained level of provincial income. Revenue from interest, premium, and discount increased materially after the debt reorganization program of 1945.

Repayments have raised steadily from year to year, the only "hump" of any consequence being the $5.6 million collected in 1939–40 as the last railway sale instalment. Repayments by government agencies of advances made to them have formed the bulk of total revenue in the category. Lethbridge Northern payments have also become significantly larger since the late 1930s. Telephones will be discussed more thoroughly later in this chapter,[19] but it should be noted that the figures in Table 7.2 are exclusive of interest paid on telephone debentures.

SOURCES AND USES OF FUNDS, 1936–51

A statement of receipts and payments gives the most comprehensive picture of the financial transactions of the government. Such a statement is provided in Table 7.6. The bulk of receipts came from revenue, and the most important payments were expenditures. These two items have been given a detailed examination immediately above.

There are also a number of other sources and uses of funds in this period. With the exception of one large, annually renewed bank loan in anticipation of the final railway instalment and a few small loans in 1937 and 1938, the practice of borrowing from banks was discontinued entirely after 1936. Hence, temporary loans play a negligible role. Of more importance were Treasury Bills to the Dominion government before 1938, and to the Imperial bank in the 1947 fiscal year. Repayments to the bank are complete, and repayments to the Dominion are scheduled to be complete in 1977.[20] In terms of debentures, the province realized no proceeds until the debt reorganization of 1945. Small payments had been made for previously issued stock, but after 1945 there were large proceeds and repayments. The debt reorganization also led to the almost complete liquidation of the sinking fund, to which the government had stopped contributing in 1936. The Special Investment Fund to which the government made positive contributions in almost every year after 1940 took its place. There were also some transfers to and from the telephones and the superannuation fund.

In addition to these relatively mundane issues, there were two that deserve closer perusal: the savings certificates and the prosperity certificates. Also of note are some of the provincial-municipal arrangements for the use of funds.

SAVINGS CERTIFICATES

Savings certificates had been a considerable source of embarrassment for a number of years because the presentation of demand certificates in any volume could easily have depleted treasury cash at critical times. Since their introduction in 1932, there had been considerable fluctuation in the balance of deposits and withdrawals. Finally, the volume of withdrawals became so heavy in 1935 that the treasury was on the verge of being stripped of all its cash, and on August 27 immediate payment of savings certificates was suspended. In a sense, this was the first of the steps that led to default on debentures on April 1, 1936.

The government adopted a policy of retiring savings certificates on an "orderly" basis; holders had to await their turn as funds were made available, but there were no announcements of the order of priority. Interest rates on the certificates were also reduced by 50 per cent in 1936, and interest arrears

Table 7.6 Sources and Uses of Funds of the Government of Alberta, April 1, 1936 to March 31, 1951 (in millions of dollars)

Fiscal year ending Mar. 31	Revenue or expenditure	Temp. Loans	Temp. bills	Treasury certificates	Savings	Prosperity certificates	Deben-tures	Sinking fund	Invest-ment Fund
Receipts:									
1937	23.6	0.0	1.6	0.4	0.4	0.0	0.1	0.8	0.4
1938	26.6	0.1	0.3	0.2	–	0.0	0.4	0.1	0.8
1939	26.9	0.4	0.0	0.2	–	0.0	0.4	0.2	0.6
1940	32.4	0.0	0.0	0.1	–	0.0	0.2	1.6	0.6
1941	27.1	0.0	0.0	0.1	0.0	0.0	0.0	1.0	0.5
1942	29.5	0.0	0.0	0.1	–	0.0	0.0	0.5	0.3
1943	30.6	0.0	0.0	0.1	–	0.0	0.0	0.8	0.3
1944	32.3	0.0	0.0	0.1	–	0.0	0.0	1.2	0.3
1945	34.5	0.0	0.0	0.1	–	0.0	0.0	0.8	0.6
1946	54.6	0.0	0.0	0.1	–	32.4	20.1	1.4	3.0
1947	45.7	0.0	0.0	0.1	–	–	0.0	3.9	2.5
1948	73.1	0.0	2.5	0.1	–	2.5	1.1	1.3	2.4
1949	74.2	0.0	0.0	0.1	–	–	0.0	0.6	4.3
1950	104.4	0.0	0.0	0.1	–	59.7	0.0	1.4	3.0
1951	126.3	0.0	0.0	0.2	–	59.7	0.0	20.9	3.0
Payments:									
1937	25.5	0.0	0.2	1.5	0.3	0.1	0.1	0.1	0.5
1938	25.9	0.0	–	1.3	–	0.0	0.0	0.1	0.7
1939	25.8	0.5	0.0	1.1	–	–	0.0	0.3	0.5
1940	26.7	5.7	–	0.8	–	–	0.0	1.5	0.2
1941	24.9	0.0	–	0.7	–	–	0.0	0.8	0.5
1942	24.9	0.0	–	0.6	–	0.0	0.0	0.9	0.2
1943	25.7	0.0	0.1	0.5	–	–	0.0	3.0	0.1
1944	27.5	0.0	0.1	0.5	0.0	0.1	0.0	2.0	–
1945	31.2	0.0	–	0.5	0.0	–	0.0	1.1	0.3
1946	57.9	0.0	–	2.1	0.0	48.4	0.0	5.0	4.8
1947	41.5	0.0	–	0.2	0.0	1.8	0.0	1.0	–
1948	54.2	0.0	15.8	0.1	0.0	7.1	0.0	1.7	–
1949	69.2	0.0	0.3	0.1	0.0	0.3	0.0	6.5	–
1950	77.1	0.0	0.4	0.1	0.0	61.1	0.0	23.7	0.7
1951	100.3	0.0	0.4	0.6	0.0	79.9	0.0	43.1	1.7

Table 7.6   (continued)

Fiscal year ending Mar. 31	Revenue or expenditure	Temp. Loans	Temp. bills	Treasury certificates	Savings	Prosperity certificates	Deben- tures	Sinking fund	Invest- ment Fund
Net proceeds:									
1937	−1.9	0.0	1.5	−1.1	–	−0.1	–	0.7	−0.1
1938	0.7	0.1	0.3	−1.1	–	0.0	0.4	–	0.1
1939	1.1	−0.1	0.0	−0.9	–	–	0.4	−0.1	0.1
1940	5.7	−5.7	–	−0.7	–	–	0.2	–	0.4
1941	2.2	0.0	–	−0.6	–	–	0.0	0.2	–
1942	4.6	0.0	–	−0.5	–	0.0	0.0	−0.3	0.1
1943	4.9	0.0	−0.1	−0.4	–	–	0.0	−2.2	0.2
1944	4.9	0.0	−0.1	−0.4	–	−0.1	0.0	−0.8	0.3
1945	3.4	0.0	–	−0.4	–	–	−0.0	−0.3	0.3
1946	−3.3	0.0	–	−2.0	–	−16.0	20.0	−3.6	−5.5
1947	4.2	0.0	–	−0.1	–	−1.8	0.0	2.9	2.5
1948	18.8	0.0	−13.3	–	–	−4.6	0.1	−0.4	2.4
1949	5.0	0.0	−0.3	–	–	−0.3	0.0	−5.9	4.3
1950	27.3	0.0	−0.4	–	–	−1.4	0.0	−22.3	2.3
1951	26.0	0.0	−0.4	−0.4	–	−20.2	0.0	−22.2	0.6

Fiscal Year Mar. 31	Total Receipts	Total Payments	Cash Surplus or Deficit (−)	Cash Balance at end of year
1937	27.3	28.3	−1.0	0.1
1938	28.5	28.0	0.5	0.7
1939	28.7	28.2	0.5	1.2
1940	34.9	34.9	–	1.2
1941	28.7	26.9	1.8	3.0
1942	30.4	26.6	3.8	6.8
1943	31.8	29.4	2.4	9.4
1944	33.9	30.1	3.8	13.0
1945	36.0	33.1	2.9	15.8
1946	111.6	118.2	−6.6	9.3
1947	52.2	44.5	7.6	16.9
1948	82.0	78.9	3.1	20.1
1949	78.1	75.3	2.8	22.8
1950	186.6	163.1	5.5	28.4
1951	210.1	226.0	−15.9	12.5

Source: See Appendix B.

amounting to nearly $1 million were paid to existing holders of certificates in 1945. In the ensuing years, saving certificates indebtedness was reduced (see Table 7.6), and on March 31, 1951, only $653,000 was outstanding in the form of savings certificates.

PROSPERITY CERTIFICATES

An interesting and short-lived experiment, which received much attention and study, was the issue of "prosperity" certificates. Since it represented an attempt to meet treasury expenditures and since it was not a Social Credit but a Gesellian[21] measure, it is discussed at this point rather than in connection with Social Credit legislation.[22] Essentially, dated stamp scrip[23] is money that is made expensive to hold by the requirement that stamps paid for in other currency be attached to it periodically. The Social Credit government in 1936 issued such scrip. The reason for the issue is obscure, but it has been suggested that it was done to appease demands of the public and legislative backbenchers for immediate implementation of social credit, or as a stop-gap measure until social credit measures could be implemented.[24]

At first it was proposed to issue scrip in order to pay "social dividends" immediately. At a caucus of the government party in December, 1935, it was suggested that the government pay monthly dividends to each eligible person by issuing five "bonds" of $5 each, bearing no interest, and payable after one year. The back of the bond was to contain spaces for placing weekly ten-cent stamps throughout the year. Consumers in their transactions would use these bonds; at the end of the year they would be redeemed in national money or Alberta credit. Thus dividends could be issued, the sale of stamps would provide a redemption fund, and the government would make 20 cents per bond.

For one reason or another the proposal to issue dividends was not adopted; it has been suggested that Social Creditors were not particularly enthusiastic because it was not a social credit technique. Instead, scrip was issued to pay civil servants and unemployed workers engaged on relief projects.[25] On June 11, 1936, the government authorized a $2 million issue of "prosperity" certificates in denominations of $1 and $5 to those who would accept them for payments on public works, relief, or other government expenditures.[26] Stamps to the value of 1 per cent per week were to be affixed to them, and the certificates were to be redeemed within two years. But the government wavered on the question of redemption. It seemed to lack faith in the general acceptability of the certificates, and its own followers were not too keen in their support of the scheme. In July, the government made provision for payment from the general revenue fund of the province for certificates presented on certain days each month, beginning in September 1936.[27] Proceeds from stamp sales were to be kept in a trust fund for redemption and other expenses incurred in issuing certificates.

The first issue was made in August 1936, to finance the road projects. After this first issue the government announced that no further issues would be made after August 6 until they had observed the effects of its circulation. By the end of the month, $239,381 had been issued to between 5,000 and 6,000 workers on road relief projects, and many retailers found themselves in possession of scrip.[28] The scrip circulated to a considerable extent in the small towns in areas where roadwork was done, while the circulation in the larger centres was almost negligible. Retailers found themselves faced with a number of difficulties which, along with the monthly redemption feature allowed by the government, doomed the scheme. First, retailers hesitated to turn down transactions in scrip; second, they hesitated to accept certificates in payment for fear of running short of cash to pay wholesalers. Most wholesalers opposed the scheme, retail store employees proved very reluctant to accept scrip as part of their wages, and farmers would not accept it in payment for produce. Consequently, the scrip "died" at the retail level, and when the first redemption came along on September 10, 11, and 12, more than 60 per cent of the certificates were redeemed. Following this the government announced that it was not issuing any more scrip for roadwork during 1936.

From November to March reissues were made at rates ranging from $11,000 to $19,000 per month as part of the salaries of civil servants. This was ostensibly done to see if the people would become accustomed to using the scrip, but it failed to attain any degree of popularity. On April 7, 1937, the provincial treasurer announced abandonment of the scheme. Altogether $359,778 had been issued and more than 95 per cent had been redeemed before April 7. Most of the balance has never been redeemed; presumably the certificates outstanding have been kept as souvenirs.

A cardinal defect of the plan was the reluctance of the government itself to accept scrip in payment of taxes and licences (except sales tax). This along with shifting policy announcements with respect to the scrip, undermined confidence in the issues made.[29] Other factors, which contributed to the failure, were the poor quality of the paper used and the small size of the stamps used, the failure of the government to establish clearing facilities, and the smallness of the issue.

An examination of Table 7.6 reveals that after the issue of 1936–37, there were small receipts from prosperity certificates until the present. These did not exceed $100 annually and arose from the sales of certificates to souvenir collectors. Redemption of certificates issued in 1936–37 ceased entirely after 1943.

The scheme might have had limited success if Social Creditors had submerged their methodological preconceptions and had adopted a more pragmatic approach. This would have induced the government to pursue a more vigorous and certain policy. It could have provided the treasury with short-term "loans" during a year when it was most hard-pressed for cash. Furthermore, multiplier effects, though limited in scope, might have provided some mild and scattered stimuli upon the economic *corpus*. The large volume of extra-provincial transactions precluded the possible supplanting of national money by scrip; the volume and the circulation of scrip would necessarily have been limited.

CASH BALANCES, SURPLUSES, AND DEFICITS

The cash balance figures in the last column in Table 7.6 represent cash and deposits of the general revenue fund in commercial banks and treasury branches. Cash was also held by other funds, by the telephone system, and substantial amounts were added to the special investment fund during the 1940s. Although the cash balance was dangerously low in the 1930s, it reached astounding heights by the latter 1940s. Despite a recent reduction in debt that has diminished balances, as of March 31, 1951, holdings of cash and investments still equalled 70 per cent of total expenditure in 1950–51, and 114 per cent of expenditure on income account.

PROVINCIAL-MUNICIPAL ISSUES

The municipalities proved far less successful in their attempts to build up cash balances. Population increases had pushed municipalities to the limit, and they began to borrow heavily after the war. Rural municipalities have tended to do better counter-cyclically than their urban counterparts due to their tax base, but both still had difficulties, and often had to call upon the provincial government for help. Table 7.7 indicates provincial grants and subventions to the municipalities. Following the report of the Judge Commission, some changes were instituted to try to help the municipalities.

The Self-Liquidating Projects Act: To meet the problems the urban centres faced because of rapid urban population growth, the province introduced a measure permitting provincial lending to cities, towns, and villages in 1950. Under the Act the government proposed to lend funds for approved self-liquidating municipal development projects at 2 per cent interest. It has proved to be a very popular measure, but it has not gone far enough to meet the needs of the two large cities.

The Municipal Assistance Act: A most interesting measure was passed in 1951 containing features that are probably unprecedented in the field of intergovernmental finance. The Municipal Assistance Act provided for the setting up of a permanent fund to be used exclusively for increased financial assistance to cities, towns, villages, municipal districts, improvement districts, and the Special Areas. The provincial treasurer is to pay into the fund annually the proportion of the gasoline tax collections of the preceding year equivalent to a tax of 4 cents per gallon, that is, 40 per cent of gasoline tax collections. For 1951–52 this amounted to $4,665,000 (40 per cent of estimated collections in 1950–51).

For the fund established, the government paid in 1951–52 a "tax reduction subsidy" not exceeding 3 mills annually to all tax-levying local governments,[30] which reduced or retained their aggregate mill rate below the highest mill rate levied on a comparable basis of assessment in any year after 1949. The amount of the subsidy in each case is one mill for each mill of tax reduction. Certain assessment limitations were defined in order to fix a benchmark.[31] The subsidy is conditional upon tax reductions, but is in effect an attempt to check the rapid rise in local government expenditure, a phenomenon about which provincial officials are deeply concerned.

After deducting the amount required for tax reduction subsidies, the entire balance remaining in the fund for the year is to be distributed as unconditional grants on the basis of the relationship, which the total assessment of each unit bears to the aggregate assessment of all units in the province. The assessments as of December 31 of the preceding year are to serve as the criteria for the apportionment. The defined limitations as to the inclusions in assessed values are the same as those mentioned in note 32, except that villages are allowed 110 per cent of their assessment values. The level of the unconditional grant depends upon the yearly appropriation and the extent to which municipalities reduce their mill rates; if few municipalities do so, unconditional grants would be larger and *vice versa*.

In his 1951 budget speech, the premier estimated that if all the municipalities took full advantage of the tax reduction subsidy, a sum of $2,175,000 would be distributed, this being equal to 3 mills on the aggregate municipal assessment in the province in 1950. A balance of $2.5 million would then remain for distribution as unconditional grants, the equivalent of 3.5 mills on aggregate assessed value in 1950.

Table 7.7 Provincial Government Grants-in-Aid and Subventions to Municipalities, 1936–1950 (in millions of dollars)

Year	1936	1937	1938	1939	1940	1941	1942	1943	1944	1945	1946	1947	1948	1949	1950
Grants-in-aid:															
Schools	1.6	1.5	.17	1.8	2.0	2.2	2.1	2.3	2.7	3.1	3.7	5.3	8.2	7.5	8.5
Hospital dists.	0.1	0.1	0.1	0.1	0.1	0.1	0.1	0.1	0.1	0.1	0.1	0.2	0.2	0.6	0.7
Highways	–	0.0	0.1	–	–	–	–	0.2	0.4	0.4	0.5	1.2	1.7	1.8	2.4
Total grants	1.7	1.6	1.8	1.9	2.1	2.3	2.2	2.7	3.2	3.6	4.4	6.7	10.1	9.9	11.5
Other:															
Mothers' allow	0.4	0.5	0.6	0.5	0.5	0.5	0.4	0.4	0.5	0.5	0.5	0.6	0.7	0.9	0.9
Indigent relief	0.2	0.2	0.2	0.2	0.2	0.1	0.1	0.1	0.1	0.1	0.2	0.2	0.2	0.2	0.1
Old age pensions[a]	1.8	2.0	2.1	2.2	2.3	2.3	3.0	3.4	3.8	4.0	4.4	5.6	6.5	9.0	10.6
Miscell.[b]	0.1	0.1	0.1	0.1	0.1	0.1	0.1	0.1	0.1	0.1	0.2	0.2	0.2	0.2	0.2
Total other	2.5	2.8	3.0	3.0	3.1	3.0	3.6	4.0	4.5	4.7	5.3	6.6	7.6	10.3	11.8
Total, all	4.2	4.4	4.8	4.9	5.1	5.3	5.8	6.6	7.7	8.3	9.7	13.3	17.7	20.2	23.2
Provincial contribution as percent of total expenditure:															
Schools	18	16	17	17	18	22	18	20	22	22	24	28	32	25	26
Hospital dists.	15	13	15	13	15	14	14	12	11	11	10	14	10	21	24
Highways[c]	–	0	2	1	–	1	1	9	11	9	10	16	20	21	25

Sources: Appendices B and C.
(a) Includes the Dominion share which was paid to the provincial government.
(b) Liquor fines and payments to cities in lieu of the service tax.
(c) Estimated from total expenditures of municipal and improvement districts for 1936–43 inclusive. Highway expenditures of these units were taken to equal 70 per cent of total expenditures. For 1944–50 inclusive, actual figures for public works and capital expenditures of these units were used.

The whole scheme is unusual in character, and it defies analysis in brief terms. Yet a few remarks are in order. The provincial government's purpose is to check the rise in the level of municipal taxation, which is felt to be becoming too high. The senior government also fears that municipalities will find themselves with a high, inflexible expenditure level in the event of a recession. Property tax levies, despite large absolute increases in recent years, are at their lowest level since World War I in relation to personal incomes. It would be good counter-cyclical policy to let tax levies continue to rise as personal incomes rise. The scheme penalizes municipalities, especially the major cities, which are undergoing rapid expansion with consequent strain on their facilities. Nevertheless, the intended check on expenditures would be desirable, not so much to prevent a higher and inflexible level, but to reduce the upward pressure government expenditures exert on the price level. But the technique of checking expenditures, if it is to be truly counter-cyclical, has to be divorced from tax reduction considerations.

The unconditional part of the scheme encourages increased overall expenditures. During an inflationary period it would be the better part of discretion to use conditional grants for specific purposes so that the principle of selection could be brought into play. In this way, special concessions could be made where overwhelming evidence can be produced to show the urgency of certain expenditures. A fortiori the major cities, which are undergoing "growing pains," could be given special attention.

If the scheme continues to be applied under recession conditions it will have more desirable effects. Tax reductions would provide relief for taxpayers whose incomes are falling. Unconditional grants would maintain municipal spending. It is difficult to predict, however, whether or not the provincial government would utilize its liquid balances and its excellent credit standing during a recession to undertake a vigorous anti-recession policy incorporating counter-cyclical municipal grants. In the light of its debt doctrines, it seems unlikely that it would incur new debt under such circumstances; the orthodoxy of a balanced budget would be more likely to prevail, all the more so in view of the Alberta experiences with debt before 1935.[32]

Municipal Assessment: The provincial government has strengthened centralized assessment procedures in recent years. This is of importance because the chief function of the provincial director of assessments is to establish and maintain an equalized assessment of the entire area of the province. This equalized assessment was used before 1947 to establish amounts payable under the social service tax, to apportion school and hospital district requisitions to the several municipalities involved in each case, and to apportion the equalization school grants. The abolition of the social service tax meant the removal of the prime reason for the establishment of an equalized assessment, but the problems of requisitioning within an overlapping municipal structure, the use of assessment criteria in paying equalization grants to schools, and the establishment of a new set of municipal grants have provided another *raison d'être*.

The Judge Commission recommended that the province appoint assessors, under the Director of Assessments, to perform all the assessing functions in all municipalities except the cities. This was implemented in 1949, the province paying 25 per cent of the costs of assessment. Cities may also request the services of provincial assessors, but they have not done so. For equalized assessment purposes, however, there are consultations between the province and the cities.

Liquor Fines and Other: The province has continued to pay $61,500 to the cities of Calgary and Edmonton in lieu of their abolition of a "service tax" (a kind of municipal income tax) in 1932. Following the recommendation of the Judge Commission, the province is paying the municipal taxes on liquor stores and treasury branches, i.e. of buildings used for self-liquidating ventures. The commission stopped short of recommending such payments on Alberta Government Telephone property since it would have widened the telephone rate differential between Calgary and Edmonton even more than has always been the case.

CHANGES IN THE COMPOSITION OF PROVINCIAL ASSETS AND LIABILITIES

Not only has the immediate liquid position of the government improved beyond expectations, but also the quality of its assets has improved in important respects. The net debt of the province has accordingly diminished to almost nothing, depending upon what assets one offsets against gross debt. A balance sheet analysis is useful to examine these points, and the basic data are set out in Table 7.8. The comparative balance sheet is a combination of the capital and income balance sheets shown in the public accounts.

ASSETS

Total assets have almost doubled in fifteen years. Many factors have contributed to this result, as shown in Table 7.8. The few asset reductions were minor in character in terms of the 1951 balance sheet, but the items subsequently reduced were of major importance in the 1936 balance sheet.

Cash: The cash balance of the government was precariously low during the late 1930s. In most years during the 1940s, however, cash on hand was probably at too high a level considering the investment possibilities which would have yielded interest, and considering the level required for ease in making financial transactions.[33] Having regard to the ability of other governments to get along with moderate cash balances and the Alberta government's holdings of liquid securities, it would seem that cash holdings could have been cut in half throughout the 1940s. It is possible that one or two million dollars in interest could have been earned accordingly throughout the ten years. Debt retirement and an increase in the investment fund account for the great decrease in the cash balance during the 1950–51 fiscal year. Debt reorganization had also imposed a drain in 1946.

The growth in cash and investments resulted partly from the government's desire to become independent of the capital market. It adopted careful expenditure policies and it met few new situations demanding action on a par with the wheat pool incident or unemployment relief because of economic recovery. The growth in liquid balances is also the result of the rise in revenue that, in recent years, has been nothing short of phenomenal.

On March 31, cash and investments equalled 9 per cent of the expenditure in the fiscal year 1936–37 just closed. By March 31, 1941, they equalled 24 per cent of the expenditure of the fiscal year closed. Thus even before the war period, the government was relatively better off in terms of liquid resources than any of its predecessors. During the war, the government stated its intention to build up a liquid surplus for post-war expenditure; it also exhorted its municipalities to do the same.[34] On March 31, 1945, the provincial government itself had cash and investments equalling 79 per cent of the expenditure for 1944–45. The emphasis upon cash balances continued after the war in order to provide a cushion for possible recession in economic conditions. The provincial government was eminently successful; on March 31, 1950, its balances stood at 88 per cent of the expenditures for 1949–50, and at 128 per cent of the more or less "inflexible" expenditures on income account. These are unprecedentedly high percentages; few, if any, public treasuries in modern times have been able to provide so well for recession. In 1950, in a well-timed move, the government refunded most of its bond indebtedness and also reduced debt by more than $20 million. Even after this reduction in liquid balances, holdings in cash and investments were still more than adequate. It is little wonder that opposition parties see little chance of winning an election until the percentages are reduced so substantially that the government would have difficulty in meeting its obligations and the expenditure demands of a recession.

Table 7.8   Assets and Liabilities of the Government of Alberta, 1936–1951
(in millions of dollars)

As at March 31	1936	1941	1946	1951
ASSETS				
Current and Income-Producing:				
Cash	2.0	5.7	14.5	14.7
Investments	1.5	0.7	8.5	55.9
Other current assets	7.0	7.8	8.4	17.2
Sinking fund	10.6	13.9	–	0.0
Fully-secured advances	13.5	6.6	5.0	6.9
Working advances	0.5	1.2	1.5	3.6
Alta. Government Telephones	16.2	16.0	20.3	31.9
Subtotal	51.3	51.9	58.2	130.2
Other:				
General Assets	66.5	74.3	77.6	157.7
Partially-secured advances	8.5	4.8	15.8	14.7
Deferred charges	18.9	20.5	16.3	12.8
Capital losses	22.8	26.3	24.0	28.5
Consolidated income deficit	17.8	3.6	0.0	0.0
Total assets	185.9	181.4	191.9	343.9
LIABILITIES				
Current Liabilities	4.0	5.0	20.5	8.5
Unfunded Debt	18.4	8.2	5.4	11.2
Funded Debt	153.6	156.1	140.8	100.6
Total debt	176.0	169.3	166.7	120.3
Reserves	9.9	12.0	9.2	144.3
Consolidated Income Surplus	0.0	0.0	15.9	79.3
Total liabilities	185.9	181.4	191.9	343.9
Net debt after deducting cash, investments and sinking fund	161.9	149.0	143.7	49.7
Net debt after deducting all current and income-producing assets	124.7	117.4	108.5	–9.9

Source: *P.A., 1936–51.* The balance sheets on income and capital accounts were combined.

Investments: The level of investments fell off after 1936 as more securities were sold than were deposited in the investment fund during 1936–37. Thereafter, the fund levelled off and there were no substantial increases until the continued surpluses and lessening prejudice against investment securities of 1949–51.

The composition of the assets of the fund is shown in Table 7.9. The initial composition of the fund impaired the liquidity of the fund as a provincial asset, for Alberta provincial bonds were naturally quite illiquid until 1945, and care had to be exercised in liquidating municipal bonds both from the point of view of the provincial government and the municipal governments. The latter would hardly appreciate substantial sales in the market by the provincial government at a time when their credit standing was most precarious. The liquidity of the fund has again been impaired during 1951 by the rise in interest rates and fall in bond prices. This, of course, is the kind of incident that can refute the argument that the government should have got along with lower cash balances.

Other Current Assets: This category consists of interest receivable, arrears of assessed taxes, accounts receivable, equipment, stores, and materials. Interest on advances of various kinds[35] has been diminished both by settlements of debtors and by write-offs. Tax arrears decreased during the 1940s. Maintenance charges for patients at mental institutions account for a large part of the accounts receivable, but most of them are non-recoverable. By and large, "other" current assets are an item that has grown in size with the rising expenditures of the government.

The Provincial Sinking Fund: The provincial sinking fund was established in 1915.[36] Contributions were set to equal 0.5 per cent of the outstanding debt; in time it was hoped that greater amounts would be contributed, but the pressure on the treasury precluded this. Interest on the holdings of the fund provided for some additional growth. The fund never came to serve any useful function except to provide funds for the purchase of Alberta government securities at appropriate times in terms of bond prices. But the amounts concerned were relatively small and the same thing could have been done without a sinking fund. The preponderance of Alberta government bonds in the portfolio of the fund proved to be a severe handicap in 1936. It is conceivable that if there had been any substantial holdings of Dominion of Canada bonds, the province could have liquidated these and provided funds for debt redemption. The composition of sinking fund investments is set out in Table 7.10.

After the default the administration ceased making contributions to the fund. Instead, from time to time, the government issued treasury bills in small amounts to the provincial treasurer, the trustee of the fund, upon which he

Table 7.9   Securities Held in the Special Investment Fund, Government of Alberta, 1936–1951 (in millions of dollars)

As at March 31	Alberta bonds[a]	Alberta municipals	Dominion of Canada	Other	Total
1936	0.5	1.0	0.0	0.1	1.5
1937	0.3	0.5	0.0	0.0	0.8
1938	0.3	0.5	0.0	–	0.8
1939	0.4	0.5	0.0	–	0.9
1940	0.4	0.4	–	–	0.9
1941	0.4	0.3	0.0	–	0.7
1942	0.5	0.2	0.3	–	1.0
1943	0.7	0.2	2.4	–	3.3
1944	1.0	0.2	2.9	–	4.1
1945	1.2	0.1	3.5	–	4.9
1946	–	0.1	7.9	0.5	8.5
1947	0.2	0.1	4.6	0.4	5.2
1948	0.5	0.1	4.5	0.5	5.6
1949	1.3	0.1	9.4	0.5	11.4
1950	1.4	–	30.4	2.9	34.8
1951	0.2	–	54.3	1.4	55.9

Source: *P.A., 1936–51.*
(a)   Includes bonds guaranteed by the province.

liquidated some of the fund's holdings to provide cash. The fund continued to grow, however, from interest earnings and from annual contributions of almost $200,000 from the Alberta Wheat Pool on the debenture issue of $5,649,000 made on October 1, 1931, and due on October 1, 1951.

With the execution of the debt reorganization program, all securities in the fund were applied to debt redemption. The Alberta bonds held were cancelled, and other holdings were sold. The fund continued to survive until June 30, 1947, when it was finally liquidated in its entirety in connection with the redemption of that remarkable *dramatis personae*, present upon all-important occasions, the Alberta and Great Waterways railway bond issue. Since the present debt of the province is on a serial basis, no valid reason exists for the retention of a sinking fund.

Fully Secured Advances: An asset that shrank both relatively and absolutely until 1949 was that of the fully secured advances. In 1936, these consisted of the balance owing from the sale of railways ($5.6 million), the

Table 7.10 Sinking Fund Investments as at Fiscal Year Ends, Government of Alberta, 1936–1947 (in millions of dollars)

As at Mar. 31	Alberta bonds	Bank – deposits	Dominion of Canada bonds	Bonds of other provinces	Alberta municipal bonds	Total
1936	8.6	0.4	0.0	0.8	0.9	10.6
1937	9.2	0.2	0.0	0.8	1.3	11.4
1938	9.6	0.3	0.0	0.8	1.3	12.1
1939	10.1	0.7	0.0	0.5	1.3	12.6
1940	11.5	0.7	0.0	0.5	0.6	13.3
1941	12.3	0.7	0.0	0.5	0.5	14.0
1942	12.6	0.8	0.4	0.5	0.3	14.6
1943	13.1	0.2	1.2	0.5	0.3	15.4
1944	13.4	0.2	1.7	0.5	0.3	16.1
1945	13.7	0.3	2.3	0.5	0.1	16.8
1946	0.0	–	0.0	0.0	0.0	–
1947[a]	0.1	–	0.0	0.0	0.0	0.1

Source: *P.A., 1936–48.*
(a) As at June 30, 1947 when the account was closed.

Alberta Wheat Pool loan ($5.0 million net), loans to Alberta cities for relief ($2.7 million), a small amount owing by the United Grain Growers amounting to $120,000 and $200,000 owed by the Dominion government for unemployment and farm relief. The Social Credit administration thus inherited some excellent accounts, the only doubtful one being that of the cities. The railway payment came through in 1939; the wheat pool reduced its balances yearly and paid its account in full in 1947 before maturity; the U.G.G. loan was paid off by the end of the fiscal year 1936–37; and the Dominion government, of course, paid its bills. The main remaining item was the loans to the cities; part of these were written off in 1947 following the Dominion-provincial agreement with respect to relief and other treasury bills. There was a substantial increase of advances in 1950–51 because of loans to the urban municipalities under the Self-Liquidating Projects Act.

Working Advances: These consist of advances outstanding made to the government printer, the schoolbooks branch, public works, and the public trustee. They represented an asset of high quality, increasing with the growth in total expenditures of the government.

The Alberta Government Telephones: There was no net investment in the telephones until 1942 when assets increased slightly. There were some additions to the plant during the war years, but the main expansion of the system has taken place during the post-war years. The telephone system, stripped of most of its rural lines and aided by economic recovery, became a provincial asset of a completely self-liquidating character. This is indicated by the data on revenue and expenditure in Table 7.11.

There were surpluses on income account in every year except 1936, but this does not tell the story correctly for the figures do not take depreciation and reduced interest payments into account. If interest payments had been made in full, the surpluses of 1936–37 to 1939–40 inclusive would have been wiped out, and revenue and expenditure would have been approximately equal in each year. In succeeding years there would have been reduced surpluses. If in addition, a depreciation allowance equivalent to one-twentieth of the book value of the system were deducted for each year, there would be substantial deficits for the first seven years, small deficits for 1943–44, 1944–45, and 1945–46, and substantial surpluses thereafter.

General Assets: This category is most important for it represents various capital expenditures that have been made by the province since 1905. Table 7.12 sets out the various categories.

From 1936 to 1946, additions to the general assets proceeded at a rate somewhat below the annual average for the preceding thirty years, reflecting the cautious expenditure policy of the Social Credit government and the restrictions imposed by wartime conditions. From 1946 to 1951, however, approximately the same amount was spent in five years as during the previous forty.[37] This was spent on the backlog of public works which had been postponed during the war; the execution of the government's 1948 policy of providing good roads and public buildings from oil revenues, and the continually rising cost of construction which augmented the dollar volume of public investment. General assets are not self-liquidating, but they are productive by virtue of their usefulness and by their contribution to the national income in the sense that they add to the future enjoyment of life.[38]

Cumulative expenditure on highways trebled between 1936 and 1951, with most of the increase taking place after 1946 (see Table 7.12). The main difference in real terms between 1936 and 1946 is one of quality of roads rather than quantity. In 1936 Alberta had practically no paved roads, and gravel mileage was limited. Today hundreds of miles of paved roads are in existence as well as greatly increased mileage of gravelled roads. Nevertheless, the government

Table 7.11 Revenue and Ordinary Expenditure of Alberta Government Telephones, 1936–1951 (in millions of dollars)

Fiscal year ending Mar. 31	Revenue	Expenditure			Total	Surplus or deficit (−)
		Maintenance	Operation	Interest		
1936	2.4	0.3	0.7	1.4	2.5	−0.1
1937	2.4	0.3	0.8	0.9	1.9	0.5
1938	2.4	0.3	0.7	0.7	1.7	0.7
1939	2.5	0.3	0.7	0.7	1.7	0.7
1940	2.6	0.3	0.8	0.7	1.8	0.8
1941	2.7	0.3	0.8	0.7	1.8	0.9
1942	2.9	0.3	0.8	0.7	1.9	1.1
1943	3.3	0.3	0.9	0.7	2.0	1.3
1944	3.8	0.3	1.0	0.7	2.1	1.7
1945	4.1	0.3	1.1	0.7	2.2	1.9
1946	4.4	0.4	1.2	0.8	2.3	2.1
1947	4.8	0.4	1.3	0.8	2.5	2.3
1948	5.3	0.5	1.6	0.7	2.7	2.6
1949	6.1	0.5	1.9	0.7	3.1	3.0
1950	8.1	0.7	2.7	0.7	4.1	4.0

Source: *P.A., 1936–51*. Expenditure on operation includes contributions to employees' pension fund. The figures for expenditure make no allowance for depreciation.

finds much more to be accomplished because of the tremendous area of the province and the growth in motor traffic.

There has been a greatly accelerated public building program during recent years. Including expenditure on the University of Alberta and the University hospital, the total has risen from $23.9 million in 1946 to $46.0 million in 1951. Many fine new buildings have been constructed, including one of the most costly university libraries on the continent.[39] These are expenditures held in high regard by the public and they stand as monuments of the accomplishments of the present administration. From the economist's point of view there appear, however, several considerations. First, buildings which prove too large during the first years of use still entail substantial increases in current expenditure on upkeep and maintenance; secondly, the money spent on ornamental features and "gadgets" might be spent more advantageously on current items; third, undertaking a large public building program in inflationary periods is not good counter-cyclical policy;[40] fourth, the emphasis on large immediate size and on permanence is not conducive to flexibility in countering the upturns and downturns in economic activity, and relatively fixed expenditures for up-keep and maintenance are embedded in the governmental expenditure structure which may prove to be a handicap if the treasury were to become hard pressed.

The government has displayed a commendable sense of priority. The construction of hospitals of various kinds was undertaken first during the post-war period in order to safeguard the physical well-being of the provincial citizens. The preservation of health and life is the prerequisite for the satisfaction to be enjoyed by individuals. University buildings for the training of technical personnel, medical and engineering, and for the provision of library facilities, which have been very inadequate in the past, have ranked high. The construction of administration buildings has been deferred to a greater degree; not until the last two years have major projects in this category been undertaken.

Unsecured or Partially Secured Advances: The most important item in 1936 was for seed grain and fodder advances made over the years, including the depression years. These were largely written off in 1939, and the chief losses were in the southeast. Unemployment relief advances to the municipalities and advances for charitable purposes under the Livestock Encouragement Act were also largely written off before the war. Thus the main items in 1936 were of a doubtful character. Those of 1951 are of a higher quality, with advances to the Lethbridge Northern Irrigation district, the "bleeder" of the provincial treasury, being much the most important. But the improved character of the Lethbridge Northern advances is very much contingent upon the continuation of the present level of agricultural prices. A notable item is the advance for clearing and breaking land; it is comparable in character to expenditures on irrigation. The miscellaneous items are too numerous to be mentioned in entirety, but they are largely of a recoverable kind.

Deferred Charges: This category has arisen as a result of a number of "emergency" and incidental expenditures, which may not be recovered. The most important is that for unemployment relief disbursed by the province; here some recoveries have been made from individuals, especially in recent years. Debenture discount less premiums was a sizeable item in 1936; it has since declined with the execution of refunding and redemption transactions yielding premiums and profits. The decline in unemployment relief payments and bond discounts accounted for practically the entire decline in total deferred charges between 1936 and 1951.

Capital Losses: This category is a kind of "graveyard" of partially secured advances and deferred charges. Here are buried some of the "mistakes" of

Table 7.12 General Assets of the Government of Alberta as at March 31 of Selected Years (millions of dollars)

	1936	1941	1946	1951
Highways, bridges, and ferries	35.9	42.1	50.1	106.8
Public buildings	17.4	18.6	20.5	32.1
Miscellaneous public works	0.8	0.8	0.6	1.4
University of Alberta	4.4	4.8	5.2	10.0
University Hospital	0.5	0.5	0.7	3.9
Lethbridge Northern Irrigation[a]	6.1	7.0	0.0	0.0
St. Mary Irrigation	0.0	0.0	0.0	1.8
Tar sands plant	0.0	0.0	0.0	0.7
Miscellaneous	1.5	0.5	0.6	1.0
Total	66.5	74.3	77.6	157.7

Source: See Appendix B.
(a) Transferred to partially secured loans and advances pursuant to the debt reorganization program in 1945.

provincial administration, chiefly the Liberal ones before 1921; others are still "hospitalized" under partially secured advances and deferred charges. Table 7.13 shows the main items written off as capital losses.

Consolidated Income Deficits Since 1905: This is the last asset category and is generally considered to be an indicator of how well governments have lived within their own means. It should be noted that annual charges do not necessarily correspond to annual surpluses or deficits because of adjustments in income asset and liabilities *vis-à-vis* capital account. The consolidated income deficit disappeared after 1941 and has instead taken up permanent residence as a consolidated income surplus on the liabilities side of the balance sheet.

Summary: The great relative change in holdings of a very liquid character (cash and investments) should be noted. The elimination of the sinking fund offsets this change somewhat, but the illiquidity of the fund in 1936 should be kept in mind in interpreting the figures. The telephone system is somewhat more important than it was in 1936, and it is of a high character financially. The current and income-producing assets group is not only larger relatively but also more liquid in 1951 than it was in 1936.

General assets have become more important quantitatively, and to some extent, qualitatively (i.e. the paved roads of 1951 are superior to the gravelled roads of 1936, new buildings are superior to the old ones, etc.). Assets representing expenditure on such a variety of objects as unproductive railroads through uninhabited territory, telephone lines in sparsely settled regions, agricultural relief in

Table 7.13 Capital Losses of the Government of Alberta as at March 31 of
Selected Years (millions of dollars)

Losses arising from:	1936	1941	1946	1951
Sale of railways	11.4	11.4	11.4	11.4
Alberta Government Telephones[a]	8.9	8.5	4.3	6.7
Seed grain and relief accounts[b]	1.5	5.2	6.1	6.3
Working advances	0.3	–	0.1	0.1
Livestock Encouragement Act	0.3	0.7	0.7	0.7
Cooperative Credit Societies	0.1	0.2	0.7	1.2
Disposal of provincial farms	–	0.1	0.2	0.2
Charitable purposes	–	–	–	0.7
Local government loans[c]	–	0.1	0.1	0.8
Miscellaneous	0.2	0.1	0.4	0.4
Total	22.8	26.3	24.0	28.5

Source: See Appendix B.
  (a) After deduction of depreciation and renewal reserve for 1936, 1941, and 1946. For 1951, the provincial accounts include the gross figures again. After deducting the depreciation reserves shown elsewhere in the accounts, however, the net figure would be zero, indicating full capital recovery since 1936. The gross figure represents chiefly amounts written off to abandonment of rural lines.
  (b) More than half of the amounts are for advances made before 1931 and especially before 1922.
  (c) School districts, municipal districts, and improvement districts.
  (d) Losses arising from the farm settlement scheme, road construction contracts, loans to normal school students, brushing contracts, advances to irrigation and drainage districts, hay relief in 1920, loans to creameries, and many small items.

drought areas, irrigation ventures which have not as yet been established to be of value in the economic sense, unemployment relief to alleviate sufferings in an economy especially hard-hit by the breakdown in world regional specialization in the 1930s, excesses of expenditure over revenue on income account, and a host of similar purposes, constituted 36.7 per cent of the total in 1936 and only 16.3 per cent in 1951. In short, the dead-weight portion of the assets was reduced by more than half in relative terms. The absolute decline was smaller; these assets fell from $68.0 million in 1936 to $56.0 million in 1951. In qualitative terms, too, the 1951 assets are somewhat superior to those of 1936, for there are greater prospects of recovering more of the partially secured advances and deferred charges in 1951 than there was in 1936. The advances to the irrigation districts constitute an important example. There can be no question that the assets position of the province is now much more liquid and economically sound from a long-run point of view than it was in 1936.

LIABILITIES

Total liabilities, of course, grew with the increase in assets. An examination of the components is needed to find out how changes took place.

Current Liabilities: This category consists of accounts payable (General Revenue Fund, Alberta Government Telephones, and the Liquor Control Board), accrued interest on the funded debt, the pension fund, unearned interest (i.e. revenue of the net fiscal year already in hand or in transit), reserves of the Alberta Liquor Control Board, and suspense consisting of cash collections not allocated on March 31 and which is eventually disbursed to other funds or refunded. Current liabilities increased little until 1943, and rose to a peak of $20.5 million in 1946 when there were large deferred liabilities ($10.8 million) in connection with the debt reorganization program,[41] and deferred revenue under the terms of the Dominion-Provincial Tax Agreement (about $3.3 million). These two items gradually diminished in size; the interest adjustment payments on immature securities were made until June 1, 1950, when the last payment was made. Finally, the amount due to the depreciation and renewal reserve of the telephone system was transferred to the general category "reserves." In 1951 the level of current liabilities, about $8.5 million, can be termed "normal."

Unfunded Debt: The unfunded debt in 1936 consisted chiefly of savings certificates outstanding and temporary loans. The former were redeemed gradually after that date. Temporary loans disappeared entirely after 1939. The most important portion of the unfunded debt is now the amount due the superannuation fund; this is growing rapidly. Since the fund is not actuarially sound on the basis of the original agreement between employees and the province, the province has assumed responsibility for additional contributions.[42]

Funded Debt: Between 1936 and 1945 the gross funded debt remained almost constant, as was the net funded debt (gross funded debt minus the sinking fund). The debt reorganization and redemptions changed this picture; by 1951 gross funded debt had fallen to $100.6 million while the net funded debt equalled the same amount since the sinking fund had been eliminated. An analysis of the funded debt is undertaken in the next chapter. Total debt declined between 1936 and 1945, but this was offset by increases in current liabilities. By 1951, total debt had fallen to $120.3 million largely because of funded debt reductions.

Reserves: This is a category with a shifting composition. Until 1941, the sinking fund was practically all the equity the province had in its assets. After that date consolidated income surpluses also began to appear. After 1945, the sinking fund disappeared, and net debt redemptions took the major place in reserves until the excess of capital expenditure over receipts became the outstanding item in 1949.

Consolidated Income Surplus Since 1905: This is also a measure of the equity of the province in its assets, and has already been mentioned. It is a net figure as shown in Table 7.8 since the excess of capital expenditure over receipts, an item shown under "reserves," is deducted. The income surplus of the telephone system, a mere $1.3 million on March 31, 1951 is included. The market increase in income surplus is evident from an examination of Table 7.8.

Net Debt: Computations are shown in Table 7.8 showing two bases on which net debt may be arrived at. Either way, no provincial government in Canada is at present in such an enviable position.

Summary: The relative changes in the composition of liabilities are shown in Table 7.14. Total debt fell from 94.7 per cent of the total liabilities in 1936 to 35.0 per cent in 1951, a decline most expressive of debt reduction and pay-as-you-go policies. It may be noted that not until March 31, 1943, did the debt ratio fall below 90 per cent, and it was still somewhat above 80 per cent on March 31, 1947. Reduction since that date has been very marked in each year chiefly as a result of heavy capital expenditures financed from revenue and substantial debt reductions out of revenue.

GOVERNMENT AND THE ECONOMY
NET INCOME-PRODUCING EXPENDITURES

Table 7.16 indicates in a very approximate manner the influence of the two levels of government upon the level of income in Alberta, Dominion government influences being ignored. Both the municipalities and the province had budget surpluses during the 1936–45 period. Interest payments, while reduced, were still substantial. Receipts from the Dominion did not rise significantly until 1946. Consequently, the total effect upon the level of income was depressive rather than stimulating. During the late 1930s this was not a beneficial state of affairs. Assuming that funds could have been borrowed, many public works projects deferred until the high-cost post-war era could have reduced the number of unemployed and increased the immediate value product of the economy as well as that of the future. During the war period, the negative influence of the provincial and local governments was in harmony with the national policy of prosecuting a war.

Table 7.14 Composition of Assets of the Government of Alberta, as at March 31, 1936 and March 31, 1951 (percentages of total)

	1936	1951	Change
Current and income-producing:			
Cash	1.1	4.3	3.2
Investments	0.8	16.3	15.5
Other current assets	3.8	5.0	1.2
Sinking fund	5.7	0.0	−5.7
Fully secured advances	7.3	2.0	−5.3
Working advances	0.3	1.0	0.7
Alberta Government Telephones	8.7	9.3	0.6
Total	27.6	37.9	10.3
Other:			
General assets	35.8	45.9	10.1
Partially secured advances	4.6	4.3	−0.3
Deferred charges	10.2	3.7	−6.5
Capital losses	12.3	8.3	−4.0
Consolidated income deficit	9.6	0.0	−9.6
Subtotal	72.4	62.1	−10.3
Total assets	100.0	100.0	0.0

Source: See Appendix B.

Table 7.15 Composition of Liabilities of the Government of Alberta as at March 31, 1936 and March 31, 1951 (percentage of total)

	1936	1951	Change
Current liabilities	2.2	2.5	0.3
Unfunded debt	9.9	3.3	−6.6
Funded debt	82.6	29.3	−53.3
Total debt	94.7	35.0	−59.6
Reserves	5.3	41.9	36.6
Consolidated income surplus	0.0	23.1	23.1
Total equity	5.3	65.0	59.6
Total liabilities	100.0	100.0	100.0

Source: See Appendix B.

Table 7.16 Net Income-Producing Expenditures of the Provincial and Local Governments in Alberta, 1936–1950 (in millions of dollars)

Year	Dominion grants	School Lands Fund	Overall Deficit less interest payments	Miscellaneous	Total
1936	5.0	0.7	−9.4	–	−3.7
1937	5.9	0.6	−11.7	–	−5.2
1938	5.8	0.8	−10.2	–	−3.6
1939	5.1	0.8	−15.2	5.6[a]	−3.7
1940	4.7	0.7	−12.1	–	−6.7
1941	4.0	0.8	−15.9	–	−11.1
1942	7.4	0.7	−16.7	–	−8.6
1943	7.7	0.8	−15.9	–	−7.4
1944	8.3	0.8	−15.8	–	−6.7
1945	21.9	0.8	−32.3	–	−6.0
1946	10.6	0.8	−16.4	–	−5.0
1947	19.2	0.8	−16.2	1.0[b]	4.8
1948	20.7	1.3	−11.0	10.0[b]	21.0
1949	24.2	1.6	−24.2	25.0[b]	26.6
1950	27.9	3.0	−22.0	35.0[b]	43.9

Sources: Appendices B and C.
(a) From the sale of railways. The fund came largely from outside the province.
(b) Estimates of provincial revenue collected from external sources. They are based on the revenue derived from the purchase price of petroleum and natural gas leases as well as rentals and fees on leases.

After the war, municipal surpluses disappeared and deficits grew yearly; Dominion payments increased; the provincial government received substantial revenues from non-provincial residents. These factors served to exert an increasing positive influence upon the economy, which aggravated the underlying inflationary tendencies of the economy. The only factor offsetting the upward surge of governmental contributions to inflation was the provincial government's policy of letting its expenditures lag behind revenues.

Except for the late 1930s, the provincial government has a good record on the counter-cyclical criterion. The municipalities also made no contribution to recovery during the 1930s and restrained themselves as to expenditures during the war. But after the war they have run with the tide of inflation, a policy that, of course, stemmed from backlogs of projects and urban expansion.

Table 7.17 Total Taxation of Alberta Governments, 1936–1950
(in millions of dollars)

Year	Provincial	Local units	Total	Total as ercentage of provincial income
1936	7.3	17.3	24.6	13.1
1937	8.7	17.4	26.1	10.4
1938	8.2	17.7	25.9	9.6
1939	8.5	17.6	26.1	10.0
1940	8.9	17.8	26.7	8.6
1941	10.2	17.5	27.7	8.6
1942	6.1	18.3	24.4	4.8
1943	6.6	18.9	25.5	5.7
1944	6.7	20.5	27.2	4.6
1945	7.5	21.6	29.1	5.2
1946	8.2	24.4	32.6	4.9
1947	9.2	28.6	37.8	5.3
1948	9.8	33.4	43.2	5.0
1949	12.4	38.2	50.6	5.7
1950	14.1	41.4	55.5	6.1

Source: Appendices B and C.

THE LEVELS OF TAXATION AND PROVINCIAL INCOME

Taxation has been far from counter-cyclical. This is indicated by the data in Table 7.17. The increasing level of Dominion taxation must, of course, be kept in mind in interpreting the data. The province was not in a position to impose additional taxes because of its agreements with the Dominion. Further, it happened to have a number of income-elastic revenue sources, which yielded increasing amounts without the necessity of raising rates to obtain such amounts. Nevertheless, the municipalities lost an opportunity to build up even greater surpluses than they did during the war years; the cities in particular maintained a stability of mill rates, which became almost a fetish of their councils and electors.

SUMMARY AND RETROSPECT, 1905–50

8

It remains to survey the broad sweep of developments and intertemporal trends for the whole 1905–50 period, with the aim of bringing into focus certain continuities in economic and fiscal developments, which were lost sight of in the detailed discussion. Underlying factors leading to the establishment of fiscal trends need to be indicated and some comparisons with other provinces can assist one in isolating Alberta trends that are out of step with those of other provinces.

ECONOMIC DEVELOPMENT

Certain economic trends and conditions are of great significance in interpreting fiscal policies. The questions of central importance are the growth, stability, and distribution of income.

THE GROWTH OF INCOME

A fact of central importance in any interpretation of the most controversial and recriminatory period in Alberta's financial history, the 1920s and the 1930s, is that between 1920 and 1940 provincial income in both money and real terms did not grow, either as an aggregate or on a per capita basis. Indeed, the trend was downward throughout most of this period.

Alberta enjoyed a period of unstable prosperity until 1920. Income settled down to a lower level during the 1920s except for the transitory rise in the 1926–28 period. It fell to even lower levels during the 1930s. Thus the 1940s constitute the first period of sustained prosperity. Table 8.1 provides a statistical summary for the various periods in per capita terms.

Table 8.1   Average Money and Real Income Per Capita in Alberta for Economic Periods Since 1906

Period	Average annual income per capita	
	Current dollars	1935–1939 dollars
1906–13	306	397
1914–20	520	453
1921–25	470	364
1926–29	496	401
1930–35	260	255
1936–39	318	317
1940–45	585	476
1946–50	940	576

Source: See Figure 4.

STABILITY OF INCOME

The instability of income in Alberta has been very great, with the predominance of agriculture among the industries of the province as the main contributing factor. Figure 8.1 shows the frequent and wide fluctuations in wheat yields and prices. Yield fluctuations are the result of weather factors; the price fluctuations have arisen from cyclical and structural changes in the demand for wheat[1] and from weather factors in various wheat-producing countries throughout the world. These changes have been indicated in previous chapters. The price stability of recent years is the result of federal government policy. Figure 8.2 illustrates the high degree of yearly instability in agricultural production as against non-agricultural production. The cyclical instability is also greater. One notes that non-agricultural production outweighed the agricultural before 1914, and that it approached or equalled the agricultural level in 1921, 1929–31, and 1941. In 1950 it exceeded agricultural production because of the high tempo of activity in the mining, manufacturing, and construction industries. Insofar as non-agricultural industries become more important, greater annual stability of production values and incomes will result. Cyclically, it is questionable whether stability will be augmented greatly since mining and construction are industries that possess no more cyclical stability than agriculture.[2] Manufacturing, too, is sensitive enough to cyclical swings.

The income instability of the past has seriously hampered the development of an adequate revenue structure, especially before 1940. It has also called for

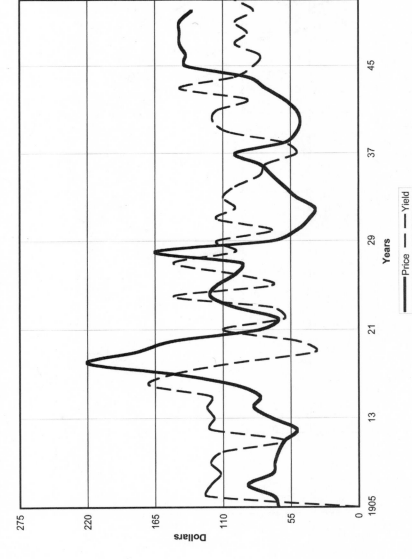

Figure 8.1 Wheat Yields Per Acre and Wheat Price Per Bushel in Alberta, 1905–1950

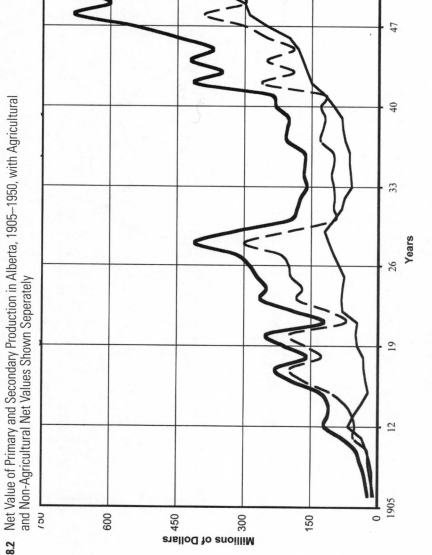

Figure 8.2 Net Value of Primary and Secondary Production in Alberta, 1905–1950, with Agricultural and Non-Agricultural Net Values Shown Seperately

emergency expenditures such as those on relief and wheat pool advances. These have, in turn, aggravated the debt problem of the provincial government.

INCOME DISTRIBUTION

Income distribution among farmers is extremely unequal in any given year. This is shown by means of the familiar Lorenz curve in Figure 8.3.[3] Since net income figures are not available on a distributive basis, gross revenue figures are used, but they serve the purpose. In 1945 half the farmers in the province received only 15 per cent of the gross revenue of farms, and two-thirds of the farmers received less than 30 per cent of the total.[4] This is explained to a minor degree by the existence of small farms since in 1945 only 6 per cent of all farms were smaller than 200 acres. A more important reason is that the incidence of drought, frost, and hail may be high in any given year.[5] These three weather factors together can lead to considerable losses. The percentage of crop area affected is one measure of incidence that is available from agricultural census figures, and it varies greatly from year to year. In 1930 the area of crop failure from all causes was 15.8 per cent of the total field crop acreage; hail accounted for more than half of this and drought ran second. By contrast, in 1940 only 2.2 per cent of the field crop acreage suffered total loss.[6] Another factor affecting agricultural income inequality in a more permanent way is the relatively high number of subsistence farms.[7] Further, there are a disproportionately large number of farms in the fringe areas and in the southeast where productivity is relatively low.[8]

The instability of farm income from year to year and its great inequality of distribution in any given year are facts which furnish an explanation of why the provincial government failed to establish an adequate revenue structure before 1940. These factors also do much to explain the difficulties of local governments with the property tax and the special provisions that have had to be made with respect to tax collections.[9] It is very dubious also whether the provincial government could have tapped the income of the farm community to yield adequate revenue by the use of a progressive income tax before 1940. Even in 1949 only 10 per cent of all farmers in Alberta paid federal income taxes, and the total yield from them was $7.2 million, less than one-fifth of personal income tax collections in the province.[10] On this basis annual collections during the 1920–40 period would have been entirely inadequate for provincial revenue purposes.[11]

Income inequality in the non-agricultural community in Alberta cannot be measured by any data available to the writer. There is, however, a

Figure 8.3 Gross Revenue from Farms in Alberta in 1945 as a Cumulative Percentage of the Total for a Cumulative Percentage of the Number of Farms

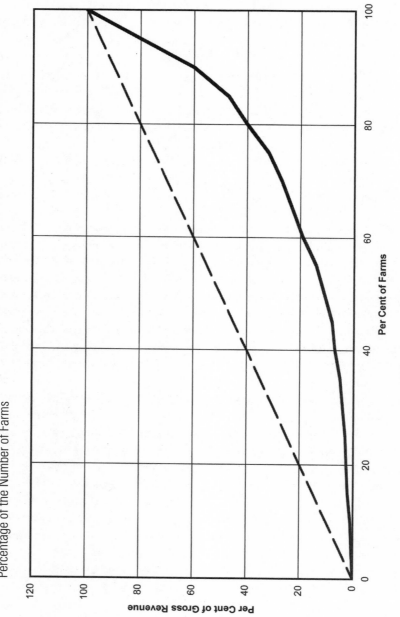

Per Cent of Gross Revenue

Per Cent of Farms

- - - Gross Revenue   ▬▬ Farms

presumption that during the present period of high employment it is less marked than in the agricultural community. The average income per person gainfully employed and the proportion of total income earned are both higher in the non-agricultural sector than in the agricultural one.

For Alberta as a whole, income inequality appears to be somewhat greater than that obtaining for all Canada if one generalizes on the basis of the incomes of federal income tax payments (see Figure 8.4). But such a generalization has dubious validity when one considers that those who do not pay income tax are not included in the data used.

GOVERNMENT EXPENDITURES

TRENDS IN TOTAL EXPENDITURES

A continuous picture of total provincial and municipal expenditures for the whole forty-five year period is shown in Figure 8.5. First, one notes the greater importance of municipal than provincial expenditures until the middle 1940s.[12] The municipal preponderance is very marked before 1920 when the urban centres were engaged in providing facilities for a rapidly growing population. The province relied upon the "guarantee" during this period, a policy that deferred actual expenditures to a large extent. Capital expenditures on the telephone system, too, were small in comparison with municipal capital expenditures before 1914, and after that date they were checked by wartime shortages of money, men, and materials.

The first fifteen years were marked by rapid increases in provincial and municipal expenditures, the former taking some time to gather momentum. At the same time, population tripled between 1905 and 1920. The period from 1920 to 1944 is marked by no upward trend in the expenditures of both levels of government while the population rose by about one-third. The post-war period has been characterized by a sharp upward turn in government expenditures that have outpaced population by a wide margin.

In real terms, provincial expenditure per capita fell somewhat during the World War I period, and rose rapidly during the 1920s and 1930s. A decline set in after 1935 as prices began to rise and provincial expenditure remained almost constant. Even the post-war average level is not much above that of the 1930–35 level. Municipal expenditures per capita in real terms fell after the boom preceding World War I and rose to pre-war levels during the depression

Figure 8.4 Lorenz Curve of Income Distribution Among Personal Income Taxpayers in Alberta and Canada in 1949

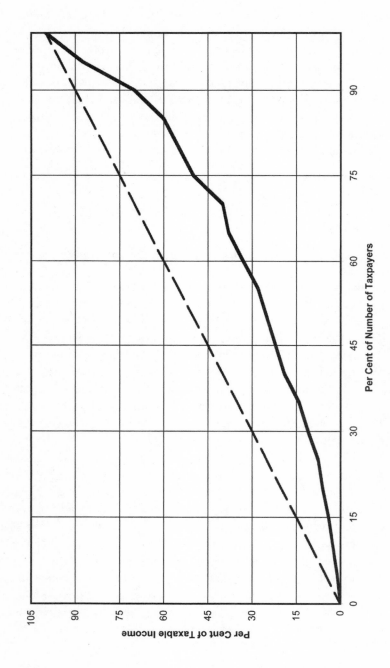

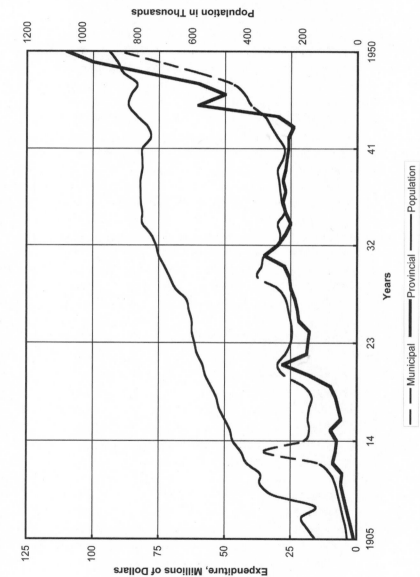

Figure 8.5 Total Expenditures of the Provincial and Municipal Governments in Alberta, 1905–1950

of the 1930s. A decline is discernible for the 1936–45 period followed by a rise to approximately the level achieved during the 1906–13 and the 1930–35 periods. Provincial expenditure per capita in real terms thus shows an upward trend while the municipal does not.[13]

A measure of the relative size and importance of government is given by the ratio of government expenditure to the national income. In the case of a province, which is a segment of a nation, there are substantial external transfers in the form of interest payments on debt that diminish the positive effects upon the level of income and employment within the province.

Despite very rapid increases in government expenditures during the late 1940s, the importance of government was no greater than during the 1920s. This is an observation that applies to both levels of government, the municipal governments being somewhat less important than during the 1920s, or for that matter, during almost any previous period. The expenditure-income ratio of the provincial government was somewhat higher than it was during the 1920s. To conclude, while government in Alberta has become more important in aggregate money terms than ever before, it certainly shows no long-run trend of becoming large relatively to the whole economy.

It is worthwhile to make some comparisons at this point. In Table 8.2 annual expenditures of various levels of government in Canada are shown as percentages of annual personal income for four selected years for which reliable data are available.[14] The importance of all governments rose during the 1930s gauged by the percentages for 1937, but there is a slight decline in 1948 as against 1937. In the light of comparisons (there are only minor differences in the results one obtains in using any income criterion), one is not convinced by the statements that government is growing at the expense of the private sector. It seems rather that government is merely keeping pace with overall economic growth, and one becomes a little weary of being told the dangers of "big government" on the one hand and of the tremendous impact government has in sustaining the "capitalistic system" on the other hand.[15]

The federal government, of course, shows great relative expansion, but much of the expenditure of 1948 for this level of government consists of interest on war-created debt, after-care of war veterans, and defence expenditures greatly in excess of those of 1937 and 1926. In 1948 these three items accounted for more than half of total federal expenditures. This suggests that even at this level of government, expenditures for social and economic purposes other than war and defence have merely kept pace with economic growth.

Expenditures of all the provinces increased relatively to income during the 1930s, fell off greatly during World War II, and rose to exceed the 1926 level

Table 8.2 Government Expenditures on Current and Capital Accounts of Canadian Governments as Percentages of Personal Income in 1913, 1926, 1937, and 1948

	1913	1926	1937	1948
All Canadian governments:				
Federal	8.1	8.7	12.8	16.8
Provincial	3.3	3.9	9.4	7.8
Municipal	7.8	7.2	7.7	4.7
Total	19.2	19.8	29.9	29.3
Alberta governments:				
Provincial	3.2	4.8	7.1	7.5
Municipal	19.3	7.8	7.8	5.5
Total	22.5	12.6	15.0	13.0

Sources: *Sirois Report*, Book 3, for 1913, 1926, and 1937 expenditures; Bank of Canada, *Statistical Summary, 1950 Supplement*, for 1948 expenditure figures for all Canadian governments; ibid., 31, for Alberta provincial expenditures in 1948; D.B.S., *Financial Statistics of Municipal Governments*, 1948, 15, for municipal expenditures in Alberta; Appendix A for income data.

in 1948. The Alberta pattern differs from the total one by the addition of a large rise in 1921, and a longer decline from 1930 until 1945. Before 1937, too, Alberta expenditures tended to be higher than the Canadian average whereas thereafter for a time they were below.

Municipal expenditures show a downward trend relatively to income. This is more marked for Canada as a whole than for Alberta. Perhaps the long-standing policy of provincial administrations in Alberta of encouraging local responsibility for governmental services and the tradition of providing the cities with a few grants are partly responsible. The urban municipal units went on an orgy of spending during the era preceding World War I; the subsequent reductions were drastic in nature. A high degree of stability is evident from 1920 to 1942, but since 1946 expenditures have doubled. Expenditures of municipal governments in Canada and Alberta have become less important in the 1940s relatively to income than ever before. Municipal expenditures in Alberta relatively to income have also rather persistently tended to exceed those in all Canada. Urban school expenditures show a similar pattern except that the 1913 bulge is less marked than in the case of the municipals. Both rural municipal and school expenditures show a steady expansion until the 1920s; they have no 1913 peak. There was little growth between 1921 and 1942. After the latter date expansion is evident. Hospital district expenditures have risen to prominence during recent years.

The combined expenditures of Canadian provinces and municipalities have remained remarkably constant over time in relation to income if one exempts the 1930s. The Alberta pattern is one of decline until the recent post-war period. Further, the Alberta percentage was considerably in excess of the overall Canadian before 1937. Between 1937 and 1945 reduced interest payments and capital expenditures brought Alberta below the national percentage. In the post-war period the percentage has risen again above the national.

INTERPROVINCIAL COMPARISONS

Figure 8.6 provides a comparison of trends in provincial expenditures on current account throughout Canada and for Alberta's neighbouring provinces.[16] The sharp rise in the expenditures of Saskatchewan during the 1930s is notable and is largely attributable to very heavy relief expenditures. The rapid rate of increase in expenditures of the three neighbouring provinces during 1947 and 1948 and the subsequent levelling off are in contrast to the steady state of increase for Alberta. Evidently the other three provinces absorbed the revenue gains accruing from their tax agreements almost immediately, while Alberta has proceeded more cautiously in the face of such revenue gains. Budget speeches of the Alberta premier indicate the reluctance of the government to increase its current expenditures by large annual increments.

Figure 8.7 shows per capita trends in Canadian and Albertan provincial and municipal expenditures. For all Canada there is an upward trend in provincial expenditure per capita from 1913 to 1948 while the Alberta pattern is irregular. The Alberta retrenchment of the early 1920s is reflected in the 1926 per capita figure; there was a similar retrenchment in 1937. Alberta expenditures per capita were considerably in excess of the Canadian before 1937; this characteristic reappeared in 1948. Thus Alberta's interest rate and capital expenditure reductions during 1936–45 are again evident.

The Canadian municipal expenditure per capita rose slowly until the 1930s and fell toward the end of the decade as senior governments assumed increasing responsibility for relief expenditures. The upward trend of the 1940s is not as great as one would expect during such an inflationary period. The Alberta pattern is similar to the Canadian one except for the abnormally high per capita expenditure of 1913, which has never been exceeded. The rise from 1945 to 1948 is more marked than that for all Canadian municipalities.

Figure 8.6 Total Expenditure on Current Account of all the Canadian Provinces, British Columbia (B.C.), Alberta, Saskatchewan and Manitoba, 1926–1950

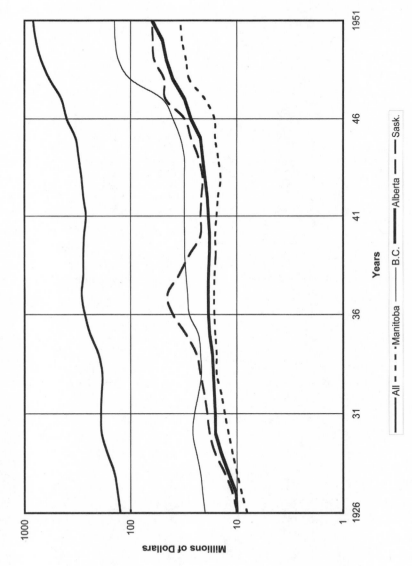

Figure 8.7a Provincial Expenditures per Capita in Canada and Alberta in Selected Years

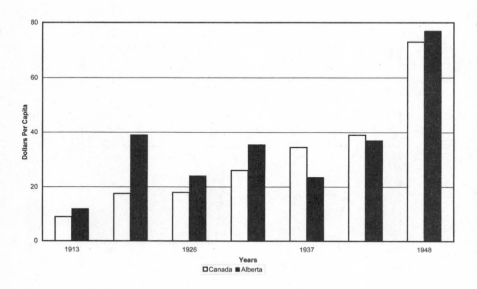

Figure 8.7b Municipal Expenditures per Capita in Canada and Alberta in Selected Years

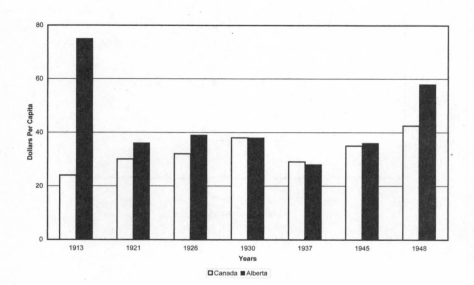

Figure 8.7c Total Municipal and Provincial Expenditures per Capita in Canada and Alberta in Selected Years

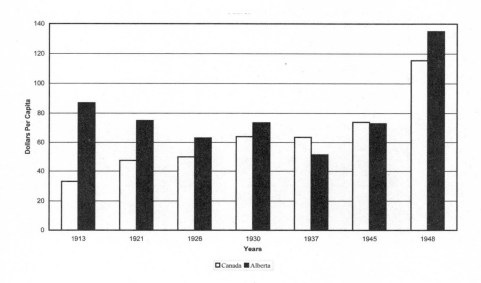

The aggregate Canadian provincial-municipal expenditure per capita is upward throughout except for the halt in the trend in 1937. The Alberta trend is downward from 1913 to 1937 and then upward. Before 1937 the Alberta average was considerably higher than the Canadian. In 1945 it was still below the national average but in 1948 it exceeded the latter.

In general, then, the Alberta provincial and municipal expenditure level has been more irregular than the national. Usually higher than the latter before 1937, it showed a tendency to decline thereafter. Only in recent years has Alberta again become one of the more liberal spenders of the Canadian federation.

EXPENDITURES IN RELATION TO INCOME FLUCTUATIONS

The counter-cyclical aspects of provincial-municipal expenditures may now be summarized. Figure 8.8 indicates the behaviour of ordinary and capital expenditures of the provincial government in relation to provincial income. Ordinary expenditures show little responsiveness to income fluctuations, one way or the other; they rose steadily throughout the whole 45-year period. The main effect

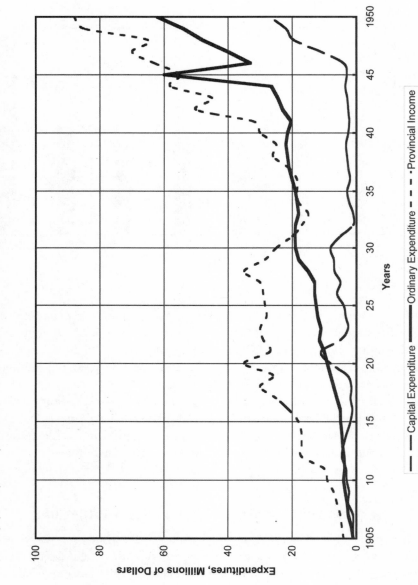

Figure 8.8 Ordinary and Capital Expenditures of the Government of Alberta and Provincial Income, 1905–1950

of income increases has been to accelerate the upward trend and income decreases have merely slowed up the steady upward climb.

The story of the capital expenditures is one of violent fluctuations. The provincial government, after a slow start, spent relatively large amounts on the construction of buildings and a telephone system during the boom period preceding World War I, and in 1912 capital expenditure exceeded ordinary expenditure. There was a rapid reduction during the pre-war depression and capital expenditure remained at low levels until 1919 when they began to rise rapidly. This rise continued into the depression year of 1921; thus there was a counter-cyclical lag of about one year before the inevitable reductions took place. The government responded to increasing prosperity again during the late 1920s, but the peak of 1921 was not reached. The government borrowed heavily during 1930 and 1931 to provide employment by means of public works until a tight capital market forced it to retrench greatly. Capital expenditures remained at very moderate levels until 1946. For the first time in the history of the province the government did not respond to recovery with a public works program of any significance. But after 1945 the government has more than contributed its share to the inflationary forces of the late 1940s.

Municipal capital expenditures have run with the cycle of income in every case. The orgy of spending before 1915 is evident from Figure 8.9. The peak expenditure of 1913 was not reached again during the whole period. The capital expenditures made before 1914 were of such a scale that the municipalities were crippled by excessive debt for decades; consequently they responded only weakly to the income upswings that occurred after 1918 and 1926. The present capital expenditure program bids fair, however, to rival the one preceding World War I. The federal government credit restrictions of 1951 and the rapid growth of the debt of the urban municipalities have, however, made the capital market very reluctant to provide the means of further financing of capital expenditures. At the moment of writing, it appears that a continuation of the municipal capital expenditure program is contingent to a considerable degree upon provincial government loans.[17]

Figure 8.10 provides a summary of fluctuations in net income-producing expenditures for the 45-year period. The provincial government exerted varying degrees of positive income stimulation throughout except during 1939–46. Counter-cyclical tendencies are discernible insofar as the early years of upswings and downswings are concerned. Thus there is no great upswing in government net expenditures before World War I; there is a cutback during World War I; the post-war increase continues well into the depression of the first half of the 1920s. There is no swing with the income cycle during the prosperity of the late

Figure 8.9 Revenue and Loan Expenditures of Local Governments in Alberta and Provincial Income, 1905–1950

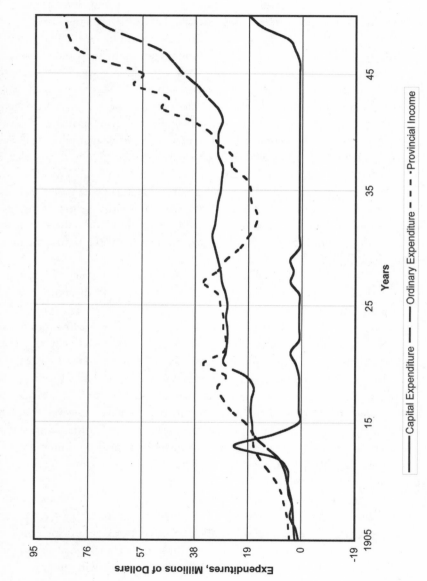

Figure 8.10a Provincial Net Income-Producing Expenditures in Alberta, 1905–1950

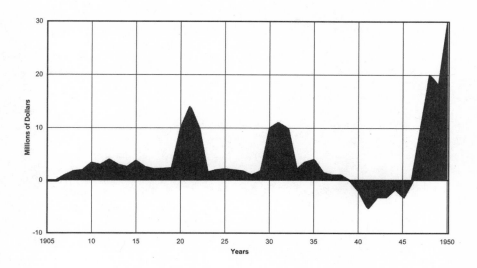

Figure 8.10b Municipal Net Income-Producing Expenditures in Alberta, 1905–1950

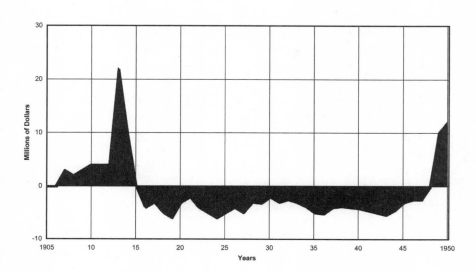

Figure 8.10c Total Provincial and Municipal Net Income-Producing Expenditures in Alberta, 1905–1950

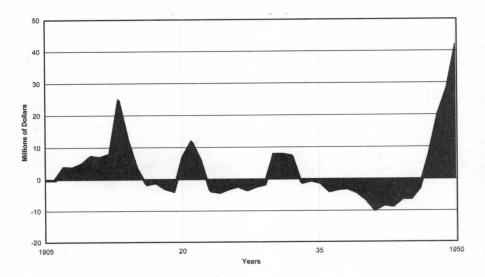

1920s, and a counter-cyclical tendency is evident during the early 1930s. The spectacular rise in net income-producing expenditures after World War II is also many years behind the initial rise in provincial income.

There is little that is counter-cyclical about the municipal net income-producing expenditures. After the upward swing in such expenditures before 1915, they became negative for thirty years, acting as a drag upon the economy. Upward trends in such expenditures coincided with the income rises of 1918–20 and 1925–27. Only during World War II was municipal fiscal policy even remotely counter-cyclical. In the post-war period, the municipalities have come back with almost every other economic unit to stimulate provincial income increases.

The net effect of the policies of both levels of government has been one of accentuating the booms of 1906–13 and 1946–50 and of counteracting, to a much smaller degree, the depressions of 1921–22 and 1931–32. There was little responsiveness to the 1926–29 upswing when governments were almost neutral with respect to income creation. The rather negative effect of governments during the 1936–45 upswing is notable; during the war years this was largely the result of various restrictions upon expenditures.

The conclusions seem to be that the provincial government has a good counter-cyclical record insofar as the early period of upswings and downswings are concerned. The municipalities seem to be more directly and quickly responsive to fluctuations in income, and have always responded in the same direction as the income change.

TRENDS IN THE PROVINCIAL EXPENDITURE PATTERN

The pattern of provincial expenditure has undergone marked changes throughout the forty-five year period. This is evident from an examination of Table 8.3, which expresses expenditures on the five main categories as percentages of total expenditures for eight economic periods and 1950.

If one considers that social and economic expenditures constitute the functional core of the government in the sense that they provide direct benefits to citizens, and that other expenditures constitute, in a sense, the "cost of government," one perceives an interesting trend. Thus social and economic expenditures fluctuated between 60 to 65 per cent of total expenditures until the 1946–50 period when they equalled more than 75 per cent. At the same time the "cost of government" is lower relatively than it has ever been.[18]

Table 8.4 expresses the different expenditure categories as percentages of provincial income, and a measure of the community's ability to pay. General government expenditures have absorbed close to one per cent of provincial income except for the initial period and the 1930s. Social expenditures have absorbed an increasing percentage except for the 1935–45 period. No persistent trend is discernible for economic expenditures, but the expenditures during the 1946–50 period are on a relatively greater scale than the developmental expenditures previous to 1921. Debt charges rose rapidly until the middle of the 1930s and then fell just as rapidly. Other expenditures have tended to rise throughout.

EXPENDITURES ON GENERAL GOVERNMENT

Expenditures on general government rose greatly during the years preceding 1914 because of outlays on buildings and the establishment of permanent government machinery. Between 1914 and 1945 there was no marked upward trend, but after 1945 there was a rapid increase. Examining Figure 8.11 reveals the trends.

Administration expenditures have become the most important within the category by far. The increasing multiplicity of government activities, the secular rise in the price and wage level, and the provision of increased office space during periods of economic expansion have led to a marked upward drift in such expenditures. Increases in governmental activities have stimulated the persistence

Table 8.3 Expenditures of the Government of Alberta Classified as to Function Expressed as Percentages of Total Expenditures, 1906–50

Period averaged	General government	Social expenditure	Economic expenditure	Debt charges	Other
1906–13	26.3	15.1	49.1	5.1	4.3
1914–20	19.8	20.2	44.0	13.5	2.4
1921–25	12.7	24.5	38.5	22.1	2.3
1926–29	11.7	24.7	34.8	25.4	3.6
1930–35	10.0	31.7	29.6	25.5	3.1
1936–39	10.8	43.8	23.2	16.8	5.2
1940–45	9.6	35.2	23.5	23.7	8.0
1946–50	8.1	40.7	35.0	9.6	6.5
1950	7.5	41.8	35.2	6.1	9.3

Source: See Appendix B.

of the upward trend. Rapid price and wage rises explain the sharp increases during and after World War I and after World War II. The construction of a new central administrative building explains the peak attained in 1931. This project, incidentally, was very well timed both with respect to resource allocation and employment; the government received very good value for its money and a complete collapse of the building trades in Edmonton was prevented before 1931. Cramped office quarters induced the government to begin constructing another administration building in 1949. In addition, various minor provincial buildings have been built throughout the province from time to time.

The graph of expenditures on justice shows sharp peaks and valleys until 1933. The provision of a provincial police force accounts for the rise after 1916; its discontinuance after 1930 accounts for the subsequent decline. In recent years, salaries and fees of court officials, reporters, and other employees have been increased in harmony with the price level.

Expenditures on legislation have fluctuated with the timing of elections. There is no upward trend, and sessional indemnities, the main item in non-election years, have not increased greatly since 1906. This expenditure is closely scrutinized by the public and the press to an extent out of all proportion to the significance of legislation expenditures in the budget. In 1906–13 they equalled 3.1 per cent of total expenditures, while in 1946–50 they equalled only 0.4 per cent of these.[19] There is little room for expenditure reductions here. It would

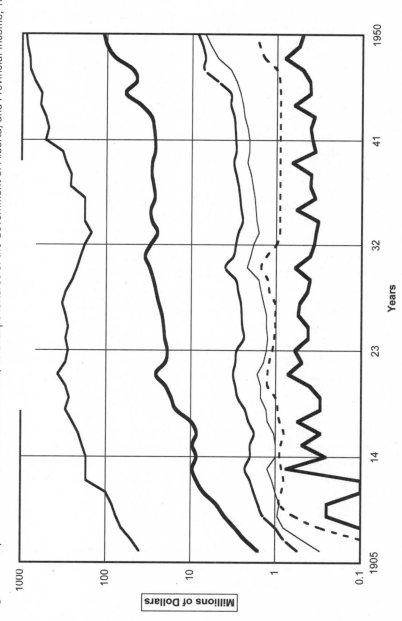

Figure 8.11 Expenditures on General Government, Total Expenditures of the Government of Alberta, and Provincial Income, 1905–1950

256

Table 8.4 Expenditures of the Government of Alberta Classified as to Function Expressed as Percentages of Provincial Income, 1906–50

Period averaged	General government	Social expenditure	Economic expenditure	Debt charges	Other	Total
1906–13	1.4	0.8	2.7	0.3	0.2	5.4
1914–20	0.8	0.8	1.8	0.6	0.1	4.2
1921–25	1.0	2.0	3.1	1.8	0.2	8.0
1926–29	0.9	1.8	2.5	1.9	0.3	7.3
1930–35	1.5	4.9	4.6	3.9	0.5	15.4
1936–39	1.2	5.0	2.6	1.9	0.6	11.3
1940–45	0.7	2.6	1.7	1.7	0.6	7.3
1946–50	0.8	3.8	3.3	0.9	0.6	9.3
1950	0.9	5.0	4.2	0.7	1.1	12.0

Source: See Appendices A and B.

be an enlightened democracy indeed if citizens scrutinized non-legislative expenditures to the high degree that legislative ones are.

Per capita expenditure on general government in selected years for the Prairie Provinces and for all provinces in the aggregate are set out in Table 8.5. Alberta expenditures per capita on this category were more than twice the national average in 1913 and 1921, indicating an administrative machine with considerable excess capacity. The spread between the two sets of figures narrowed greatly until 1945 when they were $3.89 and $3.58 respectively. Post-war expansion in administrative expenditure has been more marked in Alberta, and the gap has widened again.

The trend for all the provinces has been upward throughout the whole period while the Alberta trend was downward throughout the 1920s and 1930s. The other two Prairie Provinces show trends similar to those of Alberta but their levels of per capita expenditure have been lower.

SOCIAL EXPENDITURE

Social expenditure rose throughout the whole period without any major downswings. Generally speaking, they have tended to rise more quickly than the provincial income or total expenditures of the provincial government. Figure 8.12 is illustrative of trends. One notes an upward and unbroken trend until 1922 when economies were effected. The rise in 1924 is attributable to

Figure 8.12 Social Expenditures, Total Expenditures of the Government of Alberta, and Provincial Income, 1905–1950

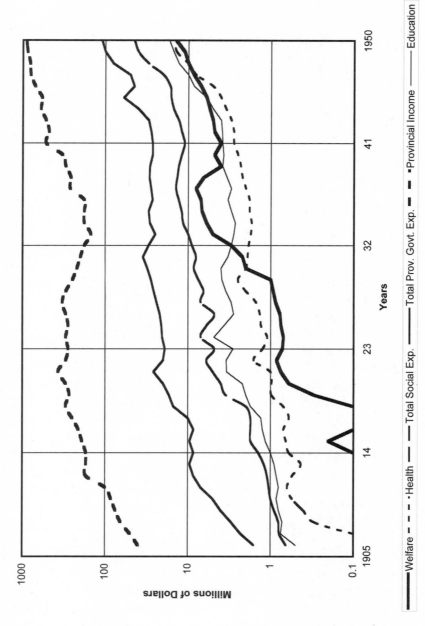

Table 8.5 Current Expenditures Per Capita on General Government by the Three Prairie Provinces and all Provinces in the Aggregate for Selected Years

Years	Alberta	Sask.	Manitoba	All provinces
1913	$3.98	$3.21	$2.13	$1.73
1921	5.17	4.13	3.45	2.49
1930	4.15	3.46	3.25	2.99
1937	3.33	2.90	2.54	3.10
1941	3.92	3.27	2.74	3.19
1945	3.89	4.49	3.53	3.58
1948	6.68	5.96	4.18	5.21

Sources: *Sirois Report*, Public Accounts Inquiry, *Dominion of Canada and Canadian National Railways and Provincial Governments, Comparative Statistics of Public Finance*, Appendix 1 (Ottawa, 1939), Statement No. 36; D.B.S., *Financial Statistics of Provincial Governments*, 1941, 1945, and 1948.

the implementation of guaranteed university debentures. The upward trend resumes after 1926, and was only broken by an economy drive in 1932. The reduction after 1938 was due to falling unemployment relief outlays. After 1942 there was a rapid upward trend exceeding the rate of increase of both provincial government expenditure and provincial income.

Education: Education expenditure, consisting largely of grants to schools and the university, rose rapidly until 1922. Between that date and 1944 there was no upward trend in contrast to other social expenditures. It is small wonder that during this period officials of the provincial education department, teachers, and school trustees acquired a cumulative sense of grievance, which has by no means been erased by the rapid rise in provincial education appropriations after 1944. Nevertheless, education services of a standard above the Canadian average (measured in terms of expenditure per capita) were maintained. There was a surplus of teachers throughout the 1930s in relation to the low salaries offered because of the high degree of unemployment and lack of liquidity in the economy. The one-year teacher-training program contributed to attract many young people into teaching rather than into occupations requiring four-year university programs which were beyond the financial capacity of any except the children of economic classes that gain by deflation. Thus Alberta, as well as other provinces, probably had teachers of a higher calibre in the 1930s than at any time before or since.[20] And the quality of teachers, rather than of buildings or curricula, is of prime importance in education.

In the light of the ability of school boards to obtain teachers of a very acceptable quality there were no impelling economic reasons for increasing provincial grants to schools; indeed, they could be reduced during the 1930s.[21] Expenditures for health and welfare, which impinge more directly upon the personal welfare of individuals, were more pressing and consequently obtained precedence. Put very simply, such expenditures had "survival importance"; many individuals would have died from starvation or ill health had they not been made. Education expenditures, on the other hand, did not assist immediate physical survival of the individual and their long-run social and economic values received lower priorities in times of stress.

The 1940s brought full employment and the withdrawal of many teachers from teaching, as well as reduced numbers of new recruits. Salaries increased in adjustment to such withdrawals. The increased birth rate during the early 1940s is now putting a strain upon school facilities. The need for new schools during the late 1940s and early 1950s was made imperative by the rundown condition of many of the old schools, the rising birth rate, and centralization of schools in rural areas. The provision of transportation facilities in rural areas because of centralization has become of importance. As a result educational expenditures have risen very rapidly, and provincial grants have risen accordingly.

Expenditures upon education by the provincial government in Alberta have been relatively high since 1916. On a per capita basis, the provincial expenditure fell to a level slightly below the Canadian average only during the first half of the 1940s.[22] In terms of provincial expenditure as a percentage of provincial income, Alberta has consistently devoted a larger proportion of income to education than all the provinces in the aggregate. The relative size of provincial grants to school districts, however, has been somewhat below the national average in Alberta throughout. As a proportion of total expenditure (both current and capital) on education within the province, the provincial grants have equalled from 10 to 30 per cent.[23] In 1948 the Alberta percentage fell somewhat below the national average. Many factors account for this phenomenon: the age distribution of the population and the degree of urbanization are two that may be mentioned. Another is simply the high level of expenditures on schools in Alberta.

The Alberta economy currently makes a greater educational effort than any other province with the possible exception of Saskatchewan. The municipalities provide by far the largest proportion of the funds, about 70 per cent. The provincial government, while contributing more on a per capita basis than most provinces furnishes a smaller percentage of the education dollar than most other provinces.[24]

One can only suggest reasons why education expenditures are relatively high in Alberta. First, the organization of school divisions has introduced collective bargaining in fixing teachers' salaries as well as systematic salary schedules with automatic upgrading features based on seniority and university degrees. In recent years, too, alternative employment opportunities have probably become more plentiful than in some other provinces.[25] Second, the centralization of rural schools has necessitated an accelerated building program and increasing expenditure on transportation.[26] Such centralization has been undertaken more rapidly in Alberta than in most other provinces. Third, the rate of urbanisation has been more rapid in recent years in Alberta than in Canada as a whole. This has necessitated extensive building programs in cities and towns to provide school facilities for new residential areas.

The provincial contribution, although not high in comparison with other provinces in a relative sense, has been increasing rapidly. The provincial government, by its system of equalization grants, has gone far to enable "poor" school divisions to provide school facilities not much below the provincial average standard. Thus a very large portion of the school grants is pumped into the school divisions of the north and west and the southeast. Whether or not this is a wise measure in terms of resource allocation is open to some question. But in the case of school grants it may be said that the appropriations may be of assistance in rendering the population more mobile than otherwise in these areas; education, by opening up new vistas and imparting skills encourages young people to seek employment in regions where their marginal productivity is higher. The provincial government, too, by its recently instituted system of making loans and grants for capital expenditures and guaranteeing the interest on school debentures is instrumental in lowering the rate of interest on Alberta school debentures in the capital market. This measure is in some degree inflationary and conducive to over expansion of school borrowing. One can only hope that the provincial government would continue the policy during a deflationary period in view of its strong cash position and credit rating in the capital market.

Public Health: The trend of provincial government health expenditure is upward throughout (see Figure 8.12), although there were decreases in expenditure during the depression of the early 1920s and 1930s, and marked upswings during the boom of World War I, the late 1920s, and the 1940s. Boom periods have been featured by construction of new hospitals, the expansion of existing services, and the initiation of new services. During deflationary periods the construction of hospitals ceased and there were reductions in existing current services. On a relative basis, however, the upward trend has been almost

Table 8.6 Public Health Expenditures of the Government of Alberta in Relation to its Total Expenditure and Provincial Income, 1936–1950

Period	Percentage of total expenditure	Percentage of provincial income
1906–13	4.5	0.2
1914–20	5.3	0.2
1921–29	6.5	0.5
1930–35	7.8	1.0
1936–45	8.3	0.7
1946–50	12.1	1.1
1950	13.4	1.6

Source: See Appendices A and B.

unbroken. Table 8.6 indicates that public health has, on the average, been absorbing an increasing proportion of provincial budgets since 1906. It also shows the increasing proportion of provincial income devoted to public health. Only during the 1936–45 period did the proportion shrink, but it rose to new peaks during the post-war years.

Public health expenditures, small before 1921, were incurred chiefly for mental institutions and grants to hospitals. These two items accounted for 73 per cent of the total in 1913; they have continued to be of basic significance for they still exceed 60 per cent of public health expenditures. The immediate period following World War I saw an expansion in general health services which were cut back in the early 1920s. It was also noted by the provision of a sanatorium for tuberculosis patients. Between 1920 and 1940 few new services were provided, and the general upward trend of expenditure is accounted for by the inexorable rise in outlays for mental institutions and by increasing grants to hospitals.[27]

In 1944 free maternity services were instituted, and in 1947 the province undertook to provide free hospitalization and medical services for old age pensioners. In 1950 these two items exceeded 20 per cent of total public health expenditure. Hospital grants were increased substantially in 1947, and in 1949 grants for hospital construction began to be made in accordance with the health grant scheme of the federal government. General services have been expanded greatly since 1948. Finally the construction of several provincial hospitals has been undertaken.

Interprovincial comparisons of public health expenditures cannot be made for the period preceding 1940.[28] Data for recent years indicate that the Alberta provincial government spends somewhat more than the national per capita average for the provinces. Thus in 1948 it spent $9.90 per capita, including capital expenditures, as against a national average of $9.10. Only provinces like British Columbia and Saskatchewan with hospitalization schemes had per capita expenditures considerably above those of Alberta. In terms of provincial personal income, the Alberta government spent 1.0 per cent, the national provincial average.[29]

Public health expenditures of the Alberta government have tended to expand and contract with upswings and downswings in the provincial income. For the whole period there has been an upward trend. In recent years there has been a very rapid increase as public health has been given high priority in the provincial budget. The emphasis during recent years has been on the expansion of hospital facilities to cope with continuous increase in the demand for space and beds. The timing of construction is not fortunate from a counter-cyclical viewpoint, and construction costs have been high. But the strong cash and credit position of the government should enable it to assist in providing additional hospital facilities as well as employment in the event of any marked recession.

Public Welfare: Public welfare expenditures were negligible before 1918 (see Figure 8.12). After 1918 several factors led to a rise to prominence of such expenditures. First, mothers' allowances began to be paid in that year; second, a provincial labour bureau was set up; third, unemployment relief was provided during the depression of 1921–22. The latter was discontinued after 1923 and public welfare expenditures did not rise appreciably again until the 1930s. After 1929 unemployment relief outlays and the inception of old age pension payments led to a large increase. A peak was reached in 1937 after which direct relief expenditures diminished rapidly yearly. Old age pensions, however, continued to increase and the payment of supplementary allowances in 1942 and subsequent years accelerated the upward trend. From 1931 to 1938 relief payments accounted for more than half of annual public welfare expenditures. In 1950 this item was of minor importance. Old age pensions made up 78 per cent of the total in that year.

In relation to the other provinces, Alberta's per capita expenditures on public welfare were approximately at the level of the Canadian average until 1930.[30] During the 1930s Alberta's per capita expenditure was somewhat less than the Canadian average and was considerably lower than that of Manitoba and Saskatchewan levels. Urban unemployment was less severe than in Manitoba and the need for agricultural relief was less than that of Saskatchewan. In 1948

Table 8.7 Economic Expenditures of the Government of Alberta in Relation to Its Total Expenditures and Provincial Income, 1906–1950

Period	Highways	Railways[a]	Tele-phones	Agriculture	Public domain	Treasury branches	Total
As percentage of total expenditures:							
1906–13	15.3	0.0	22.9	10.0	0.8	0.0	49.1
1914–20	9.9	4.8	17.4	11.0	1.0	0.0	44.0
1921–29	10.7	5.9	10.8	6.8	2.4	0.0	36.6
1930–35	11.7	–	5.5	8.0	4.5	0.0	29.7
1936–45	9.4	0.0	4.6	3.9	4.5	1.1	23.5
1946–50	20.5	0.0	7.2	1.9	4.1	1.5	35.0
1950	20.6	0.0	7.0	1.3	5.2	1.1	35.2
As percentage of provincial income:							
1906–13	0.8	0.0	1.2	0.5	0.1	0.0	2.7
1914–20	0.4	0.2	0.7	0.5	0.1	0.0	1.8
1921–29	0.7	0.5	0.9	0.5	0.2	0.0	2.9
1930–35	1.8	–	0.8	1.2	0.7	0.0	3.5
1936–45	0.8	0.0	0.4	0.3	0.4	0.1	2.0
1946–50	1.9	0.0	0.7	0.2	0.4	0.1	3.3
1950	2.5	0.0	0.8	0.2	0.6	0.1	4.2

Source: See Appendices A and B.
(a) Exclusive of interest payments on telephone debt.

Alberta's expenditure per capita was not quite as high as the national level, and as a percentage of provincial income was somewhat below the national average.

ECONOMIC EXPENDITURE

Economic expenditures were of a highly developmental character before 1921 and absorbed close to half of provincial government expenditure (see Table 8.7). They remained at a high level throughout the 1920s as many of the guarantees made before 1921 had to be implemented. They declined considerably in importance during the 1930s only to rise to prominence with the inception of an ambitious highway program during the late 1940s.

Highways: Highway expenditures have varied greatly from year to year (see Figure 8.13). Interprovincial comparisons of highway expenditures, as well as economic ones generally, are tenuous for years preceding 1940. Capital expenditure data are lacking and the distinction between current and capital expenditures are blurred because of differing accounting classifications in various provinces.[31] Current expenditure data provided by the *Sirois Report* indicate that throughout the 1920s and the 1930s Alberta spent somewhat less on highway maintenance than the Canadian average for the provinces. In any event, Alberta had very few miles of paved roads before 1940 in contrast to the situation in the central and Maritime Provinces. Between 1932 and 1946 there was no large-scale highway construction program in Alberta comparable to what was undertaken in Quebec or New Brunswick.

In 1948, a year for which both current and capital expenditure data are available, Alberta spent $21 per capita on highway construction, maintenance, and grants to municipalities. This was considerably in excess of what Saskatchewan and Manitoba spent ($11 and $15 respectively), but not much above the national average for all the provinces.[32] In short, the Alberta postwar highway program is spectacular only in relation to the past, but still falls far short of the per capita levels of such provinces as New Brunswick and Nova Scotia. This does not take into account municipal expenditures. The provincial share is much greater in the Maritimes than elsewhere in Canada, exceeding 85 per cent in all three of these provinces. For all the provinces the provincial share exceeds 60 per cent of the total. In Alberta, the provincial share, including grants to the municipalities, was about two-thirds of the total. On a per capita basis, total provincial-municipal highway expenditure in Alberta in 1948 was almost as high as in New Brunswick and Nova Scotia, about 20 per cent above the national average, and about one-third higher than in the neighbouring provinces of Manitoba and Saskatchewan. Practically all of the highway expenditures of Alberta governments, too, are paid out of current revenue while they are debt-financed to a considerable extent in other provinces.

Railways: Expenditure on railways was important between 1915 and 1930 when guarantees had to be implemented from time to time (see Table 8.7). The railway question has been discussed at some length in Chapters 3, 4, and 5 and nothing more need be said here. Examining Figure 8.13 reveals the sporadic nature of railway expenditures.

Telephones: The telephone expenditures also require little further comment. The tendency of the level of such expenditures to increase or decrease with upswings and downswings in provincial income is notable. Table 8.7 indicates the great importance of telephone expenditures before 1921 and the subsequent relative decline.

Agriculture: Expenditures on agriculture fluctuated greatly through time and have not shown a tendency to rise secularly (see Figure 8.14). Drought relief

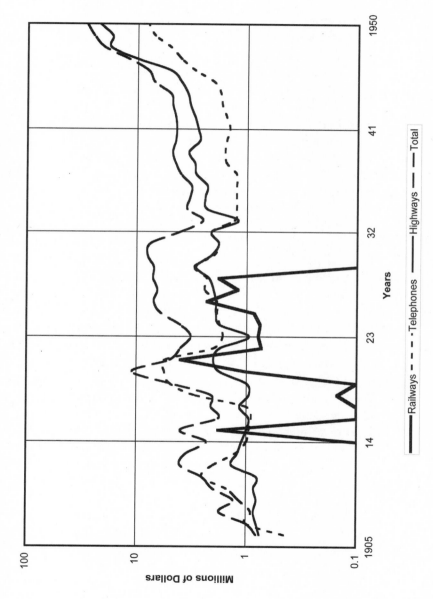

Figure 8.13 Expenditures of the Government of Alberta on Transportation and Communication, 1906–1950

and seed grain advances account for the high levels attained during the 1920s and for the rises during the 1930s. The peak of 1931 is attributable to the wheat pool guarantee. Declines in recent years can be explained by the disappearance of relief and seed grain payments and by reductions in grants to agricultural societies. In relative terms, agricultural expenditures have declined in importance. At one time they constituted about 10 per cent of total expenditure; in 1950 they were not much above one per cent (see Table 8.7). Similarly, they have declined as a proportion of provincial income except for a rather sharp rise during the early 1930s.

Comparisons with the agricultural expenditures of other provinces for selected years throughout the period indicate that Alberta has not been far out of step.

Municipal expenditures on agriculture are negligible in most years, and need not therefore be considered further. The impact of agricultural relief fell in the first instance, however, upon the municipalities in the 1930s. For most of them it became an impossible task financially, and provincial and Dominion aid had to be obtained.

Public Domain: Public domain expenditures were of little importance until the 1920s. They consisted chiefly of outlays for game enforcement, colonization propaganda, and research studies. Substantial increases resulted as assistance began to be given to irrigation and drainage districts during the early 1920s. Further increases resulted from the transfer of the public lands in 1930. Expenditures on forest administration were particularly great. There was no further upward movement until 1945 when the province assumed guaranteed irrigation bonds in connection with the debt reorganization scheme. After a temporary relapse in 1946, there has been a rapid increase in expenditures chiefly because of new irrigation projects, aerial photography surveys, and an expanded forest conservation program.

Alberta spent much less per capita on public domain before 1930 than the Canadian provinces as a group. Even after the transfer of 1930, her expenditures fell somewhat below the national average. Beginning in 1947, however, expenditures have risen relatively to other provinces so that they are approximating the average.

Treasury Branches: Outlays on treasury branches formed only about 1.5 per cent of total expenditures during the 1946–50 period and they are declining relatively to the total (see Table 8.7).

Figure 8.14 Expenditure on Public Domain, Agriculture, and Treasury Branches by the Government of Alberta, 1906–1950

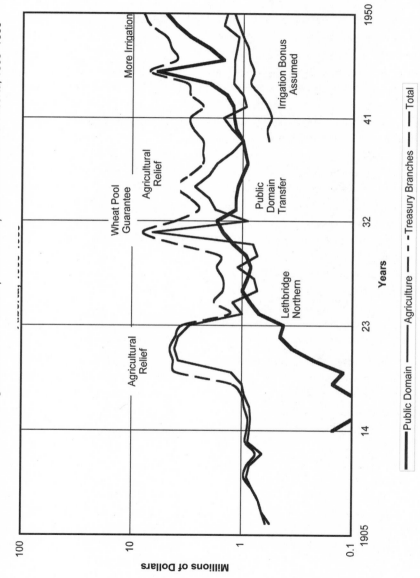

DEBT CHARGES

Debt charges rose quickly after the telephone loan of 1908. Their course can be seen in Figure 8.3. Between 1909 and 1914 they rose from about $0.2 million to $1.0 million, a fivefold increase. Their rate of increase slackened up somewhat during World War I when loan funds were difficult to get; nevertheless, they almost doubled between 1914 and 1920. Then came the large loans of the 1920–21 period with interest rates varying from 5.5 per cent to 6 per cent and in 1922 debt charges soared to $5 million, about 2.5 times the 1919 level. They rose slowly throughout the rest of the 1920s as the government endeavoured to keep new borrowing at a minimum. Thus in 1930 debt charges were only about 20 per cent higher than in 1922.

A rapid rise ensued again during the early 1930s as the government had to meet one financial crisis after another. The trough induced by debt default is very noticeable, as is the extraordinary level attained in 1945 in connection with the debt reorganization.

The relentless upward tide of debt charges before 1935 is also evident in relative terms. During the 1930s they came to absorb more than one-quarter of total expenditure and almost 4 per cent of provincial income (see Tables 8.3 and 8.4). In 1950 they had fallen to less than 6 per cent of the total budget, a level comparable to that of 1906–13.

In comparison with other provinces, Alberta early acquired per capita debt charges far above the average for all the provinces. This is evident from Table 8.8. In 1913 Alberta's debt charges were almost three times the average per capita debt charges of all the provinces. In subsequent years, Alberta continued to have exceptionally high debt charges. The debt default served to bring the per capital level down to the national average in 1937 and below it in 1941. Today, after debt reorganization, Alberta has exceptionally low debt charges per capita.[33]

OTHER EXPENDITURES

Miscellaneous expenditures have risen in absolute terms throughout the whole period but they have fluctuated rather erratically. An interesting feature is the rapid rise during the 1936–45 period when most expenditures were kept under a lid. Most of this rise was caused by a growing public works stock advances and the adoption of a policy of making advances to school districts and municipal districts with short-run financial difficulties. During the war years substantial appropriations were made to a Post-war Reconstruction Fund to be used after the war for the erection of various public works. The

Table 8.8   Debt Charges Per Capita of the Three Prairie Provinces and All the Provinces in the Aggregate for Selected Years

Year	Alberta	Sask.	Manitoba	All provinces
1913[a]	$1.30	$0.85	$1.20	$0.45
1921[a]	4.40	1.65	2.00	1.65
1930[a]	6.10	3.15	2.60	2.85
1933[a]	8.05	5.40	6.25	4.75
1937[a]	4.60	6.60	5.20	4.60
1941[b]	5.60	7.75	7.80	7.00
1948[b]	5.40	10.90	8.90	8.35

(a)   Net debt charges derived from the *Sirois Report*, Book 3.
(b)   Gross debt charges derived from the D.B.S. provincial finance statistics.

$5 million appropriation of 1950–51 for municipal self-liquidating projects accounts for the great increase in that year.

EXPENDITURES ON GUARANTEES

Expenditures on the implementation of guarantees cut across the previously discussed classifications, but are mainly economic. These expenditures furnish one of the main explanations of Alberta's financial difficulties after 1920. The guarantee was a popular device of the Alberta government before 1921. It was a convenient method of encouraging investment in transportation, irrigation, and educational facilities; it was also a device that postponed the necessity of going to the capital market for agricultural relief funds. Consequently, it tended to be used carelessly and the optimism of the early era overrode caution.

Railway, irrigation, and university bonds were guaranteed, and the province was called upon to back these promises constantly throughout the 1920s. The northern railways were in continuous financial and operational trouble following their completion immediately after World War I. Their gross earnings were pathetically small in relation to capital investment, and in almost every year during the 1920s the government had to help pay interest on bonds and even to contribute to meet operation expenses. Relief from the situation was finally obtained by the sale of the railways. The irrigation guarantees proved costly, especially the one for the Lethbridge Northern, and during the early 1920s the government was beginning to meet bond interest and maintenance costs. Most of the university bond guarantees made in 1914 had to be implemented in 1924 and 1925; a final one had to be met in the crisis year of 1936.

There were also agricultural guarantees made during 1918 to 1922 to enable farmers to purchase cattle and seed grain. These took the form of provincial backing of farmers' promissory notes with banks. Outlays on the taking up of such notes ran into millions of dollars during 1921 and 1922; they tapered off during the rest of the 1920s. The U.F.A. administration was very unfortunate in its inheritance of past promises that had to be redeemed. These implementations throughout the 1920s were the main reason why the Alberta government was financially embarrassed during that decade. Then, of course, came the wheat pool incident and the need for more agricultural relief during the 1930s.

The heavy incidence of implemented guarantees between 1921 and 1935 is evident from the figures above and from an examination of Figure 8.15. In geographic terms, it was expenditures on guarantees made to provide railways in the north and west, and to provide irrigation and agricultural assistance in the southeast, which accounted for two-thirds of the total before 1936 and for more than three-quarters of the total by 1950. Telephone expenditures in sparsely settled rural areas, the extraordinary education grants to schools in drought and fringe areas, the location of a large share of the public works of the 1930s in the same areas, and the guarantees probably accounted for about half of the direct public debt incurred before 1935. It was expensive to be a large province with large marginal areas, which were productive only sporadically.

REVENUE IN RETROSPECT

GENERAL TRENDS

The trend of revenue has been upward since 1906 (see Figure 8.16). The revenues of local governments rose rapidly during the developmental period preceding 1914 and easily outstripped provincial. They levelled off during World War I and then rose to a new level until 1922. After that date they remained practically constant until 1942, a remarkable testimony to the stability of the property tax and utility income. During the post-war era municipal revenues have risen greatly but the rise is not as spectacular as that of provincial government ones.

The tax collections of municipal governments have been far greater than provincial throughout. It was only during the 1935–41 period that provincial

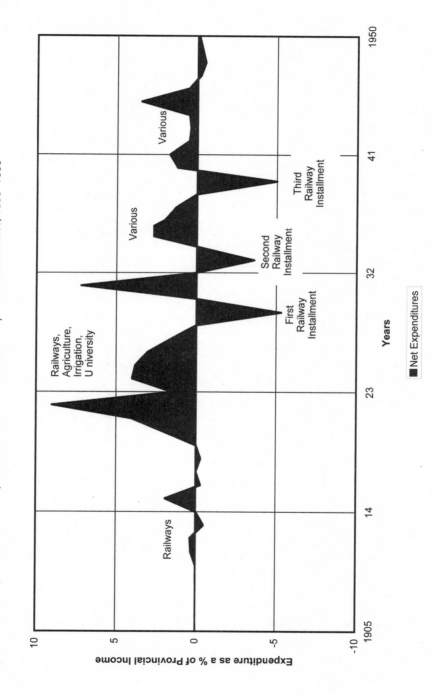

Figure 8.15 Net Expenditures Made by the Government of Alberta to Implement Guarantees, 1905–1950

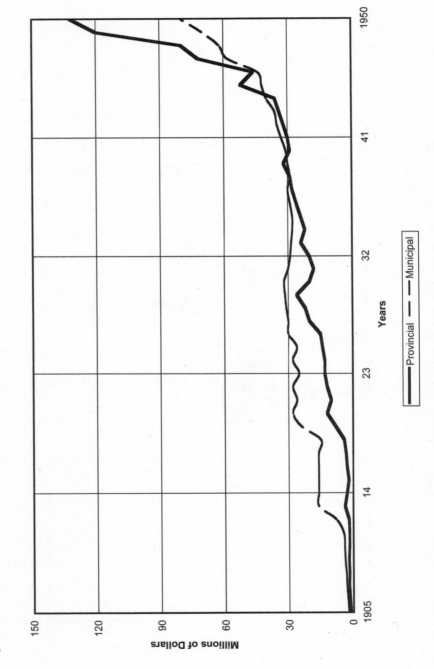

Figure 8.16 Total Revenue of the Provincial and Municipal Governments of Alberta, 1905–1950

taxes became important relatively to total taxes of the two levels of government. Then came the tax agreements with the federal government that led to the suspension of most provincial taxes. Today only the gasoline tax is significant among provincial taxes.

Provincial taxes absorbed an increasing proportion of income until 1936; this proportion declined until 1942 after which it has remained practically stable. Total taxes imposed a light burden on the economy until 1912; they rose rapidly during 1913–15 and then fell off again during World War I when income rose rapidly. After 1920 taxes relatively to income reached a higher level than at any previous time, and then remained stable until 1928. During the early depression years the tax burden became extremely heavy, reaching a peak in 1933. Subsequently there was a continuous decline to levels corresponding to those of World War I and considerably lower than those of the 1920s. During the 1942–50 period, taxes have constituted a stable proportion of income. In short, the tax burden of recent years has been the lowest since World War I.[34] This may be somewhat surprising to those who express alarm at the rapid absolute increases in property taxes. In no previous period have taxes been so easy to collect; the ratio of property tax arrears to current collections has been lower during the 1945–50 period than during any time before.

INTERPROVINCIAL COMPARISONS

The current revenue of the provincial government of Alberta has, surprisingly enough in view of criticisms that have been levelled at it (cf. *Bank of Canada Report*), been higher relatively to income and in per capita terms than that of the provincial Canadian average since 1913. The only exception to this statement applies to 1921. Figures 8.17 and 8.18 bear out these observations. It is worth noting that municipal revenues have declined relatively to provincial revenues over time.

With respect to tax revenue per capita, the provincial government lagged behind other provinces before 1921, exceeded these in 1921 and 1926, and fell behind in succeeding years. Figure 8.19 shows the changes of various years. The high Canadian average for 1948 relatively to Alberta is attributable to the tax agreements: Ontario and Quebec (which have not signed these) levy the bulk of provincial taxes. Again the tax revenue per capita of both provincial and municipal governments in Alberta exceeded the Canadian average before 1930. Since then taxes per capita have been lower than for Canadian provincial and municipal governments as a group. The much-criticized revenue policies of the Alberta

274

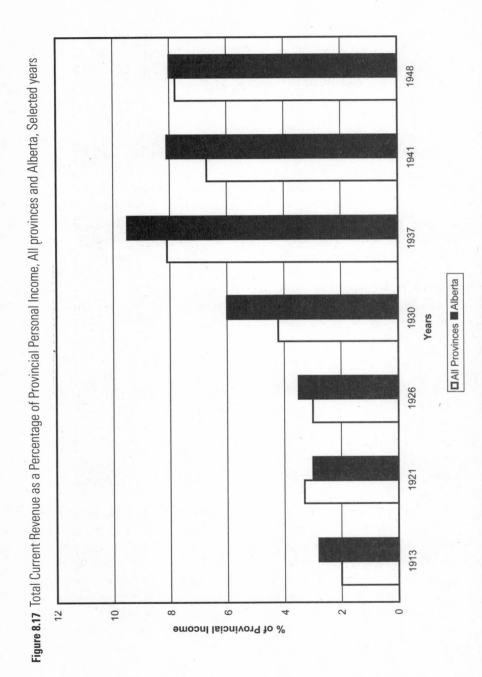

Figure 8.17 Total Current Revenue as a Percentage of Provincial Personal Income, All provinces and Alberta, Selected years

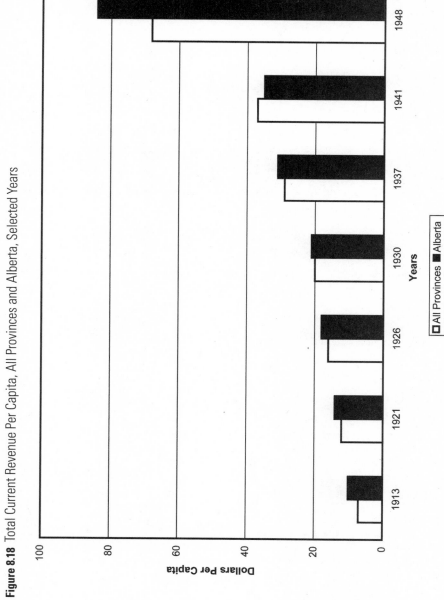

Figure 8.18 Total Current Revenue Per Capita, All Provinces and Alberta, Selected Years

Figure 8.19a Taxes Per Capita of the Provincial and Municipal Governments in Canada and Alberta, Selected Years

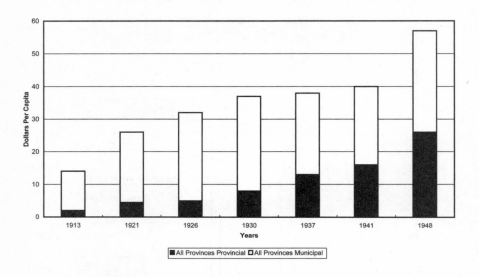

Figure 8.19b Taxes Per Capita of the Provincial and Municipal Governments in Canada and Alberta, Selected Years

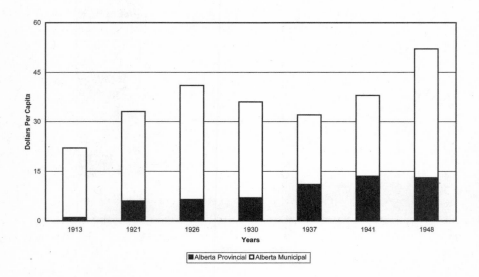

provincial government before 1930 are more understandable when one considers the high level of municipal taxation in Alberta relatively to other provinces.

PATTERNS AND TRENDS OF PROVINCIAL REVENUE

Marked changes in the relative importance of different kinds of revenues have taken place since 1906. Table 8.9 indicates those changes in relation to total revenue.

Receipts from the Dominion of Canada have varied in importance, as illustrated in Table 8.9. The statutory subsidies constituted nearly all the receipts until 1920. After that date various grants-in-aid became significant. For example, during the 1925–27 period, highway grants rose to prominence. During the 1930s, grants for unemployment relief and old age pensions rose rapidly. Finally the tax agreements of the 1940s swelled Dominion of Canada payments to the provinces to major proportions.[35]

Tax collections have risen greatly secularly, but they have fluctuated in response to income changes, rate changes, the imposition or abolition of taxes, and the tax agreements. Figure 8.20 summarizes the changes for the whole period.

In relation to total revenue, taxes were small before World War I. The imposition of property taxes, increased corporation taxes, and the introduction of a gasoline and income tax made taxes the most important category between 1914 and 1945. After the latter date only the gasoline tax has continued to be a significant revenue-producer, and taxes have fallen to third place as a revenue source.

Prior to World War I, licences and fees made up the largest local revenue category. Despite the rise of motor vehicle revenue after 1915, the whole category has declined in importance since that date (see Table 8.9). A number of fixed fees have become customary throughout the decades, and consequently revenues from licences and fees have tended to vary with volume changes induced by provincial upswings or downswings. Land titles fees are particularly cycle-sensitive. Fees from motor vehicles have been the most important relatively since the late 1920s. There are also a number of regulatory fees that were originally the most important, but they have since declined in relative importance.

The sales of commodities and services were of considerable importance before 1921 when the government was involved in the creamery business. Receipts from the sale of hay in 1920 led to a peak in that year which was not surpassed until 1947 (see Figure 8.21). With the discontinuance of government participation in creamery operation after 1920 institutional revenue constituted the main item in the whole category. The establishment of the treasury branches in

Table 8.9 Composition of the Revenues of the Government of Alberta, 1906–1950

	1906–13	1914–20	1921–29	1930–35	1936–45	1946–50
% of total revenue:						
Dom. of Canada	40.2	22.1	11.7	13.7	21.7	25.4
Taxes	7.1	21.0	22.2	23.0	22.5	11.8
Licences and fees	17.7	15.9	13.8	12.3	11.1	7.8
Public domain	0.3	1.7	1.7	4.1	6.1	23.6
School lands	3.7	5.1	3.8	3.4	2.2	1.7
Liquor control	2.8	2.4	9.8	7.4	12.0	12.0
Fines	1.3	1.4	0.9	0.5	0.3	0.2
Sales	8.7	8.8	3.5	2.6	2.1	2.5
Refunds	4.3	0.8	2.3	3.4	2.8	1.3
Interest	4.3	8.0	10.0	11.4	4.2	2.4
Repayments	0.7	0.9	9.9	11.5	8.2	4.9
Miscellaneous	0.1	0.3	0.2	0.2	0.2	0.1
Telephones, net	8.9	11.6	10.2	6.4	6.7	6.1
Total	100.0	100.0	100.0	100.0	100.0	100.0

Source: Appendix B.
Note: Telephones (net) equals gross revenues of the telephone system less interest payments of the telephone debt.

1940 has given a new fillip to revenue from sales. Nevertheless, sales are rather insignificant and constituted only 2.1 per cent of total revenue in 1950–51.

Figure 8.21 shows the dramatic rise in public domain revenue that has come to occupy first place in the Alberta revenue structure. It might be noted that the descent from the dizzy heights scaled in recent years is already on the way during the 1951–52 fiscal year. The future course of public domain revenue is, however, hazardous to predict.[36]

Revenue from the sale of liquor ranks fourth in the revenue structure. It has risen to prominence after the prohibition period of World War I. It is quite cycle-sensitive as indicated by the large decline during the early 1930s and the subsequent rapid rise.

Revenue from school lands rose rapidly until 1920 and then remained relatively stable until 1947. Since 1947 it has climbed upward sharply because of the sale of leases and mineral rights of school lands and royalties from oil and natural gas reproduction.

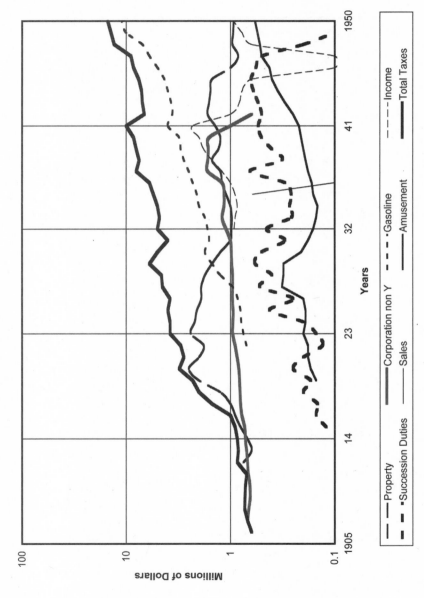

Figure 8.20 Tax Revenues of the Government of Alberta, 1906–1950

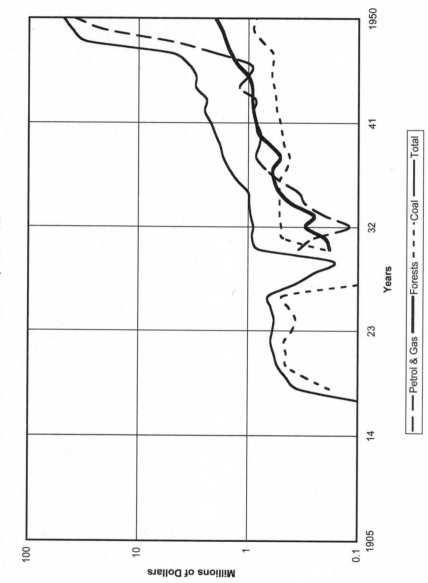

Figure 8.21 Revenue of the Government of Alberta from Public Domain, 1906–1950

Revenue from telephones rose sharply during the pre-1914 era and then levelled off until 1919 when they began to spiral upward again as facilities were extended. A levelling off took place during the depression years of the 1920s. After considerable increases during the late 1920s, large decreases took place during the first half of the 1930s. The subsequent rise has not been at as rapid a rate as the increase in provincial income because of little change in rates throughout the years, a very usual state of affairs in the telephone industry both among privately or publicly owned concerns.

Interest revenue has largely increased or decreased with corresponding changes in debt charges. Its importance has declined relatively since 1935. The changes in absolute amounts can be seen from Figure 8.22.

Repayments were unimportant before 1921. During the 1921–35 period, however, it equalled about 10 per cent of total revenue (see Table 8.9). In recent years it has declined in importance. It has fluctuated greatly because of the sporadic and occasional nature of many types of repayments; these fluctuations are shown in Figure 8.22.

INTERPROVINCIAL COMPARISONS

The composition of the provincial revenue of Alberta and that of all the provincial governments are compared in Table 8.10 for selected years. Only current revenue figures are shown. Capital revenue data are not available for all years.

Several observations may be made without going into detail. The decline in the importance of Dominion of Canada receipts for all the provinces before 1930 is evident. Heavy Dominion relief expenditures led to a rising importance of Dominion receipts in provincial budgets during the 1930s. Despite the tax agreements signed by seven provinces, there was a relative decline in the 1940s because the two largest provinces did not sign such agreements.

Taxes have provided about 40 per cent of revenues of all the provinces since 1921. Alberta's reliance upon this revenue source has always been less than in other provinces. The decrease in Alberta in this respect has become very marked during recent years.

Licences and fees have always been more important in Alberta than in all the provinces as a group. As to public domain revenue, Alberta fell behind all the provinces until the transfer of 1930. In 1948, of course, its public domain revenue greatly exceeded in importance that of any other province. Revenue from liquor control has become relatively more important in Alberta than in all the provinces only since 1937. This phenomenon can probably be explained partly in terms of the more rapid rise of Alberta income than of total Canadian income.

Figure 8.22a Revenue of the Government of Alberta from Interest and Repayments 1906–1950

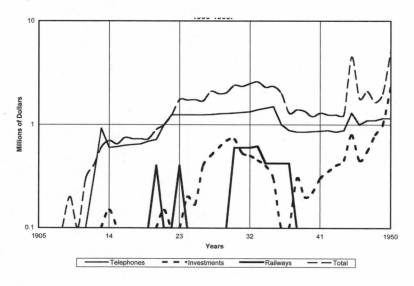

Figure 8.22b Revenue of the Government of Alberta from Interest and Repayments, 1906–1950

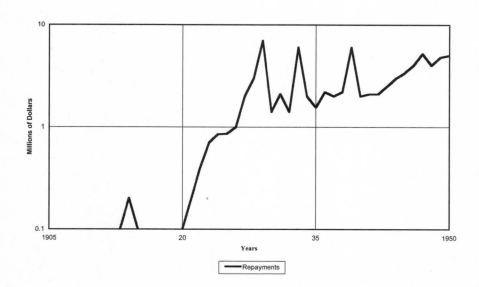

Table 8.10 Composition of Current Revenues of the Province of Alberta and All
Provinces for Selected Years (in percentages of total revenue)

	Dominion of Canada	Taxes	Licences and Fees	Public Domain	Liquor control	All other	Total current revenue
1913							
Alberta	28.4	7.3	28.2	1.3	2.9	32.0	100.0
All provinces	27.8	20.1	14.7	23.8	4.8	8.8	100.0
1921							
Alberta	21.8	34.8	21.8	5.6	3.1	12.8	100.0
All provinces	14.3	38.1	16.7	15.9	8.5	6.4	100.0
1930							
Alberta	15.4	34.0	20.5	5.5	13.1	11.5	100.0
All provinces	12.5	41.4	15.3	9.1	16.4	5.2	100.0
1937							
Alberta	29.1	35.9	11.7	6.9	10.7	5.6	100.0
All provinces	31.4	40.8	10.4	6.4	9.1	2.0	100.0
1941							
Alberta	13.9	36.5	15.2	9.1	13.9	11.5	100.0
All provinces	18.6	43.3	10.3	7.7	11.4	8.8	100.0
1948							
Alberta	29.5	14.8	9.3	23.1	14.6	8.6	100.0
All provinces	21.3	43.0	8.9	6.8	11.8	8.2	100.0

Sources: *Sirois Report*, Book 3, for 1913, 1921, 1926, 1930, and 1937, and D.B.S., *Financial Statistics of Provincial Governments*, 1941 and 1948. The data for 1913, 1930, and 1937 exclude revenue from interest which was offset against debt charges on the expenditure side. The data for 1941 and 1948 include interest; consequently the "all other" percentages are somewhat higher for 1941 and 1948 than for some previous years.

PUBLIC DEBT

TRENDS IN TOTAL DEBT

The remarkable growth of public debt in Alberta before 1921 is evident from an examination of Figure 8.23. Total provincial debt, which includes guarantees, reached about $116 million in that year. Direct provincial debt, which excludes guarantees, rose to about $63 million. The rate of increase of debt, both direct and indirect, was greater than that of provincial income. The provincial government was certainly trusting that the future would take care of its obligations. More fundamentally, it was concerned with intensifying provincial resource utilization, which, it was hoped, would eventually provide a revenue base adequate to pay interest on debt and to repay it. The guarantees were made

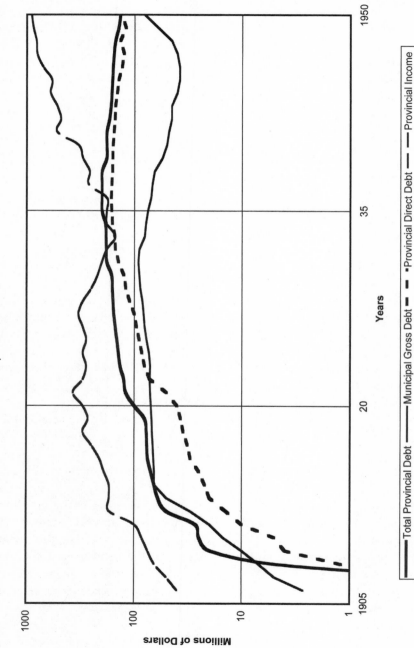

Figure 8.23 Total Debt of the Government of Alberta Municipalities, 1906–1950

on the presumption that the projects concerned would become self-liquidating. Failure to make estimates on a factual basis led to disappointment and disillusionment; the risks were not calculated. Even if calculations had been made and facts had been obtained, no one could foresee the stagnation of the two decades after 1920. As far as provincial debt was concerned, a relatively small proportion of it was incurred to provide public services of a traditional nature in the main settled parts of the province.[37]

Total municipal debt kept pace with total provincial debt until 1914; after that date it levelled off. It greatly exceeded provincial direct debt until the early 1920s. In contrast to the provincial state of affairs, most of the municipal debt was incurred to provide the standard type of urban facilities.

Total provincial debt continued to rise until 1935 but at a less rapid rate than before. The growth during the 1920–35 period arose chiefly from expenditures arising out of guarantees, highway expenditures, relief expenditures, and deficits on income account (see Table 8.11). Total debt grew from $116 million at the end of 1921 to an all-time high of $202 million at the end of the fiscal year 1935–36.[38] There was a diminution in indirect debt during this period from $53 million to $41 million because of the sale of the railways and the implementation of guarantees. The character of the indirect debt also changed because the Canadian National and Canadian Pacific Railways assumed much of it.[39] The direct debt also reached its peak[40] in 1935–36.

Municipal debt grew very slowly from 1920 to 1936. It responded little to the brief boom in the late 1920s and rose somewhat during the 1930s because of heavy relief expenditures.

Total provincial debt fell steadily after 1936, the year of the default. By 1943, the two national railway systems had redeemed all the bonds guaranteed by the province and assumed by them. The temporary loans of the province were repaid in 1939 and savings certificate redemption went on steadily after 1936. The debt reorganization program of 1945 did not lead to any immediate decrease in funded debt but paved the way for future redemption because of the introduction of call features in new debentures issued and exchanged for old ones. In 1950 a net reduction of $20 million was secured through a refunding transaction undertaken to take advantage of lower interest rates. The Alberta and Great Waterways issue was called in 1947 and retired.[41] In the same year the Dominion government wrote off $13.3 million of treasury bills owed by the province.

Municipal debt fell steadily from 1936 to 1946. Since the latter date it has risen sharply and is now rapidly approaching the level of provincial debt. The province has provided some of the loan funds. The proportion of such funds

Table 8.11 Assets of the Government of Alberta, December 31, 1921 and March 31, 1936 (in millions of dollars)

Assets:	Dec. 31 1921	Mar. 31 1936	Change
Guarantees:			
Railways	26.9	17.0[a]	−9.9
University of Alberta	4.3	4.7	0.4
Irrigation and drainage districts	6.0	12.2	6.2
Agricultural and municipal[b]	7.7	13.4	5.7
Subtotal	44.9	47.3	2.4
Telephones	19.9	24.8[c]	4.9
Relief[d]	0.0	15.2	15.2
Public buildings	9.5	18.3	8.8
Highways	9.4	33.1	23.7
Alberta Wheat Pool	0.0	4.8	4.8
Debenture discount and foreign exchange	2.3	6.3	4.0
Current deficit	2.2	15.1	12.9
All other[e]	8.9	16.1	7.2
	97.1	181.0	83.8
Less sinking fund, capital surplus account and deferred revenue	−1.2	−10.5	−9.2
Net total representing outstanding debt	95.8	170.5	74.7

Source: *Sirois Report* Public Accounts Inquiry, Appendix J, *Province of Alberta, Comparative Statistics of Public Finance*, Schedule 1.

(a) Includes the railway instalment due in 1939 as well as capital losses written off.

(b) Recoverable advances for seed grain, relief, fodder, livestock, hail insurance, co–operative credit societies.

(c) Includes capital losses of $8.9 million written off on the rural system.

(d) Includes direct relief and relief works.

(e) Includes cash, investments, accounts receivable, working funds, and miscellaneous items.

will increase in the future because smaller amounts are now obtainable by municipalities in a restricted capital market and the provincial government has indicated its intention to increase the appropriation for municipal loans for the fiscal year 1952–53.[42]

The changing relationship of the public debt of the two levels of government to the provincial income is striking. In 1920 total debt of both levels equalled 46 per cent of provincial income, a high enough proportion for an externally held debt. In 1930 it was about 100 per cent, and in 1935 it was about 150 per cent, a most excessive and critical proportion. By 1940 it had declined to 75 per cent, and by 1950 it has fallen to 22 per cent. The stagnation and retrogression of the Alberta economy during the 1920–40 period is the primary factor accounting for the onerous debt burden of that period, and the buoyancy of the Alberta economy during the 1940s is the chief reason for the great decline in the ratio of debt to income during that decade. Probably no other comparison shows so dramatically the acute debt problem of the 1930s.

TRENDS IN THE COMPONENTS OF PROVINCIAL DEBT

The changes in composition of provincial debt are set out in Table D1 of Appendix D. The province relied chiefly upon temporary loans from the banks during the pre-1913 period.[43] Such loans were obtained only sporadically after 1913 and the 1912 peak of $10.7 million was never again reached. After 1935 this type of borrowing practically ceased.

Savings Certificates grew from $0.4 million at the end of 1917 to a peak of $11.8 million at the end of fiscal 1929–30. A decline set in during the 1930s as withdrawals grew and deposits fell off. After 1936 the government began to redeem certificates gradually after the suspension of 1935. At the end of 1950–51 only $0.7 million was outstanding.

The chief items of other unfunded debt are accounts payable and the pension fund. The latter has risen rapidly during the 1940s as a consequence of enhanced payrolls.

The telephone issue of $2.0 million issued in 1908 was the first direct debenture debt incurred by the province. There was no further increase until 1912 when the province began to make its large temporary loans permanent. The net direct debenture debt reached a peak of $126.7 million by the end of fiscal 1932–33. Since then it has declined in almost every year, either from repayments or from sinking fund growth or both, and at the end of fiscal 1950–51 was only $88.8 million.

Dominion Government Treasury Bills were first issued in 1931 and the U.F.A. administration relied upon them increasingly until the end of its tenure of office. The total outstanding at the end of fiscal 1935–36 was $26.2 million. Only $0.3 million more was added to this total during 1936–37 to finance unemployment relief partially. There were no further additions in subsequent years; indeed, there were small reductions. In 1947 a total of $13.3 million was written off and a systematic schedule for retirement of the balance in 30 years was set up.

Class I Indirect Debt consists of loans and advances guaranteed by the province in the first instance. It rose rapidly after 1908 because of guarantees of railway bonds. From 1909 to 1911 it stood at $19.6 million. In 1912 it rose to $34.1 million. At the end of 1916 it reached a peak of $41.6 million. In 1917 the national railways assumed prime responsibility for $19.0 million of this, the province retaining secondary responsibility. In 1919 the railways assumed another $3.5 million of debt, and in 1929 a final $9.4 million was assumed. Implementation of a number of guarantees in the 1920s led to further reductions. At the end of 1935–36, Class I indirect debt equalled only $8.6 million. It remained close to this level until the end of 1945 when irrigation and drainage district debentures were transferred to direct debt. This brought the level of a low of $1.2 million at the end of 1945–46. It has been rising since that date because of guarantees of the debts of various provincial marketing and commercial agencies.

The nature of Class II Indirect Debt consists of railway debentures originally guaranteed by the province, but later assumed by the Canadian National Railways and the Canadian Pacific Railways. The province still remained liable in event of default by the railways. The total rose from $19.0 million at the end of 1917 to $32.2 million at the end of 1929–30. Between 1937 and 1943, the two large national railways retired all of this sum, thus relieving the province of a very remote obligation.

INTEREST RATES ON PROVINCIAL DEBT

The province has been most unfortunate in the timing of the incurrence of its debt with respect to interest rates payable. The policy of relying on temporary loans before 1913 proved to be costly in two ways: first, short-term rates were higher than long-term ones at the time, and second, the general level of interest rates rose in 1913 when the province finally issued substantial amounts of debentures. Thus debentures had to be sold at 4.5 per cent in late 1913; they

Table 8.12 Analysis of the Gross Funded Debt of the Government of Alberta by
Coupon Rates, 1913, 1921, 1931, 1936, 1946, and 1951
(in millions of dollars)

Coupon rate, per cent	Dec. 31 1913	Dec. 31 1921	Mar. 31 1931	Mar. 31 1936	Mar. 31 1946	Mar. 31 1951
0	0.0	0.0	0.0	0.0	0.0	4.8[a]
2.00	0.0	0.0	0.0	0.0	3.5	–
2.25	0.0	0.0	0.0	0.0	1.5	0.6
2.50	0.0	0.0	0.0	0.0	1.1	–
2.625	0.0	0.0	0.0	0.0	0.0	20.1
2.75	0.0	0.0	0.0	0.0	4.9	30.2
2.875	0.0	0.0	0.0	0.0	0.0	23.3
3.00	0.0	0.0	0.0	0.0	34.0	7.4
3.25	0.0	0.0	0.0	0.0	14.1	14.1
3.50	0.0	0.0	6.9	0.0	76.4	0.1
4.00	23.0	14.0	6.9	33.3	0.0	0.0
4.50	17.7	19.5	38.7	51.8	0.0	0.0
5.00	7.7	15.3	38.1	45.8	5.4	0.0
5.50	0.0	4.3	11.6	8.6	0.0	0.0
6.00	0.0	32.5	21.3	20.9	0.0	0.0
6.50	0.0	0.4	0.4	0.4	0.0	0.0
Total debt	48.4	86.1	124.0	160.8	140.8	100.6
Avg. coupon rate	4.34	5.13	4.93	4.79	3.33	2.70

Sources: *Sirois Report*, Appendix J, *Alberta*, Schedule 10, for 1913, 1921, 1931, and 1936; *P.A.*, *1945–46*, and *P.A.*, *1950–51*, for 1946 and 1951.
Note: Dominion government treasury bills and Class I guaranteed debentures are included in the totals.
(a) Interest–free Dominion government treasury bills.

could have been sold at 4 per cent in 1912 or early 1913. Table 8.12 shows the
distribution of debt according to interest rates payable.[44]

Most of the debentures issued between 1913 and 1921 were sold at 5 to
6 per cent. A university issue guaranteed by the province sold at 6.5 per cent.
Again the timing was bad, most of the debt of the 1914–21 period being incurred during 1920 and 1921 when interest rates were at their highest peak in
the western world since the beginning of the industrial revolution. For that
matter, nearly all of Alberta's debt was incurred during a period of abnormally
high interest rates.[45] Borrowing during the 1920s continued at rates between
4.5 and 5.5 per cent. Similar rates were paid during 1930 and 1931 when the
province obtained large sums in a tightening capital market. The rates on

Dominion government treasury bills varied from 3.5 to 5.5 per cent between 1931 and 1933; there were successive reductions from the high of 5.5 per cent in 1933 to 3 per cent in 1937. Table 8.12 summarizes changes in the distribution of debt according to interest rates from 1921 to 1936.

During the default period, coupon rates were not paid in full and in 1945 permanent reductions in rates were obtained. After the debt reorganization program was completed, the average coupon rate was only 3.33 per cent. Practically all of the new debt carried rates between 2.75 and 3.5 per cent. Debt refunding in 1950 brought even lower coupon rates and on March 31, 1951, the average was 2.70 per cent. By refunding in the New York market where rates were lower than in Canada, most of the issues outstanding after some redemptions carried rates between 2.625 and 2.875 per cent. Today there is no major debenture issue outstanding carrying a rate exceeding 3.25 per cent. Such rates are a remarkable reflection upon the extraordinary strength of the debentures of a province that was in default only a few years ago.

THE MATURITIES OF PROVINCIAL FUNDED DEBT

Pre-1922 Debt: No debenture issues became due until 1922. In that year a refunding process, which did not cease until 1936, began. This was another factor, beside the implementation of guarantees, which embarrassed the administration financially. Nevertheless, Alberta's credit standing in the capital market was strong enough to support refunding operations and additional issues until 1932. After that date, the province became greatly dependent upon funds from the Dominion for the retirement of old debt. Table 8.13 sets out the schedule of retirements between 1922 and 1936.

The Debenture Debt as at March 31, 1936: New debentures were not issued between 1936 and 1945, and borrowing from the Dominion almost ceased after fiscal 1936–37. The maturity dates of the debenture debt existing on March 31, 1936 ran from 1937 to 1980; the Dominion treasury bills were issued chiefly on a yearly basis and were renewable annually. Table 8.14 shows a summarized schedule of retirements called for by the maturity dates of gross debenture debt exclusive of Dominion treasury bills. On March 31, 1951 the debt would have been less than half the 1936 level assuming that Alberta had not defaulted and that the Alberta and Great Waterways issue had been called.[46] Thus substantial debt reductions were called for during the 1936–51 period. Redemptions during the 1950s would have reduced the total debenture debt to

Table 8.13 Debt Retirement and Incurrence, 1922–1936 (in millions of dollars)

Fiscal year ending	Debentures matured and retired[a]	Net charge in total debt[b]
December 31:		
1922	7.1	10.1
1923	7.4	4.7
1924	8.0	3.2
1925	4.5	3.3
1926	5.5	6.3
March 31:		
1928	5.5	8.4
1929	3.8	3.8
1930	3.0	2.4
1931	9.0	9.9
1932	13.0	17.5
1933	0.0	4.2
1934	7.0	−1.2
1935	3.9	6.3
1936	2.0	7.0

Source: *P.A., 1922–36.*
(a) Includes issues having a maturity exceeding one year.
(b) Includes increases or decreases in unfunded debt, direct funded debt, Dominion treasury bills, and indirect debt.

$17.7 million in 1961, about 12 per cent of the 1936 total. By 1971 there would have been practically no debenture debt left. A final issue of $1.0 million was due in 1980.

Actually, of course, there were practically no redemptions between 1936 and 1945. Sinking fund proceeds amounting to $0.5 million were applied to debt redemption in 1936, and some debenture stock amounting to $0.3 million was retired during the early 1940s. The debt reorganization program of 1945 cancelled the sinking funds, and this secured a reduction in debt of $20 million in that year (see Table 8.14). Redemptions under the debt reorganization program called for complete debt retirement by 1980. These were to have been made by an accelerating crescendo of payments. The third column in Table 8.14 shows the amounts involved for five-year intervals in the 1950s and for ten-year intervals during the next two decades.[47]

Table 8.14 Scheduled Retirement of Gross Debenture Debt in Existence on March 31, 1936, Government of Alberta. Direct and guaranteed debentures are included but Dominion treasury bills are excluded. (in millions of dollars)

	As Per Schedule[a]	Actual of D.R.P.[b]	Projection[c]
1. Debenture debt, March 31, 1936	135.3	135.3	
Less retirements before March 31, 1945	−35.8	−0.8	
2. Debenture debt, March 31, 1945	99.5	134.5	134.5
Less retirements in 1945–46	−6.0	−19.9[d]	−19.9[d]
3. Debenture debt, March 31, 1946	93.5	114.6	114.6
Less retirements, 1946–51	−27.7[e]	−25.8[e]	−10.1[e]
4. Debenture debt, March 31, 1951	65.8	88.8	104.5
Less retirements, 1951–56	−20.6	−13.2	−12.3
5. Debenture debt, March 31, 1956	45.2	75.6	92.2
Less retirements, 1956–61	−27.5	−18.8	−15.5
6. Debenture debt, March 31, 1961	17.7	56.8	76.7
Less retirements, 1961–71	−15.8	−49.5	−31.6
7. Debenture debt, March 31, 1971	1.9	7.3	45.1
Less retirements, 1971–81	−1.9	−7.3	−45.1
8. Debenture debt, March 31, 1981	0.0	0.0	0.0

Sources: *P.A., 1936–51*, and *Sirois Report*, Appendix J, *Alberta*, Schedule 11.

(a) The sinking funds are included in the totals. On March 31, 1936 they equalled $12.0 million. Net debt was accordingly less by this amount. Between 1936 and 1951 the funds would have fluctuated between $12 million and $15 million assuming sinking fund growth from interest only, with no direct contributions. The sinking fund levels would be smaller after 1951 because of large redemptions.

(b) According to the rearrangements following the 1950 refunding transactions for the years following 1951. The figures subsequent to 1946 are representative of net debt as against the *gross* figures shown in the first column. All sinking funds were liquidated in 1945.

(c) According to the schedule of redemption set up under the debt reorganization program (D.R.P.).

(d) The retirements made under the debt reorganization program of 1945 were made by cancelling the sinking funds. Consequently the figures under the "actual" and the "projected" columns for 1946 and subsequent years show *net* debenture debt in contrast to gross debt under the "as per schedule" column. See also footnote (b).

(e) Includes retirement by call of the Alberta and Great Waterways issue in all three cases.

The refunding transactions of 1950 not only lowered coupon rates on much of the outstanding debt but also accelerated the redemption program. The effects of these transactions on the prospective level of net debenture debt are indicated in the second ("actual") column of Table 8.14.

Comparisons of the Three Potential Schemes: In making comparisons of debt levels if there had been no debt default, many assumptions are necessary. These have been elaborated in Appendix D. Here the chief concern is with the debenture debt, and Table 8.14 sets out three bases for comparison. The first column shows gross debenture debt throughout.[48] The second and third columns show gross debt until 1946 and net debt after that date. No account is taken in Table 8.14 of additional borrowing that would have been necessary from 1936 to 1945 to meet maturing obligations. Estimates of such borrowings are indicated in Appendix D.

On the basis of the data in Table 8.14, it is seen that the debenture debt would have been consistently lower after 1936 than actually has been the case if no default had occurred. The differential widens with the passage of time. In 1961 Alberta would have been practically free of debt in the form of debentures if a sinking fund deduction from the $17.7 million for that year is made.[49] Offsetting this would be a larger new debt incurred after 1936 than has actually been the case. Estimates in Appendix D indicate that the level of all debt under the "no default" assumption would have been considerably less than the actual projected level after the year 1943.

Call Features: Any comparison of debt levels in the future must be tempered by considering the call features of the present debt. The 1936 debt contained only three callable issues. This rigidity of debt maturities proved to be a most consequential barrier to the refunding proposals made by the Alberta government before 1936.

In 1945 the Alberta government was mindful of this blocking of refunding in the 1930s and insisted upon the inclusion of call features in the bonds issued in exchange for old ones. Thus the $76.4 million of bonds issued in exchange in 1945 were callable before maturity on any interest date on or after June 1, 1950, with accrued interest at sixty days notice. The new debentures issued for cash to redeem bonds which had matured between 1936 and 1945 were not callable. Nor were the Dominion government treasury bills callable; but presumably the senior government would not be averse to complete redemption before 1977. The likelihood of this is small because a large part of the indebtedness is non-interest bearing and the balance carries a rate of 2.625 per cent.

The government took advantage of the call feature of most of its debt in 1950. It served notice on debenture-holders of its intentions in March 1950, and issued new callable debentures in New York. The interest rate on the 1945 debentures was 3.5 per cent; rates on the new ones varied between 2.625 per cent and 2.875 per cent.[50] It seems unlikely, however, that further interest rate reductions can be secured in the future in view of these low rates.[51] But insofar as the foreign exchange factor becomes favourable to the government, outright redemptions may take place in the future before scheduled dates. To this extent the comparisons in Table 8.14 for the 1951–80 period are not entirely valid. The government now has a large liquid reserve that could be used to redeem debt. It would still have almost as large a reserve if there had been no default, but re-demption opportunities would have been substantially smaller. The debt to be redeemed would, of course, have been much smaller than is now the case.

DISTRIBUTION OF PUBLIC DEBT BY CURRENCY OF PAYMENT

Foreign exchange fluctuations impose a task of prognostication upon govern-ment treasurers who must administer public debt held in foreign countries. As prophets they have no better records than other ones, and there can be little censure of decisions, which prove to be wrong in the light of subsequent events unless treasurers show a flagrant disregard of international currency fluctua-tions. Thus the heavy foreign exchange expenditures of 1931–33 in Alberta in connection with debt interest payments and bond redemptions were inevitable; the treasurer had no choice but to pay or default; it would be useless and unfair to fulminate on administrative inefficiency under the circumstances obtained at the time.

In more recent years foreign exchange fluctuations have posed the ques-tion of whether or not to redeem debt. For example, the Alberta and Great Waterways issue could have been reduced more favourably after the devaluation of the pound sterling in the fall of 1949. But devaluation was not foreseeable to any certain degree in 1947; the interest savings of 1947–49 on the issue also offset to some degree potential gains arising from waiting for devaluation.

A current problem facing the government is that of redeeming callable bonds held in the United States. The Canadian dollar has recently risen to par with the American and presumably the time would be opportune to redeem American-held debt. But another factor, the rise in the level of interest rates dur-ing 1951, has interposed itself. The average coupon rate on the external debt is in the neighbourhood of 2.75 per cent. The cash balances of the provincial treasury can be used to purchase securities of low risk yielding as much or even more.

Table 8.15 Debenture Debt of the Government of Alberta Classified According to Place of Payment, 1936 and 1951 (in millions of dollars)

Payable in:	Mar. 31 1936	Mar. 31 1951
Canada only	29.8	1.8
Canada or New York[a]	65.8	86.9
Canada, New York, or London[a]	19.9	0.1
Canada or London[a]	4.0	0.0
London only	15.3	–
Total	134.8	88.8

Sources: *P.A., 1950–51*, and *Sirois Report*, Appendix J, Schedule 13.
(a) Exact segregation is not obtainable in publications. Holders of debentures have the choice of both or all three currencies.

Foreign investors have always held a large share of the Alberta debt. The distribution of the provincial debenture debt in terms of currency of payment is accordingly shown in Table 8.15.

INTERPROVINCIAL COMPARISONS

Total Provincial Government Debts: Figure 8.24 shows the levels and trends in total provincial government debts since 1913. The Alberta debt grew so rapidly before 1913 because of railway guarantees that it exceeded that of any other western province in that year. Since 1936 it has declined consistently in contrast to other provinces, where the debt did decline during the early 1940s but rose sharply during the later years of that decade. Alberta is practically the only province that is able to pursue a pay-as-you-go policy.

Total Municipal Debt: Figure 8.25 shows levels and trends in municipal debt in Canada since 1913. The Alberta trends do not conform in all respects. The Alberta municipalities had reached their peak by 1913; after that date municipal debt remained almost stable until 1930 in contrast to the rise in the national trend. The post-war upswing has been sharper than the national one. This rise has more than offset the decline in provincial debt so that the combined

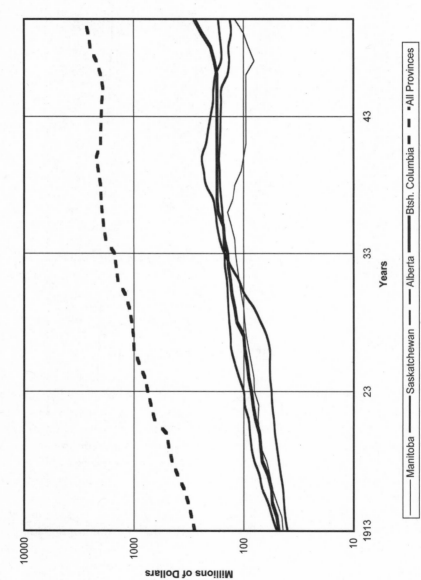

Figure 8.24 Total Debt of Provincial Governments in Canada, 1913–1950

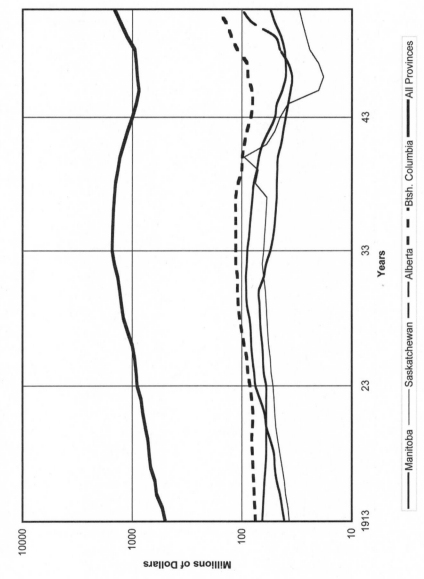

Figure 8.25 Outstanding Debt of Canadian Municipalities, 1913–1951

provincial-municipal debt has risen since 1946, but the upward trend in the combined total is less marked than is the case for the national one.

The trends in the municipal debt of the other three western provinces, in contrast to Alberta, rose with the national trend until the 1930s. The urban land boom before World War I was more marked and speculative in Alberta than in the other provinces, and it went so far that her municipalities were almost financially crippled for decades. The municipalities in the rest of Canada, including the other three western provinces, also responded to the boom in greater degree than those in Alberta. The Alberta municipalities simply did not have the credit standing required for substantial debt increases. The rate of decrease of debt after 1933 among all the four provinces varied greatly. Municipal defaults in Saskatchewan account for some of the rapid decreases there. During the post-war period the Alberta upswing was the sharpest of all as the Alberta municipalities rebounded from their long period of readjustment to the crippling blows of the 1913–15 depression.

Per Capita Comparisons: THE per capita debt of the Alberta provincial government was higher than that of all the provinces as a group before the late 1940s. In recent years it has become the lowest in Canada with the exception of Newfoundland. Table 8.16 sets out per capita debt for selected years. Alberta held the lead among the provinces until the 1930s when she was surpassed by British Columbia, and in the 1940s Saskatchewan and New Brunswick have taken over the lead.

With respect to municipal debt per capita, Alberta was surpassed only by British Columbia in 1913. After that date the per capita level fell steadily in Alberta until 1945. Then came a reversal; between 1945 and 1950 it doubled in five years.

Combined figures serve to show that Alberta had an abnormally high debt in 1913. The urban land boom assumed larger proportions, and the rate of economic development was more rapid in Alberta than in the other two Prairie Provinces. Coupled with the use of the guarantee device by the provincial government, these factors explain the high level of the Alberta debt before World War I. No per capita increase took place between 1913 and 1921; population growth and municipal stagnation offset the increase in provincial debt. But the per capita level was still the second highest in Canada, and almost twice as high as that of Saskatchewan. For the 1921–30 period the rate of increase of the combined provincial-municipal debt per capita was less than in any other province. Alberta was licking the wounds of the 1913 and 1921 downswings. The stagnation of the 1920s did not help matters, and the early downswing in income, beginning in 1928, checked both municipal and provincial expenditure

Table 8.16 Per Capita Comparisons of Provincial, Municipal, and Combined Debt of Canadian Provinces, 1913, 1921, 1930, 1936, 1945, and 1950 (in dollars)

	1913	1921	1930	1936	1945	1950
Provincial debt:						
All provinces	37	72	121	183	163	204
Alberta	122	162	196	220	195	132
Saskatchewan	70	70	110	196	233	186
Manitoba	90	119	156	175	132	149
British Columbia	119	153	196	239	183	248
Municipal debt:						
All provinces	66	92	120	128	72	86
Alberta	144	103	94	67	46	92
Saskatchewan	67	66	71	63	24	32
Manitoba	86	114	138	121	53	66
British Columbia	168	153	156	139	89	120
Combined debt:						
All provinces	103	164	241	311	235	290
Alberta	266	265	290	287	241	224
Saskatchewan	137	136	181	259	257	218
Manitoba	176	233	294	296	185	235
British Columbia	287	306	352	378	272	368

Sources: The same as for Figs. 41, 42, and 43. Population data were derived from *C.Y.B.*, 1936, and D.B.S., *Canadian Statistical Review*, various issues.

responses to the short recovery of the 1920s. Between 1930 and 1936 the per capita combined debt of all the provinces in the aggregate rose by 29 per cent. Of all the provinces, only Alberta saw its combined debt per capita fall, if only by 1 per cent.

The data suggest that Alberta had reached toleration limits in public debt many years before the other provinces. Albertans were debt conscious to a high degree in 1921, and the fuel, which ignited the blaze of debt default in 1936, had been smouldering for many years.

The picture has changed since 1936. The combined per capita debt in Alberta in 1950 was 22 per cent below the 1936 level despite the rapid rise of municipal debt between 1945 and 1950. It was 23 per cent below the average of all the provinces, and it was lower than that of six other provinces. There is a strong presumption that it will be the lowest of all within a few years. If intergovernmental debt is excluded from the computations (i.e. provincial loans to the municipalities) and the cash and investment holdings of the provincial government are deducted, Alberta's combined debt per capita is the lowest of all now,[52] with the exception of Newfoundland, most of whose debt was assumed by the Dominion government in 1949.

The default did not bring about the debt reduction which has taken place since 1936; it instead resulted in the province having at present a somewhat higher debt than if it had not defaulted.[53] The careful expenditure policy of the government has been a factor of consequence; it has learned the lessons of the past well. The phenomenal upsurge of revenue has, however, made the greatest difference. The prodigal son of the Canadian federation has returned home and the fatted calf of public domain has been killed.[54]

Debt-Income Comparisons: RATIOS of public debt to annual personal income payments provide measures of debt burdens in relation to the ability to pay. Table 8.17 provides a comparison of the debt-income ratios of the four western provinces and of all the provinces in the aggregate.

The ratio of the provincial debt of all the provinces grew from 17 per cent of personal income in 1921 to a peak of 56 per cent in 1933. The large personal income increases of the 1940s have reduced the burden greatly; in 1950 the ratio was only 21 per cent. Until 1936, Alberta's provincial debt-income ratio was almost twice the national average – it is now the lowest with the exception of Newfoundland.[55]

Alberta municipalities had a debt-income ratio exceeding the national until the middle of the 1920s. Between 1925 and 1950 it was considerably lower than the national. However, between 1946 and 1951 the debt of Alberta municipalities tripled at a rate of growth, which easily exceeds that of any other province. During the same period the debt of all Canadian municipalities grew by only 57 per cent.[56] The Alberta growth has outstripped income increases, while for Canada as a whole municipal debt has moved upward at the same rate as income.

It is little wonder, in view of its debt doctrines, that the Alberta provincial government is becoming increasingly concerned with municipal financial problems. Aside from doctrinal questions, it makes little sense to be concerned with the diminution of provincial debt and the realization of an excellent provincial credit standing when the subordinate units are forced to go to the capital market to such an extent that their credit standing deteriorates seriously. The province is accordingly increasing its advances to the municipalities at low interest rates; it could also lend its excellent credit rating to municipal bonds.

Table 8.17 Comparisons of the Debts of Provincial and Municipal Governments in Canada with Personal Income (as percentage of personal income)

	1921	1926	1930	1933	1936	1945	1950
Provincial debt:							
All provinces	17	23	29	56	52	21	21
Alberta	32	42	54	108	96	29	13
Saskatchewan	15	16	44	131	108	36	22
Manitoba	23	30	38	68	59	19	16
British Columbia	26	30	36	57	56	21	21
Municipal debt:							
All provinces	13	25	28	49	36	9	9
Alberta	20	22	26	43	27	7	9
Saskatchewan	14	15	28	52	35	4	4
Manitoba	23	30	33	51	40	8	7
British Columbia	27	26	29	45	33	10	10
Combined debt:							
All provinces	30	48 `	57	105	88	30	30
Alberta	52	64	80	151	123	36	22
Saskatchewan	29	31	72	183	143	40	26
Manitoba	46	60	71	119	99	27	23
British Columbia	53	56	65	102	89	31	31

Sources: As for Appendix B for debt data; Appendix A for income data.

APPRAISALS AND CONCLUSIONS

9

STRATEGIC FACTORS IN ALBERTA GOVERNMENT FINANCE

What are the forces and trends, which shaped the destinies of Alberta governments through the years? Which are permanent in nature and which have been more or less transitory? Major among the persisting forces are the low density and scattered nature of the population, the uncertainty of annual weather conditions, the abundance of certain physical resources, and the high degree of dependence upon external markets for the products of the Alberta economy. Among the transitory forces or trends, the major ones were the rapidity of settlement during the first decade of the province's history, the economic stagnation and depression from 1920 to 1940, the rapidity of economic development during the 1940s, and various decisions of the Dominion government.

THE LOW DENSITY AND SCATTERED NATURE OF POPULATION

Most of Alberta is uninhabited. Settlement is concentrated in about one-quarter of the area, comprising the east-central and southwestern part of the province.[1] This "core" has four-fifths of the population; it produces more than three-quarters of the gross value of agricultural products annually, more than nine-tenths of the oil, and about two-thirds of the coal. Yet its population density is only twelve per square mile if the urban population is included in averaging; it is less than six per square mile if one excludes the cities and towns. Settlements outside this "core" are scattered. The two main ones are in the southeast, which has large empty spaces, and in the remote Peace River region. Minor ones are found along the northern and western fringes of the "core" area and in such isolated spots as Fort Vermilion.

Under these conditions the costs of providing government services are high. Highways, railways, and telephone lines must conquer space even though the population is sparse; the construction of such facilities to the settlements outside the "core" area poses an even greater economic problem. The heavy drain imposed by the rural telephone system on the provincial treasury during the first three decades of the province's history is basically attributable to the large line mileage per subscriber even in the "core" area. The northern railways had to be laid through too many miles of uninhabited territory; they have earned enough revenue to cover all costs only during very few years.[2] The necessity of providing and maintaining thousands of miles of passable highways has always reduced the funds available for the extension of the mileage of gravelled and paved roads. Education costs have also been affected in large parts of the province. Under the one-room system, which was so prevalent until recent years, there were many schools with very small enrolments because of sparse populations. The economies secured in centralizing schools through the reduction in the aggregate number of classrooms within the area covered have been largely offset by additional transportation costs. The provision of hospital facilities has suffered from similar handicaps. The administrative overhead of the provincial government and small rural municipal units tends to be high.

The handicaps above are also experienced by Saskatchewan and Manitoba with one important difference. These provinces have very few scattered outposts such as those possessed by Alberta and no "southeastern vacuum."[3] They did not become involved in uneconomical railway and irrigation ventures on a large scale, or in the provision of telephone service in widely scattered areas.

WEATHER HAZARDS

Agriculture in Alberta is subject to many weather hazards. Yield fluctuations from year to year can be very severe.[4] This has made for an unstable rural municipal revenue base, and it has hampered the imposition of provincial levies upon the farming community. It has also rendered agricultural relief and the provision of seed grain necessary at frequent intervals, even when agricultural prices have been high. Saskatchewan and Manitoba are also subject to weather uncertainties to a high degree, but the incidence of hail and frost is greater in Alberta.[5] Nevertheless, the handicap of Alberta in relation to the other two provinces is not marked, and the constant threat of drought in Saskatchewan is so great as to wipe out any differential in uncertainty between the two sister provinces. The ruinously widespread incidence of drought in Saskatchewan during the 1930s, for example, was without parallel in Alberta except in the southeast.

ABUNDANCE AND VARIETY OF PHYSICAL RESOURCES

Alberta has a wider variety of physical resources than either of the other two Prairie Provinces.[6] Their fuel resources in terms of coal, petroleum, and natural gas are negligible compared to those of Alberta. They have no tar sand deposits. They lack the ranching and tourist areas of the foothills and slopes of the Rocky Mountains. Their main resource is agricultural land except for one or two mineral-producing areas and water power in Manitoba.

This greater variety of resources has given Alberta important coal, petroleum, natural gas, ranching, and tourist industries. Public domain revenue has recently provided a bonanza for the provincial government upon which the other two provinces cast envious glances. There are indications that such revenue will continue to be substantial in view of the rapid rate of resource exploitation and exploration now taking place.[7]

But there were heavy costs incurred by governments for resource development during the first four decades of provincial history. The tar sands of Fort McMurray and Waterways were an inducement to build that enfant terrible, the Alberta and Great Waterways Railway. The remote fertile prairies of the Peace River region led the province to guarantee the construction of northwestern forks of railways that needed provincial financial support until 1930. The feasibility of irrigation by the use of water from the streams of the Rockies tempted the government to guarantee irrigation projects. Considerable sums were spent annually upon the extension of coal markets. Highways were built through empty regions to reach the national parks and enable tourists to visit them by automobile. The location of the vital eastern slopes of the Rockies in Alberta cost the province large sums annually for forest protection after 1930. The physical resources have, in short, been a standing invitation for the government to spend. This was one of the factors leading to the financial strain that came to the breaking point in 1936. Now, the public domain has become the leading provider of the provincial treasury.

THE DEPENDENCE UPON EXTERNAL MARKETS

The Alberta economy is very vulnerable to changes in the world economy. It is highly dependent upon world markets for many of its products, especially agricultural ones. Weather vagaries in other wheat-producing regions of the world have created annual fluctuations in the price of Alberta wheat in the past, but the federal government's wheat policy has provided a cushion against this kind of fluctuation during recent years. The cyclical and structural decreases in demand combined with increases in the supply of agricultural products arrested economic progress in Alberta during the 1920s and 1930s. Such changes in opposite directions have been the mainspring of Alberta prosperity during the 1940s. The development of secondary industry in the province will do little to mitigate cyclical instability except under certain conditions. If such industries produce for the Alberta market their production will fluctuate with agricultural income; if they produce for external markets they will be subject to the uncertainties created by the unpredictability of world events. Only to the extent that both the secondary and primary sectors find their products absorbed by the domestic Canadian market would stability be greater. Even this is a statement open to serious question because of the high dependence of Canada upon export markets.[8]

Income fluctuations have made the revenue base of the provincial government unstable, and certain revenue sources have tended to be quite income-elastic. The gasoline tax and liquor profits are cases in point. The difficulties with provincial property taxes also stemmed from external as well as internal factors bearing upon income-generation. The problem of maintaining fiscal solvency with a large proportion of fixed expenditure was especially acute before 1940. Expenditures on agricultural and unemployment relief created new pressures upon the provincial and municipal treasuries during the depressed 1930s.

RAPIDITY OF SETTLEMENT, 1906–13

We turn now to certain dominant economic and political trends that have exercised a profound influence upon Alberta public finance. One of these is the settlement boom preceding World War I. It left a legacy of debt, both provincial and municipal, which made an imprint upon public finance until this day. Probably no period in Alberta's history would warrant a detailed study of public finance and private investment decisions more than that of 1906–13.

The main developments during this period have been discussed.[9] The provincial government made most of its railway guarantees before 1913, and it began the expensive telephone project. The municipal governments incurred a direct debt, which proved to be almost beyond their financial means for more than twenty-five years. The result was that Alberta governments had the highest per capita debt in Canada in 1913 with the exception of British Columbia. Provincial government additions to debt between 1918 and 1921 ensured Alberta's maintenance of this dubious distinction in 1921. Albertans thus acquired an early experience that made them very public-debt conscious during the 1920s. Budget speeches and debates in the legislature indicate hypersensitivity on the subject. The government constantly deplored the drain on the treasury of several million dollars annually for debt charges; yet it was faced with the necessity of borrowing more money in every year to meet guarantees and to provide public services. The opposition criticized increments in debt severely. The pressure of debt charges and the need for additional borrowing increased during the 1930s, and all political parties emphasized debt refunding. By 1936 the majority of Albertans took debt default in their stride.

ECONOMIC STAGNATION, 1920–40

The economic progress envisaged during the first fifteen years after 1905 did not materialize until the 1940s. If steady growth of the Alberta economy had taken place after 1920, the financial problems of Alberta governments would have been difficult enough in view of the early debt incurrence. But the pre-1921 level of prosperity was not maintained during the next two decades, let alone increased. Instead, the level of provincial income drifted downward; between 1920 and 1935 it fell in ten years and rose in only six. After 1935 it took seven years before the level rose to that of 1920.[10] The provincial income record of Saskatchewan is no better during the same period, and during the 1930s it was worse. But Saskatchewan entered the 1920s and the 1930s with a much smaller public debt, municipal and provincial, than Alberta.[11] Manitoba's income record was somewhat better than that of the other two provinces; its public debt was larger than Saskatchewan's but smaller than Alberta's in 1921 and 1930.

RAPID DEVELOPMENT DURING THE 1940S

Associated with the rapid economic progress during the 1940s have been annual increases in provincial government revenues, which have led to growing budget surpluses. The debt problem of the provincial government has diminished almost to insignificance. One of the most important government finance problems is here found solved. But among the municipalities debt is rising rapidly because of economic growth and the deferment of projects between 1920 and 1945. Municipal revenues have not received the same fillip from economic recovery as provincial, and the expenditure on municipal government services has grown faster than provincial income because the demand for such services is entailing capital outlays, which cannot be paid for out of current revenue. Between 1946 and 1951 the revenues and expenditures of both levels of government rose at rates exceeding the rate of increase of provincial income.[12] Since municipal revenues must come almost totally from the incomes of Alberta residents, increasing resistance to municipal taxation is encountered as such taxation comes to absorb an increasing proportion of provincial income. The provincial government obtains more than half of its revenue from two sources: the Dominion government which, of course, collects taxes from Albertans, and foreign investors and a sprinkling of local speculators. It has fewer responsibilities to meet than the municipalities in providing government services for an inflowing population. Careful consideration must accordingly be given to provincial-municipal fiscal relations.[13] The municipalities are agents delegated to perform functions that are provincial constitutionally; the provincial government cannot afford to regard itself as separate from its creatures.

DOMINION GOVERNMENT INFLUENCES

The Dominion government has made several decisions that have had a pervasive and lasting influence on provincial finance. First and foremost was the decision to make Alberta a province in 1905. Was Alberta made a province prematurely and was the northern boundary drawn too far north? Or should only one province have been formed in 1905? Secondly, there was the public domain controversy. Third, there was the Dominion government failure to handle the debt default episode in March 1936 with greater vigour and by means of closer contacts with provincial officials. Fourth, there are the tax agreements of the 1940s and the pressure brought to bear to secure debt reorganization. The senior government has made its influence felt in other ways, but these are too numerous to discuss here.

MAJOR POLICIES AND EVENTS: AN APPRAISAL

THE PREMATURE FORMATION OF THE PROVINCE

The province of Alberta was formed prematurely from a public finance point of view. This judgement is based upon the examination of events subsequent to 1905. The fiscal difficulties that beset the provincial government during the 1920s and 1930s would have been mitigated if the province had been formed in 1913 or 1914; debt default may not have taken place in 1936. The crux of the matter is that the limitation upon the incurrence of debt by the territorial government was one of real significance.[14] Provincial autonomy in 1913 instead of 1905 would at least have postponed the railway guarantees and there is evidence to suggest that they might not have been made on any large scale after 1913. Scarcities of men and materials and a shortage of funds during World War I precluded much railway construction. The post-war depression would have constituted a further deterrent. Knowledge of the economic value of the

North Country would have been greater. The direct debt would also have been smaller than was actually the case, since there would have been no legislative buildings on the "grand" scale before 1921, and the telephone project would likely have been postponed.[15]

Aside from the railway and telephone projects, provincial government services were not of crucial importance to settlers during the 1906–13 period. Neither were the expenditures on administrative buildings; makeshift structures would have sufficed for a territorial government. The residual expenditures were chiefly upon education, highways, and agriculture. Expenditures for these purposes were not unduly large and a territorial government, assisted by the Dominion, would probably have provided almost as high a level of services in these spheres as was actually the case. Table 9.1 is illustrative; it shows estimated revenues and expenditures for the 1906–13 period assuming that Alberta had been a territorial government or had part of the old territory. Actual expenditures of the provincial government as well as revenues are also shown.

It seems logical enough that while settlement of Dominion lands was going on at a rapid rate, provincial status might have been deferred. The territorial government had provided for local government organization so that the provision of local services might have been offered on the same scale as under provincial jurisdiction. Even on the score of regional self-government, the case for granting autonomy in 1905 is not convincing. There were no mass demonstrations demanding provincial autonomy. The drive for autonomy was largely the work of a comparatively small number of men who were irked by the limited means of the territorial treasury and the restrictions on borrowing. Political ambition and the desire for equal status with officials and political representatives of the provinces were also motivating factors.[16] Then there were the ambitions of citizens in such centres as Edmonton, Calgary, and Prince Albert who desired to see their home towns become provincial capitals.[17] The territorial government was both representative and responsible to the electorate. There are few, if any, unsavoury incidents that mar its legislative record; this is more than can be said for the provincial government that followed. It is the privilege of the citizens of a democracy to make mistakes, but they are entitled to some facts before they make decisions that prove faulty. The facts of the Alberta and Great Waterways guarantee were not brought to light (one is still much in the dark about them) and the early increments of the direct debt of Alberta were incurred rather surreptitiously.

Whether the federal government could have resisted the pressure for autonomy until 1913 is a question of great uncertainty. It would have found itself faced also by demands for more railway guarantees and developmental expenditures. If

Table 9.1 Actual and Assumed Expenditures and Revenues of the Government of Alberta for the 1905–1913 Period (in millions of dollars)

EXPENDITURE	Actual	Assumed
Legislation	1.3	0.7[a]
Gen. administration	6.2	2.0[b]
Justice	3.6	0.1[c]
Education	4.2	3.8[d]
Public health	1.9	1.7[d]
Public welfare	0.2	0.2[d]
Agriculture	4.2	2.5[e]
Public domain	0.4	0.4
Highways	6.5	5.8[d]
Telephones	9.6	0.0
Interest	2.2	0.0
Other	1.8	0.6[f]
Total	42.1	17.8
REVENUE		
Dominion of Canada	9.8	10.1[g]
Taxes	1.7	1.1[h]
Licences and fees	4.3	1.1[i]
School lands	0.9	0.9
Sales	2.0	0.6[j]
Interest	1.0	0.2[k]
Telephones	3.0	0.0
Refunds	1.1	0.1[i]
Other	3.7	3.7
Total	27.5	17.8

Source: See Appendix B.
(a) It is assumed that no lieutenant–governor's residence would have been constructed and that sessional indemnities and election expenses would have been smaller. The assumed level is, if anything, a little too high in relation to the level of expenditure on legislation of the territorial government before 1905.
(b) Construction and land titles office outlays of $3.8 million are subtracted from the actual as well as $0.4 million of a miscellaneous character.
(c) This function would have been largely federal.
(d) A 10 per cent reduction is assumed.
(e) The advances to the creameries are subtracted and a further 10 per cent cut assumed.
(f) Chiefly subtraction of outlays on interest on Alberta and Great Waterways bonds.
(g) A residual figure inserted to balance revenue and expenditure. On a per capita basis it is not more than 25 per cent greater than the appropriation to the territories in 1904.
(h) Railway taxation is subtracted.
(i) Land titles and legal fees are subtracted.
(j) Repayments of the creameries are subtracted.
(k) Decrease accounted for by no telephone interest reimbursements.
(l) After subtracting the Alberta and Great Waterways refund.

they had been granted, the federal treasury could have withstood the subsequent strains more easily than the provincial; the federal government assumed some of the subsequent costs of provincial guarantees anyway. And the provincial treasury of Alberta would not have been crippled from the first decade of its existence.

The municipal financial picture would not likely have been much different if provincial autonomy had been postponed. The urban local governments and all school districts possessed the legal right of borrowing, a most peculiar state of affairs in view of the limitation upon the territorial government.[18] The major cities had already had their basic charters approved by the territorial assembly before 1906. Consequently, the financial excesses of the pre-1914 era would not have been prevented. But at least it can be argued that Alberta residents would not have suffered significantly from a lack of collective services under a territorial government until 1913 because the local governments supplied by far the greatest portion of them.

Ancillary to the question of premature formation of the province is that of boundaries. The principle adopted to carve out the two new provinces was to make the sixtieth parallel the northern boundary and then to divide the territory between British Columbia and the eastern boundary of Manitoba equally. Presumably the sixtieth parallel was chosen because it was the northern boundary of British Columbia, although it was not in conformity with the northern boundary of Manitoba, which was still the "postage stamp" province in 1905. The northern boundary might well have been drawn at the fifty-fifth parallel, a distance of about one hundred miles north of Edmonton. Such a boundary would have made the new province coincide largely with the old District of Alberta and it would have been about half the present area.

Such a boundary decision would have prevented the provincial guarantees of the northern railways. The Dominion, of course, would have been under pressure to make the guarantees instead, but it would have been more impervious to local pressures than the provincial government, and its fiscal capacity was greater. To add vast and forbidding wastelands to the territory of a government, which lacks an adequate revenue structure, is to pave the way to fiscal insolvency of that government. There are examples in the local government sphere in Alberta to illustrate this point beside the example of the provincial government. When there are isolated areas containing physical resources that would be of high economic value in a location close to markets, the temptation to develop them becomes too great and expensive projects are undertaken accordingly.

THE FORMATION OF ONE PROVINCE

Perhaps the suggestion that provincial autonomy was premature is too presumptuous in the light of the pressures exerted upon the Dominion in 1905, and there are those who would cavil at the thought. Nevertheless, the remarks regarding the financial effects of the 1905 decision can stand.

There was, however, the alternative of forming only one province in the territories instead of two. This alternative had much support from members of the territorial assembly, and especially from Mr. Haultain, the territorial premier who fought to the end for the formation of only one province.[19] Dr. Lingard says: "The vast majority of the people would have received with equal satisfaction the establishment of one large province."[20] He concludes that the proposal was turned down because of local and personal ambitions in two or three communities (most notably Calgary and Edmonton), opposition of the Liberal members of parliament from the territories, and fear in the older provinces that one large province in a territory with a rapidly growing population would become preponderant in the federation.[21]

From a public finance point of view it is unfortunate that the one-province idea was rejected. The legislative members of the eastern part of such a province might have become an effective counterweight to those of Northern and Central Alberta who would have desired to make developmental expenditures north of Edmonton.[22] The telephone venture may have been undertaken on a sounder basis.[23] There would have been only one set of administrative buildings and machinery instead of two. The population of Saskatchewan exceeded that of Alberta by a considerable margin between 1905–13, and the Saskatchewan members of a one-province house would have been more numerous. The Saskatchewan government did not indulge in guarantees to nearly the same extent that the Alberta one did. The presumption is strong that some of the ill-advised policies adopted by the Alberta government before 1921, would have been rejected by a government with jurisdiction over both the areas actually made provinces.[24]

THE RAILWAY GUARANTEES

The railway guarantees of 1909 and 1912 proved to be a serious drain on the provincial treasury from 1919 to 1929.[25] This aspect has been dealt with, and it has been suggested that they had a damaging effect upon the faith of Albertans in the integrity of politicians.[26] Yet how should they be assessed on broader economic and social criteria?

The attempts at settlement and the provision of transportation facilities in the north were examples of incorrect distribution in the allocation of resources.[27]

The north is a marginal area, and the patches of good agricultural land are so scattered and remote as to make transportation costs forbidding. The railways constructed were subsidized by the provincial government until 1930 and by the federal government after that. Resources used to build railways and to maintain service would have increased the national income by being utilized elsewhere in the economy. The demand for agricultural products was such between 1920 and 1940 that any additions in quantities offered for sale tended to reduce the value of the total product.[28] Most individuals who settled in the Peace River region would have contributed a greater value product in alternative employment in Canada (or elsewhere), at least before 1940. The tar sands of Fort McMurray were not even exploitable, since the technical knowledge has been lacking until very recently and their economic potential is as yet uncertain. Development of physical resources on the margins of settlement usually has to await diminutions of supply elsewhere or increases in demand. The simple fact that Alberta is located on the periphery of North American settlement cannot be emphasized enough in interpreting both the economic and fiscal development of the province.

The provision of facilities making northern regions accessible had other resource allocation effects. Beside railways, highways and telephone lines were built and provincial education grants to schools throughout the region have been substantial.[29] The outlays involved could have been spent more usefully in other parts of the province.

From the cyclical point of view, the expenditure on the railways built was timed well enough. Most of the construction was carried out during the depression years 1913 to 1915. The provincial outlays for covering operation deficits were also counter-cyclical in character. But the interest charges were deflationary in nature as far as the Alberta economy was concerned during the 1920s.

From the point of view of equity in income distribution and for social reasons, it was clear that once the railways were built, settlers could not be left in isolation. It was for these reasons that railway services continued to be provided during the depressions of 1920–25 and 1930–39. Public health and welfare services had to be provided by the provincial government; so did education grants if a certain modicum of schooling was to be provided at all. The attendant misallocation of resources could scarcely be helped, and was only less serious than the more significant misallocation of provincial government fiscal resources. Altogether the social and private costs were high.

From the point of view of economic progress, the early attempts at northern development promoted little growth in the Alberta economy. Even during the 1940s the agricultural gross revenue of the territory north of the fifty-fifth parallel (this includes the Peace River region) approximates only six or seven per cent of total such revenue in Alberta annually. There is no other significant kind of production as yet, although the present exploratory activities in the area may result in the discovery of substantial oil-producing fields.

THE TELEPHONE POLICY

The decision to provide a rural telephone system was made early, hastily, and without technical advice.[30] It seems to have been assumed that any monopoly possesses a high and inelastic demand curve, but this was not the case with respect to the demand for rural telephones. When farm incomes fell, one of the first expenditure reductions farmers made was to discontinue paying telephone bills until their telephones were removed. When farm incomes rose, the provincial government failed to increase rates in keeping with the rising demand.

Here was another case of resource misallocation, of strain on the provincial treasury, and of incurrence of debt for a purpose that was not fully self-liquidating. The relatively heavy outlays of 1908–13 and 1927–29 ran with the cycle while those of 1920–21 ran against it. While they generated income in a depressed agricultural economy in 1920–21, prices of construction materials were high and the leakages arising from the necessity of purchasing these outside Alberta were proportionately large. The telephone system did promote economic progress, but the degree of such progress is indeterminate; it also provided marked social benefits by alleviating the solitude and isolation of farm life. But it is important to segregate economic and social benefits and costs in appraising any policy. On social grounds, there is much to be said for the telephone policy, but on purely economic and fiscal grounds there is little to commend it. The present government has learned the lessons of the past in its adoption of a cautious policy on rural electrification. The economic limitations upon the construction of rural power lines are being considered carefully.

From the point of view of equity in income distribution and resource allocation, another point emerges. The urban subscribers of the telephone system have been called upon to pay higher rates than if they had possessed their own urban systems. Calgary subscribers, for example, who are served by the Alberta Government Telephones, have paid higher rates than Edmonton residents who are served by a city-owned system. In a province whose legislature is dominated by rural voters, urban residents have found it difficult to make their voices heard effectively.

AGRICULTURAL GUARANTEES AND RELIEF

Between 1918 and 1922 the provincial government guaranteed notes to enable farmers to purchase seed grain, feed, and other production needs; it also guaranteed borrowing by the municipal districts to enable them to assist farmers in need of production requirements and relief. Hay and feed were sold to farmers during the hard winter of 1919–20, often on credit. The provincial government paid transportation costs. In general, the level of provincial expenditure and guarantees for agricultural assistance was greater annually during the 1918–22 period than even during the 1930s. The chief reasons were the extremely low yields of 1918 and 1919 and the unusually long winter of 1919–20.[31] In any event, the agricultural guarantees became another financial problem that the U.F.A. government had to cope with during the 1920s. It was forced to discontinue the previous policy in 1922 on financial grounds, except in very necessitous cases, but the policy had to be resumed again during the 1930s.[32]

The chief criticism one can make of the policy from the point of view of resource allocation is that it tended to prevent resource transfers to other sectors of the economy. It tended to encourage farmers to stay in drought-stricken areas year after year since governments financed their annual production costs. They had incurred capital investment losses in any event and could have made a greater value product contribution elsewhere by moving sooner. The policy did not prevent the depopulation of dried-out areas with many 160-acre farms; it retarded the outward movement. On humanitarian grounds, of course, there was strong justification for it. There is also the question whether or not the expenditures were made carelessly and without too much regard for need. No doubt there was a considerable degree of indiscretion in these respects. Any large-scale policy of this kind makes this unavoidable when it is first introduced without well-defined criteria of assistance.

During the 1930s increasing emphasis was put upon moving settlers out of the drought areas, and those who wished to move to the central and northern parts of the province were given financial assistance. Special areas were formed to provide administration and control of agricultural practices in the southeast. With the rising frequency of seasons with adequate rainfall during the 1940s, the enlargement of farms and outright abandonment of others, and rising agricultural prices, the productivity per farmer in the southeast now ranks favourably with that in other parts of the province. The need for agricultural relief on the scale existing during the 1918–22 period and the 1930s is likely to be less great in the future.

THE IRRIGATION GUARANTEES

The guarantee of the Lethbridge Northern Irrigation District bonds was the last major guarantee made by the province with the exception of the Alberta Wheat Pool loans guaranteed in 1930. Some additional ones were made to other districts following 1921, but they were not large in nature.

Here again were projects, which were commendable from the social point of view, but were subject to major criticisms on economic grounds. Supposed to become self-liquidating in nature, the economic stagnation of the 1920–40 period dashed any such hope to the ground. Settlers were unable to pay the capital costs, both of recovery and interest. They even had to be assisted in maintaining the systems. If the projects had been begun during the late 1930s when construction costs were low and preliminary to the agricultural price increases of the 1940s, it is entirely likely that at least some of them would have become successful financially.

THE PUBLIC DOMAIN TRANSFER

The public domain transfer was discussed and appraised in Chapter 5 where it was suggested that net revenue benefits accruing to the province of a transfer before 1930 would have been small. Further, the natural resource award of 1935 wiped out any net revenue advantage. The main feature of the public domain controversy was that it served to create an atmosphere of uneasy Dominion-provincial relationships that generated ill-feeling and the prevention of solutions to other problems. The advantage to the provincial government of possessing the public domain is now obvious. But the exceptionally strong financial position of the Alberta government at present can also serve to create provincial jealousies among the members of the federation which might be strong enough to induce pressures upon the Dominion for financial assistance to restore in some degree previous relative fiscal-capacity levels among the provinces.[33] The Alberta government is no more backward than that of other provinces in striking bargains with the federal government, and it would certainly object strongly to any financial Dominion-provincial arrangement benefiting the various provinces, which did not benefit Alberta to a substantial degree.

The future of public domain revenue is unpredictable to a large extent because the bulk of present revenue varies with exploratory activity while only a minor though increasing portion varies with the rate of output of extracted products. There is a large area to explore and the demand for oil and natural gas shows every indication of being maintained. The output of oil and natural gas is increasing annually. The recent annual decreases in coal production are not substantial enough to offset significantly gains in revenue from oil and natural gas royalties. Consequently there is a strong presumption for predicting a high level of provincial public domain revenues for years to come.[34] The fact that Alberta has become a "have" province in the Canadian federation is undeniable even on the basis of revenues received during the last four years. The cash and investment reserves of the government are almost unprecedented in relative size for a government lacking power to regulate the value of money. No province would be in a better position to adopt fiscal policies designed to counter falling economic activity if a recession were to begin.

UNEMPLOYMENT RELIEF EXPENDITURE

Alberta urban municipalities struggled with a serious unemployment relief problem during the 1930s but it was less serious than in such provinces as British Columbia, Manitoba, Ontario, and Quebec because of Alberta's smaller urban population ratio. The provincial government also had to support the municipal programs along with the Dominion government.[35]

It has been suggested that the strengthening of the agricultural sector of the Alberta economy by the decrease in the number of farmers, the larger average size of farm, the continuation of some form of federal government support of farm prices, and the adoption of regulated land use in the southeast will tend to diminish the prospective level of agricultural relief expenditures in the event of recession. Increasing urbanization, on the other hand, will tend to increase the problem of non-agricultural unemployment in such an event. But even here federal policy would mitigate conditions during the initial period of recession because of the enactment of unemployment insurance measures in 1941. The persistence of depressed conditions in the economy would require stronger medicine, and federal-provincial co-operation on works projects and direct relief measures would be called for.

DEBT DEFAULT AND REORGANIZATION

The Alberta fiscal event, which has attracted the most widespread attention, was the debt default of 1936. Fiscally, it grew out of the expenditure policies reviewed above. Consequently it deserves rather extended treatment.

REASONS FOR DEFAULT

Factors influencing the decision to default have been suggested previously. First, the early accumulation of provincial debt and the subsequent embarrassment of the treasury during the 1921–36 period cannot be ignored. Debt charges came to be looked upon as a millstone that prevented the government from performing its ordinary functions at a satisfactory standard of achievement. Since several of the projects for which debt had been incurred proved to be financial failures and since much debt had been incurred for relief purposes, a high proportion of the debt was of the dead-weight variety. A government can only carry such debt if the income of the community, that is, its taxable capacity, is keeping pace with the increase in debt charges.[36] Alberta's difficulty stemmed from the lack of growth of income after 1920; inadequacy of general revenues resulted, and revenues of the railways and telephones fell short of the expenditures required. Public debt accordingly came to be looked upon as an unmixed evil, and the administration of 1936 knew that its action would find approval among many Albertans who had become inured to individual defaults.

Secondly, the treasury was empty in 1936 and expenditures had been outrunning revenues for many years. Further borrowing was required to meet the redemption of bonds maturing. Full interest payments would also have entailed some additional borrowing or expenditure cuts or revenue rate increases or a combination of all of these measures. Social Credit doctrine condemned debt. Yet the Alberta government was prepared to seek additional loans from the Dominion government, and balked chiefly at accepting the loan council principle, especially when the chief proponent of Social Credit, Major Douglas, advised the government against acceptance. Dependence upon the federal government for years ahead to stave off default would have made it very difficult indeed to attempt to implement a Social Credit program. Attempts to put such a program into effect failed anyway, but in March 1936, the administration had sincere hopes that such a program would be feasible in both economic and constitutional terms. Consequently, the break with the federal government was made and default took place.

Third, the members of the new administration were inexperienced in financial matters and did not appreciate the fine fabric of confidence and trust out of which a specialized, interdependent society is woven. Debt defaults by single proprietorships, partnerships, small corporations, and individuals do most of their damage to the parties mainly concerned; a government default, or one by a large corporation, does serious damage not only to the parties directly concerned but also to others. Doubts as to the integrity and capacity of other governments and corporations appear in the capital and money markets and lending tends to be discouraged to the detriment of investment in capital goods and government facilities. In short, there are repercussions beyond the sphere of those most directly concerned. The Alberta administration has learned all this by now from years of experience in office; it is very much concerned with its credit standing and points with pride at its strength in this respect.

The Dominion government's part in the affair leaves something to be desired. It permitted the province to default without taking steps to secure personal negotiations with the members of the provincial administration. Telegraphic communications cannot take the place of actual conferences where points can be elaborated and explained. Probably the senior government had hopes that the provincial one would relent at the last minute; probably the provincial trusted that the senior would relent. The failure of the Dominion to bestir itself sooner cannot be dismissed on the grounds that the party in power had nothing to gain by assisting the Alberta government unconditionally or by negotiation because it had been rejected at the polls in Alberta. The indirect effects of default on the credit standing of all governments and encouragement of capital investment in Canada were of too great a consequence.

ALBERTA'S ABILITY TO PAY IN 1936

Could Alberta have met its debt obligations in full in the fiscal year 1936–37 out of its own revenue? The answer to this question is in the negative. Revenue in 1936–37 increased by $3.6 million over 1935–36, excluding the telephones. This was accomplished by various measures designed to secure more revenue, especially by increasing tax rates and the imposition of a sales tax. At the same time expenditures were reduced by $2.6 million, chiefly through the interest rate reduction on debt. Nevertheless, there was an overall deficit for the year, excluding telephones, of $1.9 million. This was met by drawing upon the liquid assets of the provincial sinking fund,[37] by liquidating securities held in the special investment fund, and by drawing down an already small cash balance. A small amount was borrowed from the federal government to meet relief costs.

To meet full interest payments over $2 million more would have been required, and to redeem debentures an additional $4 million would have been needed. A revenue increase of $9 million, from about $21 million in 1935–36 to about $30 million in 1936–37, is an unrealistic assumption. Further, millions of dollars of savings certificates were in default. The government would have had to borrow to meet its obligations. Presumably the Dominion would have provided loan funds for this was done for the other three western provinces; loans to Saskatchewan were especially great during the rest of the 1930s.

Successive annual loans by Alberta would have been required until 1941 to enable her to meet debt maturities and full interest payments unless the sales tax had been retained instead of being abolished in 1937.

THE BONDHOLDERS' REPORT

The Elliott-Walker report, prepared for the bondholders in 1936 to provide them with information on Alberta, is a long and detailed document.[38] The conclusions of the report with respect to economic and financial matters were subject to controversy at the time because of the lack of reliable national income data and because of the hypothetical nature of the various provincial government estimates. Only the main points at issue are worthy of consideration in the light of hindsight and improved national income estimates.

The report stated "there is capacity on the part of Alberta to meet full provincial interest payments from the aggregate net income of the people of the province."[39]

In an article that was highly critical of the method used by the writers of the report and of D.B.S. (Dominion Bureau of Statistics) data, Mr. D.C. MacGregor of the University of Toronto made revised estimates for 1930 and 1934.[40] It is interesting to compare the estimates of Elliott Walker and of MacGregor with "personal savings" as estimated from recent D.B.S. data. These are set out in Table 9.2.

The "net value of production" used by Elliott-Walker and MacGregor is not the same thing as "personal income" because of the exclusion of transfer payments from the former and the exclusion of corporation profits retained in the latter.[41] But the levels of the two are roughly comparable. The bondholders' representatives had an especially high estimate; they failed to appreciate the drastic impact of low agricultural prices and drought. This impact and its results are probably inconceivable to anyone who did not live in the Canadian West during the 1930s; it was not even realized by many deflation-sheltered city dwellers who had little concept of the harsh physical and economic circumstances of prairie farm life during the 1930s.[42] The more impartial MacGregor also overestimated the income of Albertans in 1934. Both overestimates are understandable too if one considers that the D.B.S. data used by both MacGregor and the bondholders' representatives were defective in nature. The collection and estimation techniques of the D.B.S. at the time left much to be desired; the development of national income accounting was in its infancy. The D.B.S. has worked assiduously and skilfully during the 1940s to revise its previous figures.

Table 9.2 Some Income Estimates, Alberta, 1930 and 1934 (in millions of dollars)

	1930	1934
Elliott–Walker:[a]		
Net value of production	269	259
Less cost–of–living (i.e. consumer expenditure)	−235	−168
"Margin of income"[b]	34	91
MacGregor:[a]		
Net value of production	251	218
Less cost–of–living (i.e. consumer expenditure)	−265	−185
"Margin of income"[b]	−14	33
D.B.S., 1952 Revision:[c]		
Wages and salaries	154	103
Interest, dividends, and rentals	26	19
Net income of farmers[d]	47	36
Net income of other unincorporated business[d]	24	16
Government transfer payments	8	11
Total personal income	259	183
Less consumption expenditures[e]	−290	−216
"Margin of income"	−31	−33
(personal savings plus direct taxes)		

(a) From D.C. MacGregor, "Income and Expenditure in Alberta," 533.
(b) Income available after consumer expenditure on goods and services.
(c) From D.B.S., National Accounts, Income and Expenditure, 1926–50 (Ottawa, 1952).
(d) These two categories are not segregated in the source material, but they are in the *Sirois Report*, MacGregor and others, *National Income*, and for 1938 and subsequent years in D.B.S. publications. From these sources estimates were made by the writer of the proportion accruing to farmers.
(e) This is not available directly in the source material. The per capita consumer expenditures for Canada were computed. This figure was multiplied by the Alberta population for the year concerned. On the same basis the "margin of income" in Alberta for the years 1926–1950 would have been as follows in millions of dollars:

A controversy over income levels of the kind dealt with here would rage over a much smaller range in the future.[43]

Details of how consumer expenditures were estimated in the Elliott-Walker Report and by MacGregor cannot be enumerated here.[44] Both estimates were smaller than those inserted by the writer who used the Canadian average per capita consumption expenditure multiplied by the Alberta population. This was probably too high for Alberta in 1930 and certainly altogether too high in 1934. The degree to which Albertans reduced their consumer expenditures below the Canadian average is not known, but the use of the Canadian average serves to accentuate the fact of greatly depressed economic conditions in Alberta throughout the 1930s.[45]

The residual income, that is, personal savings, of Albertans after purchasing consumer goods and services was probably negative for the whole decade of the 1930s even after severe reductions in consumer expenditures. Data presented in previous chapters indicated the economic extremities of Albertans during that decade and further data could be marshalled. The simple fact emerges that there was little ability on the part of Albertans to pay additional provincial-municipal taxes during these years. It is not too difficult to have high financial morals when income is high and stable over time; those who enjoy such income but who stray from the paths of virtue can rightly be condemned. When incomes are so low that a large proportion of the population is reduced to a subsistence standard of living, many people do not find it possible to practise the principles of financial morality. Both the Elliott-Walker Report and the Bank of Canada Report seemed to imply that Albertans were improvident and amoral in financial matters. One gets the impression of listening to sermons. If this was the intention of the writers, one must protest that it was an ill-considered, superficial judgement, which can be condoned only by the writers' ignorance of income levels in Alberta. Lacking alternative economic opportunities in a land-locked area with a specialized economy, Albertans sought political means of regaining self-confidence and self-respect, and the debt default was one direct way of manifesting their protests. Even the approximate $3 million or so of interest reductions constituted a significant sum in 1936, and in terms of the 1933 net income of farmers it was about one-half.

A second main contention of the bondholders' report was that the Alberta budget for 1936–37 as estimated in early 1936 could have been balanced on income account even after paying full interest. This, it was contended, could have been done chiefly by discontinuing sinking fund contributions,[46] by borrowing from the Dominion government to finance relief expenditures,[47] by postponing the change in the automobile licence year,[48] and by some minor expenditure reductions. All of these suggestions were reasonable enough; the budget could have been balanced on income account on this basis both in the estimates and in terms of actual realization. But wrangling over income account items is of greater significance in an accounting sense than a real one. The fact remained that even if the budget on income account had been balanced by the measures suggested the provincial government was still faced with borrowing more than $6 million to finance relief expenditures and redemptions of debentures maturing in 1936–37. The writers of the report certainly faced up to this and suggested additional borrowing. Alberta debentures were not very acceptable in the capital market at the time and presumably the additional loan funds were to come from the Dominion. In view of its financial support of the other three western provinces by providing loan funds, it is not an unreasonable supposition that the Dominion would have extended similar aid to Alberta as needed. To obtain these funds, of course, the Alberta government would have had to accede to the loan council principle and any other conditions that the Dominion might have imposed.[49]

PROVINCIAL FINANCE ASSUMING NO DEBT DEFAULT

Several questions present themselves in any discussion of the debt default. How would the provincial government have met all of its debt obligations if they had been paid in full? What would have been the financial position of the Alberta treasury today? How much would the debt have increased to finance debt charges and redemptions? These questions cannot be answered without making certain assumptions.

With respect to the first question it has already been suggested that it would be heroic to assume that the Dominion would have provided loan funds. The province would also in all likelihood have obtained an annual fiscal subsidy from 1937 to 1947 like Saskatchewan and Manitoba. Additional funds could also have been obtained by retaining the sales tax.

The treasury obtained considerable relief from debt default during 1936–45. In the long-run, debt default has not helped; indeed, there is a presumption that in terms of dollars and cents[50] the treasury is going to lose by default. The skilful debt management of the administration in recent years has, however, minimized the after-effects of default on treasury balances.

It is not sufficient to assess the debt default in terms of the effects upon the provincial treasury only. Whether the treasury would or would not have been somewhat better off one way or the other is a question that would be of basic significance only if national income and the value of money did not fluctuate.

For example, it is misleading to compare provincial government revenues in 1935 and 1950 on a dollar basis without taking income and price changes into account for a "dollar is not a dollar" at all times. Similarly, the easing of the pressure on the treasury in 1936 is of more significance in real terms than any equivalent dollar reduction in 1951. Further, the question of the broader effects of default has to be considered.

Full payment of interest on debentures existing in 1936 and on additional debt incurred would have imposed a considerable real burden on the Alberta economy during the late 1930s and early 1940s. The additional burden during these years, expressed as a percentage of provincial income or the total revenue of the government, would easily offset any lessening of the real burden measured similarly during recent years. Full payment would have increased the depressive influence of provincial fiscal policy upon provincial income during the late 1930s.

From the point of view of equity, debt default spread depression sacrifices among a larger number of people. In such times the question arises whether or not it is fair that the remuneration of capital investors who made their investments previously should remain stable while that of other groups falls. There is another aspect also. Many holders of Alberta debentures lost heavily by selling their holdings before 1945; ultimate holders were thus the ones who benefited from debt reorganization. Consequently the incidence of debt default on bondholders is not easy to assess.

From the point of view of economic progress, debt default was a deterrent to new capital investment in Alberta before 1945 and it did not encourage maintenance of confidence in other government bonds. Nevertheless, all is now well with Alberta bonds in the capital markets; they are quoted at yields nearly as low as those of Dominion government bonds. Since 1946, the level of private investment in Alberta has been unparalleled, that is, if one exempts the pre-1914 period. Only municipal debentures are sagging in the capital market, and this is a condition that the provincial government could ease by guaranteeing such securities. In addition, it is in a position to make direct substantial advances to the municipalities out of its own cash balances.

It may seem that memories are short in the capital market, although it is rather the case of an increase in the demand for Alberta's products. Investors do not like to stay out of an area whose products have high demand schedules and which has very promising growth potentialities. When the government of such an area goes out of its way to encourage private investment both by word and deed its debt instruments are going to be strong in the capital market, especially if its revenues are closely and positively related to resource development. It might be that without default the credit standing of Alberta now would be better than it is.

Alberta has definitely emerged as a "have" province in the Canadian federation; it can no longer be regarded, as was done by the Sirois Commission, as standing between the "haves" and the "have-nots." This emergence is the result of the phenomenal rise in public domain revenue and the expansion in other revenue bases induced by the current investment boom. The other provinces cannot accuse Alberta of having been assisted in achieving its present strong financial position by means of the debt default. The default hampered, rather than facilitated, the achievement of this position.

PROVINCIAL INCOME ESTIMATES

Appendix A

There are no estimates of the national income or the personal income of Alberta before 1919. The D.B.S. had an old series of both kinds of income beginning in 1919 which was discontinued in 1938. It made intensive revisions during the 1940s and has prepared for publication a new series of personal income from 1926 to 1950. For Canada as a whole, there are estimates for 1911–20 made by J.J. Deutsch.

An attempt is made here to make income estimates for Alberta beginning in 1906 on the basis of the sketchy and scattered data available; these are checked against existing estimates or projections thereof. The estimates are to be regarded as rough approximations. But these approximations should be useful in gauging relative levels and fluctuations of income and in analysing public finance data.

The estimates made by J.J. Deutsch (see "War Finance and the Canadian Economy, 1914–1920," *C.J.E.P.S.*, Toronto, November, 1940, 538–39) for Canada from 1911 to 1920 inclusive are shown on a per capita basis in the first column of Table A1. These estimates have been multiplied by the population of Alberta to obtain the income estimates for Alberta from 1911 to 20 in the first column of Table A2. The figures for these years, then, are based on the assumption that Albertans received per capita incomes equal to the Canadian average. According to the old D.B.S. series, which is not too reliable, Alberta had a higher per capita income than Canada as a whole in 1919.

The income estimates for 1906–10 in the first column of Table A2 are based on the slope of the trend of the Deutsch estimates for 1911–20. The Canadian per capita income in 1911 was deflated by the Canadian wholesale price index for each of the years 1906–10 inclusive, and multiplied by the population of Alberta in each year of the same period. Thus the whole series from 1906 to 1920 is obtained on the basis of the Deutsch estimates. This series provides a check on, and comparison with, the independent estimates made by the writer. The Deutsch figures, as applied to Alberta in this case, have the weakness of reflecting Canadian economic fluctuations rather than Alberta ones; another weakness, as applied to Alberta, is that they are based on the Canadian average income level per capita.

The D.B.S. series for 1919–38 furnishes provincial breakdowns of national income produced and of aggregate income payments (see D.B.S., *National Income of Canada, 1919–1938*, Part I, Ottawa, 1941). The per capita figures of aggregate income payments for Canada and Alberta set out in the second and third columns respectively of Table A1 are based upon this old D.B.S. series. The aggregate figures for Alberta of both national income and income payments are shown in the second and third columns respectively of Table A2. These data, now seriously questioned by the D.B.S. itself, are used to bridge the gap between 1920 and 1926.

The series currently compiled and published by the D.B.S. starts with 1926. (See D.B.S., *National Accounts, Income and Expenditure, 1926–1950*, Ottawa, 1952.) The per capita figures of the personal income for Canada and Alberta are found in the fourth and fifth columns respectively of Table A1. The aggregate figures for Alberta are given in the fourth column of Table A2. The D.B.S. does not at present publish a national income series for the provinces.

The 1926–37 series prepared for the Sirois Commission was referred to at points, especially in preparing Table A7. The Bank of Nova Scotia series was not utilized at all.

The writer's own estimates of national income produced are found in the fifth column of Table A2. These are the results of using procedures and sources of data similar to those employed by Mr. Deutsch. The procedures are set out in detail in Tables A3 to A6 inclusive. The estimates obtained in this manner are set out in the sixth column of Table A2 for the years 1906–18 inclusive; the 1941 D.B.S. estimates of income payments fill the gap between 1918 and 1926; the new D.B.S. personal income series covers the 1926–50 period. Thus the 1906–18 figures represent national income produced while the 1919–50 figures are representative of personal income payments. In national income accounting there is a rough equivalence in the magnitude of these two quantitative concepts. The early D.B.S. series tends to overstate incomes in depressed periods. Consequently, the writer's estimate for 1921 and the D.B.S. one were averaged to obtain provincial income for that year. The resulting series, set out in the sixth column of Table A2, is termed *provincial income*, a term used throughout the treatise where reference is made to Alberta income unless otherwise specified.

Table A1 National Income and Personal Income Per Capita in Canada and Alberta, 1911–1950 (in dollars)

Year	Deutsch estimates, Canada	D.B.S. 1941 Income payments		D.B.S. 1952 Personal income	
		Canada	Alberta	Canada	Alberta
1911	290				
1912	300				
1913	310				
1914	290				
1915	290				
1916	340				
1917	410				
1918	460				
1919	510	480	600		
1920	520	520	640		
1921		430	520		
1922		410	460		
1923		430	500		
1924		420	460		
1925		420	460		
1926		440	470	430	480
1927		450	490	450	550
1928		470	490	470	500
1929		480	490	460	420
1930		450	450	430	360
1931		390	370	360	280
1932		330	320	290	230
1933		300	290	260	190
1934		310	290	290	240
1935		330	310	310	240
1936		350	310	330	240
1937		380	330	360	320
1938		380	340	370	340
1939				390	330
1940				430	390
1941				510	410
1942				640	660
1943				690	570
1944				750	720
1945				760	680
1946				790	830
1947				820	860
1948				910	1030
1949				940	1020
1950				970	1010

Table A2   Provincial Income Estimates for Alberta, 1906–1950 (in millions of dollars)

Year	Hanson via Deutsch, national income produced	D.B.S. 1941		D.B.S. 1952 Personal Income	Hanson, national income produced Alberta	Provincial income
		National Income Produced	Income Payments			
1906	46				41	41
1907	65				53	53
1908	73				60	60
1909	83				73	73
1910	94				88	88
1911	108				130	130
1912	120				168	168
1913	133				165	165
1914	131				164	164
1915	140				183	183
1916	166				259	259
1917	209				308	308
1918	238				253	253
1919	274	333	325		314	325
1920	291	375	365		373	365
1921		299	304		233	269
1922		277	271			271
1923		305	296			296
1924		278	275			275
1925		298	280			280
1926		311	287	293		293
1927		336	313	350		350
1928		360	326	328		328
1929		359	335	290		290
1930		298	315	259		259
1931		235	271	201		201
1932		196	234	169		169
1933		187	214	146		146
1934		202	217	183		183
1935		220	236	186		186
1936		241	240	188		188
1937		266	257	252		252
1938		268	268	268		268
1939				262		262
1940				310		310
1941				324		324
1942				512		512
1943				447		447
1944				589		589
1945				564		564
1946				666		666
1947				709		709
1948				870		870
1949				896		896
1950				907		907

Table A3 Estimates of National Income Produced in Alberta, 1906–1921 (in millions of dollars)

Years	1906	1907	1908	1909	1910	1911	1912	1913	1914	1915	1916	1917	1918	1919	1920	1921
Agriculture	13	14	19	23	25	55	52	58	75	109	168	197	127	164	198	75
Mining[a]	3	4	4	5	7	5	10	12	11	8	11	14	19	18	33	30
Other primary[b]	2	2	2	2	2	2	3	2	2	2	2	2	2	3	6	4
Total primary	18	20	25	30	34	62	65	72	88	119	181	213	148	185	237	109
Manufacturing[c]	2	4	5	7	9	10	11	11	10	9	17	26	25	34	32	26
Electric power[d]	1	1	1	1	1	1	1	2	2	2	2	2	3	3	4	4
Custom and repair[e]	1	1	2	2	2	2	2	2	2	2	2	2	3	3	4	4
Construction	5	7	6	8	14	23	53	39	23	9	7	2	2	7	10	13
Total secondary	9	13	13	18	26	36	67	54	37	22	28	32	33	47	50	47
Total income from production of goods	27	33	38	48	60	98	132	126	125	141	209	245	181	232	287	156
Income from production of services	14	20	22	25	28	32	36	39	39	42	50	63	72	82	86	77
Total income	41	53	60	73	88	130	168	165	164	183	259	308	253	314	373	233

(a) The net values are derived from the gross data available. During the 1920s and 1930s the net value in each year approximated 85 per cent of the gross value. The gross values for 1906–21 were accordingly multiplied by 85 per cent to obtain the figures in the table, rounded off to the nearest million dollars.

(b) This includes forestry, fishing, and trapping. Data from *C.Y.B.*, 1909–23, were used.

(c) Before 1917, figures are available only for 1905, 1910, and 1915. The figures for intervening years are estimates based on the three years for which data are available and on the tempo of economic activity as gauged by construction values.

(d) The figures before 1920 are estimates. Data for 1920 and 1921 were derived from *Facts and Figures*.

(e) The figures were obtained in the same way as those for electric power.

Table A4 Estimates of the Net Value of Agricultural Production in Alberta, 1906–1921

Year	Price index 1935–39 is 100	Converted expense per acre	Field crop acreage (millions)	Expenses and depreciation	Gross value (millions)	Net value (millions)
1906	70	$2.25	0.9	2	$15	$13
1907	76	2.45	1.3	3	17	14
1908	76	2.45	1.4	3	22	19
1909	77	2.45	1.9	5	28	23
1910	77	2.47	2.6	6	31	25
1911	80	2.55	3.4	9	64	55
1912	84	2.70	3.6	10	62	52
1913	83	2.65	3.7	10	68	58
1914	84	2.70	3.4	9	84	75
1915	88	2.82	4.0	11	120	109
1916	97	3.10	5.4	17	185	168
1917	125	4.00	6.7	27	224	197
1918	147	4.70	7.7	36	163	127
1919	158	5.10	8.2	42	206	164
1920	179	5.75	8.4	48	246	198
1921	152	4.85	9.4	46	121	75
Avg., 1938–42	111	3.55	13.6	46	228	182

Note: The gross values of production are derived from *Canada Year Books*. There are some duplications in the gross value series which probably make the net value estimates a little high; no allowance could be made for this. Expenses deducted include payments for seed, feed, various miscellaneous expenses, and depreciation. Payments of wages, interest, rent, and taxes have not been deducted. It should be emphasized that the net value of production of agriculture is not synonymous with personal income of farm operators. The latter would be lower in magnitude than the former.

Estimates of expenses were made by adding farm expense items for 1938–42 inclusive as set out in the D.B.S. publication, *Quarterly Bulletin of Agricultural Statistics*, Jan.-March 1947, 25. Field crop acreages, a series available for every year from 1906 to the present, were averaged for 1938–42. The average expense per field crop acre for these years equalled $3.55. This figure was equated with the average index for 1938–1942 of the cost of commodities purchased by farmers in Western Canada. Estimates of expenses for 1906–21 were then made by multiplying $3.55 by the given year price index and dividing by the index average for 1938–42. The wholesale price index for Canada was used for 1906–13, since the other index is not available before 1914. The resulting amounts per acre were multiplied by field crop acreages for the given years, and the products rounded off to the nearest million dollars.

Table A5   Estimates of the Net Value of Construction in Alberta, 1906–1921 (in millions of dollars)

Year	Building permits, Edmonton & Calgary	Railway construction[a]	Governments[b]	Other value[c]	Gross value	Net[d]
1906	3.0	2.4	1.3	1.8	8	5
1907	4.4	1.4	4.1	2.0	12	7
1908	3.6	0.7	4.4	1.4	10	6
1909	4.5	2.7	4.9	2.4	14	8
1910	7.8	5.2	6.4	4.3	24	14
1911	16.7	6.4	7.5	7.7	38	23
1912	34.8	20.0	15.2	18.2	88	53
1913	17.9	13.0	23.6	10.3	65	39
1914	8.3	10.3	12.7	6.2	38	23
1915	0.5	7.8	4.0	2.8	15	9
1916	0.9	5.4	3.6	2.1	12	7
1917	0.9	0.0	1.8	0.3	3	2
1918	1.5	0.3	1.0	0.6	3	2
1919	3.1	3.2	2.5	2.1	11	7
1920	6.1	1.2	6.8	2.4	17	10
1921	3.9	2.3	13.0	2.1	21	13

Note: There are lags with respect to the construction of buildings and the taking out of permits. Further, some building may not have been undertaken at all although permits were taken out. The estimates above should be regarded as being very rough approximations; they are, however, indicative of the timing of fluctuations.

(a)   The mileage added in each year was multiplied by $15,000 in 1906, by $16,000 in 1907, by $17,000 in 1908, and so forth up to $25,000 for 1916–21 inclusive. This was done to allow for rising costs, and the figures were originally arrived at by reported costs of railway construction at the time.

(b)   Provincial, municipal, and school.

(c)   This is an arbitrary figure designed to include building permits in smaller centres and miscellaneous items. It is taken to equal one-third of the sum of the figures in the first two columns for each year.

(d)   The net value is taken as being approximately 60 per cent of gross value in keeping with the average percentage relationship during the 1920s.

Table A6   Estimates of Income from Production of Services in Alberta, 1906–1921

Year	Thousands		Dollars		Millions of $	
	Population Alberta	Working force, 40% of population	Service producers, 30% of working force	Income per capita, Canada	Income per gainfully employed	Income from Services, Alberta
1906	185	74	22	252	630	14
1907	236	95	29	275	688	20
1908	266	106	32	275	688	22
1909	301	120	36	275	688	25
1910	336	134	40	280	700	28
1911	374	150	45	289	702	32
1912	400	160	48	300	750	36
1913	429	172	52	309	752	39
1914	459	184	55	286	702	39
1915	480	192	58	291	728	42
1916	496	198	60	335	838	50
1917	508	203	61	410	1025	63
1918	522	210	63	456	1140	72
1919	541	217	65	507	1268	82
1920	565	226	68	515	1288	86
1921	588	235	71	433	1083	77

Note: The 1921 census classified 65 per cent of the working force in primary and secondary industry. In addition, 4.6 per cent were classified as "labourers" in secondary and tertiary industries. On this basis somewhat more than 30 per cent of the working force, including some of the labourers mentioned, were producing services. Here it is assumed that 30 per cent of the working force was so engaged each year, the working force in turn being assumed to be 40 per cent of the total population.

The income per gainfully employed is obtained by multiplying the Canadian national income per capita by 2.5, the number of gainfully employed being taken as being 40 per cent of the total population. The Deutsch per capita figures are used for 1911–20 inclusive, while the D.B.S. 1941 estimate is used for 1921. The figures for 1906–10 are projections of the Deutsch figures deflated by the wholesale price index in each year.

Table A7   Components of Personal Income, Alberta, 1926–1950 (in millions of dollars)

Year	Wages and salaries[a]	Farm operators' net income[b]	Unincor- porated business[b]	Invest- ments[c]	Transfer payments	Total
1926	135	104	22	27	6	293
1927	142	146	25	32	6	350
1928	153	111	28	31	7	328
1929	164	62	29	29	7	290
1930	154	47	24	26	8	259
1931	132	14	22	25	10	201
1932	107	15	18	20	11	169
1933	96	6	16	18	11	146
1934	103	36	16	19	11	183
1935	109	31	18	18	12	186
1936	117	20	19	19	12	188
1937	130	67	20	22	14	252
1938	127	81	24	25	13	268
1939	132	68	24	26	12	262
1940	151	89	28	29	13	310
1941	182	72	30	29	11	324
1942	209	209	34	40	20	512
1943	242	110	40	42	13	447
1944	273	207	45	46	18	589
1945	287	141	49	47	40	564
1946	285	182	61	55	83	666
1947	307	206	76	61	59	709
1948	362	306	80	64	58	870
1949	403	279	85	68	63	896
1950	430	245	90	75	69	907

Source: D.B.S., *National Accounts, Income and Expenditure, 1926–1950* (Ottawa, 1952).
(a)   Includes military pay and allowances.
(b)   The source material reports the net income of farm operators and unincorporated business without segregating them. The writer deducted the *Sirois Report* estimate of the income of unincorporated business from the total to derive the net income of farm operators for the years 1926–37. For 1938–50, data on the net income of farm operators was available from D.B.S., *Quarterly Bulletin of Agricultural Statistics*. Thus for 1938–50, net income of farm operators was deducted from the total reported in the source material to derive the net income of unincorporated business.
(c)   Interest, dividends, and net rentals.

PROVINCIAL GOVERNMENT STATISTICS

Appendix B

Data on provincial government revenue, expenditure, and debt have been derived from Government of Alberta, *Public Accounts*, and to some extent from various *Sirois Report* appendices which are noted as sources in various tables in the text. The classifications employed by the government accountants have undergone change through time. Only during the last two decades has there been approximate uniformity of categories of revenue and expenditure. The writer consequently set up his own classification as outlined below, and examined the public accounts of 1905–51 in detail. Thus, uniformity of categories through time has been substantially achieved.

The government accountants have also segregated "capital" and "income" items in the public accounts since 1912. The writer has adopted the overall approach and has made no distinction between these two kinds of items for the purpose of analysing budgets and of measuring the impact of government upon the economy. References are made in the text to surpluses and deficits on "income account" and to revenue and expenditure on "capital account." These references apply to the categories and classification used by the government accountants.

CLASSIFICATION OF REVENUE

Revenue is defined here as receipts which improve the net condition of the treasury. They are receipts – for example, taxes – which increase the useable funds of the treasury without increasing its debt obligations, or which reduce its debt obligations without reducing its usable funds.[1] Thus proceeds from bond issues, bank loans, treasury bills, etc. are not included in revenue although some of the earlier provincial treasurers did so in presenting their budgets. Even in the classification employed in the present public accounts, such proceeds are included under "capital account." But just as loan proceeds of individuals are not income, so loan proceeds of governments are not "revenue," or if one likes, government "income."

DOMINION OF CANADA

This category consists of statutory subsidies received since 1905; receipts under the wartime tax agreement from 1941 to 1947; receipts under the post-war tax agreements of 1947; and grants-in-aid for agriculture, public health, public welfare, education, and public works. At the present time the government receives statutory subsidies under the heads of population, government and legislation, debt allowance, and compensation in lieu of public lands. It receives what is called a tax rental payment in lieu of levying corporation taxes of all kinds, personal income taxes, and succession duties. Grants-in-aid are paid for the maintenance of farm labour exchanges, tuberculosis patients who are wards of the Dominion government, hospitals, cancer research, internees and evacuees, vocational training, schools of agriculture, and forest conservation. Finally, the Dominion pays the major portion of the old age and blind pensions.

TAXES

This category includes the educational tax on land; the supplementary revenue tax of 1918–36 inclusive; the social service tax on land for 1936–46 inclusive; the taxes on railways, electric power, pipelines, and corporations generally; taxes on the entrance charges of places of amusement and on pari-mutuel betting; personal income taxes; succession duties; gasoline taxes; and taxes on retail sales. Many of these taxes are no longer levied by the province. The chief tax remaining is the one on gasoline.

LICENCES, FEES, AND PERMITS

This is a category consisting of a very large number of sources. Motor vehicle licences are most important; they accounted for about 70 per cent of total revenue of this category in 1950–51. Incorporation fees provided 3 per cent; court and legal fees, more than 4 per cent; land title fees, almost 9 per cent; inspection and regulatory activities, about 8 per cent; educational and other fees accounted for the balance.

PUBLIC DOMAIN

This includes revenue from coal royalties, fees, and rentals; petroleum and natural gas royalties, fees, rentals, and leases; taxes on mineral rights; forestry fees, rentals, and leases; grazing fees and leases; land leases; fur licences and taxes;

fishing and game licences; and hay leases. In recent years this category has become by far the largest revenue producer.

SCHOOL LANDS

This category includes the interest received from the school lands fund as well as fees and rentals and royalties on mineral rights, grazing, hay, and timber.

LIQUOR CONTROL

This includes revenue from the licensing of beverage rooms and from profits on the sale of beer, wine, and other liquor in retail stores. All legal retail sales in the province are made by the government stores.

FINES

This is a minor category and consists of fines and penalties collected under provincial and Dominion statutes.

SALES OF COMMODITIES AND SERVICES

This category includes sales of supplies to the inmates and staff of provincial institutions such as mental hospitals and jails, sales of agricultural produce of these institutions, sales by the government printer, profits on working advances, hail insurance premiums (1906–11), sales of dairy products, sales of hay, and sundry items.

REFUNDS OF EXPENDITURES

This category includes the following: payments made by municipalities to the province on account of old age pensions, indigents, mothers' allowances, unemployment relief, and seed grain; amounts charged as administrative expense against improvement districts; old age pension contributions of other provinces; voluntary salary deductions of civil servants; and sundry refunds.

INTEREST, PREMIUM, AND DISCOUNT

This category includes the following: earnings on bank balances, investments in securities, and on advances to the wheat pool, railways, school districts, normal school students, drainage districts, irrigation districts, cities, etc.; interest paid by the telephone system.

REPAYMENTS

This category includes repayments of advances made for a variety of purposes: seed grain; government printer; public works stock advance; school books branch; school districts; normal school students; drought relief; agricultural pest control; livestock purchases; irrigation and drainage districts; elevators; co-operative credit societies; unemployment relief; and various sundry items.

TELEPHONES

Telephone revenue is defined as the gross income of the telephone system minus interest paid on debt. The latter is included under "interest, premium, and discount."

MISCELLANEOUS

This is a small category made up of sundry departmental receipts.

CLASSIFICATION OF EXPENDITURE

An *expenditure* is here defined as a payment which reduces the usable funds of the treasury without reducing its debt obligations. They worsen the condition of the treasury.[2] Thus repayments of debt are excluded while interest charges on debt are included. The provincial accounts, on the other hand, include sinking fund contributions and debt repayments in expenditures on "income account." Expenditures, as well as revenues, have been classified mainly with the classification of the *Sirois Report* as a guide. The major classifications are those suggested by Mrs. U.K. Hicks (see Hicks, *Public Finance*, Chapter I).

GENERAL GOVERNMENT

This category consists of expenditures on legislation, general administration, and the administration of justice. The objects of expenditure within each of these three classes are listed below.

Legislation: Elections, sessional indemnities, legislative library, maintenance and construction of the residence of the lieutenant-governor, legislative counsel, and consolidation of statutes.

General Administration: Salaries of cabinet ministers, general departmental offices (salaries, supplies, maintenance and construction of buildings), land titles offices (salaries, supplies, maintenance and construction of buildings), collection of statistics, investigations and commissions, inspection and supervision of public works, government contributions to workmen's compensation and superannuation funds, special ceremonies, and minor sundry items.

Administration of Justice: Supreme and district courts, legal proceedings and prosecutions, police magistrates, provincial police, Royal Canadian Mounted Police, jails, maintenance and construction of jails and police barracks, and the maintenance and construction of court houses.

SOCIAL EXPENDITURE

This category includes expenditures on education, public health, and public welfare. The objects of expenditure within each of these three classes are listed below.

Education: Grants to schools; grants to university; operation, construction, and maintenance of agricultural schools, technical schools, and normal schools; construction of university buildings; school inspection; examinations; school texts; deaf and blind children; school organization; English schools for foreigners; special summer schools; truancy enforcement; scholarships; teachers' pensions; advances to school districts and normal school students.

Public Health: Control of diseases (administration, distribution of vaccines and sera, treatment of patients in hospitals, diagnostic and clinical work, social hygiene, mental hygiene, insulin, polio sufferers, cancer treatment and prevention); general services (hospitalization of incurables, health laboratories, travelling clinics, inspection services, public health education, entomology, health units, nursing aides, sanitary engineering, public wells); mental institutions; sanatoria; hospital grants; medical care of pensioners; maternity care and hospitalization; veterans' hospitals; and construction of hospitals.

Public Welfare: Child welfare; mothers' allowances; old age pensions; pensions to the blind; unemployment relief; indigent relief; Board of Industrial Relations; inspection of steam boilers; labour bureaus; welding and electrical inspection; factory inspection; rural housing committee; fire protection; veterans' welfare advisory committee; Alberta Women's Bureau; public administrators; cultural activities; miscellaneous grants; construction of shelters and hostels.

ECONOMIC EXPENDITURE

This category includes expenditures on agriculture, public domain, highways, railways, telephones, and treasury branches. The objects of expenditure within each of these six classes are listed below.

Agriculture: Demonstration farms; experimental farms; extension services; district agriculturists; boys' and girls' clubs; stock inspection; stock shows; dairy work promotion; poultry; livestock commissions; dairy commissioners; recording of brands; provincial veterinarians; Livestock Encouragement Act; advances to marketing services; grants to agricultural societies, exhibition associations, school fairs, livestock breeders' associations, seed fairs, stock shows, and irrigation associations; farm relief advances; moving of settlers; implementation of notes under the Livestock Encouragement Act; seed grain advances; short courses; destruction of agricultural pests; agricultural publications; supervision of grazing; destruction of noxious weeds; encouragement of co-operative marketing; tree planting; agricultural machinery; soil surveys; and advances to elevator companies (the Alberta Farmers Cooperative Elevator Company, 1913–18, and the Alberta Wheat Pool, 1930–31).

Public Domain: Forest fires; fire ranging and forest services; mine inspection; land agencies; grazing; water resource surveys; administration of irrigation and drainage districts; advances to such districts (Lethbridge Northern Irrigation District being the most important by far); game inspection and enforcement; bird sanctuaries; fish hatcheries; petroleum and natural gas conservation; research councils and organizations; colonization; parks and beaches; trade commissioners; publicity; and extension of coal markets.

Highways: Construction and maintenance of main highways, secondary highways, district and local roads (in part only), and colonization roads; ferries and bridges; grants to municipalities for road construction; surveys, ditches, drains, and airports.

Railways: Advances for construction and maintenance to (1) the Central Canada Railway in 1915 and 1921–29 inclusive, (2) the Lacombe and Blindman Valley Railway in 1917–30 inclusive, (3) the Alberta and Great Waterways Railway in 1920–30 inclusive, (4) the Edmonton, Dunvegan, and British Columbia Railway in 1920–30 inclusive, and (5) the Pembina Valley Railway in 1926–30 inclusive. The provincial government disposed of all its railway holdings in 1930.

Telephones: Maintenance, operation and construction of a provincial system covering most of the settled part of the province except the city of Edmonton which has its own system. Interest charges on the telephone debt are not included in this class of expenditures.

Capital expenditure data for the telephones had to be obtained from several sources. The figures for 1906–22 were obtained from the provincial public accounts; for 1923–28 resort was had to Government of Alberta, Department of Railways and Telephones, *Annual Reports, 1923–28*, since they were not available in the public accounts; for 1929–42 they were obtained from the capital account statement in the public accounts for the period; for 1942–51 they were obtained from the office of the comptroller of the Alberta Government Telephones through the courtesy of Mr. J.P. Ogilvie, Comptroller.

The telephone data, both on the revenue and expenditure side, have not been easy to deal with because of several changes in the accounting procedures. In some years the telephone accounts are incorporated with the general revenue statements; sometimes they are not.

Treasury Branches: These were first set up in 1938. The expenditures include salaries, supplies, and maintenance of buildings.

INTEREST ON DEBT

This category includes the following: interest on direct bonds and temporary loans; interest on guaranteed debts (chiefly railways and irrigation projects); interest on provincial savings certificates and deposits; foreign exchange charges; commissions and other charges of management; interest on miscellaneous items such as municipal sinking funds, superannuation funds, etc. deposited with the province. All interest charges on the telephone debt are included in this category.

OTHER EXPENDITURE

These include the following: Working advances to the government printer, public works, school book branch, and liquor stores; payment of taxes to municipalities on forfeited lands; and a miscellany of refunds, remissions, rebates, and contingent payments.

LOCAL GOVERNMENT STATISTICS

Appendix C

The financial data on local governments in the tables throughout the text are both actual and estimated figures. For the sake of clarity of presentation and of facility of interpretation they have been rounded off in most instances. It is not claimed that they are correct in the accounting sense since estimates had to be made in various cases. Special adjustments, too, have been made to adapt figures to the purposes at hand. For example, estimates were made to segregate interest payments on debt, debt repayments, and sinking fund payments from data in financial reports for the purpose of computing total expenditures (the writer's definition) and debt charges. In many cases, sinking fund contributions and debt repayments were included under expenditures in the financial statements and reports; these had to be eliminated to fit the writer's definition. The adjustments made are described below. Despite the use of estimating procedures, the writer feels that the data are sufficiently accurate to serve the purpose of analysing the levels of fluctuations of local government revenue, expenditure, and debt.

SOURCES OF DATA

REPORTS OF THE GOVERNMENT OF ALBERTA

Public Accounts were used to obtain information on (1) revenue and expenditure of the unorganized local improvement districts administered by the province since 1905, (2) revenue and expenditure of the Special Areas administered by the province since 1937, and (3) grants and advances of the provincial government to local governments.

The Annual Reports of the Department of Public Works, Local Improvement Branch cover the 1905–12 period and provide data on tax levies and collections in local improvement districts, both organized and unorganized, before 1912.

The Department of Municipal Affairs' Annual Reports from 1912–50 were also used. These were first published in 1912. The early reports contain data on the assessment, tax levies, and debenture debt of cities, towns, villages, and municipal districts. They have become more elaborate since 1920, but unfortunately, many series are broken since there have been rather frequent changes in the methods of organizing and assembling the reports. Consequently adjustments and estimates were necessary at various points to secure reasonably consistent series. After 1942, the department adopted the methods of financial reporting recommended by the Continuing Committee appointed by the Dominion–Provincial Conference on Municipal Statistics held in July, 1937. The 1943–50 reports provide data on cities, towns, villages, and municipal and local improvement districts. School and hospital district requisitions are also reported.

The Annual Reports of the Department of Education, 1905–50, are very satisfactory for they provide consistent series from 1906 to the present in many respects. Some adjustments were made during the early 1940s because of the formation of school divisions and the inclusion of some towns and villages in these. The work of the statisticians in the department is commendable, all the more so because of the thousands of districts involved. As an example of governmental reporting, the education ranks high on the score of consistency of organization; instead of dropping old series in all cases, many have been retained along with the new ones added from time to time. The revenue, expenditure, and debt data for school districts were obtained from these reports.

The Department of Public Health, Hospital Division, also produces Annual Reports. These reports, running from 1929 to 1950, provide financial data for the hospital districts since 1929. All hospitals in the province are included in the data and the hospital district data had to be separated from the totals reported. Early data on hospital district debt are lacking; consequently estimates were used.

Finally, the annual reports of the Department of Public Health, Alberta Municipal Hospitals, were used to provide municipal hospital district data after 1937.

LOCAL GOVERNMENT REPORTS

The City of Edmonton's Financial Statements and Departmental Reports, 1905–50, were relied upon heavily for the early years. Figures extracted from these reports from 1906 to 1912 are the basis of various estimates for the urban centres.

The City of Calgary produces Auditors' Reports. The earliest report available to the writer was that of 1913; they continue into the present.

The Financial Statements of the City of Lethbridge are available from 1911–50.

The City of Medicine Hat also produces Financial Statements, 1911–50
The earliest report available to the writer was that of 1911.

REVENUE DATA

The definition of revenue set out in Appendix B is also applicable to the local
government revenue data.

CITIES

The revenue data consist of two categories, *taxes* and *other revenues*. It would be
a task requiring several research assistants to attempt a finer classification than
this twofold one. The figures on taxes were derived from tax levies, not actual
collections. Data on collections are very sketchy for the early years. Further, the
new system of municipal accounting in use incorporates the levy under revenue
rather than collections. School taxes and provincial government taxes are not
included in the series presented in the tables throughout the text. Property tax
levies constitute the major part of total city taxes; business and income taxes
account for the rather small balance.

For 1906–29 inclusive tax data were extracted from the financial reports of
the cities mentioned above. The Edmonton data are basic for 1906–12 because
estimates for other centres are made on the strength of them. Thus Calgary
revenues for 1906–12 were assumed to equal 80 per cent of the Edmonton
ones on the basis of the 1913–15 relationships between tax levels in the two
cities. The Lethbridge figures for 1906–10 are 20 per cent of Edmonton's on a
similar basis. The Medicine Hat figures for 1906–10 are 7 per cent of those for
Edmonton. The other cities were Red Deer and Wetaskiwin which had about
2 per cent of the total population of all the cities; accordingly this percentage
was used to estimate their tax levels until 1930. The data in the reports of the
Department of Municipal Affairs were not used until after 1929 because school
taxes are included in the figures reported during 1913–29. Further, no city data
are given in the 1922 report. The figures for 1930–50 inclusive were derived
from the reports of the Department of Municipal Affairs.

Other revenue includes receipts from licences, fees, miscellaneous departmental items, and public utilities. The utility revenues are gross figures and
constitute about 90 per cent of the whole category of other revenue in most
years. The Calgary figures for 1906–12 were taken to equal 70 per cent of the
Edmonton ones in keeping with the 1913–15 relationship. The Lethbridge and

Medicine Hat figures for 1906–10 are 13 and 7 per cent respectively of the Edmonton ones. For the other two cities, 2 per cent of totals is used.

TOWNS

Again revenues are classified as taxes and other revenue. Tax estimates for 1906–12 were made by taking one-sixth of the total tax levies of the cities in keeping with the approximate relationship in 1913–15 and in relation to the growth in the number of towns. For 1913–50 the figures were obtained from the reports of the Department of Municipal Affairs. The tax levies between 1913 and 1925 are inflated considerably by high assessments in some towns in financial difficulties. These levies were far from being collectible in full. After 1925, assessments were reduced greatly, not only in towns, but also in other municipal units. For 1930–42 inclusive the figures were obtained from the reports of the department mentioned above subject to adjustment. Thus trust taxes received by the towns were added and trust taxes paid to the provincial government were subtracted. For 1943–50 inclusive, the school requisition, the hospital requisition, and the social service tax requisition in each year were subtracted from the total tax levy reported.

As to other revenue, the utilities portion was estimated at 30 per cent of the tax levies of the towns for the years 1906–18. The 1919 utility figure is an actual one derived from the municipal affairs report. The utility figure was 30 per cent of the tax levy in that year. The utility figures for 1920–23 are estimated on the basis of the actual figures for 1919 and 1924. For 1924–50, the utility figures presented (or incorporated in total revenues) are actual ones obtained from the reports of the Department of Municipal Affairs for 1924–50. Miscellaneous revenue for 1906–24 was estimated to be 10 per cent of the total revenue; for 1925–50 the figures were obtained from the reports mentioned above.

VILLAGES

The same sources were used as in the case of the towns. Estimating procedures were also similar.

MUNICIPAL DISTRICTS

Data were obtained from the reports of the Department of Municipal Affairs for 1913–50. Tax revenue figures are the levies reported. For 1913–29 the figures presented are taken directly from the reports for 1913–29. For 1930–35 trust taxes received were added to the levy reported and trust taxes paid were subtracted. For 1936–42 the figures were taken directly from the reports for 1936–42 since trust tax adjustments no longer had to be made. For 1935–50, the school requisition, the hospital requisition, and the social service tax requisition were subtracted from the levy in each year. Other revenue for 1913–25 was estimated by the procedures used for other units.

ORGANIZED LOCAL IMPROVEMENT DISTRICTS

Tax levy figures for 1907 and 1909 were obtained from the annual reports of the Department of Public Works for the same years. An actual figure was available from the report of the Department of Municipal Affairs for 1917. For other years estimates had to be made; these were made on the basis of changes in the number of districts and with reference to municipal district levies. To obtain other revenue, 10 per cent was added to the tax levy in each year.

UNORGANIZED IMPROVEMENT DISTRICTS

Data were obtained from the provincial public accounts for the years 1906–16 and 1923–51, and from reports of the Department of Municipal Affairs for 1917–22. The latter source had to be used for 1917–22 because cash balances on hand were lumped with receipts for these years in the public accounts. All figures are for tax collections, not levies. The figures for 1927–44 correspond to the fiscal year of the province; for all other years they cover calendar years.

SPECIAL AREAS

Data were obtained from the provincial public accounts for 1938–51. Taxes are equal to tax collections reported less school, hospital, and social service tax requisitions.

SCHOOL DISTRICTS

Data were obtained from the reports of the Department of Education, 1906–50.

HOSPITAL DISTRICTS

Data before 1929 are very sketchy. The tax levies were available in the reports of the Department of Municipal Affairs for 1919–28, and provincial grants from the provincial public accounts for the same years. For 1929–50 the data were obtained from the reports of the Department of Public Health. All figures before 1929 are estimates except for the provincial grants.

EXPENDITURE DATA

Expenditures of local governments are defined in the same way as those of the provincial government. They are divided into two categories only, ordinary or tax-financed, and capital or loan-finances.

CITIES

Ordinary expenditure figures for Edmonton were obtained from the financial reports of that city for 1906–29. The Calgary figures for 1906–12 were estimated by applying 1913–15 relationships to the Edmonton figures; for 1913–29 the financial reports of the city were used. The Lethbridge figures for 1906–10 were estimated on a similar basis; for 1911–29 the Lethbridge reports were used. The Medicine Hat figures were obtained similarly. To complete the picture, the expenditures of other cities were added to the total by the addition of 2 per cent to the total for the four main cities. For 1930–50, total expenditure of all the cities was obtained from the reports of the Department of Municipal Affairs. The figures presented for these years equal total ordinary expenditure given in the reports less debenture payments reported plus estimated debenture interest payments. Depreciation allowances of utilities have been excluded wherever they were reported; if they had been available on any consistent basis they might well have been included. School requisitions and provincial tax requisitions have been excluded.

Data on capital expenditures are very sketchy. These expenditures are shown in some reports of the cities, but not in others. They are not given in the reports of the Department of Municipal Affairs in most years. As a last resort, capital expenditures were estimated on the basis of annual increases in debt. Spot checks for years when data on capital expenditures were available in the reports of the cities indicate that the annual debt increase is a fairly reliable measure of capital expenditure, but there are both leads and lags. Accumulated surpluses were also checked against sinking fund deposits; this checking revealed no serious discrepancies between funds expended and debt increases. Much temporary debt before 1926 consisted of tax arrears bonds; these were funded during 1924–26 in the two major cities and account for the increasing debenture debt in those years. These increases are not included in making capital expenditures for the years in question. Figures on temporary debt are available after 1926 from the reports of the Department of Municipal Affairs for 1926–50, and increases are considered as capital expenditures. Decreases in debt are not subtracted from expenditure. Throughout the tables in the text, total expenditure only is shown; this is the sum of ordinary and capital expenditure. Gross expenditures of the utilities are included.

TOWNS

For 1906–29 inclusive, ordinary expenditure is assumed to equal total revenue as estimated in each year. Expenditure data are completely lacking in the reports of the Department of Municipal Affairs before 1923 and the 1924–30 series provided is of little use since it includes trust taxes which cannot be segregated. For 1930–50 figures were obtained from the reports in question. Hospital, school, and social service tax requisitions were deducted from totals reported. Capital expenditure estimates were obtained by noting debt increases each year. Throughout the tables, only total expenditures are shown, and they include both ordinary and capital expenditures. Gross utility expenditures are included in the total.

VILLAGES

The same sources and similar estimating procedures were used as in the case of the towns.

MUNICIPAL DISTRICTS

Ordinary expenditures for 1913–25 were taken to equal estimated revenues. Figures for 1926–50 were taken from the reports of the Department of Municipal Affairs for the years in question. Capital expenditures were derived from increases in debt.

ORGANIZED LOCAL IMPROVEMENT DISTRICTS

Expenditure is assumed to equal revenue in each year between 1906 and 1918 when these units were disorganized.

UNORGANIZED IMPROVEMENT DISTRICTS

All data were obtained from the provincial public accounts from 1906 to 1950 inclusive.

SPECIAL AREAS

All data were obtained from the provincial public accounts from 1938 to 1950.

SCHOOL DISTRICTS

All data were obtained from the reports of the Department of Education for 1906–50 inclusive.

HOSPITAL DISTRICTS

The figures for 1919–28 are estimates from the scattered data in the reports of the Department of Municipal Affairs. The figures for subsequent years were obtained from reports of the Department of Public Health.

DEBT DATA

CITIES

Debenture debt data for 1906–29 inclusive were obtained from the same sources as revenues and expenditures for these years. For 1930–42 inclusive, city reports were used because the debt figures reported in the reports of the Department of Municipal Affairs include school debenture debt. For 1943–50 inclusive, the figures were derived from the reports of the aforementioned department. Temporary debt figures were obtained from the reports of the same department and from city reports. The latter had to be resorted to in order to obtain the indebtedness of the cities to the provincial government.

TOWNS

Debenture debt for 1906–12 was estimated by comparing the figures reported in the reports of the Department of Municipal Affairs with the Edmonton debt. (The 1913 report of the department was used.) In 1913, the debt of the towns equalled 12 per cent of the Edmonton debt. This percentage was applied to obtain the 1906–12 estimates. The figures for 1913–50 were obtained from the reports of the Department of Municipal Affairs. Temporary loan data were obtained from the same source after 1926. No such data are available for years preceding 1926.

VILLAGES

The same sources and similar procedures were used as in the case of the towns.

MUNICIPAL DISTRICTS

All debt figures are actual ones derived from the reports of the Department of Municipal Affairs for the years 1913–50 inclusive. Figures for seed grain indebtedness, the chief kind of municipal district debt, were obtained from the same source except for the years 1919–20 which were not reported. Data for these two years were obtained from the provincial public accounts.

SCHOOL DISTRICTS

Data were obtained from the reports of the Department of Education, 1906–50 inclusive.

HOSPITAL DISTRICTS

Data for the early 1920s were obtained from an examination of various orders of the Board of Public Utility Commissioners. No aggregate data are available to the knowledge of the writer. The order of magnitude of hospital district debt, however, is small. Data for 1929 to 1950 inclusive were obtained from the reports of the Department of Public Health.

PROVINCIAL DEBT

Appendix D

Certain statistical material relating to the provincial debt and the conditions of the debt reorganization program of 1945 are set out below. Most of this appendix, however, is devoted to the presentation of tables showing detailed procedures used in estimating the provincial debt position in the event of no default.

CHANGES IN THE LEVEL AND COMPOSITION OF PROVINCIAL DEBT, 1908–51

Changes in the annual level and composition of provincial debt from 1908 to 1951 are set out in Table D1. *Temporary loans* include loans obtained from the banks and of treasury bills sold to banks and other financial institutions. It is notable that such borrowing ceases after 1935 except for a treasury bill issue in 1947 which was redeemed before the fiscal year ended, and is therefore not reflected in the year end total. *Savings certificates* include both demand and term certificates of various denominations sold. They were redeemed gradually after 1936 following the suspension of payment on demand and on maturity dates in August, 1935. They now constitute a negligible part of the provincial debt. *Other* unfunded debt includes accounts payable and various miscellaneous liabilities; at the present time the chief item consists of the provincial obligation to the pension fund of civil servants. No entry is made in Table D1 for the years 1908 to 1923 inclusive to show the amount of this category of debt because the public accounts for those years had no balance sheets. *Net debenture debt* consists of direct debentures and stock after deducting sinking fund assets. This is the most important constituent of the provincial debt at the present time. *Treasury bills, Dominion of Canada,* consist of bills sold to the Dominion of Canada during the 1930s to finance relief expenditures and the redemption of maturing debentures. A large reduction was effected in 1947 when the Dominion government wrote off more than $5 million and applied the natural resource award of about $8 million against them. The balance is repayable over thirty years, the first payment to be made in 1977. A portion of the remaining bills is interest-free. *Class I indirect debt* consists of debentures of railways, irrigation and drainage districts, the University of Alberta, etc. which the province guaranteed, and of guarantees of seed grain notes, loans for the purchase of livestock, loans of co-operative credit societies, etc. *Class II indirect debt* consists of railway debentures originally guaranteed by the province but later assumed by the Canadian National Railways and the Canadian Pacific Railways. The province still remained liable in the event of default by the railways. These debentures were completely retired by the railways in 1942.

THE DEBT REORGANIZATION PROGRAM OF 1945

The following is a reproduction of the statement of the details of the debt reorganization program of 1945 as set out in the public accounts of the fiscal year 1945–46 (see Government of Alberta, *Public Accounts, 1945–46*, 14–17):

> Under the provisions of The Provincial Debt Reorganization Act, 1945, being Chapter 1 of the Statutes of Alberta, 1945 (Second Session), the Lieutenant Governor in Council by Order-in-Council, numbered 1168/45 and dated July 17, 1945, authorised the Provincial Treasurer, for and on behalf of the Government of the Province, to make an offer to the several holders of the outstanding securities issued or guaranteed by the Province excepting (a) Alberta and Great Waterways Railway bonds and treasury bills held by the Dominion Government, upon which interest has always been paid in full. (b) Savings certificates in connection with which a plan of adjustment was authorised under authority of Chapter 3, Statutes of Alberta, 1945 (Second Session), and Order-in-Council numbered 1362/45 as amended by Order-in-Council numbered 1428/45. The said plan is as nearly as practicable comparable to the Debt Reorganization Programme. (c) Two small matured issues of guaranteed irrigation and drainage districts debentures originally amounting to $64,000.00 with respect to which the province proposes to make an adjustment similar to that contained in the Debt Reorganization Programme.

The Debt Reorganization Programme provided for in the Offer was declared operative on October 24, 1945, and contained the following provisions as to payments to be made to holders of matured and unmatured securities:

A – MATURED SECURITIES:

Holders who surrender to the Province any of the Matured Securities described in Columns 1, 2, 3 and 4 of Schedule "A" and release all claims for principal, interest or otherwise in respect thereof will receive from the Province in consideration of such surrender and release the total cash payment per $1,000 Debenture of £100 Stock, as the case may be, set forth in Column 9 of Schedule "A" in respect of the Matured Securities so surrendered. Such payment will be made in the currency, or in one of the alternative currencies at holder's option, set forth in Column 10 of Schedule "A," being the same currency or currencies in which the Matured Securities so surrendered are payable as set forth in Column 3 of Schedule "A." The said payment comprises the following:

(a) The principal amount of the Matured Securities so surrendered.

(b) An adjustment of interest unpaid in the nine years from June 1, 1936, to June 1, 1945, as set forth in Columns 5, 6, and 7 of Schedule "A." The method of computing this adjustment is as follows: Each of the Matured Securities has been valued on a 3.25% yield basis as of 1st June, 1936, on the assumption that the maturity date thereof was June 1st, 1945. To the premium so ascertained, as shown in Columns 5 and 6 of Schedule "A" is added the difference between interest at a 3.25% rate and interest at 50% of the contract rate for said nine-year period, as set forth in Column 7 of Schedule "A."

(c) An amount equal to accrued interest on the Matured Securities so surrendered at 50% of the respective contract rates as shown in Column 4 of Schedule "A" calculated to 1st June, 1945, from the last preceding interest payment date subsequent to 1st December, 1944, as set forth in Column 8 of Schedule "A" and with the exception that all adjustments, computations and calculations with respect to the $2,198,000 4.5% Debentures due 15th June, 1945, have been made to 15th June, 1945 instead of to 1st June, 1945.

B – UNMATURED SECURITIES

Holders who surrender to the Province any of the Unmatured Securities described in Columns 1, 2, 3 and 4 of Schedule "B" and release all claims for principal, interest or otherwise in respect thereof will receive from the Province in exchange therefor the following:

(a) The total payments per $1,000 Debenture of £100 Stock, as the case may be, set forth in Columns 11 and 12 of Schedule "B," in respect of the Unmatured Securities so surrendered. Such payments will be made in the currency, or in one of the alternative currencies at holder's option, set forth in Column 15 of Schedule "B," being the same currency or currencies in which the Unmatured Securities so surrendered are payable, as set forth in Column 3 of Schedule "B." The said payments comprise the following:

1) An amount equal to accrued interest on the Unmatured Securities so surrendered at 50% of the respective contract rates as shown in Column 4 of Schedule "B," calculated to 1st June, 1945 from the last preceding interest payment date subsequent to 1st December, 1944, as set forth in Column 10 of Schedule "B."

2) An adjustment of interest unpaid in the nine years from 1st June 1936 to 1st June 1945 and an adjustment in respect of contract interest rates to future maturity or call dates as set forth in Column 9 of Schedule "B." The method of computing this adjustment is as follows: Each of the Unmatured Securities has been valued on a 3.5% yield basis as of 1st June, 1936, computed to the actual maturity or earliest call date. The total amount of the premium so ascertained is divided between the portions thereof which pertain respectively to the periods prior to and subsequent to 1st June, 1945, as shown in Columns 5, 6 and 7 of Schedule "B." To the total premium is added the difference between interest at a 3.5% rate and interest at 50% of the contract rate for said nine-year period as set forth in Column 8 of Schedule "B." Payment of the premium and additional interest as thus computed will be made 50% in cash (including the full amount of the premium payment which pertains to the period from 1st June, 1945, to maturity or earliest call date as shown in Column 7) to which is added the accrued interest shown in Column 10 of Schedule "B," resulting in the total cash payment shown in Column 11 of Schedule "B," and 50% in five equal annual instalments (without interest) payable on 1st June in each of the years 1946 to 1950 (both inclusive), and are presented by special interest adjustment coupons or obligations to be issued with, attached to, or provided for in the New Debentures

and Alberta Government Stock referred to in (b) below and to be payable in the same currency or currencies and at the same place or places as therein respectively stipulated. (Adjustments in this 50% division have been provided for in Columns 11 and 12 of Schedule "B" to avoid fractions in calculating the amount of the five equal annual instalments referred to above.)

(b) New Debentures or New Alberta Government Stock, as the case may be, in the same principal amount and payable in the same currency or in the same alternative currencies, at holder's option, as the Unmatured Securities so surrendered."

Schedules A and B referred to above are very detailed and are not shown in the public accounts.

COMPUTATIONS OF ASSUMED PUBLIC DEBT IN THE EVENT THAT NO DEFAULT HAD TAKEN PLACE

The question of the prospective level of public debt in the event that there had been no default was raised in Chapter 11. The assumptions set out in an attempt to answer the question were set out in that chapter. Tables D2 and D15 inclusive set out the basis for the computations.

The sources of data are as follows: (1) *Sirois Report*, Public Accounts Inquiry, *Province of Alberta, Comparative Statistics of Public Finance*, Appendix J (Ottawa, December 1, 1938), especially Schedules 10 to 14 inclusive; (2) Government of Alberta, *Public Accounts, 1935–36 to 1950–51* inclusive. The first is referred to simply as *Sirois Report*, Appendix J, throughout the tables following; the second is designated the usual abbreviation of *P.A.* used throughout. Schedules referred to in the public accounts by number refer to the 1950–51 accounts unless otherwise specified. Since the numbers used for each specific kind of schedule in the 1950–51 accounts have not been used uniformly to apply to each kind of schedule in every issue of the public accounts, any other procedure would make references cumbersome; the reader should be aware of different numbering in issues previous to 1950–51, but the number in the 1950–51 accounts furnishes a guide as to what kind (i.e. funded debt, sinking fund, receipts and payments, etc.) of schedule is meant.

Table D1 Public Debt of the Province of Alberta, 1908–1951 (in millions of dollars)

Year end	Temp. loans	Savings certificates	Other unfunded	Total unfunded	Debentures, net	Treasury bills, Dominion	Total funded debt	Total direct debt	Class I indirect debt	Class II indirect debt	Total indirect debt	Total debt	Annual change
1908[a]	1.2	0.0	0.0	1.2	0.0	0.0	0.0	1.2	0.0	0.0	0.0	1.2	1.2
1909	1.0	0.0	0.0	1.0	2.0	0.0	2.0	3.0	19.6	0.0	19.6	22.6	21.4
1910	3.4	0.0	0.0	3.4	2.0	0.0	2.0	5.4	19.6	0.0	19.6	25.0	2.4
1911	7.3	0.0	0.0	7.3	2.0	0.0	2.0	9.3	19.6	0.0	19.6	28.9	3.9
1912	10.7	0.0	0.0	10.7	6.9	0.0	6.9	17.6	34.1	0.0	34.1	51.7	22.8
1913	3.7	0.0	0.0	3.7	15.3	0.0	15.3	19.0	37.2	0.0	37.2	56.2	4.5
1914	0.0	0.0	0.0	0.0	22.7	0.0	22.7	22.7	41.6	0.0	41.6	64.4	8.2
1915	0.0	0.0	0.0	0.0	26.7	0.0	26.7	26.7	41.6	0.0	41.6	68.4	4.0
1916	0.0	0.0	0.0	0.0	28.6	0.0	28.6	28.6	41.6	0.0	41.6	70.3	1.9
1917	0.4	0.4	0.0	0.8	30.0	0.0	30.0	30.8	22.7	19.0	41.6	72.4	2.1
1918	1.2	1.1	0.0	2.3	30.7	0.0	30.7	33.1	22.8	19.0	41.7	74.8	2.4
1919	0.3	1.7	0.0	2.0	33.7	0.0	33.7	35.6	20.9	22.5	43.4	79.1	4.3
1920	1.0	2.8	0.0	3.8	40.8	0.0	40.8	44.5	25.2	22.5	47.8	92.3	13.2
1921	2.0	3.7	0.0	5.7	57.5	0.0	57.5	63.2	30.4	22.5	52.9	116.1	23.8
1922	2.9	4.4	0.0	7.3	65.7	0.0	65.7	72.9	30.7	22.5	53.3	126.2	10.1
1923	0.3	4.7	0.0	5.0	71.8	0.0	71.8	76.8	31.6	22.5	54.1	130.9	4.7
1924	0.8	5.5	0.4	6.7	76.9	0.0	76.9	83.6	28.0	22.5	50.5	134.1	3.2
1925	1.5	7.7	0.6	9.8	79.5	0.0	79.5	89.2	25.6	22.5	48.2	137.4	3.3
1926	0.5	10.1	0.9	11.4	84.5	0.0	84.5	95.9	25.3	22.5	47.8	143.8	6.4
1928[b]	2.0	11.8	0.9	15.7	87.7	0.0	87.7	103.4	26.3	22.5	48.8	152.2	8.4

Table D1 (continued)

1929	1.5	11.6	1.5	14.6	92.8	0.0	92.8	107.4	25.8	22.8	48.6	156.0	3.8
1930	0.0	11.8	2.5	14.3	102.4	0.0	102.4	116.7	9.5	32.2	41.7	158.4	2.4
1931	0.0	11.0	3.0	14.0	111.5	0.0	111.5	125.5	10.6	32.2	42.8	168.3	9.9
1932	0.0	9.2	3.7	12.9	126.2	4.3	130.5	143.4	10.2	32.2	42.4	185.8	17.5
1933	3.1	9.2	2.4	14.6	126.7	6.5	133.2	147.8	10.0	32.2	42.2	190.0	4.2
1934	3.4	9.2	2.7	15.4	121.6	10.5	132.1	147.5	9.1	32.2	41.3	188.8	-1.2
1935	4.2	10.9	2.7	17.8	119.8	16.3	136.1	153.9	9.0	32.2	41.2	195.1	6.3
1936	5.7	9.3	3.4	18.4	117.7	25.2	142.9	161.3	8.6	32.2	40.8	202.1	7.0
1937	5.7	8.1	3.2	17.1	117.3	26.2	143.5	160.6	7.8	32.2	40.0	200.6	-1.5
1938	5.8	7.0	2.9	15.7	117.1	26.5	143.0	159.3	8.3	32.2	40.5	199.8	-0.8
1939	5.7	6.1	3.0	14.8	116.9	26.5	143.4	158.2	9.1	20.1	29.2	187.4	-12.4
1940	0.0	5.4	3.2	8.6	116.4	26.5	142.9	151.5	9.3	20.1	29.4	180.9	-6.5
1941	0.0	4.9	3.4	8.2	115.7	26.5	142.2	150.4	8.5	20.1	28.6	179.0	-1.9
1942	0.0	4.4	3.5	7.9	115.0	26.5	141.5	149.4	7.6	5.5	13.1	162.5	-16.5
1943	0.0	4.0	3.7	7.7	114.1	26.4	140.5	148.2	6.8	5.5	12.3	160.5	-2.0
1944	0.0	3.6	4.0	7.6	113.3	26.3	139.6	147.2	6.3	2.4	8.7	155.9	-4.6
1945	0.0	3.1	4.3	7.4	112.6	26.2	138.8	146.2	5.9	0.0	5.9	152.1	-3.8
1946	0.0	1.1	4.3	5.4	114.6	26.2	140.8	146.2	1.9	0.0	1.9	148.1	-4.0
1947	0.0	1.0	4.7	5.8	113.0	26.2	139.2	145.0	1.2	0.0	1.2	146.2	-1.9
1948	0.0	1.0	5.5	6.5	108.5	12.9	121.4	127.9	1.3	0.0	1.3	129.2	-17.0
1949	0.0	1.0	8.0	9.0	108.3	12.5	120.8	129.9	2.3	0.0	2.3	132.2	3.0
1950	0.0	1.1	8.3	9.4	109.0	12.2	121.2	130.6	3.2	0.0	3.2	133.8	1.6
1951	0.0	0.7	10.6	11.2	88.8	11.8	100.6	111.8	4.1	0.0	4.1	115.9	-17.9

(a) As at Dec. 31, 1908 to 1926.
(b) As at March 31, 1928 to 1951.

Table D2 Net Assumed Debt, 1936–1951 (in millions of dollars)

As of Mar. 31	Funded Debt			Other[d]	Total funded debt	Unfunded debt[e]	Total net debt[f]
	Net direct debenture debt[a]	Net indirect debt[b]	Dominion treasury bills[c]				
1937	112.5	7.8	32.6	0.7	153.6	17.1	170.7
1938	110.1	8.3	36.0	1.1	155.5	15.7	171.2
1939	104.6	8.9	43.3	1.5	158.3	14.8	173.1
1940	101.4	9.3	47.9	1.7	160.3	8.6	168.9
1941	100.6	8.4	48.4	1.7	159.1	8.2	167.3
1942	94.2	7.5	49.9	1.7	153.3	7.9	161.2
1943	90.6	6.7	49.8	1.7	148.8	7.7	156.5
1944	83.0	6.1	49.7	1.7	140.5	7.6	148.1
1945	82.3	5.7	49.6	1.7	139.3	7.4	146.7
1946	76.1	5.4	49.6	1.7	132.8	5.4	138.2
1947	67.6	4.7	49.6	1.7	123.6	5.8	129.4
1948	56.2	4.7	33.4	1.7	96.0	6.5	102.5
1949	55.5	5.7	32.5	1.7	95.4	9.0	104.4
1950	51.8	6.3	31.6	1.7	91.4	9.4	100.8
1951	47.8	7.2	30.7	1.7	87.4	11.2	98.6

(a) Assuming redemptions as per maturity dates and call of the Alberta and Great Waterways issue in 1947 and of another $3 million issue in 1949. See Table D3 for details of derivation of assumed net direct debenture debt.
(b) See Table D4 for details of derivation of assumed "net" indirect debt.
(c) See Table D5 for details of derivation of assumed loans from the Dominion of Canada.
(d) Treasury bills are held by the provincial treasurer. The amounts here are equal to the actual ones.
(e) It is assumed that there would have been no change in annual amounts in "unfunded debt." Thus the figures above are actual ones. This, for example, assumes that the redemption of savings certificates would have proceeded at the same rate as was actually the case.
(f) The sum of "total funded debt" and "unfunded debt."

Table D3 Assumed Debenture Debt, 1936–1951 (in millions of dollars)

Fiscal year[a]	Gross debenture debt at beginning of year[b]	Less redemptions[c]	Gross debenture debt at end of year	Less sinking fund at end of year	Net debenture debt at end of year[d]
1936–37	128.1	−4.1	124.0	−11.5	112.5
1937–38	124.0	−1.6	122.4	−12.3	110.1
1938–39	122.4	−5.5	116.9	−12.3	104.6
1939–40	116.9	−3.8	113.1	−11.7	101.4
1940–41	113.1	0.0	113.1	−12.5	100.6
1941–42	113.1	−7.8	105.3	−11.1	94.2
1942–43	105.3	−3.2	102.1	−11.5	90.6
1943–44	102.1	−8.6	93.5	−10.5	83.0
1944–45	93.5	0.0	93.5	−11.2	82.3
1945–46	93.5	−6.0	87.5	−11.4	76.1
1946–47	87.5	−8.8	78.7	−11.1	67.6
1947–48	78.7	−12.2	66.5	−10.3	56.2
1948–49	66.5	0.0	66.5	−11.0	55.5
1949–50	66.5	−3.0	63.5	−11.7	51.8
1950–51	63.5	−3.7	59.8	−12.0	47.8

(a) April 1 to March 31.
(b) Excluded are guaranteed debentures which are dealt with in Table D4.
(c) As per schedule of maturities of the debt existing on March 31, 1936, and assuming callable issues are called on the earliest call date.
(d) See Table D6 for sinking fund estimates.

Table D4 Assumed Indirect Debt, 1936–1951 (in millions of dollars)

Fiscal year	Gross debt at beginning of year[a]	Annual change[b]	Gross debt at end of year	Less sinking fund at end of year[c]	Net indirect debt at end of year
1936–37	9.9	−0.7	9.2	−1.4	7.8
1937–38	9.2	0.6	9.8	−1.5	8.3
1938–39	9.8	0.7	10.5	−1.6	8.9
1939–40	10.5	0.4	10.9	−1.6	9.3
1940–41	10.9	−0.6	10.3	−1.9	8.4
1941–42	10.3	−0.7	9.6	−2.1	7.5
1942–43	9.6	−0.6	9.0	−2.3	6.7
1943–44	9.0	−0.4	8.6	−2.5	6.1
1944–45	8.6	−0.1	8.5	−2.8	5.7
1945–46	8.5	−0.2	8.3	−2.9	5.4
1946–47	8.3	−0.6	7.7	−3.0	4.7
1947–48	7.7	0.1	7.8	−3.1	4.7
1948–49	7.8	1.1	8.9	−3.2	5.7
1949–50	8.9	0.8	9.7	−3.4	6.3
1950–51	9.7	1.0	10.7	−3.5	7.2

(a) Includes debentures of irrigation and drainage districts and various minor guarantees.
(b) Annual change as per *P.A.*
(c) See Table D7 for derivation of this column.

Table D5 Actual and Assumed Loans from the Dominion of Canada, 1936–1951 (in millions of dollars)

As at Mar. 31	As per public account		Assumed		Total actual plus assumed
	With interest[a]	Interest free[a]	With interest[b]	Interest free[b]	
1937	26.2	0.0	6.4	0.0	32.6
1938	26.5	0.0	9.5	0.0	36.0
1939	26.5	0.0	16.8	0.0	43.3
1940	26.5	0.0	21.4	0.0	47.9
1941	26.5	0.0	21.9	0.0	48.4
1942	26.5	0.0	23.4	0.0	49.9
1943	26.4	0.0	23.4	0.0	49.8
1944	26.3	0.0	23.4	0.0	49.7
1945	26.2	0.0	23.4	0.0	49.6
1946	26.2	0.0	23.4	0.0	49.6
1947	26.2	0.0	23.4	0.0	49.6
1948	7.6	5.3	18.5	2.0	33.4
1949	7.3	5.2	17.8	2.0	32.3
1950	7.2	5.0	17.2	1.8	31.2
1951	7.0	4.8	16.6	1.7	30.1

(a) Actual year end levels as per the public accounts.
(b) Assumed loans are the additional funds that would have to have been obtained from the Dominion government to meet relief expenditures and the redemption of debentures on maturity dates. It is assumed that there would have been an additional $4 million of loans incurred for relief expenditures; thus another $2 million would have been written off in 1947 and the balance would have been free of interest.

Table D6   Assumed and Actual Sinking Fund of the Direct Debentures, 1936–1951 (in millions of dollars)

Fiscal year	Assumed Sinking Fund					Sinking fund at end of year	Actual sinking fund at end of year[c]
	Sinking fund at beginning of year	Contri-butions[a]	Earnings[b]	Total	Less applied on redemptions		
1936–37	10.6	0.5	0.5	11.6	−0.1	11.5	11.4
1937–38	11.5	0.3	0.5	12.3	−	12.3	12.1
1938–39	12.3	0.2	0.6	13.1	−0.8	12.3	12.6
1939–40	12.3	0.2	0.6	13.1	−1.4	11.7	13.3
1940–41	11.7	0.2	0.6	12.5	0.0	12.5	14.0
1941–42	12.5	0.2	0.6	13.3	−2.2	11.1	14.6
1942–43	11.1	0.2	0.6	11.9	−0.4	11.5	15.4
1943–44	11.5	0.2	0.6	12.3	−1.8	10.5	16.1
1944–45	10.5	0.2	0.5	11.2	0.0	11.2	16.8
1945–46	11.2	0.2	0.6	12.0	−0.6	11.4	
1946–47	11.4	0.2	0.5	12.1	−1.0	11.1	0.1
1947–48	11.1	0.2	0.4	11.7	−1.4	10.3	0.0
1948–49	10.3	0.2	0.5	11.0	0.0	11.0	0.0
1949–50	11.0	0.2	0.5	11.7	0.0	11.7	0.0
1950–51	11.7	0.2	0.5	12.4	−0.4	12.0	0.0

(a)   The contributions shown here are the actual ones made until 1945–46. The telephone system contributed small amounts in 1936–37 and 1937–38. The Alberta Wheat Pool made a contribution every year until 1945, when the debt was reorganized. Here it is assumed that the Alberta Wheat Pool issue had run to maturity and contributions would have continued. It is assumed that all other contributions would have ceased after 1936.

(b)   Earnings have been computed and estimated on the basis of the full rate on fund holdings of Alberta bonds. Earnings on bonds purchased by the fund in the market would have depended on yields; consequently earnings shown in the table may be understated or overstated. It is believed that the cumulative possible margin of error should not exceed one million dollars one way or the other. Amounts applied on debenture redemptions have also been estimated on the basis of the application of compound interest at a rate about 2 per cent higher than that actually earned. Again there is some margin of error here, possibly another million dollars one way or the other. Most of the bonds held by the sinking fund in 1936 were Alberta ones. That is the prime reason why sinking fund earnings suffered by the default.

(c)   *P.A., 1936–51.*

Table D7   Assumed and Actual Sinking Fund of the Indirect Debentures, 1936–1951
(in millions of dollars)

Fiscal year	Sinking fund at beginning of year	Contribu- tions[a]	Earnings[b]	Less redemptions[c]	Sinking fund at end of year, assumed	Sinking fund at end of year, actual
1936–37	1.4	0.0	0.1	0.0	1.4	1.4
1937–38	1.4	0.0	0.1	0.0	1.5	1.5
1938–39	1.5	0.0	0.1	0.0	1.6	1.5
1939–40	1.6	0.0	0.1	0.0	1.6	1.6
1940–41	1.6	0.1	0.1	0.0	1.9	1.8
1941–42	1.9	0.1	0.1	0.0	2.1	2.0
1942–43	2.1	0.1	0.1	0.0	2.3	2.2
1943–44	2.3	0.1	0.1	–	2.5	2.4
1944–45	2.5	0.1	0.1	0.0	2.8	2.6
1945–46	2.8	0.0	0.1	0.0	2.9	0.0
1946–47	2.9	0.0	0.1	0.0	3.0	0.0
1947–48	3.0	0.0	0.1	0.0	3.1	0.0
1948–49	3.1	0.0	0.1	0.0	3.2	0.0
1949–50	3.2	0.0	0.1	0.0	3.4	0.0
1950–51	3.4	0.0	0.1	0.0	3.5	0.0

(a)   These were actual contributions to the Lethbridge Northern Irrigation District sinking fund.
(b)   Earnings are estimated similarly to the procedures used for the provincial government sinking fund shown in Table D6.
(c)   A small issue matured in 1943.

Table D8   Assumed Receipts if Full Payment of Interest Had Been Made and Matured Debentures Had Been Redeemed, 1936–51 (millions of dollars)

Fiscal year	Net receipts[a]	Sinking fund applied on loans[b]	Fiscal need subsidy[d]	Wartime tax agreements[e]	Debt reorgani- zation[f]	New deben- tures[g]	Tax collections lost[h]	Total assumed receipts
1936–37	26.5	0.0	0.0	0.0	0.0	0.0	0.0	26.5
1937–38	28.4	–	0.6	0.0	0.0	0.0	0.0	29.0
1938–39	28.5	0.8	0.6	0.0	0.0	0.0	0.0	29.9
1939–40	33.3	1.4	0.6	0.0	0.0	0.0	0.0	35.3
1940–41	27.6	0.0	0.6	0.0	0.0	0.0	0.0	28.2
1941–42	29.9	2.2	0.6	5.9	0.0	0.0	–3.8	34.8
1942–43	31.0	0.4	0.6	2.3	0.0	0.0	–0.1	34.2
1943–44	32.7	1.8	0.6	2.1	0.0	0.0	–0.1	37.1
1944–45	35.2	0.0	0.6	2.2	0.0	0.0	–0.1	37.9
1945–46	110.2	0.6	–1.8	–8.9	–55.9	0.0	0.0	44.2
1946–47	48.2	1.0	0.6	0.1	–0.8	0.0	0.0	49.1
1947–48	67.5	1.4(c)	0.0	–3.3	–0.6	–2.5	0.0	62.5
1948–49	77.4	0.0	0.0	0.0	–0.6	0.0	0.0	76.8
1949–50	167.3	0.0	0.0	0.0	–0.6	–59.7	0.0	107.0
1950–51	189.2	0.4	0.0	0.0	–0.6	–62.3	0.0	126.7

(a)   As per *P.A.*, Statement No. 9, after deducting cash balances on hand and sales of investment as per Statement No. 143.

(b)   These are estimates of sinking fund applicable to matured debentures assumed redeemed on the basis of Alberta bond holdings in 1936 and subsequent holdings assumed acquired in the market. The rate earned on most of the assets of the fund would then have been an average of bond rates held in 1936 and of bond yields of bonds acquired subsequently.

(c)   Estimate was based on data in Statement No. 17, last appearing in *P.A., 1945–46*, compound interest being applied to the residual shown in that statement. The $1.4 million includes $0.8 million applying to the Alberta and Great Waterways debenture issue.

(d)   It is assumed that the province would have received $0.6 million in fiscal need subsidies annually between 1937 and 1947 because both Saskatchewan and Manitoba received such subsidies for this period. Under the debt reorganization program, $2.4 million was received for 1937 to 1941 in the fiscal year 1945–46. No allowance was made for the wartime tax agreement years under the actual conditions.

(e)   These are net differences between actual receipts and assumed ones. See Table D10 for details.

(f)   For details see Table D18.

(g)   These are debentures issued apart from the debt reorganization program but which were largely made possible by call features in the new bonds issued in 1945. An issue of $2.5 million was made in 1947–48; it is here assumed that it would not have been floated. The figures for 1949–50 and 1950–51 are for bonds issued under the 1950 refunding scheme; it is assumed that this transaction would not have taken place. In fact, it could not have been made without an agreement with the bondholders.

(h)   It is assumed that the wartime tax agreement on the debt option basis would have been made effective beginning April 1, 1941. Thus the taxes affected would not have been collected in 1941–42. The amounts for the following years are estimates of arrears applicable to 1941–42 levies.

Table D9   Assumed Payments if Interest on Debt Had Been Paid in Full and Maturing Debentures Had Been Redeemed, 1936–51 (millions of dollars)

Fiscal year	Net payments[a]	Additional interest on funded debt[b]	Interest on additional loans[c]	Assumed debt redemption[d]	Debt reorganization program[e]	Other debt redemption[f]	Total assumed payments
1936–37	28.2	2.2	0.0	4.0	0.0	0.0	34.4
1937–38	27.9	2.4	0.2	1.6	0.0	0.0	32.1
1938–39	28.9	2.5	0.3	5.5	0.0	0.0	37.2
1939–40	33.4	2.2	0.5	3.8	0.0	0.0	39.9
1940–41	26.0	2.0	0.7	0.0	0.0	0.0	28.7
1941–42	25.7	2.0	0.7	7.9	0.0	0.0	36.3
1942–43	26.4	1.7	0.7	3.4	0.0	0.0	32.2
1943–44	28.1	1.6	0.7	8.5	0.0	0.0	38.9
1944–45	32.1	1.4	0.7	0.0	0.0	0.0	34.2
1945–46	113.1	1.1	0.7	6.2	−77.8	0.0	43.3
1946–47	43.5	0.6	0.7	8.8	−4.2	0.0	49.4
1947–48	63.9	0.6	0.7	4.8	−3.9	2.0	68.1
1948–49	68.8	0.0	0.7	1.1	−2.8	0.0	67.8
1949–50	129.4	−0.1	0.7	4.1	−2.8	−59.7	81.6
1950–51	182.9	0.7	0.6	4.9	−3.0	−79.6	106.5

(a)   As per *P.A.*, Statement No. 9, after deducting purchases of investments as per Statement No. 141.
(b)   Difference between full interest and interest actually paid on debt in existence on March 31, 1936.
(c)   On Dominion government loans additional to those secured in the actual case. An interest rate of 3 per cent is assumed.
(d)   Assumed redemptions as per maturities of issues.
(e)   Debt redemptions and interest payments. See Tables D16 and D17.
(f)   Chiefly redemptions in connection with the 1950 refunding transaction.

Table D10 Actual and Assumed Revenue from Tax Agreements with the Dominion Government, 1941–1951 (in millions of dollars)

Fiscal year	Actual[a] WTA	FNS	1947 TA	Assumed Total	WTA [f]	FNS	Actual 1947 TA	Total	less assumed
1941–42	0.0[b]	0.0	0.0	0.0	5.9	0.6	0.0	6.5	−6.5
1942–43	3.6[c]	0.0	0.0	3.6	5.9	0.6	0.0	6.5	−2.9
1943–44	3.86[c]	0.0	0.0	3.8	5.9	0.6	0.0	6.5	−2.7
1944–45	3.76[c]	0.0	0.0	3.7	5.9	0.6	0.0	6.5	−2.8
1945–46	14.8[d]	2.4	0.0	17.2	5.9	0.6	0.0	6.5	10.7
1946–47	5.8	0.0	0.0	5.8	5.9	0.6	0.0	6.5	−0.7
1947–48	3.3[e]	0.0	9.9	13.2	0.0	0.0	9.9	9.9	3.3
1948–49	0.0	0.0	14.0	14.0	0.0	0.0	14.0	14.0	0.0
1949–50	0.0	0.0	15.3	15.3	0.0	0.0	15.3	15.3	0.0
1950–51	0.0	0.0	17.3	17.3	0.0	0.0	17.3	17.3	0.0

Note: WTA refers to Wartime Tax Agreement; FNS refers to Fiscal Need Subsidy; 1947 TA refers to 1947 Tax Agreement.

(a)   As per P.A., Statement No. 7.

(b)   The first receipt of the province from the Dominion under the Wartime Tax Agreement came on April 29, 1942; thus nothing was received in the fiscal year 1941–42.

(c)   Portions were deferred until the termination of the agreement after tax arrears were determined by subsequent collections. The province was finally entitled to $4.1 million per year for the years 1941–42 to 1946–47 inclusive under the tax option.

(d)   Pursuant to the debt reorganization program, the Dominion government permitted the province to transfer to the debt option on a retroactive basis. This entitled the province to $5.8 million per year for each of the six years. In 1945–46 the province received $7.0 million being the aggregate of the amounts by which the payments under the debt service option exceeded the payments under the tax option for the fiscal years 1941–42 to 1944–45 inclusive. In the same year it also received $2.0 million of the deferred portion under the tax option and $5.8 million applying to the current year as per the debt option.

(e)   This was the final settlement of the portion deferred under the tax option since 1941.

(f)   The writer estimates the net debt interest charges for 1940–41 to have been about $6.3 million under assumed conditions. From this is deducted succession duties of $0.4 million in 1940–41.

Table D11 Actual Interest Expenditures and Revenues, 1936–51 (in millions of dollars)

Fiscal year	Excluding Debt Reorganization			Debt Reoganization			Total net interest charges
	Payments	Less revenue	net interest charges	Payments	Less revenue	Net	
1936–37	5.6	−1.6	4.0	0.0	0.0	0.0	4.0
1937–38	4.8	−1.3	3.6	0.0	0.0	0.0	3.6
1938–39	4.8	−1.3	3.5	0.0	0.0	0.0	3.5
1939–40	4.7	−1.3	3.4	0.0	0.0	0.0	3.4
1940–41	4.7	−1.1	3.6	0.0	0.0	0.0	3.6
1941–42	4.7	−1.2	3.5	0.0	0.0	0.0	3.5
1942–43	4.7	−1.1	3.6	0.0	0.0	0.0	3.6
1943–44	4.7	−1.2	3.5	0.0	0.0	0.0	3.5
1944–45	4.7	−1.2	3.5	0.0	0.0	0.0	3.5
1945–46	5.6	−1.8	3.8	18.8	−2.8	16.1	19.9
1946–47	5.0	−1.1	3.8	2.3	−0.6	1.7	5.5
1947–48	4.2	−1.1	3.1	2.2	−0.6	1.6	4.7
1948–49	4.0	−1.0	3.0	2.1	−0.6	1.5	4.5
1949–50	4.3	−1.4	2.9	2.1	−0.6	1.5	4.4
1950–51	3.7	−4.8	−1.1	2.3	−0.6	1.7	0.6

Sources: See Tables D13 and D16 for details of derivation of the amounts shown.

Table D12 Assumed Interest Expenditures and Revenues, 1936–51
|(in millions of dollars)

Fiscal year	Interest on old debt[a]	Interest on new debt[b]	Total interest payments	Less inteest revenue[c]	Net assumed interest charges	Assumed net less the actual net
1936–37	8.3	0.0	8.3	−2.1	6.2	2.2
1937–38	7.9	0.2	8.1	−1.9	6.2	2.6
1938–39	7.9	0.3	8.2	−1.9	6.3	2.8
1939–40	7.4	0.5	7.9	−1.8	6.1	2.7
1940–41	7.2	0.7	7.9	−1.6	6.3	2.7
1941–42	7.2	0.7	7.9	−1.7	6.2	2.7
1942–43	6.7	0.7	7.4	−1.4	6.0	2.4
1943–44	6.5	0.7	7.2	−1.4	5.8	2.3
1944–45	6.1	0.7	6.8	−1.2	5.6	2.1
1945–46	6.1	0.7	6.8	−1.2	5.6	−14.3
1946–47	5.7	0.7	6.4	−1.3	5.1	−0.4
1947–48	4.8	0.7	5.5	−1.1	4.4	−0.3
1948–49	3.9	0.7	4.6	−0.9	3.7	−0.8
1949–50	3.9	0.7	4.6	−1.1	3.5	−0.9
1950–51	3.9	0.6	4.5	−1.7	2.8	2.2

(a) See Table D14 for details of derivation of amounts.
(b) Assumed interest on Dominion government borrowings required to meet annual cash deficits after 1936. The rate applied is 3 per cent.
(c) See Table D15 for details of derivation of amounts.

Table D13 Actual Interest Expenditure and Revenue Excluding Debt Reorganization Program Transactions, 1936–51 (in millions of dollars)

Fiscal year	Expenditure				Revenue		Net Other[f]	Total	Expend-iture
	FD[a]	SC[b]	PF[c]	0[d]	Total	Tel.[e]			
1936–37	5.0	0.2	0.1	0.3	5.6	0.9	0.7	1.6	4.0
1937–38	4.3	0.2	0.1	0.3	4.8	0.7	0.6	1.3	3.6
1938–39	4.3	0.1	0.1	0.3	4.8	0.7	0.6	1.3	3.5
1939–40	4.3	0.1	0.1	0.1	4.7	0.7	0.6	1.3	3.4
1940–41	4.3	0.1	0.1	0.1	4.7	0.7	0.4	1.1	3.6
1941–42	4.3	0.1	0.2	0.1	4.7	0.7	0.5	1.2	3.5
1942–43	4.3	0.1	0.2	0.2	4.7	0.7	0.4	1.1	3.6
1943–44	4.3	0.1	0.2	0.2	4.7	0.7	0.5	1.2	3.5
1944–45	4.3	0.1	0.2	0.2	4.7	0.7	0.5	1.2	3.5
1945–46	4.8	–	0.2	0.5	5.6	0.6	1.2	1.8	3.8
1946–47	4.6	–	0.2	0.1	5.0	0.7	0.4	1.1	3.8
1947–48	4.0	–	0.1	–	4.2	0.7	0.4	1.1	3.1
1948–49	3.8	–	0.2	–	4.0	0.7	0.4	1.0	3.0
1949–50	3.9	–	0.2	0.1	4.3	0.7	0.8	1.4	2.9
1950–51	3.2	–	0.2	0.3	3.7	0.6	4.1	4.8	−1.1

(a) Interest payments on funded debt (FD). This includes interest on general revenue direct debentures, the Alberta Government Telephones share of direct debentures, Dominion of Canada treasury bills, treasury bills held by the Provincial Treasurer, and irrigation and drainage district debentures.
(b) Interest on savings certificates (SC). This was also reduced by one-half in 1936 (or to 2 per cent).
(c) Interest on the pension fund (PF).
(d) Interest on other (0) items such as bank loans. It also includes foreign exchange discounts and expenses of management of debt.
(e) Interest on the telephone portion of the debt.
(f) Interest payments of the Alberta Wheat Pool; interest earned on the final railway instalment (until 1939); interest earned on the special investment fund and on bank deposits; interest on advances to the cities; profits and foreign exchange premiums on debentures sold; and a miscellany of other items.

Table D14 Assumed Expenditure on Interest, 1936–51, Excluding Interest on Assumed Additional Borrowing (in millions of dollars)

Fiscal year	Funded debt[a]	Foreign exchange[b]	A.G. & W. bonds[c]	Savings certificates[d]	Other[e]	Total assumed expenditure
1936–37	7.4	–	0.0	0.4	0.4	8.3
1937–38	7.2	–	0.0	0.3	0.4	7.9
1938–39	7.2	–	0.0	0.3	0.4	7.9
1939–40	6.9	–	0.0	0.3	0.2	7.4
1940–41	6.7	0.1	0.0	0.2	0.2	7.2
1941–42	6.7	0.1	0.0	0.2	0.2	7.2
1942–43	6.3	0.1	0.0	0.2	0.2	6.7
1943–44	6.1	0.1	0.0	0.2	0.2	6.5
1944–45	5.7	0.1	0.0	0.1	0.2	6.1
1945–46	5.7	0.1	0.0	0.1	0.2	6.1
1946–47	5.4	–	0.0	–	0.2	5.7
1947–48	4.9	–0.1	–0.2	–	0.2	4.8
1948–49	4.1	–0.1	–0.3	–	0.2	3.9
1949–50	4.1	–0.2	–0.3	–	0.2	3.9
1950–51	4.1	–0.2	–0.3	–	0.2	3.9

(a) Includes interest on general revenue fund debentures, telephone debentures, guaranteed Class I debentures (irrigation and drainage districts), Dominion government treasury bills, treasury bills held by the Provincial Treasurer, and the Alberta and Great Waterways bonds. See *Sirois Report*, Appendix J, Schedule 11, for all the issues included. With assumed redemptions, bond interest was deducted in subsequent years accordingly, the reduction being assumed to take effect in the year following redemption.
(b) Estimated from composition of bonded debt in terms of currency of payment as set out in ibid., and from foreign exchange rates as set out in Bank of Canada, *Statistical Summary, 1950 Supplement*, 134–35, and ibid., *August 1951*, 127.
(c) Estimated reduction in interest after redemption after taking exchange into account.
(d) The actual figures were doubled and rounded off to the nearest $100,000.
(e) As per *P.A., 1936–51*, after adjusting for foreign exchange actually paid. Complete accuracy cannot be claimed for the foreign exchange estimates.

Table D15 Assumed Interest Revenue, 1936–51 (in millions of dollars)

Fiscal year	AGT[a]	AWP[b]	Cash and investments[c]	Other	Total
1936–37	1.38	0.24	0.09	0.37	2.1
1937–38	1.27	0.25	0.04	0.34	1.9
1938–39	1.27	0.25	0.04	0.33	1.9
1939–40	1.19	0.25	0.04	0.33	1.8
1940–41	1.19	0.25	0.04	0.11	1.6
1941–42	1.19	0.25	0.04	0.21	1.7
1942–43	1.04	0.25	0.04	0.11	1.4
1943–44	0.93	0.25	0.08	0.12	1.4
1944–45	0.77	0.25	0.04	0.11	1.2
1945–46	0.77	0.25	0.12	0.11	1.2
1946–47	0.77	0.25	0.14	0.10	1.3
1947–48	0.60	0.25	0.13	0.08	1.1
1948–49	0.60	0.25	0.04	0.04	0.9
1949–50	0.60	0.25	0.22	0.04	1.1
1950–51	0.60	0.25	0.80	0.09	1.7

(a) Interest received from Alberta Government Telephones (AGT). The amounts payable by the telephone system would have been diminished with the retirement of debt attributed to the telephones; allowance is made for this.
(b) Interest at full rate on bonds issued to meet the Alberta Wheat Pool emergency of 1931.
(c) It was assumed that the province would have had a minimum cash and investment balance of $2 million. Thus loans from the Dominion government are assumed to have equalled the cash deficit if the cash and investment balance on hand was exactly $2 million; they are assumed to have been more if the balance was less than $2 million and less if the balance was more than $2 million. The balance would have been close to the minimum in almost every year until 1945. Earnings of 2 per cent on the balance are assumed to have been made.

Table D16 Interest Expenditure and Revenue Under the Debt Reorganization Program, 1946–51 (in millions of dollars)

Fiscal year ending Mar. 31	1946	1947	1948	1949	1950	1951
Expenditure:						
Interest adjustments	18.6	2.2	2.1	2.1	2.1	2.1
Expenses	0.3	0.2	–	–	–	0.2
Total	18.8	2.3	2.2	2.1	2.1	2.3
Revenue:						
Alberta Govern't Tel.	3.6	2.0	1.6	1.2	0.8	0.4
Alberta Wheat Pool	0.8	0.4	0.3	0.2	0.2	0.1
Irrigation and drainage districts	1.3	0.7	0.5	0.4	0.3	0.1
Total	5.8	3.0	2.4	1.8	1.2	0.6
Less deferred portion	–3.0	–2.4	–1.8	–1.2	–0.6	0.0
Net total for year	2.8	0.6	0.6	0.6	0.6	0.6
Net Expenditure:	16.1	1.7	1.6	1.5	1.5	1.7

Table D17 Expenditure Under the Debt Reorganization Program, 1946–51 (in millions of dollars)

Fiscal year ending Mar. 31	1946	1947	1948	1949	1950	1951
Income Account:						
Expenses	0.3	0.2	–	–	–	0.2
Interest adjustments	18.6	2.2	2.1	2.1	2.1	2.1
Total	18.8	2.3	2.2	2.1	2.1	2.3
Capital Account:						
Redemption of debentures and treasury bills	48.4	0.0	0.0	0.0	0.0	0.0
Advances to irrigation and drainage districts	7.6	0.2	–	. –	–	–
Advances to Alberta Governent Telephones	3.0	0.0	0.0	0.0	0.0	0.0
Total	59.0	0.2	–	–	–	–
Combined Total:	77.8	2.5	2.2	2.2	2.2	2.3

Table D18 Cash Collected Under the Debt Reorganization Program, 1946–51 (in millions of dollars)

Fiscal year ending March 31	1946	1947	1948	1949	1950	1951
Income Account:						
Fiscal need subsidy	2.4	0.0	0.0	0.0	0.0	0.0
Tax agreements	7.3	0.0	0.0	0.0	0.0	0.0
Interest	2.8	0.6	0.6	0.6	0.6	0.6
Total	12.4	0.6	0.6	0.6	0.6	0.6
Capital Account:						
Proceeds of new debentures	28.6	0.0	0.0	0.0	0.0	0.0
Provincial sinking funds applied on debt	14.5	0.0	0.0	0.0	0.0	0.0
Irrigation and drainage districts:						
Guaranteed debentures surrendered in exchange for direct issues	3.8	0.2	—	—	—	—
Sinking fund applied on advances	2.6	0.0	0.0	0.0	0.0	0.0
Alberta Wheat Pool:						
Sinking fund applied	3.0	0.0	0.0	0.0	0.0	0.0
Reimbursement	0.3	0.0	0.0	0.0	0.0	0.0
Profit on redemption of stock issues	0.2	0.0	0.0	0.0	0.0	0.0
Total	53.1	0.2	—	—	—	—
Total, Both Accounts	65.5	0.8	0.6	0.6	0.6	0.6
Less Dominion receipts	−9.7	0.0	0.0	0.0	0.0	0.0
	55.9	0.8	0.6	0.6	0.6	0.6

NOTES

CHAPTER 1: GEOGRAPHIC, HISTORICAL, AND STRUCTURAL BACKGROUND

1 For a discussion of resource appraisal, see E.W. Zimmerman, *World Resources and Industries* (New York, 1933), I–III. For a brief analysis of the resource concept, see V.W. Bladen, *An Introduction to Political Economy* (Toronto, 1943), I, 3–4.

2 For a description of the weather conditions under which agriculture is carried on in the Prairie Provinces, see A. Thomas and A.J. Connor, "The Climate of Canada," *Canada Year Book* (henceforth *C.Y.B.*), 1948–49, 52.

3 For a description of the physical features of the whole prairie region, see W.A. Mackintosh, *Prairie Settlement, The Geographical Setting* (Toronto, 1935), I, 3–8.

4 *Editors' note:* In fact, since the 1970s at least, energy revenues have served to increase the variability of provincial revenues substantially.

5 *Editors' note:* Contrary to Hanson's prediction, oil revenues continued to outweigh agricultural production, and do so to this day. The role of energy in Alberta is further discussed in chapters seven and eight.

6 See W.A. Mackintosh, *Economic Problems of the Prairie Provinces* (Toronto, 1935), I, 10–11. *Editors' note:* Alberta's debt default is analysed in some detail in chapter six.

7 *Editors' note:* See Palmer and Palmer's *A New History of Alberta* (Edmonton: Hurtig, 1990), chapters eight and nine, for more information on agrarian discontent.

8 Dr. Stanley mentions such settlements at St. Albert, Lac Ste. Anne, Lac la Biche, and Victoria. See George F.G. Stanley, *The Birth of Western Canada* (Toronto, 1936), 186.

9 *Editors' note:* The Riel Rebellion of 1885, called the Half Breed Rebellion by Hanson and his contemporaries, would have been a key element in forming and maintaining such fears. Such concerns combined with a variety of other factors such as poor transportation and lack of information about Alberta's farming potential (discussed by Hanson in chapters one and ten) to make settlement a reluctant process.

10 J.B. Hedges, *Building of the Canadian West* (New York, 1939), 126–27, and A.S. Morton, *History of the Prairie Settlement* (Toronto, 1938), IV.

11 Mackintosh, Economic Problems, I, esp. 8–9.

12 *Editors' note:* The "Dominion government" refers to the federal government, or the Government of Canada. The term "Dominion" derives from Canada's official name: The Dominion of Canada.

13 Professor Hedges points out that close co-operation between the Dominion government and the Canadian Pacific Railway Company made the immigration drive very effective. The policy itself was almost perfectly timed to supplement the basic factors favouring settlement. See Hedges, op. cit., VI, *passim*.

14 A.K. Cairncross, "Die Kapitaleinfuhr in Kanada, 1903–13. Eine Nachprüfung," *Weltwirtschaftliches Archiv* (Kiel, Nov. 1937), 593–634; Jacob Viner, *Canada's Balance of International Indebtedness, 1900–1913* (Cambridge and London, 1924); Mackintosh, *Economic Problems*, I–III; Dominion of Canada, *Report of the Royal Commission on Dominion–Provincial Relations* (henceforth the *Sirois Report*) (Ottawa, 1940), Book I, Chap. III. The first two works are primarily concerned with the problems of adjustments in the transfer of

international payments, which arise in association with the boom. The two latter ones deal more specifically with Western Canada in relation to the Canadian economy.

15   The gross value of agricultural production was about $550 per farm in 1906 (estimate from data drawn from *Statistical Progress*). The net income per farm would be considerably smaller.

16   All figures were obtained from the Dominion census of 1891 and 1901, and from the census of the Prairie Provinces in 1906.

17   The development of wheat varieties, which ripened in a shorter time than previous ones, pushed the wheat frontier farther northward after 1906. The incidence of frost also seems to have declined as more land was cleared and drained. Finally, "wet" years were more frequent than "dry" ones at the turn of the century, a factor that may have contributed to frosts.

18   For accounts of company rule and controversies regarding the claims of the company, see Chester Martin, *"Dominion Lands" Policy* (Toronto, 1938), I–II; A.O. MacRae, *The History of Alberta* (Calgary, 1912), XIII–XV and XVII; and C.M. McInnes, *In the Shadow of the Rockies* (London, 1930), I–III. A compilation of charters, statutes, and orders-in-council with reference to the Hudson's Bay Company is provided by *The Charters, Statutes, Orders-in-Council, Etc. Relating to the Hudson's Bay Company* (London, 1931).

19   For a treatment of the controversy in relation to Dominion–provincial financial relations throughout Canada, see J.A. Maxwell, *Federal Subsidies to the Provincial Governments in Canada* (Cambridge, 1937), VI and XII. For a discussion of the question in relation to the land policy of the Dominion government, see Martin, op. cit., XII and XIII.

20   The statute of 1875 provides that an electoral district might be formed when an area of 1,000 square miles contained a population of not less than 1,000 adults. Such a district was entitled to elect a member of the council.

21   In 1877 the council consisted of three nominative members. In 1886 there were six nominative and fourteen elected members.

22   Adam Shortt and A.G. Doughty, editors, *The Prairie Provinces, Canada and its Provinces*, Volume 19 (Toronto, 1914), 220–21.

23   North-West Territories Act, 1888, 51 Vict., c. 19.

24   See Shortt and Doughty, op. cit., 227–39, for a detailed account of the conflict.

25   Haultain originally proposed a subsidy along the lines of the subsidies paid to the provinces.

26   The most valuable, thorough, and recent treatment of the struggle for autonomy between 1897 and 1905 is that of C. Cecil Lingard, *Territorial Government in Canada, The Autonomy Question in the Old North-West Territories* (Toronto, 1946). Dr. Lingard emphasizes the constant financial embarrassment of the territorial government and stressed the influence of Sir Frederick Haultain throughout the long and wearisome negotiations between Ottawa and Regina. Shortt and Doughty, op. cit., 248–70, gives a shorter and much older account of political developments during the 1897–1905 period. An interesting and detailed contemporary narrative of the autonomy legislation with much reference to the separate school controversy that arose is given in *The Canadian Annual Review* (henceforth *C.A.R.*), 41–119. Controversies broke out in Eastern Canada in 1905 with respect to the education clause in the autonomy legislation. *Editors' note:* For a recent discussion of the push for provincial status, see Palmer and Palmer, *Alberta: A New History* (Edmonton: Hurtig, 1990) chapter 6.

27   See A.N. Reid, "Local Government in the North-West Territories," *Saskatchewan History* (Saskatoon, 1949), Vol. II. No. 3, 1949, 1–14. Professor Reid concludes that "the expense involved was out of all proportion to the benefits conferred," that there was divergence of interests between rural and urban residents and between different parts of the municipalities because of their size, and that "unorganized areas do not appear to have been at any great disadvantage and certainly were not felt to be so at the time."

28   Saskatchewan provided for a uniform city charter early in its history. In Alberta, the provincial government has discussed the question for decades but not until 1951 was legislation passed to secure uniformity.

29   E.J. Hanson, "Local Government Reorganization in Alberta," *Canadian Journal of Economics and Political Science* (henceforth *C.J.E.P.S.*) (Feb. 1950), 53–62.

30   Shortt and Doughty, op. cit., 457. The erection of both Protestant and Catholic schools was, of course, accompanied by many lengthy debates on the religious aspects of school organization. The public lands question also got attention, especially with respect to school lands. In 1884 a number of elected members of the territorial council requested that the Dominion government either grant money on the security of the potential value of the school lands in the territories in amounts sufficient to meet requirements for school expenditures or hand over the school lands to the territorial government.

31   From Shortt and Doughty, op. cit., 155. Separate figures for Alberta are not available.

32   *Editors' note:* As part of its fiscal reforms, the Klein government made fundamental changes to municipal finance, especially the school property tax. Formerly set by individual school boards, the Province moved to provincial assessment, a uniform school property-tax rate, and redistribution to equalize school funding across the province. Needless to say, this move was greeted with dismay by more prosperous, mostly urban school boards and is a source of much ongoing controversy.

33   See MacInnes, op. cit., V and VI, for a detailed account of the work performed by the police force.

34   A considerable part of the expenditure on Dominion lands was spent in Manitoba, especially before 1900.

35   The first function, that of defence, was assumed implicitly by the Dominion government. The second function is justice.

36   Adam Smith, *The Wealth of Nations* (New York, 1937), 681.

37   *Editors' note:* Mrs. Hicks, née Lady Ursula Kathleen Webb, was a scholar at Oxford University where she worked in applied economics with an interest in less developed countries. She often worked with her husband Sir John Hicks (winner of a Nobel Prize for his work in Economics) whom she married in 1935. A number of her publications are available at Oxford University.

38   Aggregate time series data on such expenditures are not available. The tax revenue series for Edmonton in Table 1.8 is indicative of both revenue and expenditure trends.

39   See Lingard, op. cit., II–V and IX, for a detailed and documented account of memorials, representations, requests, and the degree to which the Dominion government met these. Lingard tends to make the senior government the villain of the piece. The tenor of his treatment is denoted by the following passage: "Nevertheless, the Cabinet as a whole and Parliament with only a bare half-dozen members virtually interested in the Territories, followed a penurious policy with respect to the petitions of the government of the vast, new, and bustling West," (II, 20). The territorial premier, F.W.G. Haultain, is the central figure who championed the cause of the territorial government. The Dominion government, of course, was playing the traditional role of governments in the matter of finance, namely, that of establishing priorities for a large number of expenditures of various kinds. Each kind of expenditure usually does not lack vigorous support by those most vitally concerned, and the territorial premier was exerting the kind of pressure one would expect from a strong official in his position. He was a very able, forthright, and fearless man, but there seems to be no need to make him a shining knight in armour. The financial need of the territories is undeniable in the light of their rapid development. On a per capita basis, however, the grant to the territories compared favourably with subsidies to the provinces at the time while the Dominion government also spent large sums on railways, public lands, and the Northwest Mounted Police.

40   Government of Alberta, Department of Education, Annual Report, 1905.

41   *C.A.R.*, 1901, 206.

42   ibid., 1902, 208.

43   ibid., 1903, 525.

44   Special clauses were also passed with respect to Manitoba and Saskatchewan as well as the other provinces which became partners of the Canadian federation after 1867. *Editors' note:* Alberta's premier when Hanson was writing was Ernest Manning, leader of the Social Credit Party.

45   For a list of the powers and functions of the Canadian provinces, see the *British North America Act*, 1867 (30–31 Vict.c.3. and amendments), Section 92. See also *Canada Year Book*, 1948–49, 103–04.

46   The first legislature consisted of 25 members. There are now 60 members while during the 1930s there were 63. *Editors' note:* As of December 1998, there were 83 members of the Alberta Legislative Assembly.

47   The present premier is also the provincial treasurer. *Editors' note:* Hanson's "present" premier was Ernest Manning, leader of the Social Credit Party.

48   For general accounts of the place of the provinces in the Canadian federation and of jurisdictional disputes see the following: Clokie, H. McD., Canadian Government and Politics (Toronto, 1946), VIII; Robert MacGregor Dawson, Democratic Government in Canada (Toronto, 1949), IV and VIII; J.A. Corry, Democratic Government and Politics (Toronto, 1946), XIII.

49   In 1951 the department was subdivided into a department of public works and a department of highways and transportation.

50   *Editors' note:* There is some change in where spending occurs. In the 1999–2000 budget, the following four departments were allocated the bulk of the resources: Health, Education, Family and Social Services, Advanced Education and Career Development.

51   The revenue statement in the public accounts of 1949–50 is a classification with about 290 items, many of which can be broken down further.

52   *Editors' note:* Sources of the Alberta government's estimated revenues for the 2002–03 fiscal year as percentages of the total: income taxes, 31.4%; non-renewable resources, 18.6%; other taxes, 13.2%; investment income, 5.9%; premiums, fees and licenses, 7.8%; income from commercial operations, 9.4%; federal government transfers, 10.9%; other, 2.8%.

53   *Sirois Report*, Book 1, 46.

54   See Government of Alberta, *Public Accounts*, any recent year, for a complete list.

55   The story of the Dominion subsidies has been told in detail by J.A. Maxwell, op. cit., and by W. Eggleston and C.T. Kraft, *Dominion–Provincial Subsidies and Grants* (Ottawa, 1939). The latter is a study made for the Royal Commission on Dominion–Provincial Relations appointed in 1937. *Editors' note:* Transfers of money from the federal to provincial governments remain a constant item of discussion and negotiation. For comparison, however, transfers from Ottawa to Alberta are projected to be $2.18 billion , or 10.9% of revenue in Alberta's 2002–03 budget.

56   *The Alberta Act*, Sections 18–22.

57   The early accounts are something of a nightmare to accountants and research workers. *The Edmonton Journal* once said (in 1913) that they were like Chinese puzzles. One cannot help thinking that some of the haphazardness was contrived to facilitate the announcement of surpluses when such surpluses were non-existent and to obscure embarrassing items. If this is not so, the accountants of the early period were rather indifferent to their work or they were short staffed, or both.

58   *Editors' note:* Recently, the province has made major progress in improving the quality and timeliness of its financial reporting. Following the recommendations of the Financial Review Committee (1993) and the Auditor General, the Province now provides clear, consolidated financial statements on a quarterly basis.

59   *Statutes of Alberta*, 1911–12, Ch. 3. Saskatchewan and Manitoba were the only other provinces which had such a department at the time.

60   Adjustments were made so that the shore lines of the larger rivers and lakes became the boundary lines.

61   *Statutes of Alberta*, 1907, Ch. 11. This act was a revision of the territorial ordinance of 1903.

62   There were some exceptions that need not be made explicit here.

63   Government of Alberta, Department of Municipal Affairs, *Annual Report*, 1912, 7.

64   The rural municipalities were termed municipal districts by this act.

65   See A.S. Abell, "Rural Municipal Difficulties in Alberta," *C.J.E.P.S.* (Toronto, 1940), 555–61, for an analysis of the problems of the municipal districts in the 1930s.

66   See Mackintosh, *Economic Problems*, Appendix B, 291–94.

67   See E.J. Hanson, op. cit. for an account of the reorganization process.

68   The city of Edmonton, for example, has been taxing land on 100 per cent of its assessed value, business buildings on 60 per cent of assessed value, and residential buildings on 50 per cent of assessed value. These percentages vary greatly for different cities, towns and villages.

69   This brief sketch of school organization does not do full justice to the topic. A detailed explanation of local government organization would require at least one or two full chapters.

70   This system tends to complicate municipal budgeting, especially in rural areas where the annual yield of the tax levy is more variable than in urban municipalities. School districts have a first claim upon the total revenues of the municipalities because of the requisitioning procedure; a municipality must pay on demand.

71   L.G. Thomas, "The Liberal Party in Alberta, 1905–21," *The Canadian Historical Review* (Toronto, 1947), 411–27. See especially 420–23.

72   Government of Canada, Bank of Canada, *Reports on the Financial Position of the Provinces of Manitoba, Saskatchewan, and Alberta* (Ottawa, 1937), 34.

73   Thomas, op. cit., 425–27. The United Farmers of Alberta are henceforth referred to as the U.F.A.

74   *Editors' note:* The Social Credit Party remained in power in Alberta until 1971 when it lost to the Conservatives under Peter Lougheed, but began losing support as a national force in the mid 1950s.

75   Professor Thomas says: "After such a washing of dirty linen as occurred in 1910 the voters of Alberta never quite believed in their politicians, especially in those politicians who were identified with the old line parties or who had been long in power." See ibid., 420.

76   *Editors' note:* Laissez faire philosophy is a theory of governance which holds that the government should refrain from becoming involved in the working of the market. It is interesting to speculate on what Hanson would think of the political philosophy of Albertans in the 1990s. Out of the Canadian provinces, Alberta has been called the least accepting of government intervention, yet the size of government today is huge by Hanson's standards.

77   H.A. Innes, "The Rowell-Sirois Report," *C.J.E.P.S.* (Toronto, November, 1940), 56. See the following for a more detailed treatment of the topic: Thomas, op. cit.; John A. Irving, "The Evolution of Social Credit," *C.J.E.P.S.* (Toronto, August, 1948), 321–41; A.F. McGoun, "Social Credit Legislation: A Survey," ibid. (Toronto, November, 1936), 512–24.

CHAPTER 2: THE INVESTMENT BOOM, 1906–13

1   *Editors' note:* Immigration to Alberta in 1912 was 48,000, or 11.4 per cent of the population, which remains the peak both in absolute numbers and in percentage. For comparison, in 1996–97 immigration was 13,905, or 0.5 per cent of the population (CANSIM Matrices D10 and D83).

2   *C.Y.B.*, 1910–15.

3   *C.Y.B.*, 1915, 249.

4   An estimate by *Canadian Finance* of Winnipeg, Sept. 17, 1913, placed loans outstanding to the farmers in Alberta by these companies at $64 million in 1913 or about $1,000 per farm. (See *C.A.R.*, 1913, 35.)

5   *Editors' note:* Hanson's "marginal efficiency of capital" is currently referred to as "productivity."

6   *C.A.R.*, 1913, 41.

7   John T. Moore, Liberal member for Red Deer, in the debate on the budget said: "Looking at the expenditures, I say that these figures read like a fairy tale, a wonderful romance, all the more fascinating because it rests upon substantial facts." (From *Edmonton Bulletin*, May 10, 1906.) Moore was a flowery orator who did yeoman service for the government side in debate.

8   *C.A.R.*, 1907, 597–98.

9   *C.A.R.*, 1909, 554.

10 Presumably, J.P. Morgan and Company retained $740,000. There were many rumours, however, to the effect that Clarke, his associates, and even members of the Rutherford administration had received large slices of the $740,000. In any event, and whatever the facts may be (no one knows them to this day), the bond rate had been set too high. Whether this was done intentionally or was the result of misjudgment of investor appraisal is not known. *Editors' note:* Hanson's account of the sale of these bonds is a bit confusing. What seems to have occurred is that to produce $7.4 million, J. P. Morgan and Company sold 74 000 bonds at $110 each, thus producing $8.14 million. If the Alberta and Great Waterways Railway Company received $7.4 million, then there is $740 000 left unaccounted for. This could be the percentage retained by the bank in payment for its services, but it could also have been put to other uses.

11 *C.A.R.*, 1910, 509.

12 *C.A.R.*, 1910, 513.

13 *Edmonton Bulletin*, December 1, 1910.

14 *C.A.R.*, 1911, 595.

15 See *C.A.R.*, 1910–13, for detailed accounts of the case.

16 Ibid., 1912, 587.

17 Ibid., 1913, 646.

18 *Edmonton Bulletin*, February 2, 1913.

19 There was no budget speech in 1911 as the government grappled with the monetary problems incurred by the Alberta and Great Waterways Railway. In 1912 a new treasurer, Mr. Malcolm Mackenzie, had been appointed. He never presented a budget for he was stricken ill in March, 1913, and died shortly afterward. Consequently, Premier Sifton assumed the portfolio again and made his 1913 budget speech on very short notice.

20 *The Edmonton Journal*, February 17, 1913. This paper claims that Sifton was very touchy about the public accounts. The issue of March 6, 1913, states: "He was so afraid that the people of the country might learn full details about the public accounts last year that he actually sat with his foot on them until an hour before the house adjourned, and then watched the clerk of the house lock them in the vault."

21 The interest rates on short-term loans were higher than those on long-term loans, a customary relationship before the 1930s. Thus the province paid 5.75 per cent on short-term treasury bills at a time when it could have issued long-term debentures at 4 per cent.

22 *Edmonton Bulletin*, February 7, 1912.

23 A general policy of erecting more temporary, smaller structures would make a counter-cyclical public works policy more flexible. It would make for easier adaptation to change in a dynamic and progressive economy in which rates of growth of economic and social variables are uneven. For example, there are at present large school buildings, durably built, but partially empty, in the centres of cities, while schools in the suburbs become overcrowded as

soon as they are built. There would, of course, be some sacrifice of aesthetic and engineering values if such a policy were adopted.

24 It is not argued that the cost of administering justice should be fully met by fees.

25 Due to the difficulties inherent in using either a multiplier concept akin to that devised by Fritz Machlup in international trade (see Fritz Machlup, *International Trade and the National Income Multiplier*, Philadelphia, 1943, VII.), or an analysis of provincial fiscal policies in terms of the categories suggested by Harold Somers (see Harold M. Somers, *Public Finance and National Income*, Philadelphia and Toronto, 1949, XXIII), one finds oneself confined to the use of rather crude measures of the impact of expenditures and revenues upon the provincial economy. Net income-producing expenditures and overall deficits, as well as the expenditure and revenue magnitudes themselves, are indicative of trends and enable one to detect the expansionary or restrictive effects of fiscal policies. Expenditures and revenues expressed as percentages of provincial income do give a rough measure of the magnitude of direct governmental impact upon the economy. On the other hand, per capita measures tend to lose significance when they are used in any analysis involving considerable passage of time. Federal government expenditures and revenues are ignored in calculating net income-producing expenditures because they cannot be separated out for the province, because the province operates under much the same known federal fiscal conditions as other provinces and adjusts to them accordingly, and because this is a treatise on provincial–municipal finance. The Dominion subsidy, however, and other payments of the Dominion to the province are included.

CHAPTER 3: THE WORLD WAR I PERIOD, 1914–20

1 *Editors' note:* The 1915 wheat yields of 32.8 bushels per acre were first exceeded in 1980 with 33.0 bushels per acre (CANSIM Matrix D230023).

2 *Facts and Figures*, 131.

3 *C.Y.B.*

4 *Editors' note:* Interestingly, government views on the benefits of counter-cyclical spending have now come full circle. Today, it is widely held that governments can never respond quickly enough with discretionary spending to offset normal downturns in the economy. At the same time, however, it is well recognized that the major counter-cyclical thrust of government comes from so-called automatic stabilizers such as the decline in income tax receipts and increase in unemployment insurance and social assistance payments that occur without any deliberate intervention by government.

5 Government of Alberta, *Sessional Papers*, Budget Speech, 1920.

6 Mitchell complained in his 1920 budget speech of the "highly organized" state of society and the continual pressure for social expenditures, "... all very worthy in themselves" but which could be "... carried to such an extent as to over-reach not only our annual sources of revenue but even such resources as remain latent." Cf. also his speech to automobile users in Red Deer in July, 1920. A note of weariness and irritation is indicated by the following statement: "You are too impatient and want everything hand made, and are not content to do the pioneer work." See *C.A.R.*, 1920, 792.

7 Government of Alberta, *Sessional Papers*, Budget Speech, 1917.

8 *Editors' note:* Through the 1970s and 1980s, the Province followed a very activist policy of promoting economic development by direct investment in the economy. Such investments went far beyond the provision of infrastructure to include ownership of grain terminals, airlines, and even private companies. Today the pendulum has swung back. Given the

disappointing results of some government forays in the private sector, it is generally held that government should confine its efforts to the provision of high quality infrastructure and social programs such as health care and education.

9   *Editors' note:* In his recent investigation of the Alberta Debt Default, Robert Ascah agrees that the stigma of default is a large check against the event occurring. However, he notes conditions under which bankruptcy could become an option to a government: "One of the conditions is the co-existence of a large segment of the population that is heavily indebted with a likewise heavily indebted government. A second condition is a precipitous fall in income that results in the rise of interest payments as a percent of spending and revenue. At this historical moment, another condition is critical – the identification of "external forces" (e.g., Montagu Norman, Bay Street, International Monetary Fund) outside the geographical area as causes of economic and social collapse. An "us versus them" psychological dynamic thus reinforces the "righteousness" of default. Finally, equally important is the emergence of a theory that can be rapidly popularized and translated to the mass public that attaches blame to these external forces" (pp. 141–42).

10   The drought which hit the southeast in 1914 had previously evoked Dominion aid on a smaller scale.

11   *C.A.R.*, 1916, 728.

12   *C.A.R.*, 1920, 787–88.

13   *Editors' note:* See Palmer and Palmer, *Alberta: A New History* (Edmonton:Hurtig, 1990), Chapter eight, for a discussion of the UFA.

14   These figures are inclusive of interest on the telephone debt.

15   One writer says: "Then in 1913 the tax base was broadened, by receipt of the new unearned increment tax, and in the following year by receipts for new taxes on wild lands, timber areas, education tax on leased land, and amusement tax. But unfortunately they were all imposed, just when the land boom was beginning to deflate. This made evident to Alberta (as it did to Saskatchewan) that revenues were too closely dependent on the level of agricultural income, the fall in revenue from 1914 to 1917 reflecting the agricultural conditions of that period." (*Sirois Report*, Stewart Bates, *Financial History of Canadian Governments*, Ottawa, 1939, 265.) It should be pointed out that none of the new taxes affected the farming community to any marked degree; they were imposed on land values in urban centres, on absentee landowners, and on amusements in urban centres. Alberta revenues were not directly dependent on the level of agricultural income at this time. As a matter of fact, as has been indicated in the first part of this chapter, agricultural income rose phenomenally during the 1914–17 period.

16   This grant was earmarked and the funds received put in a special fund. The writer, however, has included receipts and payments of this fund in all revenue and expenditure totals.

17   Government of Alberta, *Sessional Papers*, Hon. C.R. Mitchell, *Budget Speech*, March 21, 1918.

18   *C.A.R.*, 1916, 743.

19   This might be more properly classified under taxes, but the writer has adhered to the classification of the *Sirois Report* here as well as in his whole revenue classification scheme.

CHAPTER 4: DEPRESSION, STAGNATION, AND RECOVERY, 1921–29

1   "Wheat prices were high (1917–20) and, though yields were low, the memory of the phenomenally high yields of 1915 was strong. Farmers, calculating the incomes which would result, when the yields of 1915 were multiplied by the prices of 1917–20, bid up

the price of land." (See *Sirois Report*, W.A. Mackintosh, *The Economic Background of Dominion–Provincial Relations*, Appendix 3 (Ottawa, 1939), 39).

2   *Editors' note:* Canada's primary export market was shifting from England to the United States in the post World War I period, but the United States was entering a protectionist period. These two tariffs were a reflection of this protectionist bent, and were part of a series of tariffs that culminated in the 1930s.

3   *C.Y.B.*

4   D.B.S., *Quarterly Bulletin of Agricultural Statistics*, Oct.–Dec, 1944, 162.

5   *Editors' note:* The value of agricultural production has not yet exceeded the 1929 figure of 60 per cent of provincial income, indicating that agriculture's importance to the economy was at its peak in the 1920s.

6   Source: Appendix A.

7   Professor Thomas says: "The provincial Liberal party, old and tired after 16 years of power, a period long enough even by Canadian standards, was scarcely likely to be able to cope with these problems. It was beset by troubles on every side and some were beyond its control. The post-war recession struck at the western farmers with especial vehemence and old parties and old governments are apt to be the victims of such economic blizzards. In such climates new parties flourish and the U.F.A., even before it had made up its mind to be a party, found these adverse winds most bracing. It was not, curiously enough, except in the most general way, critical of the Government's policies. The government indeed was willing to make any concessions to retain the rural vote that had so long sustained it. The Liberals, instead of growing more conservative the longer they enjoyed power, grew more radical. During the war years they had matched the introduction of direct legislation with such measures as an act for female suffrage and they had not hesitated to allow the institution of prohibition by petition and referendum, grievous though that measure may have been to some of the more bibulous. The Liberals were quite willing to be radical agrarians; so were the Conservatives. But the public or the majority of the public, was openly sceptical of the likelihood of the realisation of any agrarian utopia by the old parties and by 1921 was politely oblivious of any claim Liberals and Conservatives might have upon its votes." See L.G. Thomas, "The Liberal Party in Alberta, 1905–1921," *Canadian Historical Review* (Toronto, 1947), 426. The U.F.A. and its supporters were tired of "government from the throne" and wanted "direct government from the people." See ibid., 426.

8   Legislative Assembly of Alberta, *Sessional Papers*, Budget Speech, March 13, 1922.

9   Legislative Assembly of Alberta, *Sessional Papers*, Budget Speech, March 18, 1924.

10 See Chester Margin, op. cit., especially XII, and James A. Maxwell, op. cit., XII and XIII. The actual transfers did not take place until 1930 after the agreements had been ratified by the Dominion parliament and provincial legislature.

11 *Editors' note:* Both these governments were Liberal, and the provincial Liberals were trying to refrain from embarrassing the federal Liberals. In contrast, Alberta Premier Don Getty and Canadian Prime Minister Brian Mulroney were both Tories, and were both in office between 1985 and 1992. The fact that they were both Conservatives did not stop them from opposing one another on issues like the GST, or from making their opposition known.

12 Government of Alberta, *Journals of the Legislative Assembly*, 1910, 47.

13 The Alberta legislature debated the natural resources question between February 22 and March 7, 1921, and passed a resolution on March 7 which was very moderate and conciliatory in tone. See *C.A.R.*, 1921, 837–38.

14 From the debate on the bill in the Alberta legislature, May 22, 1926. See *C.A.R.*, 1925–26, 496.

15 Maxwell, op. cit., 153.

16 Dominion of Canada, *Report of the Royal Commission on the Transfer of the Natural Resources of Manitoba* (Ottawa, 1929).

17 Dominion of Canada, *Report of the Royal Commission on the Natural Resources of Saskatchewan* (Ottawa, 1935), and *Report of the Royal Commission on the Natural Resources of Alberta* (Ottawa, 1935). For appraisals of all three reports, see Maxwell, op. cit., 154–63 and 166–74.

18 *Editors' note:* Hanson is likely correct in concluding that public domain revenues could not have been prolific revenue producers before 1930, but he underestimates the potential of public domain revenues for the future. In the 1970s, revenues from natural resources formed nearly a third of total revenues, thus encouraging Albertans to expect substantial income from this source.

19 Seed grain and other advances served a useful purpose in aiding destitute farmers. On the other hand, they tended to encourage farmers in the drought area to remain there to await a good crop. Settlers in these areas remembered 1915 when the southeast harvested its heaviest crop in history. Another heavy crop materialized in 1923 and it served to check the exodus out of the southeast.

20 *Editors' note:* Disrepair of roads still causes the electorate to grumble, and considerable sums are still spent on infrastructure, but the hot points for Albertans are currently schools and the health care system.

21 *C.A.R.*, 1925–26, 49.

22 Ibid., 185.

23 Ibid., 185.

24 Ibid., 1926–27, 198.

25 Ibid., 1927–28, 530.

26 Ibid., 530.

27 Ibid., 531.

28 Summarized from official statement made by Premier Brownlee on September 20, 1928. See *C.A.R.*, 1928–29, 179.

29 Ibid., 180.

30 In making this statement, account is not taken of the sale of railways in 1929 which temporarily increased revenue.

31 See *Report of the Bank of Canada*, 11–12. The report states: "The years 1925 to 1929 were exceptionally prosperous, but the tax system was extremely limited in scope, and the level was said in Alberta budget speeches to be lower than in any province west of Quebec." (See pp. 11–12.) In the light of income data now available, one has to take issue with the phrase "exceptionally prosperous" as applied to the 1925–29 period. Prosperity was not sustained and income reached a peak in 1927 (see <XREF=2nd page, ch5>) and fell in both 1928 and 1929. No account was taken by the writers of the report of the extreme income inequality in the occupation of farming. During the years 1925–29, too, there was a high proportion of pioneers in the farming group; these pioneers were debt-laden and had little ready cash. Under such conditions the provincial government hesitated to extend the scope of taxation. The report goes on to say: "The province could scarcely have expected a more favourable opportunity than that presented in the years 1925–29 to recoup itself from the rural areas for some of the large expenditures made on them. The opportunity was allowed to pass, and no reduction in the dead-weight debt took place." (See p. 12.) This statement is the one to which particular reference is made here.

32 For details, which are quite lengthy, see Government of Alberta, *Report of the Alberta Taxation Inquiry Board on Provincial and Municipal Taxation* (Edmonton, 1935), 74–79.

33 *Editors' note:* Although Alberta has no sales tax, and lower personal income tax rates than the Canadian average, the province's corporate taxes are on par with those of the other provinces. (Source: *Budget 2002: The Right Decisions for Challenging Times*, Government of Alberta, p. 101.)

34 *Editors' note:* Similar charges are still leveled at the Alberta Government, especially with regard to Video Lottery Terminal revenues.

35   It seems logical to classify this revenue under repayments since the proceeds were fundamentally a recovery of advances made in previous years.

CHAPTER 5: THE GREAT DEPRESSION, 1930–35

1   For a detailed analysis of the impact of the world depression on the Canadian prairies see *Sirois Report*, Book I, 138–60, and ibid., W.A. Mackintosh, *The Economic Background of Dominion Provincial Relations*, Appendix 3 (Ottawa, 1939), VI. *Editors' note:* For a full analysis of the Great Depression, see Peter Temin's *Lessons from the Great Depression* (Cambridge, MA: MIT Press, 1989).

2   As a matter of fact, income paid out to agricultural enterprisers in Alberta had already declined from $146 million in 1927 to $62 million in 1929, a drop of 57 per cent.

3   Source: same as for Table 5.1.

4   The writer has a vivid memory of his father once receiving seventy-five cents for a hog after the trucker had been paid. There were cases where nothing was left after paying transportation charges, especially in the Peace River region.

5   It has been said that this frost sealed the doom of the U.F.A. government and clinched the Social Credit victory in the provincial election which took place a week after the occurrence of the frost.

6   Calculated from data obtained from the Government of Alberta, Department of Agriculture, *Statistics of Principal Grain Crops by Census Divisions*, 1921–40 inclusive (Edmonton, April, 1941).

7   Dominion of Canada, D.B.S., *Unemployment Among Wage-Earners for the Provinces of Manitoba, Saskatchewan, and Alberta* (Ottawa, 1937), 7.

8   Ibid. Comparable figures for every year between 1931 and 1936 are not available since the figures quotes here are derived from census data.

9   Government of Canada, Department of Labour, *Labour Gazette* (Ottawa, December, 1948), 1486.

10   George Britnell, *The Wheat Economy* (Toronto, 1939).

11   The government had to be very careful about its cash balance in the 1920s also, but access to the money markets was easier than in the early 1930s. During the latter period the government could not be sure when its securities might become unmarketable.

12   *P.A., 1930–31*, Statement No. 3.

13   Government of Alberta, *Sessional Papers*, Budget Speech, February 20, 1931.

14   *P.A., 1931–32*, Statement No. 13.

15   It was oversubscribed at this yield. See *C.A.R.*, 1932, 291.

16   *C.A.R.*, 1933, 290–91.

17   Government of Alberta, *Sessional Papers*, Budget Speech, March 3, 1933.

18   *P.A., 1933–34*, Statement No. 13.

19   The amount authorized was $2,000,000. See ibid.

20   The total discount exceeded $2,000,000 for the three years 1931–32, 1932–33, and 1933–34.

21   *Sirois Report*, Public Accounts Inquiry, Province of Alberta, Comparative Statistics of Public Finance, Appendix J (Ottawa, 1938), 20.

22   Ibid.

23   *C.A.R.*, 1933, 263. Mr. Duggan was speaking in the debate on the address in reply to the speech from the throne which took place between February 10 and February 23, 1933.

24   Ibid., 1934, 302.

25   The average coupon rate on Alberta debentures was nearly 5 per cent during the first half of the 1930s.

26   Government of Alberta, *Sessional Papers*, Budget Speech, March 8, 1935.

27   *Sirois Report*, Book I, 170. Relief expenditures in Alberta for 1930–37 as a percentage of provincial income was 3.6 (see ibid., Table 58, 164). In Manitoba it was 4.2 and in Saskatchewan it was 13.3.

28   Ibid., A.E. Grauer, *Public Assistance and Social Insurance*, Appendix 6 (Ottawa, 1939), 17.

29   It was 25 per cent in the five eastern provinces.

30   For an appraisal of unemployment relief administration in Canada during the 1930–37 period see ibid., II.

31   *Facts and Figures*, 316–17.

32   Calculated from *P.A., 1906–1936*.

33   *Editors' note:* Despite the continuing solvency of the publically owned telephone system, it was sold in 1989 as part of the privatization policy of Premier Don Getty.

34   W.A. Mackintosh, *Economic Problems*, 51. But see H.S. Patton, *Grain Growers' Cooperation in Western Canada* (Cambridge, 1928), for a detailed account of this episode, as well as for an account of grain growers' organizations from the beginning.

35   Ibid., 51–52. See Chapter IV of this book for a discussion of marketing problems on the prairies before 1935.

36   During 1928–30 the price of wheat in Winnipeg was higher than in Liverpool.

37   A.F. McGoun, "Social Credit Legislation: A Survey," *C.J.E.P.S.* (Toronto, November, 1936), 513.

38   *Sirois Report*, Book I, 171.

39   A.S. Morton, *History of Prairie Settlement* (Toronto, 1938), 175.

40   Mackintosh, *Economic Problems*, 258.

41   See Government of Alberta, *The Case for Alberta*, 115.

42   The total net income for the eight years 1930–37 was $316.3 million according to the estimates made by the Royal Commission on Dominion–Provincial Relations. See *Sirois Report*, D. Macgregor and others, National Income. The heavy burden of interest charges, of course, was a factor depressing the net income of farmers.

43   See Government of Alberta, The Case for Alberta, 136, for details.

44   See ibid., 136–37.

45   See ibid., 137.

46   *Editors' note:* Improvements in macroeconomic management by governments and central banks have reduced the likelihood of a 1930s-like depression substantially. Interestingly, the most serious threat to the Canadian federation today is the rise in Quebec nationalism that has resulted in two separate referenda on separation in that province.

47   *C.A.R.*, 1935–36, 349.

48   Ibid., 350.

49   Ibid.

50   Ibid.

51   Ibid., 351.

52   Ibid.

53   Government of Alberta, Report of the Alberta Taxation Inquiry Board on Provincial and Municipal Taxation (Edmonton, 1935).

CHAPTER 6: DEFAULT, RECOVERY AND PROSPERITY, 1936–50

1   *Editors' note:* Federal subsidies in the grain industry currently consist of subsidies made directly to grain farmers.

2   Source: Government of Alberta, Department of Industries and Labour, Bureau of Statistics. Data are originally those of the D.B.S.

3   Details are provided in Chapter VIII.

4   Government of Alberta, Department of Industries and Labour, Bureau of Statistics.

5   The preamble of the Social Credit Measures Act (*Statutes of Alberta*, First Session, 1936, Chapter 5), which was the first social credit statute of the new government, states that "under modern scientific conditions, productive capacity is unlimited"; that the existing economic chaos demonstrated "that the present monetary system is obsolete and a hindrance to the efficient production and distribution of goods," that the processes of invention and discovery and organization have so changed social and economic conditions that "abundance of production has itself created new problems"; and that "the electors of the province are favourable to the adoption of... a measure based on what are generally known as social credit principles, their general objects being to bring about the equation of consumption to production."

6   See J.R. Mallory, "Disallowance and the National Interest," *C.J.E.P.S.* (Toronto, August, 1948), 342–57, for an interpretation of the events in question. Detailed accounts of the statutes passed are given by Hugh J. Whalen, *The Distinctive Legislation of the Government of Alberta, 1935–1950*, M.A. thesis (University of Alberta, 1951).

7   *Statutes of Alberta*, First Session, 1936, Chapter 5.

8   For details see Whalen, op. cit., 75–77.

9   *Statutes of Alberta*, Second Session, 1936, Chapter 1.

10   Some Social Credit backbenchers attacked the "orthodoxy" of the budget. So did the Liberal and Conservative members who, as a matter of strategy, pressed for the execution of Social Credit policies in order to establish to the electorate their impracticability. In his budget speech, the treasurer insisted upon the need to balance the budget and certain taxes were increased to attempt to secure such a balance.

11   *Editors' note:* The "Aberhart" wing is called after William Aberhart, premier and leader of the Social Credit party. The "Douglasite" wing is named for Major C.H. Douglas, originator of the Social Credit concept.

12   See Whalen, op. cit., 86–118.

13   *Statutes of Alberta*, First Session, 1937, Chapter 10.

14   *Editors' note:* Section 91 of the BNA Act establishes which areas are federal jurisdictions. In essence, it says that everything not specifically allocated to the provinces is of federal responsibility.

15   Ibid., Second Session, 1937, Chapter 1.

16   Ibid., Chapter 2.

17   Ibid., Chapter 5.

18   See Whalen, op. cit., 96, and Mallory, op. cit., 350.

19   Government of Alberta, *Sessional Papers*, Third Session, 1937, Bill 1.

20   Ibid., Bill 9.

21   *Editors' note:* Section 92 of BNA Act enumerates the provinces' powers and jurisdiction, which include, under part 13, property and civil rights.

22   *Statutes of Alberta*, First Session, 1938, Chapter 3.

23   Ibid., Second Session, 1938, Chapter 3.

24   Government of Alberta, Social Credit Board, *Alberta's Treasury Branches* (Edmonton, no date), 9. For a detailed account of the objectives and administration of the treasury

branches, see Bruce Powe, *The Social Credit Interim Program and the Alberta Treasury Branches*, M.A. thesis (University of Alberta, 1951).

25 See Powe, op. cit., III.

26 The interested reader is referred to ibid., which is a very exhaustive treatise on the subject.

27 *Editors' note:* Alberta Treasury Branches continue to provide services in competition with chartered banks. As of 2002, there were 144 branches and 130 agencies, and in 90 communities the Alberta Treasury Branches were the only provider of financial services. Total deposits for the 2001–02 fiscal year were $11 billion.

28 *Statutes of Alberta*, 1946, Chapter 30. The demand for legislation reached its peak at the annual meeting of the Social Credit League in December, 1945.

29 But see Whalen, op. cit., 107–13.

30 *Editors' note:* There were not any Social Credit measures after 1951 either.

31 It is convenient to use the word "default" in the narrative that follows. There was much controversy as to whether or not the government's action did not constitute repudiation. *Editors' note:* For a more recent examination of the debt default, see Robert Ascah's *Politics and Public Debt: The Dominion, the Banks, and Alberta's Social Credit* (University of Alberta Press, 1999).

32 J. Russell Love, the provincial treasurer, cited the Australian case in some detail in the budget speech of 1935. For an account of Australian and New Zealand economy measures early in the depression, see Hugh Dalton and others, *Unbalanced Budgets, A Study of the Financial Crisis in Fifteen Countries* (London, 1934), 395–421.

33 *Editors' note:* There are currently neither mechanisms nor regulation to manage bond or loan issues between provinces and the federal government. However, borrowing from the federal government is now rarely, if ever, done by the provinces.

34 *Edmonton Journal*, February 19. The contents of the telegram were divulged to the legislature on this date.

35 He said: "If the provinces of Canada allow their remaining autonomies in regard to the most important factor in the constitution – that of finances – thus to be filched away from them, then I have little doubt that democracy is doomed." See Edmonton Journal, Feb. 11, 1936.

36 Government of Alberta, *Sessional Papers*, Budget Speech, March 2, 1936.

37 *Edmonton Journal*, March 5, 1936.

38 From correspondence read by Mr. Dunning to the Canadian House of Commons on April 1, 1936. See *C.A.R.*, 1935–36, 85.

39 Ibid.

40 Ibid.

41 Ibid.

42 Ibid., 86.

43 *Statutes of Alberta*, First Session, 1936, Chapter 6.

44 Order-in-Council 734, 1936. Naturally the government did not want to jeopardize its receipt of the last railway sale installment.

45 *Editors' note:* more detailed attention to this report and to the associated controversy over Alberta's ability to pay is given in Chapter IX.

46 *Edmonton Journal*, Oct. 2, 1936.

47 "Alberta, Economic and Political": G.E. Britnell, "The Elliott-Walker Report: A Review," *C.J.E.P.S.* (Toronto, November, 1936), 524–32, and ibid., D.C. Macgregor, "Income and Expenditure in Alberta: A Revision," 533–43.

48 Government of Alberta, *Sessional Papers*, Budget Speech, March 1, 1943.

49 *Statutes of Alberta*, Second Session, 1936, Chapter 11.

50 Ibid., Chapter 12.

51 Ibid., First Session, 1937, Chapter 11.

52 Ibid., Chapter 12. Securities of the Lethbridge Northern Irrigation District were in the *guaranteed* category.

53   For interpretations and accounts of the *Sirois Report*, see J.A. Maxwell, *Recent Developments in Dominion–Provincial Fiscal Relations in Canada*, New York, 1948, 3–11, and H.A. Innes, op. cit.

54   Government of Alberta, ibid., Budget Speech, March 9, 1945.

55   See A.E. Buck, op. cit., 295. Buck quotes the following extract from the letter of Ilsley: "On grounds of financial cost alone, I have no doubt that the plan I have suggested is the preferable one from the point of view of the selfish interest of your province. On more general grounds the argument is even more powerful. In these days when billions of dollars worth of government bonds are held by millions of persons, many of whom are persons of small or modest incomes who have never before bought securities, it is of vital importance to establish and maintain the faith of the people in the pledged word of governments. I would like the public to have the complete assurance that when any Canadian government gives its promise to pay it will abide by its undertakings. If we can establish that assurance, all governments should be able to borrow whatever they may require on more favourable terms."

56   Government of Alberta, *Sessional Papers*, Budget Speech, March 4, 1946.

57   The provincial government obtained another $291,000 for the period April 1, 1945 to June 1, 1945. See P.A., 1945–46, 86.

58   Government of Canada, *House of Commons Debates*, Budget Speech, October 12, 1945.

59   Government of Alberta, *Sessional Papers*, Budget Speech, March 2, 1936.

60   The writer has arrived at somewhat different results on an overall basis because of some differences in revenue and expenditure classifications. For example, retirement of debentures on the serial basis is included in expenditure in the public accounts in contrast to the writer who excludes them.

61   Sinking fund contributions were included under expenditure on income account according to the accounting practice of the provincial government. The writer has excluded them from expenditure entirely in his series.

62   *Editors' note:* For clarification, the pay-as-you-go policy is simply a policy of having balanced budgets and reducing debt; a policy of paying for one's expenses immediately, instead of incurring debt.

63   See Buck, op. cit., 80. Professor Buck comments on how uncannily close British revenue officers can be in making their estimates. Canadian and American governments have poor records in this respect. It should be remembered, however, that the North American economy is a very dynamic one.

64   Government of Alberta, *Sessional Papers*, Budget Speech, March 10, 1941.

65   See Chapter 8, pages 283–301.

CHAPTER 7: FISCAL POLICIES AND TRANSACTIONS, 1936–51

1   Government of Alberta, J.W. Judge (Commissioner), *Report of the Royal Commission on Taxation* (Edmonton, 1948).

2   These are convenient approximations.

3   One year's residence in the province is required to qualify for benefits. One of the results of this service is pressure on existing hospital facilities.

4   *Editors' note:* The concept of universal health care with which Canadians are now familiar was not introduced until the 1960s under Prime Minister Lester Pearson. In 1957 public health insurance was introduced (shared 50/50 between the provinces and the federal government), and in 1968 public medical insurance. These were quickly combined into health insurance, and although division of financial responsibility has changed, the cost is still shared between the provinces and the federal government.

5   *Editors' note:* Kenneth Norrie examines the evolution of Canadian social programmes in his article "Intergovernmental Transfers in Canada: An Historical Perspective on Some Current Policy Choices," in *A Partnership in Trouble: Renegotiating Fiscal Federalism.*

6   This amount is not shown as revenue in the provincial public accounts for 1947–48 but it is listed under transactions relating to public debt.

7   For further details, see *C.Y.B.*, 1946, 79–80.

8   All the provinces accepted the dominion's proposal.

9   See Government of Alberta, *Sessional Papers*, Budget Speech, March 7, 1947, 22. Ontario and Quebec did not accept either proposal.

10   See *C.Y.B.*, 1950, 238–39, for details.

11   See *C.Y.B.*, 1951, 687–90, for details.

12   See *C.Y.B.*, 1951, 631–34. Each province designates the route of the highway within its borders, provided adjacent provinces agree where it crosses provincial boundaries and that routes selected are the shortest practical east-west routes. The standards are defined in detail, and provide for a hard-surfaced two-lane highway.

13   *Editors' note:* Hanson predicted that Dominion subsidies would become the largest, most reliable and most important income source for Alberta. Ironically, federal transfers are today one of the smallest and least predictable sources of provincial revenue.

14   The provincial public accounts show no distinction between collections of personal and corporation taxes.

15   It was pointed out in Chapter 1 that the provincial government has title to the mineral rights on more than 80 per cent of the area of Alberta.

16   *Statutes of Alberta*, The Mines and Minerals Act (consolidated), Section 231. When a discovery is made, the lessee must return one-half of the property under lease to the Crown, and he continues to pay one dollar per acre rental on the half returned.

17   Order-in-Council 322, 1949, and Order-in-Council 122, 1951. The fees are $250 for each reservation (not to exceed 100,000 acres) for the first four months, 7 cents per acre for a first renewal period of three months, and 8 cents per acre for a further three-month renewal period.

18   *Editors' note:* Hanson's dire predictions regarding the slackening of oil revenue have proved inaccurate, in part because of on-going discoveries of new reserves of oil, natural gas, and related energy resources.

19   See page 222.

20   *Editors' note:* In fact, the treasury bills issued in 1938 were repaid well in advance of 1977.

21   *Editors' note:* "Gesellian" refers to the works of Silvio Gesell (1862–1930), a philosopher and economist who had significant influence on the more well known John Maynard Keynes. Gesell's principle economic text is Die Nauterliche Wirschaftsordung, which contains the theories that Hanson is making reference to: change the nature of money so that it benefits everyone, not just the creditor class.

22   V.F. Coe says in introducing his study of dated stamp scrip in Alberta and in listing reasons for his undertaking: "The second reason is the paradox that the Social Credit government's first monetary innovation was not the installment of Social Credit but the adoption of a rival monetary reform, the dated stamp money of Gesell." J.M. Keynes and Irving Fisher had both been interested in scrip, and the latter even wrote a book on it in 1933. See V.F. Coe, "Dated Stamp Scrip in Alberta," *C.J.E.P.S.* (Toronto, February, 1938), 60.

23   *Editors' note:* Essentially, scrip is state-issued money that loses value over time unless special stamps are affixed. Its purpose is to keep money in circulation.

24   See ibid., 60–65. Coe's study is comprehensive and little can be added to it. The interested reader is referred to it for details of the issue. See also Powe, op. cit., 59–66, for a discussion of its relationship to the "interim program."

25   "The more prominent Social Credit members were committed to a particular plan; they refrained from saying that the stamp money was Social Credit, and contented themselves

with maintaining that the provincial issue of scrip made it a step toward Social Credit." See Coe, op. cit., 70.

26   Order-in-Council, 815, 1936.

27   Ibid.

28   In September the legislature confirmed the order-in-council by passing The Prosperity Certificates Act, *Statutes of Alberta*, Second Session, 1936, Chapter 4.

29   For an account of a short-run success of scrip to "defrost" the frozen local accounts and payments transactions of a New Jersey county, see H.L. Lutz, *Public Finance* (New York, 1947), 613–15.

30   This excludes school and hospital districts, which use the requisitioning method of obtaining local revenue.

31   Assessment of lands was to be recognized up to 100 per cent on the basis of 1942 values; assessment of improvements in the case of cities was to be recognized up to 60 per cent on the basis of 1942 values; assessment of improvements in the case of all other units was to be recognized up to 100 per cent on the basis of 1942 assessment values. These limitations were in alignment with assessment practices in the various units.

32   *Editors' note:* Interestingly, the former mayor of Calgary, Al Duerr, proposed that municipalities be allocated a portion of the gasoline tax.

33   Cash holdings shown in Table 8.8 do not agree with those shown in Table 8.6 because the latter shows only cash in the general revenue fund.

34   It was suggested by officials of the Department of Municipal Affairs that a municipality should attempt to build up liquid balances equaling about half of annual expenditure.

35   Chiefly seed grain and drought relief advances, school lands sales, loans to school districts, and implemented guarantees of co-operative credit societies.

36   See page 66.

37   About $7.5 million of Lethbridge Northern expenditure was transferred to loans and advances in 1945. This means that not quite as much was spent during the five years as in the previous forty.

38   See Harold M. Groves, *Financing Government* (New York, 1950, 3rd ed.), 463.

39   *Editors' note:* Hanson comments on how huge, and even excessive, Rutherford Library was when built, but despite its large original size, Rutherford library has subsequently been expanded to more than double its original size. Currently, The Rutherford Library complex is only one of four libraries on the University of Alberta Campus.

40   The Alberta government cannot be judged harshly on this point when one considers the relative youth of the province and the fifteen years of "starvation" in the sphere of public buildings. Many buildings simply had to be built to alleviate highly unsatisfactory conditions, e.g. hospitals and university library facilities.

41   They were payments of a portion of the interest adjustment on immature securities deferred until June 1, 1946 to 1950 inclusive.

42   The provincial auditor reported as follows on August 25, 1950: "Contributions to the Pension Fund have been made by the employees at the rate of 5% of gross salaries with a like contribution from the employers. The actuarial report as at April 1, 1947, on the Public Service Pension Act indicates that to provide the benefits under the Act a contribution of 7.9% of gross salaries should be made by the government." The report points out that under Section 5 (7) of the Act the government has a general obligation to pay into the fund amounts sufficient to enable all the benefits to be paid, therefore, while such funding is of an indefinite nature this general guarantee establishes the technical solvency of the fund. See *P.A., 1949–50*, 10.

CHAPTER 8: SUMMARY AND RETROSPECT, 1905–50

1   Since annual averages are used, there are no seasonal fluctuations shown in the graph.

2   *Editors' note:* Today, the value of energy production (which Hanson incorporates into mining) far outweighs agricultural receipts, but this has not lead to more stability in income. Although the expansion of the energy industry has lead to increased fluctuations in income, it has also made a tremendous contribution to the province.

3   *Editors' note:* A Lorenz Curve is a measure of income distribution. In these graphs, the greater the area between the two lines, the wider the income gap.

4   The returns for Saskatchewan were checked for the same year, and almost the same degree of inequality was found to exist there.

5   The incidence of hail is higher than in any other agricultural region in the world for which hail statistics are available.

6   D.B.S., *Census for Agriculture, Alberta,* 1941 (Ottawa, 1945), 19.

7   A subsistence farm is defined by the D.B.S. as one for which the value of farm products consumed equals or exceeds 50 per cent of its gross revenue. In 1946 about 10 per cent of all farms were in this category.

8   The following table indicates the relationship between gross revenue and number of farms for Regions A, D, E, and F (southeast, northeast, Peace River, and north and west) for the last three census years for which data are available:

Year	% of provincial gross revenue	% of provincial gross revenue
1935	32.1	43.0
1940	33.7	44.2
1945	32.4	43.6

9   Cf. The Tax Consolidation Act of the 1930s, which provided for the payment of arrears by the installment method over a period of five years.

10   Government of Canada, Department of National Revenue, Taxation Division, *Taxation Statistics,* 1951, 133–34. A reflection upon the weakness of the income tax as applied to agricultural communities is that the proportion of farmers paying income tax was highest in Alberta with Saskatchewan a close second. Farmers in these two provinces paid 77 per cent of the total paid by all farmers in Canada. The fact that so many farms in these two provinces are grain farms selling produce directly through government agencies is a partial explanation of this percentage. Farm incomes in the Maritimes and Quebec are low. The reasons why Ontario farmers pay such a low proportion are so complex that explanation is not attempted here.

11   The Alberta government collected practically nothing from farmers under the provincial income tax in force between 1932 and 1941.

12   Gross expenditures of municipal utilities are included in the totals; so are the gross expenditures of the provincial telephone system as well as provincial payments to the northern railways to meet deficits.

13   From expenditure and price data presented in tables in previous chapters. The averages for periods were computed by obtaining the per capita figure for each year, and then averaging the year averages.

14   The expenditure data in Table 8.2 do not include the gross expenditure on municipal and provincial utilities. This is the chief respect in which the data differ from those used by the writer for Alberta.

15   The relative level was lower in the 1920s than in the 1930s and 1940s, and in this respect one must yield a bit to the critics in both camps. Nevertheless, the growth of ordinary functions of governments and expenditure thereon has, in the opinion of the writer, been greatly exaggerated. Among the ramifications of economic growth resulting from the adoption of more highly developed techniques, more intense utilization of resources (or failure to utilize all of them), and increasing capital formation are the impacts upon the occupational structure of the population, the geographic shifts in resource use, and the growing complexity generally in the interdependence of economic processes. Government grows accordingly to provide the proper (equilibrium?) proportionality of general and collective wants. The so-called "welfare state" is a case in point. Philosophical, religious, and ideological factors retard or accelerate governmental growth; it is unfortunate that more often than not these serve to throw more heat than light upon issues to such an extent that pragmatic solutions to social and economic problems may not be adopted. There is the nostalgic who advocates a return to "the good old days" when men were "moral" and "self-reliant"; there is the visionary who advocates a drastic overhaul, if not replacement of the existing "system." Both can point to extreme examples to illustrate their points because of a more or less "normal" distribution of a population of phenomena subjected to statistical analysis. But it would be a dull democracy indeed if we did not have these people.

16   The graph is based on data for 1926, 1930; 1933, 1937, 1940, 1943, and 1945 to 1951 inclusive.

17   *Editors' note:* True to Hanson's prediction, the municipal capital expenditure programme continued to be contingent on provincial government loans. In the late 1970s, though, the provincial government paid off the municipal loans with the surplus from oil revenues.

18   There are some outlays for direct services among "other" expenditures. Also debt charges are not, strictly speaking, wholly part of the "cost of government." They represent outlays incurred because of debt incurred in previous periods to provide government services on a large scale within a shorter period of time. Capital expenditures so financed provide services for years.

19   *Editors' note:* In the estimated 2001–02 budget, $58 million, or 0.27% of the total expense budget was allocated to the Legislative Assembly, the large part of which is to pay the Members of Parliament. Total allocation for all salaries in the provincial budget amounts to 7%.

20   This is a very broad statement which would require much elaboration in its support. Such elaboration is not deemed relevant here, but objective data in terms of high school performance of teacher-training candidates in the 1920s, 1930s, and 1940s are indicative of the general validity of the statement.

21   School districts in the southeast and north and west received more provincial aid than others in the 1930s to enable them to keep their schools open. Many of them lacked sufficient cash to pay for operation for even one or two months in the year.

22   This statement is made as the result of a per capita analysis of education expenditures of the Canadian provinces since 1913, data being derived from the *Sirois Report* and the D.B.S.

23   *Editors' note:* The Department of Education was scheduled to receive 18% of the 1999–2000 budget, and the Department of Advanced Education and Career Development a further 8%.

24   In 1948 school grants constituted a smaller percentage of current revenue than Alberta only in Manitoba and Quebec.

25   For the school year 1947–48 the median salary of Alberta school teachers was the highest in Canada with the exception of British Columbia. See *C.Y.B.*, 1951, 296.

26   In areas, however, where pupil enrolment per room in scattered one-room schools is low, transportation costs are counterbalanced by the reduction in the number of rooms attendant to centralization.

27 *Editors' note:* For comparison, it is estimated that 36% of the 2002–03 budget will be allocated to Health.

28 The *Sirois Report* accountants did not segregate public health expenditures but included them in a general category called "other public welfare" which included all public welfare expenditures except those on relief.

29 *Editors' note:* For 2001–02, Alberta's forecast to spend $2,377.71 per capita on health care, while the Canadian average is $2,226.46 (sources of data: Canadian Institute for Health Information 2001).

30 From computations made on the basis of the *Sirois Report* figures.

31 The *Sirois Report* statistics indicate a current expenditure of $82,000 on highways in Alberta in 1913. This was far below the current expenditures of Saskatchewan and Manitoba in the same year. An examination of the public accounts of Alberta for 1913 reveals that nearly all the highway expenditures were charged to capital account.

32 D.B.S., *Financial Statistics of Provincial Governments*, 1948 (Ottawa, 1950).

33 *Editors' note:* Alberta's debt charges per capita for 2002–03 are projected to be about $200.

34 *Editors' note:* What Hanson calls the tax burden is now commonly called the effective tax rate, and now usually includes federal taxes and CPP/UIC premium contributions as well as provincial and municipal tax. Using Hanson's method of calculation, the current tax burden for Alberta is 10.98 per cent; using today's more common calculations, the effective tax rate is 26.75 per cent (CANSIM Matrices D42118, D42344, and D42355).

35 Data on Dominion of Canada receipts is drawn from Appendix B, as for licenses and fees, sales of commodities and services, and liquor revenue.

36 *Editors' note:* Contrary to Hanson's pessimism, public domain revenues have continued to be important. In 1997, a boom year, $4,034 million in revenue (28 per cent of total revenues) came from non-renewable resources alone. An additional $754 million came from resource taxes, fees, and licenses (Government of Alberta, Public Accounts 1997).

37 It was about one-third of total debt and one-half of direct debt in 1921.

38 See Table D1.

39 This portion of indirect debt is labeled Class II indirect debt. It is excluded in Table 9.11. For the amounts involved, see Table D1.

40 See ibid.

41 This was not included in the debt reorganization program of 1945 and the government had always paid full interest on it. It was one of the two pre-1935 issues with a call feature.

42 The total appropriation in 1951–52 was $10 million for self-liquidating projects ($7 million) and school buildings ($3 million).

43 See page 43.

44 The $7.7 million of 5 per cent debt at the end of 1913 consisted chiefly of the Alberta and Great Waterways issue, sold at a high premium.

45 The 1915–32 period had higher interest rates than any other period of equal length between 1750 and 1950. Incidentally, the rates obtaining throughout the 1940s were certainly not the lowest for any decade during the 200-year period; they were not far below the average for the whole period.

46 This issue was redeemable in whole or in part on six months notice at 112.5 and accrued interest at any time prior to maturity. In 1947 the government redeemed all of this issue. Since it was a London issue foreign exchange rates were favourable to the government.

47 *Editors' note:* According to plan, there was no debenture debt of any type left by the 1981–82 fiscal year.

48 For strict comparability the sinking fund should be deducted. Estimates correcting for this factor are set out in Appendix D.

49 Accumulations by virtue of compound interest between 1936 and 1961 on the issues outstanding in 1961 would have been substantial.

50 The rate was 2.625 per cent on the shorter maturities and 2.85 per cent on the longer ones. This is in accord with interest rate structures at the present time.

51 *Editors' note:* Time has borne out Hanson's predictions; there have been no further interest rate reductions, and rates are now much higher than 2.875 per cent.

52 April, 1952.

53 This point is elaborated at length elsewhere. See Appendix D.

54 *The Report of the Bank of Canada* practically called Alberta the prodigal member of the Prairie Provinces; it might as well be taken to apply with respect to all the provinces. See W.W. Waines, "Federal Public Finance: Canada," *C.J.E.P.S.* (Toronto, May, 1937), 195. He says: "The prodigal son in the prairie family is at last revealed" (i.e. revealed by the Bank of Canada).

55 *Editors' note:* Alberta's debt-income ratio is lowest in Canada.

56 Data for comparisons are derived from Bank of Canada, *Statistical Summary.*

CHAPTER 6: APPRAISALS AND CONCLUSIONS

1 See Figure 1.3.

2 They did so during the early 1940s when they were used to transport materials for such major defense projects as the construction of the Alcan Highway and the Canol pipeline.

3 The southeast of Alberta is the most sparsely populated part of the so-called Palliser triangle in the Prairie Provinces.

4 See page 1.

5 Cf. 1918–20. See page 61. Manitoba and Saskatchewan did not suffer serious droughts in 1918 and 1919 like large portions of Alberta.

6 See also page 1.

7 *Editors' note:* Hanson's predictions in this chapter regarding the energy industry are of cautious optimism, curiously at odds with the pessimism he voiced in the previous chapter.

8 *Editors' note:* Unfortunately, Hanson's uncertainty regarding the future has proven to be justified. Alberta's economy remains the most volatile of the Canadian provinces.

9 See, *passim.*

10 See page 233.

11 It emerged from the depression of the 1930s with a larger one.

12 Between 1946 and 1951 municipal revenues increased annually at an average rate of about 13 per cent while provincial grew at rates varying from 19 to 41 per cent. Municipal expenditures increased at rates varying from 11 to 26 per cent annually; provincial rose at annual rates between 10 and 30 per cent.

13 *Editors' note:* Municipalities currently have two principal sources of funding: municipal property taxes and provincial grants.

14 See page 8.

15 *Editors' note:* It should be noted that in 1905 there were no portents of the problems to come. Unless the Dominion had reasonable indications that these problems would develop, it is difficult to place for the premature formation of the province on the Dominion government. Further, it is unclear whether later formation of the province would have avoided the problems or merely delayed them.

16 *Editors' note:* It is also worth noting that there were no strong reasons not to grant provincial standing in 1905. Indeed, the Dominion government may have been worried that the ambitions of the men who pushed for provincial status would lead to another incident like the Riel Rebellion if not attended to.

400

17 For a full account of the steps and motives leading to autonomy, see Lingard, *The Autonomy Question*.

18 The limitation upon territorial borrowing was presumably imposed because of the supposed temporary nature of the territorial government.

19 See Lingard, op. cit., 67–75 and 202–06. Cf. Mr. Haultain's sent an eminently sensible letter to the Canadian prime minister on March 11, 1905. He deplored the duplication of elaborate administrative machinery implicit in the two-province idea, and stressed the political "individuality and identity" of the people of the territories. See ibid., 203.

20 Ibid., 203.

21 Ibid., 205.

22 The decision to make Edmonton the capital instead of Calgary is also one with public finance implications. Members of the legislative assembly would probably have been under less pressure from Edmonton enterprisers, speculators, and merchants if they had met in Calgary annually instead of Edmonton. Northern projects may thus have been scrutinized more carefully.

23 In Saskatchewan the provision of rural telephone service was a "grassroots" proposition. Rural service in any given area was contingent upon the formation by residents of a local company. See Mackintosh, *Economic Problems*, 149–55.

24 *Editors' note:* It is interesting to speculate on what the effects of one province from the North-West Territories might have on the balance of political power in Canada today, or on sentiments of Western alienation.

25 See Chapter 2 for details.

26 See page 37.

27 I.e. of agents of production.

28 The demand curves were not only tending to shift downward; they were also inelastic. The effect of an increase in supply is obvious under these conditions. The northern Alberta increment to world production, however, was small and the point made should not be overemphasized.

29 The provincial government is currently paying from 50 to 75 per cent of the cost of education in the northern school divisions.

30 See page 36

31 The municipalities and the federal government also made large expenditures on agricultural assistance. See page 73.

32 The provincial public accounts distinguish between "old" (pre-1931) and "new" (post-1931) agricultural assistance accounts.

33 *Editors' note:* Hanson makes an uncanny prediction of the forces that ultimately led to the federal government's National Energy Program in the early 1980's.

34 The Alberta premier forecast the maintenance of the 1951 estimated level during 1952 in his budget speech of March, 1952.

35 See page 137.

36 This is assuming that at the initial point of growth there was a tolerable balance between income and debt charges.

37 They consisted chiefly of interest earnings of the fund.

38 See page 176.

39 Quoted from newspaper reports and checked with the review article of G.E. Britnell, "The Elliott-Walker Report: A Review," *C.J.E.P.S.* (Toronto, November, 1936), 527. The writer made repeated attempts from August, 1950 until early 1952 to secure a copy of the report through libraries. The only known copy extant in a Canadian library is at the University of Toronto which would not permit it to be taken out and sent to the writer. Personal conversation with Mr. Elliott, one of the co-authors, revealed that he was not sure himself whether or not he had a complete copy.

40 See D.C. MacGregor, "Income and Expenditure in Alberta: A Revision," *C.J.E.P.S.* (Toronto, November, 1936), 533–43.

41 There are some further minor differences.

42 The net income of farmers in Alberta fell continuously from 1927 to 1933 from $146 million to $6 million. In 1934 it rose to $36 million only to fall to $31 million in 1935 and to $20 million in 1936.

43 *Editors' note:* The DBS (Dominion Bureau of Statistics) is the predecessor of Statistics Canada. The controversy in question was over methodology as this department was trying to establish itself as a statistical authority.

44 But see MacGregor, op. cit.

45 See bottom of Table 9.2 for estimates of the level of personal savings and direct taxes in Alberta from 1926 to 1950, assuming the average Canadian level of consumer expenditure. The levels are negative in eleven years between 1926 and 1941. For Canada they are negative in only three years. Saskatchewan would show even greater negative levels and more of them.

46 The Alberta government did this anyway after the estimates for 1936–37 were passed.

47 The Alberta government transferred such expenditures from capital account to income account in its 1936–37 budget.

48 See page 188.

49 For a contemporary symposium of the debt default controversy, see "Alberta, Economic and Political," *C.J.E.P.S.* (Toronto, November, 1936), 512–49. Here are found the two articles of Britnell and MacGregor referred to above. In addition there is an article on legislation by A.F. McGoun and a reply to Britnell and MacGregor by Elliott and Walker. *Editors' note:* For an account contemporary to readers in 1999, see Robert Ascah's *Politics and Public Debt: The Dominion, the Banks and Alberta's Social Credit*, University of Alberta Press, 1999.

50 This is not a valid economic measure over time because of the changing value of money, and the writer hastens to make clear that he is not concerned with economic effects in this connection.

APPENDIX B

1 See Philip E. Taylor, *The Economics of Public Finance* (New York, 1948), II, 33.

2 See ibid. Professor Taylor calls such a payment a *cost* outlay.

AUTHOR'S BIBLIOGRAPHY

Only books, monographs, articles, and documents to which reference has been made in the text and notes have been included. Other works were consulted but were not utilized directly.

GENERAL WORKS

Bladen, V.W., *An Introduction to Political Economy*, Toronto, 1943.

Britnell, G., *The Wheat Economy*, Toronto, 1939.

Buck, A.E., *Financing Canadian Government*, Chicago, 1949.

Clokie, H. McD., *Canadian Government and Politics*, Toronto, 1946.

Corry, J.A., *Democratic Government and Politics*, Toronto, 1946.

Dalton, Hugh, and others, *Unbalanced Budgets, A Study of the Financial Crisis in Fifteen Countries*, London, 1934.

Dawson, R.M., *Democratic Government in Canada*, Toronto, 1949.

Groves, Harold M., *Financing Government*, New York, 1950.

Hansen, Alvin H., and Perloff, Harvey S., *State and Local Finance in the National Economy*, New York, 1944.

Harris, Seymour (ed.), *Postwar Economic Problems*, New York, 1943.

Hedges, J.B., *Building the Canadian West*, New York, 1939.

Hicks, U.K., *Public Finance*, London and Cambridge, 1948.

Lingard, C. Cecil, *Territorial Government in Canada, The Autonomy Question in the Old North-West Territories*, Toronto, 1946.

Lutz, H.L., *Public Finance*, New York, 1947.

McInnes, C.M., *In the Shadow of the Rockies*, London, 1930.

MacRae, A.O., *The History of Alberta*, Calgary, 1912.

Mackintosh, W.A., *Economic Problems of the Prairie Provinces*, Toronto, 1935.

Mackintosh, W.A., *Prairie Settlement, The Geographical Setting*, Toronto, 1935.

Machlup, Fritz, *International Trade and the National Income Multiplier*, Philadelphia, 1943.

Martin, Chester, *"Dominion Lands" Policy*, Toronto, 1938.

Maxwell, J.A., *Federal Subsidies to the Provincial Governments in Canada*, Cambridge, 1937.

Maxwell, J.A., *Recent Developments in Dominion–Provincial Fiscal Relations in Canada*, New York, 1948.

Morton, A.S., *History of the Prairie Settlement*, Toronto, 1938.

Patten, H.S., *Grain Growers' Cooperation in Western Canada*, Cambridge, 1928.

Powe, Bruce, *The Social Credit Interim Program and the Alberta Treasury Branches*, M.A. thesis, University of Alberta, Edmonton, 1951.

Shortt, Adam, and Doughty, A.G., eds., *The Prairie Provinces, Canada and Its Provinces*, Volume 19, Toronto, 1914.

Smith, Adam, *The Wealth of Nations* (Everyman's ed.), New York, 1937.

Somers, Harold M., *Public Finance and National Income*, Philadelphia and Toronto, 1949.

Stanley, George F.G., *The Birth of Western Canada*, Toronto, 1936.

Stewart, Andrew, *Crop Insurance in Alberta*, Edmonton, 1945, unpublished.

Taylor, Philip E., *The Economics of Public Finance*, New York, 1948.

Viner, Jacob, *Canada's Balance of International Indebtedness, 1900–1913*, Cambridge and London, 1924.

Whalen, Hugh J., *The Distinctive Legislation of the Government of Alberta*, M.A. thesis, University of Alberta, Edmonton, 1951.

Wyatt, F.A., and others, *Soil Survey of Lethbridge and Pincher Creek Sheets*, Edmonton, 1939.

Zimmerman, E.W., *World Resources and Industries*, New York, 1933.

ARTICLES

Abell, A.S., "Rural Municipal Difficulties in Alberta," *Canadian Journal of Economics and Political Science*, Toronto, November, 1940.

Britnell, G.E., "The Elliott-Walker Report: A Review," *Canadian Journal of Economics and Political Science*, Toronto, November, 1936.

Cairncross, A.K., "Die Kapitaleinfuhr in Kanada, 1900–1913, Eine Nachprufung," *Weltwirtschaftliches Archiv*, Kiel, November, 1937.

Coe, V.F., "Dated Stamp Scrip in Alberta," *Canadian Journal of Economics and Political Science*, Toronto, February, 1938.

Deutsch, J.J., "War Finance and the Canadian Economy, 1914–20," *Canadian Journal of Economics and Political Science*, Toronto, November, 1940.

Elliott, J. Courtland, "The Elliott-Walker Report: A Rejoinder," *Canadian Journal of Economics and Political Science*, Toronto, November, 1936.

Innes, H.A., "The Rowell-Sirois Report," *Canadian Journal of Economics and Political Science*, Toronto, November, 1940.

Irving, John A., "The Evolution of Social Credit," *Canadian Journal of Economics and Political Science*, Toronto, August, 1948.

Hanson, E.J., "Local Government Reorganization in Alberta," *Canadian Journal of Economics and Political Science*, Toronto, February, 1950.

MacGregor, D.C., "Income and Expenditure in Alberta: A Revision," *Canadian Journal of Economics and Political Science*, Toronto, November, 1936.

McGoun, A.F., "Social Credit Legislation: A Survey," *Canadian Journal of Economics and Political Science*, Toronto, November, 1936.

Mallory, J.R., "Disallowance and the National Interest," *Canadian Journal of Economics and Political Science*, Toronto, August, 1948.

Reid, A.N., "Local Government in the North-West Territories," *Saskatchewan History*, Saskatoon, Vol. II, 1949.

Thomas, L.G., "The Liberal Party in Alberta, 1905–21," *Canadian Historical Review*, Toronto, December, 1947.

Waines, W.J., "Federal Public Finance: Canada," *Canadian Journal of Economics and Political Science*, Toronto, May, 1937.

PERIODICALS AND NEWSPAPERS

Hopkins, Castell (ed.), *Canadian Annual Review*, Toronto, 1901–38.
Edmonton Bulletin.
Edmonton Journal.

GOVERNMENT DOCUMENTS AND PUBLICATIONS
GOVERNMENT OF CANADA

Bank of Canada, *Report on the Financial Position of the Provinces of Manitoba, Saskatchewan, and Alberta*, Ottawa, 1937.

Bank of Canada, *Statistical Summary*, 1946–52.

Canada Year Book, 1905–51.

Census of Agriculture, 1881, 1891, 1901, 1911, 1921, 1931, 1941.

Census of the Prairie Provinces, 1906, 1916, 1926, 1936, 1946.

Department of Interior, *Annual Reports*, 1883 and 1888.

Department of Labour, *Labour Gazette.*

Department of National Revenue, Taxation Division, *Taxation Statistics*, 1951.

Dominion Bureau of Statistics (henceforth D.B.S.), *Canadian Statistical Review*, 1948–51.

D.B.S., *Financial Statistics of Municipal Governments*, 1941–49.

D.B.S., *Financial Statistics of Municipal Governments*, 1941–48.

D.B.S., *National Accounts, Income and Expenditure, 1926–1950*, Ottawa, 1952.

D.B.S., *National Income of Canada, 1919–1938*, Part I, Ottawa, 1941.

D.B.S., *Price Index Numbers of Commodities and Services Used by Farmers, 1913 to 1948*, Ottawa, 1948, and also April, 1950 and April, 1951.

D.B.S., *Prices and Price Indexes, 1944–47*, Ottawa, 1948.

D.B.S., *Quarterly Bulletin of Agricultural Statistics*, 1919–51 (monthly before 1940).

D.B.S., *Types of Farming* (Bulletin No. XXXV), Ottawa, 1938.

D.B.S., *Unemployment Among Wage-Earners for the Provinces of Manitoba, Saskatchewan, and Alberta*, Ottawa, 1937.

Dominion Census, 1881, 1891, 1901, 1911, 1921, 1931, 1941, 1951.

Dominion–Provincial Conference on Reconstruction, various monographs, no-date, no-place.

Report of the Royal Commission on Dominion–Provincial Relations, Books I–III, Ottawa, 1940. Other documents published under the direction of the commission are prefixed *Sirois Report* below.

Sirois Report, Bates, Stewart, *Financial History of Canadian Governments*, Ottawa, 1939.

Sirois Report, Eggleston, W., and Kraft, C.T., *Dominion–Provincial Subsidies and Grants*, Ottawa, 1939.

Sirois Report, Grauer, A.E., *Public Assistance and Social Insurance*, Appendix 6, Ottawa, 1939.

Sirois Report, MacGregor, D.C., and others, *National Income*, Appendix 4, Ottawa, 1939.

Sirois Report, Mackintosh, W.A., *The Economic Background of Dominion–Provincial Relations*, Appendix 3, Ottawa, 1939.

Sirois Report, Public Accounts Inquiry, *Dominion of Canada and Canadian National Railways and Provincial Governments, Comparative Statistics of Public Finance*, Appendix 1, Ottawa, 1939.

Sirois Report, Public Accounts Inquiry, *Province of Alberta, Comparative Statistics of Public Finance*, Appendix J, Ottawa, 1938.

Report of the Royal Commission on the Natural Resources of Alberta, Ottawa, 1935.

Report of the Royal Commission on the Natural Resources of Manitoba, Ottawa, 1929.

Report of the Royal Commission on the Natural Resources of Saskatchewan, Ottawa, 1935.

Statutes of Canada, The Alberta Act, 1905.

Statutes of Canada, The North-West Territories Act, 1875.

GOVERNMENT OF ALBERTA

Alberta Gazette

Department of Agriculture, Publicity and Statistics Branch, *Statistics of Progress*, Edmonton, 1929.

Department of Education, *Annual Reports*, 1905–50.

Department of Industries and Labour, Bureau of Statistics, *Facts and Figures*, Edmonton, 1950.

Department of Municipal Affairs, *Annual Reports*, 1912–50.

Department of Public Health, Alberta Municipal Hospitals, *Annual Reports*, 1937–50.
Department of Public Health, Hospital Division, *Annual Reports*, 1929–50.
Department of Public Works, Local Improvement Branch, *Annual Reports*, 1905–12.
Report of the Alberta Taxation Inquiry Board on Provincial and Municipal Taxation, Edmonton, 1935.
Report of the Royal Commission on Taxation (J.W. Judge, Commissioner), Edmonton, 1948.
Sessional Papers, Budget Speeches, 1906–1951.
Sessional Papers, Public Accounts, 1905–1951.
Social Credit Board, *Alberta's Treasury Branches*, Edmonton, no-date.
Statutes of Alberta, 1905–50.
The Case for Alberta, Edmonton, 1938.

GOVERNMENT OF THE NORTH-WEST TERRITORIES

Department of Public Works, *Annual Reports*, 1901–04.
North-West Gazette.
Ordinances of the North-West Territories.
Public Accounts, 1885–1905.
City Governments
City of Calgary, *Auditors' Reports*, 1913–50.
City of Edmonton, *Financial Statements and Departmental Reports*, 1905–50.
City of Lethbridge, *Financial Statements*, 1911–50.
City of Medicine Hat, *Financial Statements*, 1911–50.

MISCELLANEOUS

Statutes of Great Britain, British North America Act, 1867.
The Charters, Statutes, Orders in Council, Etc. Relating to the Hudson's Bay Company, London, 1931.

EDITORS' BIBLIOGRAPHY

Ascah, Robert. *Politics and Public Debt: The Dominion, the Banks and Alberta's Social Credit*. Edmonton: University of Alberta Press, 1999.

Boothe, Paul. *The Growth of Government Spending in Alberta*. Toronto: Canadian Tax Foundation, 1995.

Gesell, Silvio. *Die Nauterliche Wirschaftsordung.*

Government of Alberta. *Public Accounts 1997.* 1997.

Government of Alberta. *Budget 99: The Right Balance.* 1999.

Norrie, Kenneth. "Intergovernmental Transfers in Canada: An Historical Perspective on Some Current Policy Choices." *A Partnership in Trouble: Renegotiating Fiscal Federalism*. Peter Leslie, Kenneth Norrie and Irene Ip. Ottawa: Howe Institute, 1993.

Palmer, Howard with Tamara Palmer. *Alberta: A New History of Alberta*. Edmonton: Hurtig, 1990.

Statistics Canada. CANSIM Matrices D10, D28, D83, D6367–6379, D42118, D42344, D42355, and D230023.

Temin, Peter. *Lessons from the Great Depression*. Cambridge, MA: MIT Press, 1989.

Toronto Dominion Bank. *Toronto Dominion Bank Report on Provincial Government Finances*. 1997.

INDEX

on debt reorganization program, 180–
83, 285
effect on economy (territorial period),
18
establishment of Employment Offices,
72
expansion, 242
grants, 99, 154, 200
grants-in-aid, 79, 110, 277, 338
guarantee of provincial gasoline tax
revenues, 199
immigration policy, 6, 18
and inflation of post-war years, 161
influences on provincial finances, 303,
308
interest on Grand Trunk Pacific bonds,
103
irrigation surveys, 74
lender of last resort, 128
loan council, 173–76
loans to Alberta, 130–31, 153, 319–20
management of revenue from school
lands, 80–81
mining area roads, 202
old age pensions, 195–96, 338
receipts, 277, 338
interprovincial comparison, 281
as revenue source, 129, 131, 197,
199–202, 308, 338 (*See also*
Dominion subsidy)
and Social Credit legislation, 166–68
stabilization policy, 157
statutory subsidies, 338
taxation, 231
Treasury bills, 125, 135, 288, 290
unemployment and agricultural relief in
Alberta, 59, 73, 81, 137, 139,
175, 277
wheat policy, 305
wheat pool, 142
withdrawal of Northwest Mounted
Police, 64, 70
Dominion Lands Act of 1872, 23

Dominion-provincial agreements, 22, 221
Dominion-provincial conferences
1945, 199
1950, 202
Dec. 1935, 136
financial position of provinces, 172
Dominion-provincial relations, 178–79,
199, 316
Dominion-Provincial Tax agreement, 227
Dominion subsidy, 22–23, 52, 78, 110,
382n, 394n
Rutherford on, 35–36, 42
Sifton on, 43
Dominion-territorial relations, 18
Dominion Unemployment Relief Act of
1930, 137
Dominion youth training program, 200
Douglas, Major C. H., 149, 172, 174, 318
Social Credit plan, 149
drainage and irrigation outlays, 152
drought, 61, 78, 87, 90, 122, 143, 157
1914, 59
1921, 62
of 1918 and 1919, 73
relief, 114, 137, 139, 264
The Drought Area Relief Act 1922, 146
Duggan, D. M., 129, 135, 173–74
Dunning, Charles Avery, 174–75

E

earmarked funds, 54
economic development, 3, 307
1921–29, 85–86
1936–50, 157–64, 307
trends, 233–39
economic expenditure, 263–66, 342
1906–13, 50–51
1913–20, 72–76
1920–29, 100
1930–36, 152
1936–50, 196–97
1936–51, 196
trends, 253